Fodor's 2013

LAS VEGAS

Fodor's Travel Publications   New York, Toronto, London, Sydney, Auckland
www.fodors.com

W9-AQQ-358

FODOR'S LAS VEGAS 2013

Editor: Eric B. Wechter
Writers: Andrew Collins, Xazmin Garza, Alexis C. Kelly, Swain Scheps, Matt Villano, Mike Weatherford

Production Editor: Evangelos Vasilakis
Maps & Illustrations: David Lindroth, *cartographers;* Rebecca Baer, *map editor;* William Wu, *information graphics*
Design: Fabrizio La Rocca, *creative director;* Tina Malaney, Chie Ushio, Jessica Ramirez, *designers;* Melanie Marin, *associate director of photography;* Jennifer Romains, *photo research*
Cover Photo: (Limousine on Las Vegas Boulevard): Rudy Sulgan/Corbis
Production Manager: Angela L. McLean

ISBN 978-0-87637-121-3

ISSN 1542-345X

SPECIAL SALES

This book is available at special discounts for bulk purchases for sales promotions or premiums. Special editions, including personalized covers, excerpts of existing books, and corporate imprints, can be created in large quantities for special needs. For more information, write to Special Markets/Premium Sales, 1745 Broadway, MD 3-1, New York, NY 10019, or e-mail specialmarkets@randomhouse.com.

AN IMPORTANT TIP & AN INVITATION

Although all prices, opening times, and other details in this book are based on information supplied to us at press time, changes occur all the time in the travel world, and Fodor's cannot accept responsibility for facts that become outdated or for inadvertent errors or omissions. So **always confirm information when it matters,** especially if you're making a detour to visit a specific place. Your experiences—positive and negative— matter to us. If we have missed or misstated something, **please write to us.** Share your opinion instantly through our online feedback center at fodors.com/contact-us.

PRINTED IN CHINA

10 9 8 7 6 5 4 3 2 1

CONTENTS

Fodor's Features

ABOUT THIS GUIDE

Fodor's Ratings

Everything in this guide is worth doing—we don't cover what isn't—but exceptional sights, hotels, and restaurants are recognized with additional accolades. Fodor'sChoice ★ indicates our top recommendations; ★ highlights places we deem **Highly Recommended**; and **Best Bets** call attention to notable hotels and restaurants in various categories. Care to nominate a new place? Visit Fodors.com/contact-us.

Trip Costs

We list prices wherever possible to help you budget well. Hotel and restaurant price categories from **$** to **$$$$** are noted alongside each recommendation. For hotels, we include the lowest cost of a standard double room in high season. For restaurants, we cite the average price of a main course at dinner or, if dinner isn't served, at lunch. For attractions, we always list adult admission fees; discounts are usually available for children, students, and senior citizens.

Hotels

Our local writers vet every hotel to recommend the best overnights in each price category, from budget to expensive. Unless otherwise specified, you can expect private bath, phone, and TV in your room. For expanded hotel reviews, facilities, and deals visit Fodors.com.

TripAdvisor ◎◎

Our expert hotel picks are reinforced by high ratings on TripAdvisor. Look for representative quotes in this guide, and the latest TripAdvisor ratings and feedback at Fodors.com.

Restaurants

Unless we state otherwise, restaurants are open for lunch and dinner daily. We mention dress code only when there's a specific requirement and reservations only when they're essential or not accepted. To make restaurant reservations, visit Fodors.com.

Credit Cards

The hotels and restaurants in this guide typically accept credit cards. If not, we'll say so.

Ratings		Hotels & Restaurants	
★	Fodor's Choice	🏨	Hotel
★	Highly recommended	🛏	Number of rooms
☾	Family-friendly	⑩	Meal plans
Listings		✕	Restaurant
✉	Address	⟨	Reservations
✉	Branch address	👔	Dress code
☎	Telephone	💳	No credit cards
🖷	Fax	$	Price
⊕	Website		
✎	E-mail	**Other**	
✉	Admission fee	⇨	See also
⊙	Open/closed times	☞	Take note
Ⓜ	Subway	🏌	Golf facilities
✛	Directions or Map coordinates		

Experience
Las Vegas

1

LAS VEGAS PLANNER

When to Go

For the most part, the Vegas climate's bark is worse than its bite. Sure, summer highs exceed 100°F, but with low humidity and ever-present air-conditioning, you can stay comfortable as long as you have water on hand and limit your time outside to short intervals. Even in the hottest months (late June through September) you can bear the heat, provided you stay hydrated and don't try to walk too far. Luckily, with more than 300 days of sunshine a year, the chances of a rain-out are slim.

On the other hand, nights can be chilly between late fall and early spring, so bring a sweater or windbreaker for your evening strolls beneath the neon-bathed skies.

Las Vegas doesn't have a high or low season by the standard definition, but you'll find it least crowded between November and January. Hotels are at their fullest July through October. Specific events—New Year's Eve, spring break, major conventions, sporting events—draw big crowds, so plan accordingly.

Getting Around

CAR TRAVEL

If you're exploring the Strip or Downtown, it's best just to park your car (it's free at most casinos) and walk. If you think you'll be operating beyond the Strip during your stay, get a rental car.

BUS TRAVEL

Public bus transportation's available (on Citizens Area Transit, or CAT) but is geared more to locals than visitors. Both CAT buses and trolleys ply the Strip but can take forever in traffic—the fare on both is $2.

The Deuce is geared more to the tourist. The double-decker buses run up and down the Strip 24/7—the fare is $5. Stops are located every quarter mile, and are marked with signs or shelters; from transfer points, you can connect to other city buses that go all over town.

TAXI TRAVEL

If your itinerary's centered on the Strip, plan on walking or using cabs. Cabs aren't cheap ($3.30 initial fare plus $2.60 per mile) but can be very convenient and worthwhile, especially if you're splitting a fare (no more than five people allowed in a cab). You may save a few bucks renting a car, but you'll pay a price in aggravation.

MONORAIL TRAVEL

The Las Vegas Monorail costs $5 per ride (or $12 for a one-day pass) and runs from the MGM Grand to Harrah's before making a jog out to the Convention Center and terminating at the Sahara. It's no sightseeing tour; the train runs along the back sides of the resorts. But it's a fast way to travel the Strip, especially on weekends when even the Strip's backstreets are full of traffic. The trains run 7 am–2 am weekdays; 7 am–3 am weekends.

Other monorails include Mandalay Bay to Excalibur (only stopping at Luxor when it heads south), one that runs from Monte Carlo through CityCenter to Bellagio, and a third that runs between the Mirage and Treasure Island. Rides are free; trains run 24 hours a day.

Safety Tips

Few places in the world have tighter security than the casino resorts lining the Strip or clustered together Downtown (just ask the fabled "Bellagio Bandit" of early 2011). Outside of these areas, Las Vegas has the same urban ills as any other big city, but on the whole, violent crime is extremely rare among tourists, and even scams and theft are no more likely here than at other major vacation destinations. Observe the same common-sense rituals you might in any city: stick to populated, well-lighted streets, don't wear flashy jewelry or wave around expensive handbags, keep valuables out of sight (and don't leave them in unattended cars), and be vigilant about what's going on around you.

Reservations

Many attractions don't require reservations; some places don't even accept them. But any activity with limited availability—a stage show, a restaurant, a guided tour—deserves a call ahead.

Use common sense. Ask yourself these questions:

- Am I bringing a big party (six or more people) to this event?

- Is this a weekend event at a popular time of day (6–9 pm for dinner, 10 am–2 pm for golf)?

- Is the venue very popular?

- Will I be disappointed if I arrive to find the venue full?

- Will the people I'm traveling with hold me personally responsible for ruining their morning/day/evening?

If you answered "yes" to one or more of these questions, then you need to make a reservation, or you need someone to call ahead for you. Who would be willing to do such a thing? Your hotel's concierge, that's who. And don't wait until you check in; call the concierge before you leave home to get a jump on the crowd.

Las Vegas Hours

Hoping for sushi at 4 in the morning, or looking to work out at a gym at midnight? Sounds like you're a night owl, and that means Vegas is your kind of town. There are all kinds of businesses that run 24/7 in this city of sin, from supermarkets to bowling alleys. Oh yeah, and they have casinos, too.

Attractions, such as museums and various casino amusements, tend to keep more typical business hours, but you can almost always find something to keep you entertained no matter the hour.

Visitor Centers

The Las Vegas Convention and Visitors Authority (LVCVA) operates a visitor center (☎ *702/892–0711* ⊕ *www.visitlasvegas.com*) at 3150 Paradise Road, open weekdays from 8 to 5. Stop by for brochures and advice on what to see and do in town.

The LVCVA also operates the Las Vegas Hotline (☎ *877/847–4858*), with operators who are plugged into every major resort and restaurant in the region. Think of them as a concierge service for all of southern Nevada.

WHAT'S WHERE

1 South Strip. Between fight nights at the MGM Grand and concerts at Mandalay Bay, the section of Strip between the sprawling CityCenter and the iconic "Welcome to Las Vegas" sign could be considered the entertainment hub of Vegas. Resorts in this area include the Tropicana, Monte Carlo, New York–New York, Excalibur, MGM Grand, and Luxor. Rooms on this side of town generally are within 15 minutes of the airport and are slightly more affordable than their Center and North Strip counterparts. After major renovations at the Tropicana and New York–New York in 2010 and 2011, the South Strip's the most recently updated section of Sin City's most famous street.

2 Center Strip. The heart of the Strip is home to CityCenter and iconic casinos such as Bellagio, Planet Hollywood, Bally's, Harrah's, Flamingo, the Mirage, and Caesars Palace. This section, a 20-minute cab ride from the airport, stretches north from CityCenter to the Venetian. Room rates in

the Center Strip tend to be in the mid range, with smaller resorts being the most affordable. Another draw is the mega-boutique shopping inside CityCenter, Planet Hollywood, and Caesars.

3 North Strip. The North Strip is defined by luxury. Wynn Las Vegas, Encore, the Venetian, and the Palazzo have some of the swankiest rooms in town. Rooms at Trump International Las Vegas are pretty nice, too. About a 30-minute ride from the airport, the North Strip is well worth the journey—clubs and restaurants here are some of the best in town. Rates here tend to be among the most expensive in town.

4 Downtown. Hotels are cheaper and favored for their strictly adult pleasures: dice and drinks. They maintain the old Vegas tradition, when guests were expected to spend most of their hours in the casinos, not their rooms; consequently, with

the exception of the Golden Nugget, rooms range from scuzzy to mediocre. Stay here if you want to spend less than $50 per night and enjoy lower table limits.

5 Paradise Road. Parallel to the Strip, a short drive or 15-minute walk east, is the mellower Paradise Road area, which includes the Convention Center. There's less traffic, and there's monorail service along one stretch. Hotel options include The LVH (formerly known as the Las Vegas Hilton), Hard Rock Hotel, and the Platinum.

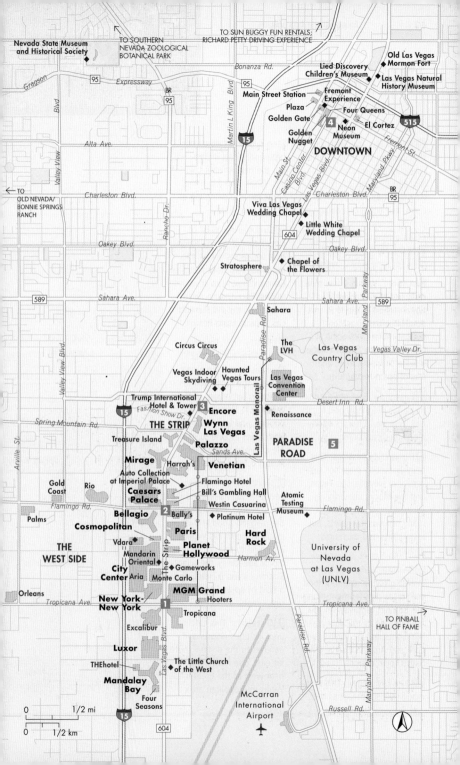

WHAT'S WHERE

6 **West Side.** Due west of the Strip, on the other side of Interstate 15, are the Palms, Rio, and the Orleans. This isn't a glamorous section of town, and you'll be cabbing or driving to and from the Strip. Chinatown and the city's only In-N-Out Burger are short rides (or long walks) away.

7 **Airport.** Within a few-mile radius of McCarran International Airport is the M Resort, South Point, a bunch of budget motels, economical time-shares (i.e., Tahiti Village), a huge shopping mall, and lots of chain restaurants.

8 **East Side.** East of Paradise Road is a neighborhood locals call "Sunrise," after its eponymous medical center.

9 **University District.** This neighborhood comprises University of Nevada, Las Vegas, and the blocks immediately surrounding it. There aren't many noteworthy hotels, but restaurants and museums abound.

10 **Boulder Strip.** Las Vegas's fastest growing neighborhood comprises development along the Boulder Highway, on the far east side of the Valley. Highlights include Mystic Falls Park and Arizona Charlie's and Sam's Town casinos.

11 **Lake Las Vegas.** This man-made lake southeast of the Strip is a resort area with high-end hotels including the new Ravella Lake Las Vegas. Check out the shopping and gambling at MonteLago Village.

12 **Summerlin.** West of Downtown, this tony neighborhood looks out on the gorgeous Red Rock National Conservation Area. It's home to Red Rock Casino, Resort & Spa and the JW Marriott Las Vegas Casino Resort.

13 **Henderson.** Southeast of the Strip but west of Lake Las Vegas, the area's perhaps the most stereotypically "suburban" in the valley. Still, its outlets are popular, and locals come from miles around to gamble at Green Valley Ranch Resort & Spa Casino.

14 **North Side.** This area, between Summerlin and the Boulder Strip, encompasses the neighborhood known on maps as North Las Vegas. It's home to the Las Vegas Motor Speedway, the Aliante Station Casino & Hotel, and a host of up-and-coming restaurants.

15 **Outskirts.** This catchall area includes resorts and eateries to the distant south, far east, due north, and near west of the greater Las Vegas metropolitan area.

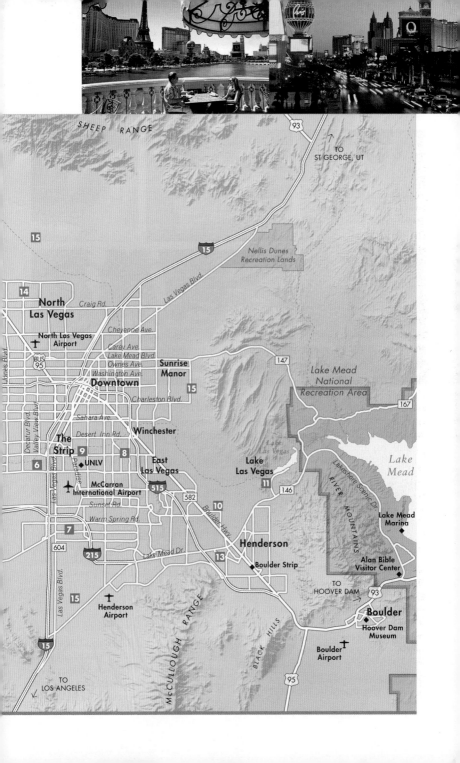

LAS VEGAS TOP ATTRACTIONS

Spectacular Spectaculars

(A) Will it be an acrobatic Cirque du Soleil extravaganza? A standing act by a musical legend? An afternoon comedy show, or Broadway-lite (90-minute cut-downs of the original productions from the Great White Way)? A classic feather revue, or a spooky hypnotist show? Maybe you're just in the mood for a plain old lounge show where the microphones squeal, the singer is slightly out of tune, and a great time is all but guaranteed. It's practically against the law to be bored in Vegas.

World-Class Restaurants

(B) The $2.95 lobster dinner has gone into hiding, but those cheap chow deals of yesteryear are hardly missed; Las Vegas has become a foodie's dream destination. Every major resort offers a half dozen fine-dining options in addition to the ubiquitous snack bars and fast-food places. If you stayed in Vegas for a year, you'd never have to eat at the same place twice—or leave the Strip.

Hitting the Tables

(C) Never mind those buffets, swimming pools, spas, traffic jams, dancing girls (and boys, and water), wedding chapels, and circus acts. It's Vegas, baby, and you're here to roll the bones and go all in.

Nature versus Nurture

(D) Consider heading out of the casino and taking in one of the many natural wonderlands surrounding Las Vegas. Explore Lake Mead or Red Rock Canyon. During the winter months, hit the ski slopes at Mt. Charleston. There's more to this town than neon.

The Stratosphere Thrill Rides

(E) If you're an adrenaline fiend, you can't miss the incredibly scary (and fun) rides perched atop the 112-floor Stratosphere tower. The Big Shot fires you 160 feet up the Stratosphere needle, and both the X Scream and Insanity dangle you over

the edge of the Stratosphere tower. These aren't for the faint of heart.

Shopping at Crystals at CityCenter

(F) This chichi shopping and dining mall designed by Daniel Liebskind has taken the retail and culinary scene in Vegas to an even higher level. In addition to stellar restaurants like Mastro's Ocean Club and Social House, this austere space contains dozens of fine stores, including Gucci, Fendi, and Tom Ford, as well as dozens of pieces of public art.

Legendary Nightlife

Sky-high bars with valley-wide views. Thumping bass lines and flashing lights. Semiclothed Adonises and Venuses swinging overhead. Whether you're looking for a wild dance club or a sophisticated lounge scene, Vegas comes alive after dark. So dress to the nines, grab a cosmo, and join the 24-hour party.

Over-the-Top Pools

(G) The tanning booth is now a ubiquitous feature in the Anytown strip mall, but it still can't compare with the old-fashioned poolside sun soak—especially if that soak is in Las Vegas, land of toned bodies, cocktails, cabanas, Euro-style bathing, man-made beaches, and swim-up blackjack.

Hoover Dam and Lake Mead

(H) If you have time for just one trip outside of town, make it to this Depression-era concrete monstrosity, considered one of the seven wonders of the industrial world. You'll see why when you tour the interior and see the massive turbines that make the lights go on in Pasadena. Combine the trip with a visit to nearby Lake Mead, where you'll enjoy numerous watery activities.

FREE THINGS TO DO

Yes, Vegas brims with cash, glitz, and glamour, but that doesn't mean you can't find freebies (or cheapies).

Experience Fremont Street. The Downtown casinos' answer to the spectacle of the Strip is the Fremont Street Experience, played out on a 90-foot-high arced canopy that covers the entire street. Every hour between sunset and midnight it comes alive with an integrated video, graphics, and music show. Several different programs run each night, and contribute to a festive outside-in communal atmosphere that contrasts with the Strip's every-man-for-himself ethic.

Watch a Free Show. You can easily spend $100 or more on seats at a typical Vegas concert or big-name production, but several casinos offer fabulous, eye-catching extravaganzas that won't cost you a penny. There's the erupting volcano at the Mirage and the over-the-top *Sirens of TI* at Treasure Island. Relax to the graceful Fountains of Bellagio, or see any of a handful of free animal exhibits, like the Wildlife Habitat (with a flamboyance of flamingoes!) at the Flamingo Las Vegas.

See the New Old Downtown. The Downtown casinos make no attempt to compete with the opulence of the Strip, but Fremont and connecting streets have a charm all their own. For cheapskate gamblers, take advantage of the free slot pulls and roulette spins offered at many of the Downtown casinos. You can also view many of the Neon Museum's signs along Fremont as well. And check out the art deco–inspired Smith Center, a world-class performing arts facility.

Be a Guinea Pig. Vegas is home to several preview studios, where you're asked to watch and offer feedback on TV shows. Some studios offer a small cash stipend for your time; for others you'll have to be satisfied with free refreshments, coupons, and the thanks of a grateful nation. We like **CBS Television City research center** (✉ *3799 S. Las Vegas Blvd., South Strip* ☎ *702/891–5752* ☉ *Daily 10–8*) at the MGM Grand. ⚠ No kids under 10.

Cruise the Strip. You haven't done Vegas until you've been caught—either intentionally or unwittingly—in the slow-mo weekend-night crawl of traffic down the Strip. You can handle the experience like a been-there local, or you can play the delighted tourist: relaxed, windows down, ready to engage in silly banter with the carload of players in the convertible one lane over. We suggest the latter, at least once. Just be mindful of all the pedestrians, who can crowd the crosswalks like belligerent cattle and are just as dazed as you are by the cacophony.

Step Back in Time. Don't miss out on the opportunity to explore bits and pieces of bygone days that are there if you look hard enough. Drop by **The Mob Museum** (✉ *300 Stewart Ave., Downtown* ⊕ *www. lasvegasnevada.gov*), which examines the city's ties to the mafia, and resides in the formal federal courthouse and U.S. Post Office. Also check out hacienda-style El Portal Theatre built in 1928 and the Mission-style 5th Street and Westside schools. Beyond Downtown, Vegas is full of well-preserved examples of fine architecture, mid century—we like the Morelli House—and modern, like the Frank Gehry–designed Cleveland Center. Wander through the older hotels on the Strip and Downtown that will, eventually and inevitably, be torn down to make way for new construction. You'll be able to say you were there.

HISTORY, VEGAS-STYLE

by Matt Vilano

Over the last few years, we've all heard the brilliant marketing slogan "What happens in Vegas stays in Vegas." But a whole lot has happened in Vegas in the last few hundred years, and most of the stories *have* made it into the history books.

Archaeologists believe civilization in the area now known as Sin City stretches back almost 2,000 years. This once lush area was home to numerous Native American tribes, including the Kawaiisu, Kitenamuk, and Serrano. In the 1820s, Spaniards traveling from Mexico to northern California on the Old Spanish Trail named the area "Las Vegas" (meaning "The Meadows"). When the area became part of the U.S. in 1855, the name stuck.

The railroad arrived in 1905, and, over the next decades, Las Vegas grew from a rail hub to a leisure destination. The Hoover Dam, built in the 1930s, played a large part in development, but gambling put the city on the map. Since 1940, Las Vegas has seen casinos rise, fall, and rise again—bigger than before. These casinos have launched some of the greatest names in show business, including Frank Sinatra, Dean Martin, and Wayne Newton.

Today, Las Vegas and its environs (population: 2 million) shelter those who make the casinos whir. And nothing here sits for long; the town becomes hipper, bolder, and more sophisticated every year. The city is now home to 18 of the 21 largest hotels in the world. From a place nicknamed Sin City, you'd expect nothing less.

1829: water-rich Las Vegas valley (the Meadow) gets its name.

1855: Mormons build fort.

1864: Nevada becomes 36th state.

1885: State Land Act attracts farmers.

COL. FREMONT

(left) Detail from poster for John C. Fremont 1856; (above) Las Vegas circa 1895; (right) construction workers working Hoover Dam spillway between 1936 and 1946.

1500s–1800s Native Occupation

Cultural artifacts indicate that human settlers including the Kawaiisu, Kitanemuk, Serrano, Koso, and Chemehuevi occupied the area as far back as the 100 or 200 A.D. Archaeologists have said the land would have been hospitable—the region's artesian wells would have provided enough water to support small communities, and skeletal remains indicate wildlife was prevalent. It also stands to reason that many of the earliest inhabitants took advantage of the lush meadows after which the region ultimately was named; excavated pieces of detailed weavings and basketry support these theories.

1820s–90s Early Settlers

Spaniards settled the area in the 1820s, but John Fremont, of the U.S. Army Corps of Engineers, quickly followed on a scouting mission in 1844. After annexation, in 1855, Brigham Young sent a group of missionaries to the Las Vegas Valley to convert a number of modern Native-American groups, including the Anasazi. The missionaries built a fort that served as a stopover for travelers along the "Mormon Corridor" between Salt Lake City and a thriving colony in San Bernardino, California. Dissension among leaders prompted the Mormons to abandon Las Vegas by the 1860s, leaving only a handful of settlers behind.

1890s–1920s Industrialization Arrives

Everything in Las Vegas changed in the 1900s. Just after the turn of the century, local leaders diverted the spring and resulting creek into the town's water system. The spring dried up and the once-vibrant meadows turned into desert. Then, in 1905, the transcontinental railroad came through on its inexorable push toward the Pacific. The city also began to serve as a staging point for all the area mines; mining companies would shuttle their goods from the mountains into Las Vegas, then onto the trains and out to the rest of the country. With the proliferation of railroads, however, this boom was short-lived.

| 1905: Las Vegas is founded as a city. | 1911: Divorce laws are liberalized in Nevada | 1931: construction begins at Hoover Dam sight. Population booms. Gambling is legalized. | 1941: El Rancho Vegas, first hotel and casino on the Strip. | 1951: First Atomic Bomb is detonated north of Las Vegas. |

1920   **1940**   **1960**

1

(above) The Flamingo Hotel; (below) Bugsy Siegel; (top right) The Rat Pack.

1930s Early Casinos

Las Vegans knew they needed something to distinguish their town from the other towns along the rails that crisscrossed the United States. They found it in gambling. The Nevada State Legislature repealed the ban in 1931, opening the proverbial floodgates for a new era and a new economy. Just weeks after the ban was lifted, the now-defunct Pair-O-Dice opened on Highway 91, the stretch of road that would later become known as the Las Vegas Strip. The city celebrated another newcomer—dedicating the Boulder (now Hoover) Dam on the Colorado River in 1935.

1940s–50s Bugsy Takes Charge

No person had more of an impact on Las Vegas's gambling industry than gangster Ben "Bugsy" Siegel. The Brooklyn, New York native aimed to build and run the classiest resort-casino in the world, recruiting mob investors to back him. The result was the Flamingo Hotel, which opened (millions of dollars over budget) in 1946. Though the hotel was met with historic fanfare, it initially flopped, making Siegel's partners unhappy and suspicious of embezzlement. Within six months, Siegel was "rubbed out," but the Flamingo lived on—a monument to the man who changed Vegas forever.

1950s–60s Rat Pack Era

Frank Sinatra, Dean Martin, Sammy Davis, Jr., Peter Lawford, and Joey Bishop were a reckless bunch; upon seeing them together, actress Lauren Bacall said, "You look like a goddamn rat pack." The name stuck. The quintet appeared in a number of movies—who can forget the original *Ocean's Eleven?*—and performed live in Las Vegas. Their popularity helped Sin City grow into an entertainment destination. They also played an important role in desegregation—the gang refused to play in establishments that wouldn't give full service to African-American entertainers, forcing many hotels to abandon their racist policies.

TIMELINE

| 1966: Howard Hughes arrives in Las Vegas. | 1971: Hunter S. Thompson writes *Fear and Loathing in Las Vegas*. | 1970s: Elvis Presley and Liberace are Las Vegas's top performers. | 1980: MGM Grand catches fire. It's the worst disaster in the city's history. | 1989: Steve Wynn opens The Mirage |

1970   **1980**   **1990**

(left) Howard Hughes; (center top) Frank Rosenthal interviewing Frank Sinatra; (center bottom) Elvis Presley; (top) Liberace; (right top) Steve Wynn; (right bottom) Siegfried and Roy; (right) Bellagio's dancing fountains.

1960s
A Maverick Swoops in

Multimillionaire Howard Hughes arrived in Vegas in 1966 and began buying up hotels: Desert Inn, Castaways, New Frontier, Landmark Hotel and Casino, Sands, and Silver Slipper, to name a few. He also invested in land—then mostly desert—that today comprises most of the planned-residential and commercial community of Summerlin. Hughes also wielded enormous political and economic influence in Nevada and nearly single-handedly derailed the U.S. Army's plan to test nuclear weapons nearby. His failure in this matter led to a self-imposed exile in Nicaragua until his death in 1976.

1960s–80s
Mob Era

Elvis Presley made his comeback in 1969 at The International (now the Las Vegas Hilton) and played there regularly until the middle of the next decade. In the same era, East Coast mobsters tightened their grip on casinos, prompting a federal crackdown and forcing some to return to the east when gambling was legalized in Atlantic City, New Jersey, in 1976. Frank "Lefty" Rosenthal, largely seen as the inventor of the modern sports book, narrowly survived a car bomb in 1982. Others, such as Tony "The Ant" Spilotro, were not as lucky—Spilotro and his brother, another casino gangster, were beaten and strangled to death in 1986 and buried in a cornfield in Indiana.

Late 1980s–90s
Era of Reinvention

The years immediately following the mob crackdown weren't pretty. The nation was in a recession, and tourism was down. Large fires at major resorts such as MGM Grand, Aladdin, and Monte Carlo killed visitors and devastated the city's economy and image. Gradually, Las Vegas recovered. Big corporations purchased hotels off the scrap heap, and several properties underwent major renovations. With the help of clever marketing campaigns, properties began attracting tourists back to experience the "new" Vegas. In 1989, Steve Wynn opened the city's first new casino in 16 years—the Mirage—and triggered a building boom that persists today.

| 1993: Work begins on Fremont Street Experience. | 1996: Las Vegas Motor Speedway opens. | 2001: Green Valley Ranch Resort and Spa opens. | 2005: The Wynn opens; Las Vegas celebrates its centennial. | 2010: The new Las Vegas CityCenter is completed. |

2000　　　　　　　　**2010**　　　　　　　**BEYOND** 1

IN FOCUS HISTORY, VEGAS-STYLE

1990s Age of the Mega-Hotel

In all, more than a dozen new mega-resorts opened in the 1990s. The Mirage, which opened in 1989, started the domino effect of new hotels up and down the Strip. It was followed by the Rio and Excalibur in 1990; Luxor and Treasure Island (now TI) in 1993; the Hard Rock Hotel in 1995; the Stratosphere and the Monte Carlo in 1996; Bellagio in 1998; and Mandalay Bay, the Venetian and Paris Hotel & Casino in 1999. These, coupled with the $72-million, 1,100-acre Las Vegas Motor Speedway, which took the city from exclusively gambling destination to a NASCAR destination, made the city incredibly visitor-friendly. Tourists obliged, arriving in record numbers.

2000s Variations on a Theme

Never fans of complacency, Vegas hoteliers have continued to innovate. Steve Wynn, of Mirage and Bellagio fame, opened arguably the city's most exquisite resort, Wynn Las Vegas, in 2005. Sheldon Adelson, CEO of Sands Corporation, countered by opening The Palazzo next door to the Venetian, giving the two properties 7,000 rooms combined. Off the strip, multimillion dollar mega-resorts such as the Palms and Red Rock offered more exclusive, intimate experiences. Then, toward the end of this decade, Vegas experienced a new trend: hotels without casinos of any kind, outfitted for nothing but complete relaxation.

2012 & Beyond What's Next

Growth—which once advanced in Sin City at breakneck speed—has slowed in recent years, but a number of big projects are on the horizon. For starters, **The Nobu Hotel**, at Caesars Palace, will transform the Centurion Tower into a Japanese-themed micro-resort with 180 rooms, 16 suites, and a penthouse. Conceived in partnership with chef Nobu Matsuhisa, the resort will operate as a hotel-within-a-hotel, and will feature a **Nobu Restaurant and Lounge**. It's scheduled to open in early 2013.

Other big Strip plans include two competing observation wheels—one from Caesars Entertainment and one from MGM Resorts. Both will be like the London Eye.

LAS VEGAS GOLF

With an average of 315 days of sunshine a year and year-round access, Las Vegas's top sport is golf. The peak season is any nonsummer month; only mad dogs and Englishmen are out in the noonday summer sun. However, most of the courses in Las Vegas offer reduced greens fees during the summer months, sometimes as much as 50% to 70% lower than peak-season fees.

If you want to play on a weekend, call before you get into town, as the 8 to 11 am time slots fill up quickly. Starting times for same-day play are possible (especially during the week), but if you're picky about when and where you play, plan ahead. Some of the big Strip resorts have a dedicated golf concierge who can advise you on a course that fits your tastes. In some cases, these people can get you access to private courses.

Best Courses

★ **Fodor's Choice** **Bali Hai Golf Club.** This island-theme 18-hole, 7,002-yard, par-72 course is dotted with palm trees, volcanic outcroppings, and small lagoons. The entrance is a mere 10-minute walk from Mandalay Bay. The clubhouse includes a pro shop and restaurant. Peak greens fees begin at $249 midweek, going up to $295 on weekends. ⊠ *5160 Las Vegas Blvd. S, South Strip* ☎ *888/427–6678* ⊕ *www.balihaigolfclub.com.*

Bear's Best Las Vegas. Jack Nicklaus created this course by placing replicas of his 18 favorite holes (from the 270 courses he's designed worldwide) into a single 7,194-yard, par-72 course. If that doesn't make you reach for your ugly pants, then consider that the clubhouse has enough Nicklaus memorabilia to fill a small museum. A huge dining area doubles as a banquet hall, and an even bigger pavilion provides beautiful views of the mountains and the Strip. Peak-season greens fees start at $169 during the week and $249 on weekends. ⊠ *11111 W. Flamingo Rd., Summerlin* ☎ *702/605–0649* ⊕ *www.clubcorp.com/Clubs/Bear-s-Best-Las-Vegas.*

The Golf Club at SouthShore. Technically, the Jack Nicklaus–designed Signature Course at this Lake Las Vegas golf club is members-only, but a relatively new change in the bylaws allow guests of Loews Lake Las Vegas, Ravella at Lake Las Vegas, and a handful of other hotels play as if they were card-carrying stalwarts. Hardcore enthusiasts say the par-71, 6,917-yard championship layout is challenging; there are nearly 90 bunkers in all. Still, with views of Lake Las Vegas and the surrounding River Mountains, the experience is second to few others in the Las Vegas Valley. ⊠ *100 Strada di Circolo, Lake Las Vegas, Henderson* ☎ *702/506–0081.*

Las Vegas National Golf Club. Built in 1961, this historic 6,815-yard, par-72 course has played host to Vegas royalty and golf's superstars over the years. Tiger shot 70 on the final round of his first PGA Tour win during the 1996 Las Vegas Invitational, and Mickey Wright won two of her four LPGA Championships here. You'll find five difficult par-3s and a killer 550-yard, par-5 at the 18th. Peak greens fees start at $74 during the week and $84 on weekends. The course is a $12 cab ride from most properties on the Strip. ⊠ *1911 E. Desert Inn Rd., East Side* ☎ *702/734–1796, 888/584–6531* ⊕ *www.lasvegasnational.com.*

Paiute Golf Resort. You can play three Pete Dye–designed courses here: Wolf, Snow Mountain, and Sun Mountain. Snow Mountain fits most skill levels and has been ranked by *Golf Digest* as Las Vegas's

best public-access course. Sun Mountain is a player-friendly course but its difficult par-4s make it marginally more challenging than Snow. Six of those holes measure longer than 400 yards, but the best is the fourth hole, which is 206 yards over water. Wolf, with its island hole at No. 15, is the toughest of the three and arguably the most difficult in the area. Greens fees at 7,146-yard, par-72 Snow Mountain and 7,112-yard, par-72 Sun Mountain go up to $149, and premium weekend tee times on Wolf get into the $169 range. If you want to play last-minute, all courses offer great twilight 9-hole rates. ✉ *10325 Nu-Wav Kaiv Blvd., Summerlin* ☏ *702/658–1400, 800/711–2833* ⊕ *www.lvpaiutegolf.com.*

Rhodes Ranch Golf Club. One of the better courses in the Las Vegas Valley, the 6,909-yard, par-72 Rhodes Ranch course was designed by renowned architect Ted Robinson to provide enough challenges for any skill level—numerous water hazards, difficult bunkers, and less-than-even fairways. Peak-season greens fees start at $139 Sunday through Thursday and $123 Friday and Saturday; twilight rates have been known to drop to around $65 or lower. ✉ *20 Rhodes Ranch Pkwy., West Side* ☏ *702/740–4114, 888/311–8337* ⊕ *www.rhodesranchgolf.com.*

Royal Links Golf Club. Similar in concept to Bear's Best, this 7,029-yard, par-72 is a greatest-hits course, replicating popular holes from 11 courses in the British Open rotation. You can play the Road Hole from the famed St. Andrews, and the Postage Stamp from Royal Troon. It's a rare chance to play links golf without having to cross an ocean, and the Las Vegas weather usually has far more sunshine and warmth. Also on-site is

Stymie's Pub. Peak-season greens fees start around $175 weekdays and $199 weekends. ✉ *5995 Vegas Valley Dr., East Side* ☏ *702/450–8181, 888/427–6678* ⊕ *www.royallinksgolfclub.com.*

TPC Las Vegas. The PGA manages this 7,063-yard, par-71 championship layout next to the JW Marriott. The course features a number of elevation changes, steep ravines, and a lake. It also is one of the venues for the Las Vegas Invitational, a stop on the PGA Tour. During peak season, fees start at $179 during the week and $249 on weekends. ✉ *9851 Canyon Run Dr., Summerlin* ☏ *702/256–2000, 888/321–5725* ⊕ *www.tpc.com/tpc-las-vegas.*

★ **The Wynn Golf Club.** Tom Fazio's lavish urban golf course is built on the site of the old Desert Inn Golf Course, but bares little resemblance to the original. You're up against significant elevation changes and water hazards are in the mix on 11 of the 18 holes. The 37-foot Wynn waterfall on the 18th hole caps the 7,042-yard, par-70 course. Open to hotel guests only, the greens fee is $500. ✉ *Wynn Las Vegas, 3131 Las Vegas Blvd. S, North Strip* ☏ *702/770–7100, 877/321–9966* ⊕ *www.wynnlasvegas.com.*

TIE THE KNOT

Vegas wedding chapels: They're flowers and neon and love ever after (or at least until tomorrow's hangover). They're also mighty quick, once you get that marriage license.

★ **Chapel of the Flowers.** Enjoy a brief facsimile of a traditional ceremony at this venue, designed to be a turnkey wedding operation, with three chapels, on-site flower shop, photography studio, and wedding coordinators. Sure, it's still Las Vegas, so an Elvis impersonator is available for all ceremonies. ⊠ *1717 Las Vegas Blvd. S, North Strip* ☎ *800/843–2410, 702/735–4331* ⊕ *www.littlechapel.com.*

Clark County Marriage License Bureau. A no-wait marriage certificate can be yours if you bring $60 cash ($65 credit card), some identification (prison IDs are accepted on a case-by-case basis), and your beloved to the Clark County Marriage License Bureau. It's open from 8 am to midnight (as well as 24 hours on holidays such as New Year's Eve and Valentine's Day). ⊠ *201 E. Clark Ave., Downtown* ☎ *702/671–0600.*

Little Church of the West. This cedar-and-redwood chapel is one of the city's most famous. The kitsch is kept under control, and the setting borders on picturesque (it's even listed on the National Register of Historic Places—ah, Vegas). No wonder it appealed to part-owners Angelina Jolie and Billy Bob Thornton in 2000. ⊠ *4617 Las Vegas Blvd. S, South Strip* ☎ *702/739–7971, 800/821–2452* ⊕ *www.littlechurchlv.com.*

Little White Wedding Chapel. The list of LWWC alums is impressive: Demi Moore and Bruce Willis, Paul Newman and Joann Woodward, Michael Jordan, Britney Spears, and Frank Sinatra. Try the Hawaiian theme, where the minister plays a ukulele and blows into a conch shell to close out the ceremony. Or, get hitched in a pink Cadillac while an Elvis impersonator croons. There's even a drive-thru for the ultimate in shotgun weddings. ⊠ *1301 Las Vegas Blvd. S, North Strip* ☎ *800/545–8111, 702/382–5943* ⊕ *www.alittlewhitechapel.com.*

★ **Madame Tussauds Las Vegas.** The wax museum features the full-service Chapel of Dreams. You can take a guided tour of the museum before exchanging vows in front of a small gathering of friends (and wax statues). For larger weddings (or other events), book the Spirit of America room. Imagine the delight on your grandmother's face when she sees the wedding pictures featuring you, your new spouse, and your guests of honor: Zac Efron, Lady Gaga, and President Obama. ⊠ *Next to the Venetian, 3377 Las Vegas Blvd. S, North Strip* ☎ *702/862–7805, 866/841–3739* ⊕ *www.madametussauds.com/LasVegas.*

Office of Civil Marriages. Elsewhere in town, at the Office of Civil Marriages, a commissioner will do the deed for $50 cash ($55 credit). Exact change and one witness are required, and the facility is open from 8 am until 10 pm on weekends. No appointment required. ⊠ *309 S. 3rd St., Downtown* ☎ *702/671–0577* ☉ *Sun.–Thurs. 2–6 pm, Fri. and Sat. 8 am–10 pm.*

Viva Las Vegas Wedding Chapel. An endless variety of wedding themes and add-on shtick is available, ranging from elegant to casual to camp; say your vows in the presence of Elvis, the Blues Brothers, or Liberace. The chapel features a live webcam on its website that lets you track the nuptials in real time. ⊠ *1205 Las Vegas Blvd. S, North Strip* ☎ *702/384–0771, 800/574–4450* ⊕ *www.vivalasvegasweddings.com.*

Exploring Las Vegas

WORD OF MOUTH

"My favorite attractions are walking on the Strip in the stretch from MGM to the Venetian, watching the Bellagio Fountain, and making excursions to the Valley of Fire and Red Rock Canyon."

—happytrailstoyou

Matt Villano

Easter Island, Machu Picchu, and other celebrated wonders of the world are certainly impressive. But Las Vegas . . . Las Vegas is a land where jungles thrive and fountains dance in the middle of the desert. It's a place that unites medieval England and ancient Egypt with modern-day Venice, Paris, and New York. It's a never-ending source of irony and improbability where you can turn a chip and a chair into a million dollars, or celebrate your shotgun wedding by shooting machine guns. Where else does such a wonderland exist? In a word, nowhere. But Vegas.

The smallish city (geographically) is larger than life, with a collective energy (and excess) that somehow feels intimate. Maybe it's the agreeable chimes and intermittent cheers from the casino floor that fade to tranquillity when you enter a sumptuous spa. Maybe it's the fish flown in nightly from the Mediterranean that lands on your plate. For each individual, Vegas is an equation where you + more = more of you: more chances to explore aspects of your personality that may be confined by the routine of daily life. It's for this reason alone that the "what happens here stays here" phenomenon is shared by so many visitors.

The city itself has a number of different faces. For the history, head Downtown, and explore everything from old casinos to a museum that pays homage to the mobsters who built them. For fun, glitz and glamour, head to the Strip, which itself has three distinct vibes *(see below)*. For outdoor adventure, head west and south, either to the Spring Mountains beyond Summerlin or out to Hoover Dam and Lake Mead—manmade accomplishments of an entirely different sort. Along the way, you can pamper yourself at world-class spas and restaurants, engage in retail therapy at some of the best shopping in the world, dance the night away at rocking nightclubs, or—of course—court Lady Luck long enough to strike it rich. With the right itinerary, Vegas even can work for kids (or families with young kids).

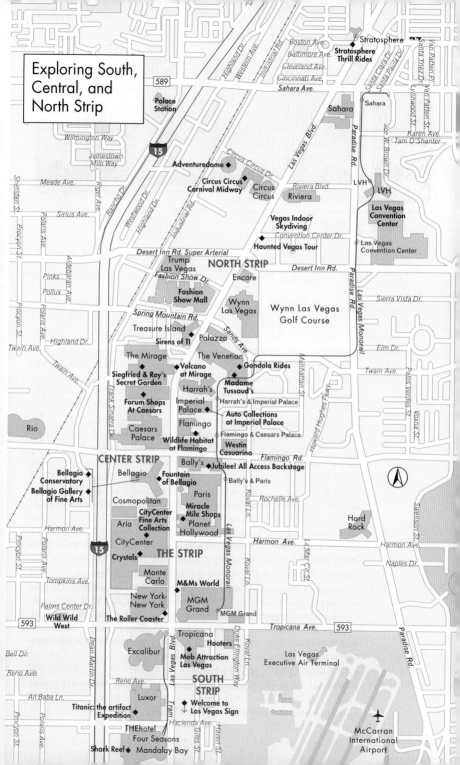

Exploring South, Central, and North Strip

SOUTH STRIP

Dining
★★★★☆

Sightseeing
★★★★☆

Shopping
★★★☆☆

Nightlife
★★★☆☆

Fun and fantasy collide on the South Strip. Whether it's a man-made beach lagoon, a glass pyramid, a medieval castle, or an Oz-like complex, imagination in these parts most certainly runs wild.

A first-time tour should start at the iconic "Welcome to Las Vegas" sign south of Frank Sinatra Drive. From there, swing through the shark habitat at Mandalay Bay, check out the "Sphinx" in front of Luxor, and the circa-1950 stained-glass skylights inside the renovated Tropicana Las Vegas.

The jousting in the Tournament of Kings at Excalibur is topped only by the gravity-defying loops of the roller coaster at New York–New York. Then, of course, there's the MGM Grand—still the largest hotel in the world. And Monte Carlo, with fountains and marble staircases that evoke the style and panache of the European city by the same name.

Dig deeper and you start to appreciate the details of the South-Strip resorts. The palm-frond fans inside Mandalay Bay. The South-Beach white of the Tropicana. Even New Yorkers say the West Village–inspired food court at New York–New York feels like home. And the giant bronze lion in front of MGM Grand is a throwback to the hotel's affiliation with the movie company, but it's also a veiled reference to the "Wizard of Oz," which inspired the building's green hue.

Non-casino destinations are worth visiting, too; GameWorks attracts serious gamers, while M&M World satisfies sweet tooths of every age. Compared to the rest of the Strip, which is more modern and, at times, stuffy, the South Strip is whimsical and just plain neat. It's also a perfect introduction to the grandeur, luxury, and history quite literally down the road.

GETTING HERE AND AROUND

Everything on the South Strip is relatively close. Most resorts are within a 10- or 15-minute cab ride from the airport, and all are accessible by public transportation. A monorail connects Mandalay Bay with the Luxor and Excalibur. What's more, a pedestrian bridge across Las Vegas Boulevard links New York–New York and the MGM Grand. If it's not July or August a walking tour of this area is a fun activity (⇨ *see feature box*). From ground level, the heft of casinos never gets old.

> ### TAXI!
>
> You're never far from a taxi, but it's downright impossible to hail a cab on the Strip. Hotels welcome you onto their taxi stand lines in the hope that you'll come back and play in their casinos.

The Las Vegas Monorail begins (or ends) on this part of the Strip at the MGM Grand station. CAT (Citizens Area Transit) services this part of the Strip with public buses and double-deckers (⇨ *see also Bus Travel in Travel Smart*).

TOP ATTRACTIONS

Mob Attraction Las Vegas. Since it opened in 2010, this mafia-themed attraction inside Tropicana Las Vegas has been plagued by poor technology, controversial exhibits, and flagging visitation. When The Mob Museum opened up Downtown, the plight only got worse. Nevertheless, history buffs will appreciate artifacts such as the diary of mobster Meyer Lansky, Tony "The Ant" Spilotro's gun, and family photos and home movies from other infamous criminals. Visitors can interact with life-size holograms of chatty gangsters and have a chance to get "made." The museum itself is about a 10-minute walk from the main entrance of the casino. ⊠ *Tropicana Las Vegas, 3801 Las Vegas Blvd. S* ☏ *702/739–2662* ⊕ *www.troplv.com/entertainment* ⊠ *$25 adults, $15 kids 6–11* ☉ *Daily 10–9.*

Fodor's Choice
★ **The Roller Coaster.** There are two reasons to ride the Coney Island–style New York–New York roller coaster (aka Manhattan Express): first, with a 144-foot dive and a 360-degree somersault, it's a real scream; and second, it whisks you around the amazing replica of the New York City skyline, giving you fabulous views of the Statue of Liberty, Chrysler building, and, at night, the Las Vegas lights—you climb to peak heights around 200 feet above the Strip. Get ready to go 67 mph over a dizzying succession of high-banked turns and camelback hills, twirl through a "heartline twist" (like a jet doing a barrel roll), and finally rocket along a 540-degree spiral before pulling back into the station. ⊠ *New York–New York, 3790 Las Vegas Blvd. S* ☏ *800/689–1797* ⊕ *www. nynyhotelcasino.com* ⊠ *$14; all day-ride pass $25* ☉ *Sun.–Thurs. 11–11, Fri. and Sat. 10:30 am–midnight, weather permitting.*

★ **Shark Reef.** You start your journey through the mysterious realm of deep water at the ruins of an old Aztec temple. Here the heat and humidity may be uncomfortable for humans, but it's quite nice for the golden crocodiles, endangered green sea turtles, water monitors, and tropical fish. Descend through two glass tunnels, which lead you deeper and deeper under the sea (or about 1.6 million gallons of it), where exotic tropical fish and other sea creatures swim all around you. The tour saves the best for last—from the bowels of a sunken galleon, sharks swim below, above, and around the skeleton ship. Elsewhere you'll find something like a petting zoo for marine life plus a special jellyfish

GREAT WALKS: SOUTH STRIP

Mummies to Big Apple: Inside Luxor's pyramid follow the enclosed walkways to Excalibur. From there, it's an easy walk across a pedestrian bridge to New York–New York's new gaming floor. Total time: 15 minutes.

All about M's: Inside the MGM Grand, resort guests can explore the grounds—both the MGM Grand and the area surrounding the Signature towers. Then you can join the masses and hit the Strip heading north toward M&Ms World, the town's biggest candy store. Total time: 30–40 minutes.

See an Icon: Head south on Las Vegas Boulevard from Mandalay Bay and you'll spot the famous "Welcome to Las Vegas" sign. If you want to take a picture directly under the sign, be careful crossing the street; the sign sits in the center median and there's no crosswalk. Total time from Mandalay and back: 40 minutes.

habitat. ⊠ *Mandalay Bay, 3950 Las Vegas Blvd. S* ☎ *702/632–7777* ⊕ *www.mandalaybay.com* ✉ *$18 adults, $12 kids 5–12* ⊙ *Fri. and Sat. 10–10, Sun.–Thurs. 10 am–8 pm.*

"Welcome to Fabulous Las Vegas" sign. This neon-and-incandescent sign, in a median of Las Vegas Boulevard south of Mandalay Bay, is one of Sin City's most enduring icons. The landmark dates back to 1959, and was approved for listing on the National Register of Historic Places in 2009. Young Electric Sign Company currently leases the sign to Clark County but the design itself was never copyrighted, and currently exists in the public domain. (This, of course, explains why you see so many likenesses all over town.) There is a parking lot in the median just south of the sign. If you prefer to go on foot, expect a 10-minute walk from Mandalay Bay. ⊠ *5100 Las Vegas Blvd. S.*

WORTH NOTING

GameWorks. GameWorks is the biggest, most boisterous arcade in town. The multilevel arcade has more than 250 games, loosely arranged by genre, including shoot-em-ups, sports games, and virtual dance stations. There are also several casual restaurants and 21-and-over bars with pool tables. ⊠ *3785 Las Vegas Blvd. S, next to MGM Grand, South Strip* ☎ *702/432–4263* ⊕ *www.gameworks.com* ✉ *Free entry, games cost $1–$2 each, $35 all-day pass* ⊙ *Sun.–Thurs. 10 am–midnight, Fri. and Sat. 10 am–1 am.*

Titanic: The Artifact Exhibition. Travel down to the bottom of the North Atlantic where the "ship of dreams" rests after grazing an iceberg in 1912. The 25,000-square-foot exhibit inside Luxor Las Vegas includes a replica of guest compartments, the grand staircase, and a promenade deck that movie fans will recognize from a little film by James Cameron. There's plenty of emotionally arresting artifacts: luggage, clothing, a bottle of unopened champagne, and pieces of the ship including a massive section of the iron hull, complete with bulging rivets and portholes. ⊠ *Luxor Las Vegas, 3900 Las Vegas Blvd. S* ☎ *702/262–4444* ⊕ *www. luxor.com* ✉ *$32 adults, $24 kids 4–12* ⊙ *Daily 10–10.*

GREAT ITINERARIES: SOUTH STRIP

TWO HOURS TO KILL

If you only have a couple of hours to burn, head to **Mandalay Bay** at the south end of the Strip. You can tour the **Shark Reef** in about 45 minutes and then spend the rest of your time shopping at **Mandalay Place**, lunching at trendy **Burger Bar** or Hubert Keller's other restaurant, **Fleur**. You could also avoid the Strip entirely and head to the recently expanded **Hard Rock Hotel**. Grab some margaritas at **Pink Taco** and take in views of the pool complex. If you need to stay near the airport, drive five minutes east of McCarran to the **Town Square**, an open-air dining, shopping, and entertainment complex with something for everyone.

THE VEGAS VIRGIN

Head for the heart of the Strip to take in all that glitz and glamour you came to see. Walk across the miniature version of the Brooklyn Bridge at **New York–New York**, take in some of the modern art collection at **Aria** inside CityCenter, check out the dancing fountains at **Bellagio,** and do as the Romans would and take a stroll through **Caesars** (the Forum Shops have great lunch options).

Head back to your hotel to freshen up before your night on the town. Splurge on dinner at MGM Grand's **Joël Robuchon** or at **Switch Steak** inside **Encore**. Later on? Try **The Deuce**, the new lounge/high-roller pit inside Aria, or **Mix**, a lounge atop **THEhotel** at Mandalay Bay for the view of the Strip. Then finish off with some gambling or a show—we love Cirque du Soleil's **O**.

CENTER STRIP

Dining
★★★★☆
Sightseeing
★★★★★
Shopping
★★★★★
Nightlife
★★★★☆

It's fitting that this part of the Strip comprises the heart of today's Las Vegas. Even before the $8.5-billion CityCenter project was completed, this stretch captured the American consciousness like no other. It is, quite literally, where modern Vegas was born.

It began with the Flamingo more than 60 years ago, and then the Mirage ushered in the age of the modern megaresort in the late 1980s. That renaissance gained momentum with Bellagio and snowballed from there. Today the stretch includes other classics such as Caesars Palace and Bally's, as well as thematic wonders such as Paris and Planet Hollywood. The centerpiece is, fittingly, CityCenter, a city-within-the-city that includes everything from public art to apartment-style living and more. Then, of course, there's the relative new kid on the block: the uber-hip Cosmopolitan, Las Vegas.

There's no shortage of spectacles in this part of town. From the fountains in front of Aria and Bellagio to the Eiffel Tower at Paris and the volcano in front of the Mirage, the Center Strip truly is a feast for the eyes. Art is on display here as well; CityCenter has a $42-million collection for visitors to enjoy, and the Bellagio has one of the most highly regarded galleries in town. Another popular pastime: shopping. A day of exploration here should include strolls through vast retail destinations such as Crystals, Miracle Mile, and Forum Shops—all of which offer some of the finest boutiques and shops in the United States.

No visit to the Center Strip would be complete without a little pool time. For an intimate vibe, check out The Cosmopolitan's eighth-floor pool deck that looks down on the Strip. To live like royalty, check out the seven-pool Garden of the Gods Pool Oasis at Caesars Palace. Reclining on a lounger, soaking up the sun, you'll be experiencing Vegas the way countless others have over the years. The more things change, apparently, the more they stay the same.

GETTING HERE AND AROUND

CityCenter makes the Center Strip challenging to navigate; at some point, almost all pedestrian traffic along the Strip must go through the Crystals Retail & Entertainment Center. Another bottleneck: the fountains at Bellagio, especially on weekend evenings when the most crowds gather. One way to avoid these backups is to take advantage of the Las Vegas Monorail between Monte Carlo and Bellagio. If you're traveling by cab, expect anywhere from 15 to 20 minutes to the airport, and 10 to 15 minutes to get to other parts of town.

> ### COOLING MIST
>
> Numerous casinos and restaurants have public water misters. Our favorites: outside Diablo's Cantina at the Monte Carlo; the frozen-margarita bar outside Caesars Palace (northwest corner of Flamingo and the Strip); and various shops outside Fashion Show Mall in the North Strip.

Las Vegas Monorail stations here include the Bally's/Paris station, Flamingo/Caesars Palace station, and farthest north, the Harrah's Imperial Palace station. CAT (Citizens Area Transit) services this part of the Strip with public buses and double-deckers (⇨ *see also Bus Travel in Travel Smart*).

TOP ATTRACTIONS

★ **Auto Collections at Imperial Palace.** Collectively billed as the "world's largest classic car showroom," the 250 antique, classic, and special-interest vehicles inside the IP's "Auto Collections" exhibit will keep gearheads entertained for hours. All the vehicles on the lot are for sale, so the collection is constantly changing. But at any given time you might see "famous" cars, like the Trans Am that acted as the pace car at the 1983 Daytona 500, or cars that once belonged to famous people, like the 39 Chrysler the late Johnny Carson rode in to his senior prom. Many of the cars are just vintage rides: a supercharged 57 T-Bird, or the immaculate 29 Rolls-Royce Springfield Phantom I straight out of *The Great Gatsby*. Free admission coupons are available online. ⊠ *Imperial Palace, 3535 Las Vegas Blvd. S* ☎ *702/794–3174* ⊕ *www.autocollections. com* ⊠ *$8.95 adults, $5 kids under 12* ☉ *Daily 10–6.*

★ **Bellagio Conservatory.** The flowers, trees, and other plants in the atrium are fresh and live, grown in Bellagio's 5-acre greenhouse. They change each season, and the lighted holiday displays in December (for Christmas) and January (for Chinese New Year) are particularly dramatic. ⊠ *Bellagio, 3600 Las Vegas Blvd. S* ☎ *702/693–7111, 888/987–6667* ⊕ *www.bellagio.com* ⊠ *Free* ☉ *Daily 24 hrs.*

Bellagio Gallery of Fine Art. This gallery—one of the last of its kind inside Strip hotels—originally was curated from Bellagio founder Steve Wynn's private collection. Today, with Wynn long gone, the gallery operates independently, bringing in traveling exhibits from some of the most famous art museums in the world. Recent shows have featured works by Lichtenstein and Monet. But you're just as likely to see works by Picasso, Hopper, and others. Also, on the second Wednesday of each month, the gallery pours select wines from Bellagio's cellar, and patrons

GREAT WALKS: CENTER STRIP

See the Fountains: Catch the dancing fountains outside Bellagio. Showtimes are every half hour. It's best to go at night, when the fountains are illuminated with spotlights. Total time: 20–30 minutes.

Retail Therapy: Start by circling the stores in Crystals at CityCenter, then hit the Miracle Mile Shops at Planet Hollywood. To wrap things up, cross the street and explore the Forum

Shops at Caesars Palace. Total time: three hours, depending on stops and dressing-room time.

Molten Fun: The Mirage's volcano is worth a gander, but the best views are from the opposite side of the Strip. From Bally's, head north and stop in front of the Casino Royale. It's best to go at night, when the "lava" glows like the real stuff. Total time: 25 minutes.

can interact with the hotel's director of wine. ⊠ *Bellagio, 3600 Las Vegas Blvd. S* ☎ *702/693–7871, 888/957–9777* ☎ *$15 adults (includes audio guide)* ⊙ *Daily 10–8.*

CityCenter Fine Art Collection. CityCenter includes $42 million in public art. Pieces range from sculptures to paintings and elaborate fountains. Our favorite: "Big Edge," an amalgam of kayaks and canoes by Nancy Rubins. ⊠ *CityCenter* ⊕ *www.citycenter.com* ⊙ *Daily 24 hrs.*

★ **Fountains of Bellagio.** Bellagio's signature water ballet has more than 1,000 fountain nozzles, 4,500 lights, and 27 million gallons of water. Fountain jets shoot 250 feet in the air, tracing undulations you wouldn't have thought possible, in near-perfect time with the music. The best view's from the Eiffel Tower's observation deck, directly across the street (unless, you've got a north-facing balcony room at The Cosmopolitan). Paris and Planet Hollywood have restaurants with patios on the Strip that also offer good views. Every first-time visitor to Vegas should take in this show. ⊠ *Bellagio, 3600 Las Vegas Blvd. S* ☎ *888/987–6667* ⊕ *www.bellagio.com* ⊙ *Weekdays 3–7 every ½ hr, 7–midnight every 15 mins; weekends noon–7 every ½ hr, 7–midnight every 15 mins.*

Fodor'sChoice **Siegfried & Roy's Secret Garden & Dolphin Habitat.** The palm-shaded sanc-
★ tuary has a collection of the planet's rarest and most exotic creatures. Animals are rotated regularly, but at any time you're likely to see white tigers, as well as lions, a snow leopard, a panther, and an elephant. (The tiger that mauled Roy in 2003 is not on view.) Atlantic bottle-nosed dolphins swim around in a 2.5-million-gallon saltwater tank at the Dolphin Habitat. Pass through the underwater observation station to the video room, where you can watch tapes of two dolphin births at the habitat. In addition to the regular admission, there are VIP edu-tours as well as a deluxe trainer-for-a-day program that gets you up-close and personal with the animals if you've got the time and $500 or so. ⊠ *The Mirage, 3400 Las Vegas Blvd. S* ☎ *702/791–7111* ⊕ *www. mirage.com/attractions/secret-garden.aspx* ☎ *$19.95 adults, $14.95 kids 4–12* ⊙ *Weekdays 11–6:30, weekends 10–6:30.*

Volcano at Mirage. This erupting volcano, a 54-foot mountain-fountain surrounded by a lake of miniature fire spouts, is a must-see free attraction on the Strip. Several times an hour the whole area erupts in flames, smoke, and eerily backlighted water that looks like lava. The thundering island percussion sound track was created by Grateful Dead drummer Mickey Hart. The best vantage point is near the main drive entrance, or on the East Side of Las Vegas Boulevard in front of Casino Royale. ⊠ *Mirage, 3400 Las Vegas Blvd. S* ☎ *702/791–7111* ⊕ *www. mirage.com* ⊠ *Free* ☉ *Daily 6–11 pm, every hr on the hr.*

WORTH NOTING

Jubilee! All Access Backstage Walking Tour. Admit it—you're just as mesmerized by all the sequins and fancy headpieces of a classic feather show as we are. On this tour, a real showgirl (or male dancer, depending on the day) escorts you backstage to see firsthand the workings behind the curtains for this $50-million stage production. The hourlong tour shows you the mechanics of the stage, costumes, and dressing rooms. Visitors must be 13 years or older and should be able to move up and down several cases of stairs. ⊠ *Bally's, 3645 Las Vegas Blvd. S* ☎ *702/967–4938* ⊕ *www.ballyslasvegas.com* ⊠ *$17; $12 with purchase of show ticket* ☉ *Mon., Wed., and Sat. 11 am.*

★ **Wildlife Habitat at Flamingo.** Just next to the Flamingo's pool area, a flamboyance of live Chilean flamingos, swans, ducks, koi, goldfish, and turtles live on islands and in streams surrounded by sparkling waterfalls and lush foliage. ⊠ *Flamingo Las Vegas, 3555 Las Vegas Blvd. S* ☎ *702/733–3111* ⊕ *www.flamingolasvegas.com* ⊠ *Free* ☉ *Daily 24 hrs.*

NORTH STRIP

Dining
★★★★★
Sightseeing
★★★★☆
Shopping
★★★★☆
Nightlife
★★★★☆

Like the best nights out, the North Strip is the perfect mix of luxury and opulence, fun and debauchery—a blend of the very best that Vegas has to offer in high-end, low-brow, and laugh-out-loud diversion. Wynn, Encore, Palazzo, and Venetian are posh celebrity favorites. And cheap beers at Treasure Island, carnival acts at Circus Circus, and thrill rides at the Stratosphere entertain the masses. In between, the Trump Hotel offers elegant, apartment-style living in a nongaming environment.

Sister properties dominate the landscape in this part of town—resorts that complement each other wonderfully. One pair, the Venetian and Palazzo, whisks visitors to Italy, where they can ride gondolas and marvel at indoor waterfalls. Another pair, Wynn and Encore, offer a different kind of luxury, one that Steve Wynn himself has sharpened after years in the business. Encore in particular is a one-of-a-kind blend of classic (authentic antiques pervade the property) and modern (windows in the casino). Also not to be missed: the Encore Beach Club, a thumping day-lounge experience.

Farther north, this part of the Strip embraces the circus. In the Adventuredome, behind Circus Circus, visitors can participate in an actual carnival, complete with cotton candy and midway games. On top of the Stratosphere tower the attractions are not for the faint of heart, considering that they suspend you about 900 feet over the ground.

The North Strip has improved upon a number of familiar Vegas experiences, too. Still campy, the Sirens of TI show in front of Treasure Island has been updated and is always worth the price (free). The golf course behind Wynn is a premier experience. And the "sports book" at Palazzo doubles as a casual restaurant from Emeril Lagasse. The North Strip presents a number of familiar sights; it just does them better.

GETTING HERE AND AROUND

The North Strip is far enough from the airport (20 to 25 minutes) that if a cabby opts to take the Interstate, it's probably not worth arguing for him to change course. A pedestrian bridge between the Palazzo and Wynn makes exploring these two properties easy. The journey from Trump and Encore to Circus Circus and the Stratosphere is deceptively long; on hot days, it pays to take a cab or public transportation. Be warned, from the Stratosphere, it's still 10 to 15 minutes to Downtown.

Las Vegas Monorail stations here include the Harrah's/Imperial Palace station, the Las Vegas Convention Center station, the LVH station, and the Sahara station. CAT (Citizens Area Transit) services this part of the Strip with public buses and double-deckers (⇨ *see also Bus Travel in Travel Smart*).

TOP ATTRACTIONS

Gondola Rides. Let a gondolier "o sole mio" you down Vegas's rendition of Venice's Canalozzo. We love this attraction because it's done so well—owner Sheldon Adelson was obsessed with getting the canals *just right*: he had them drained and repainted three times before he was satisfied with the hue, and the colossal reproduction of St. Mark's Square at the end of the canal is authentic right down to the colors of the façades. The gondoliers who ply the waterway are professional entertainers and train for two weeks to maneuver the canals. It all makes for a rather entertaining way to while away an hour on the Strip. Outdoor gondola rides along the resort's exterior waterway are also available, weather permitting. A gondola carries up to four passengers. ⊠ *The Venetian, 3355 Las Vegas Blvd. S* ☎ *702/414–4300* ⊕ *www.venetian. com* 🎫 *$16 per person (gondolas seat 4) or $64 total for a 2-seater* ⊙ *Sun.–Thurs. 10 am–11 pm, Fri. and Sat. 10 am–midnight.*

Fodors Choice ★ **Stratosphere Thrill Rides.** High above the Strip at the tip of the Stratosphere tower are three major thrill rides that will scare the bejeezus out of you, especially if you have even the slightest fear of heights. Don't even think about heading up here if you have serious vertigo. People have been known to get sick just watching these rides.

The **Big Shot** would be a monster ride on the ground, but starting from the 112th floor—and climaxing at more than 1,000 feet above the Strip—makes it twice as wild. Four riders are strapped into chairs on four sides of the needle, which rises from the Stratosphere's observation pod. With little warning, you're flung 160 feet up the needle at 45 mph, then dropped like a rock. The whole thing is over in less than a minute, but your knees will wobble for the rest of the day.

The **XScream** tips passengers 27 feet over the edge of the tower like a giant seesaw again and again. Sit in the very front to get an unobstructed view of the Strip, more than 800 feet straight down!

Another unobstructed view can be seen by dangling over the edge of the tower off the arm of **Insanity**. The arm pivots and hangs you out 64 feet from the edge of the tower; then it spins you faster and faster, so you're lifted to a 70-degree angle by a centrifugal force that's the equivalent of 3 g-forces. ⊠ *2000 Las Vegas Blvd. S* ☎ *702/380–7711, 800/998–6937* ⊕ *www.stratospherehotel.com/Tower/Rides/* 🎫 *Tower $16 adults, $10*

GREAT WALKS: NORTH STRIP

Viva Italy: The Strip has plenty of Italy to explore. To immerse yourself, stroll the canals around the Venetian's shops, then follow signs toward Barney's New York and Palazzo. All told, you never have to step outside. Total time: 45 minutes.

Wynn Nature: Conservatory gardens in both Wynn Las Vegas and Encore feature seasonal flowers and trees—both rarities in the middle of the Las Vegas desert. To care for this greenery, Wynn employs more than 50 gardeners. Total time: 40 minutes.

Mall and Trump: On superhot days, avoid the sun with a stroll through Fashion Show Mall, then cross Fashion Show Drive and head into the Trump Hotel Las Vegas for a martini at DJT. Total time: 45 minutes.

kids; *Big Shot $13, XScream or Insanity $12, unlimited rides and tower day pass $34* ⊗ *Sun.–Thurs. 10 am–1 am, Fri. and Sat. 10 am–2 am.*

Fodor'sChoice
★
Vegas Indoor Skydiving. Here you can get the thrill of skydiving without leaving the ground. A vertical wind tunnel produces a powerful stream of air that lets you float, hover, and fly, simulating three minutes of freefall after 20 minutes of training. Airspeeds reach 120 mph. You can make reservations a minimum of 48 hours in advance for parties of five or more. It closes for private parties from time to time; it's wise to call ahead. ⊠ *200 Convention Center Dr.* ☎ *702/731–4768, 877/555–8093* ⊕ *www.vegasindoorskydiving.com* ✉ *$85 for 1st flight; $50 per repeat flight* ⊗ *Daily 9:45 am–8 pm; classes every ½ hr.*

WORTH NOTING

Adventuredome at Circus Circus. If the sun is blazing, the kids are antsy, and you need a place to while away a few hours, make for the big pink dome behind Circus Circus. The 5-acre amusement park has more than 25 rides and attractions for all age levels, and is kept at a constant 72°F. Check out the Canyon Blaster, the world's largest indoor, double-loop roller coaster, a huge swinging pirate ship, a flume ride, bumper cars, several kiddie rides, a laser-tag room, a rock-climbing wall, and much more. And who wouldn't enjoy the Inverter, which whips you upside down over and over. The Fun House Express, designed exclusively for Circus Circus, uses computer-generated images to portray a fast-paced roller-coaster ride through a spooky world called Clown Chaos. ⊠ *Circus Circus* ☎ *702/794–3939, 866/456–8894* ⊕ *www.adventuredome. com* ✉ *$5–$8 per ride; all-day pass $26.95* ⊗ *Call for hrs.*

☺ **Madame Tussauds Las Vegas.** Audition in front of Simon Cowell or stand toe-to-toe with Muhammad Ali as you explore the open showroom filled with uncanny celebrity wax portraits from the worlds of show business, sports, politics, and everywhere in between. Crowd-pleasers include the figures of Lady Gaga, Tom Jones, Hugh Hefner, and Abe Lincoln. An interactive segment lets you play golf with Tiger Woods, shoot baskets with Shaquille O'Neill, play celebrity poker with Ben Affleck, dance with Britney Spears, or marry George Clooney. Discount tickets are available online. ⊠ *Next to the Venetian, 3377 Las Vegas*

FAMILY FUN

WILDLIFE

This may be Sin City, but there are plenty of great family-oriented activities. There's wildlife galore, starting with exotic birds at **Flamingo** and the fish and reptiles at **Shark Reef at Mandalay Bay**. Next, head to the **Mirage** to see the white tigers of the **Secret Garden** and the eponymous mammals of the **Dolphin Habitat**.

FAST TIMES

If your family prefers adrenaline-based bonding, scream your way up the strip, starting at the **Roller Coaster** at **New York–New York**. Next, head to the multifaceted entertainment complex **GameWorks** in the Showcase Mall (next to **MGM Grand**). Continue north along the Strip, stopping at **Circus Circus's** indoor theme park **Adventuredome** on your way to the **Stratosphere**

Tower. Here the Big Shot, XScream, and Insanity–The Ride fly high above the Strip at 1,149 feet. Can't decide between wild animals and wild rides? Go Downtown for both at The Tank at **Golden Nugget,** where a three-story waterslide includes a ride through a glass tube into the heart of a 200,000-gallon shark tank.

DOWNTIME

For a mellower afternoon, head to the Venetian's **Madame Tussaud's Wax Museum**. After posing next to Denzel and J-Lo, check out the exploding volcano at the **Mirage**. Since you're at the Mirage, grab last-minute tickets for ventriloquist **Terry Fator's** one-of-a-kind musical puppet act. You can minimize your kids' sinful intake by staying at the **Trump Hotel Las Vegas**, a posh accommodation unusual for being smoke- and casino-free.

Blvd. S ☎ *866/841–3739* ⊕ *www.madametussauds.com/lasvegas* ▭ *$25 adults, $15 kids 7–12* ☉ *Sun.–Thurs. 10–9:30, Fri. and Sat. 10–10:30.*

Sirens of TI. If *Saturday Night Fever* and *Pirates of the Caribbean* had a baby, it would be something like this oversexed, 20-minute outdoor spectacle. The musical naval battle between voluptuous Sirens and a greedy gang of pirates is full of groan-inducing lip-synched double entendres, explosions, and backflips from the crow's nests. The finale loosely mimics what happened at the Battle of Trafalgar in 1805 (and by loosely we mean that we're pretty sure the original battle didn't include a Siren deejay scratching out a funky beat during an ensemble song-and-stomp routine). Still it's a spectacle and certainly worth a stop on this part of the Strip. ⊠ *Treasure Island Las Vegas (TI), 3300 Las Vegas Blvd. S* ☎ *702/894–7111* ⊕ *www.treasureisland.com* ▭ *Free* ☉ *Daily 5:30 (winter only); 7, 8:30, 10, and 11:30 pm (spring/summer only).*

DOWNTOWN

Dining
★★★☆☆

Sightseeing
★★★☆☆

Shopping
★☆☆☆☆

Nightlife
★★☆☆☆

With neon lights, single-deck blackjack, and a host of new attractions that spotlight yesteryear, old Vegas is alive and well Downtown.

This neighborhood revolves around Fremont Street, a covered pedestrian walkway through the heart of the Downtown gambling district. Originally, this attraction was nothing more than a place to stroll; today, however, the canopy sparkles with millions of lights, and outfitters have set up everything from zip lines to band shells on street level down beneath. Use Fremont Street to access resorts such as the Golden Nugget (our fave in this neighborhood), Four Queens, the Plaza Hotel & Casino, and others. Just be prepared for sensory overload.

Old is new again all over Downtown. The Mob Museum, which opened in February 2012, pays homage to Las Vegas's mafia years; the Smith Center, a world-class performing arts center that opened in March 2012, was designed to invoke the same art deco style that inspired the Hoover Dam. Both facilities are worth exploring (especially if there's a good concert at the Smith). Then, of course, there's the Neon Museum, where visitors can behold the glow of original Las Vegas neon signs.

Old casinos Downtown seem to announce renovations just about once a month, and Zappos.com is planning a move into the building formerly occupied by the city government. A vibrant arts and mixology scene has developed here, too—the "First Friday" walkabout celebrates local art and artists on the first Friday of every month, and a burgeoning Arts District attracts fans of the avant-garde from all over the world.

No visit to Downtown Vegas would be complete without a pilgrimage to one of the neighborhood's most lasting legacies: Luv-It Frozen Custard. Flavors here change regularly, but cinnamon and almond chip are mainstays in the rotation. Try some in a homemade waffle cone with chocolate sauce on top.

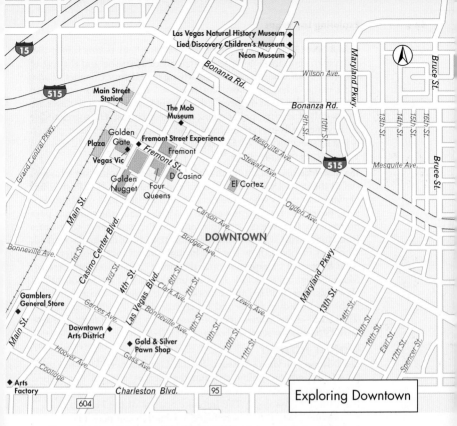

Exploring Downtown

GETTING HERE AND AROUND

Taxi and public transportation are the easiest ways to get to Downtown from the South, Central, and North Strip, but be warned that city buses must stick to Las Vegas Boulevard and often get stuck in terrible traffic around rush hour. Once you're Downtown, everything is walkable. Do not stray from populated areas, and travel in pairs at night. And if you've had too much to drink, it's admirable but not advisable to walk back to the North Strip *and above properties*: It's more than an hour on foot. Best to take a taxi.

TOP ATTRACTIONS

Fremont Street Experience. If you're looking for something a little different, head to this eardrum-rupturing, eye-popping show that takes place on the underside of a 1,450-foot arched canopy 90 feet overhead. The 12.5 million synchronized LED modules, 180 strobes, and eight robotic mirrors per block treat your eyes, while the 208 speakers combine for 550,000 watts of fun for your ears. The shows play five to seven times a night depending on the time of year and the six-minute presentations change regularly. In 2010, the "Experience" also added a zip line that spans the length of the pedestrian walkway. ⊠ *Fremont St. from Main to 4th Sts.* ⊕ *www.vegasexperience.com* ⊡ *Free* ☉ *Daily.*

Gold & Silver Pawn Shop. Reality television fans flock to this run-of-the-mill pawn shop for a glimpse of owner Rick Harrison and the rest of the staff, all of whom appear regularly on the History Channel's *Pawn Stars* reality television show. On any given night, the line waiting to get in might be 30 or 40 people deep. Inside, dozens of glass cases are chock-full of jewelry, poker chips, and other curios. The merchandise area, which sells everything from G&S T-shirts to G&S shot glasses, is just as spacious. ⊠ *713 Las Vegas Blvd. S* ☎ *702/385–7912* ⊕ *www. gspawn.com* ⊗ *Daily 9–9.*

The Mob Museum. It's fitting that the new, $42-million Mob Museum sits in the circa-1933 former federal courthouse and U.S. Post Office Downtown; this is where the Kefauver Committee held one of its historic hearings on organized crime in 1950. Today the museum pays homage to Las Vegas's criminal underbelly, explaining to visitors (sometimes with way too much exhibit text) how the mafia worked, who was involved, how the law brought down local mobsters, and what happened to gangsters once they were caught and incarcerated. Museum highlights include bricks from the wall of the St. Valentine's Day Massacre in 1929, and a mock-up of the electric chair that killed mobsters including Julius and Ethel Rosenberg. ⊠ *300 Stewart Ave.* ☎ *702/229–2734* ⊕ *www.themobmuseum.org* ⊠ *$18 adults, $12 kids 5–17* ⊗ *Sun.–Thurs. 10–7, Fri. and Sat. 10–8.*

WORTH NOTING

⟳ **Lied Discovery Children's Museum.** The Lied (pronounced *leed*) has more than 100 hands-on exhibits covering the sciences, arts, and humanities. It hosts several excellent traveling exhibits each year that have ranged from fun ("Grossology: The Impolite Science of the Human Body") to sobering ("My Life as a Refugee"). Children can play a laser harp, experience a hurricane, perform on a stage, and more. ⊠ *833 Las Vegas Blvd. N* ☎ *702/382–5437* ⊕ *www.ldcm.org* ⊠ *$9.50 adults, $8.50 kids 1–17* ⊗ *Tues.–Fri. 9–4 (summer all weekdays 10–5), Sat. 10–5, Sun. noon–5.*

Neon Museum. After years of legal wrangling (and years of desperately trying to come up with the cash), Las Vegas' Neon Museum received a $1.9 million grant from the Bureau of Land Management and in May 2011 "opened" this gated park with dozens of historic neon signs on display. Some of the more notable signs include those for the Bow & Arrow Motel, the Silver Slipper, and Binion's Horseshoe. At this writing, the park was still waiting to build a formal visitor's center, but it's available for prescheduled guided tours, held Tuesday through Saturday at 12 and 2 pm. ⊠ *810 Las Vegas Blvd. N* ☎ *702/387–6366* ⊕ *www. neonmuseum.org* ⊠ *$15* ⊗ *Tours ues.–Sat. noon and 2 pm.*

Vegas Vic. The 50-foot-tall neon cowboy outside the Pioneer Club has been waving to Las Vegas visitors since 1947 (though, truth be told, he had a makeover and was replaced by a newer version in 1951). His neon sidekick, Vegas Vicki, went up across the street in 1980. ⊠ *Fremont St. and Las Vegas Blvd..*

2

PARADISE ROAD AND THE EAST SIDE

Dining
★★★☆☆

Sightseeing
★★☆☆☆

Shopping
★☆☆☆☆

Nightlife
★★★☆☆

The East Side of Las Vegas, an area that includes Paradise Road and stretches to the University District, is as eclectic as it is convenient. Much of the area is residential, save for a handful of (older) resorts that rise from the landscape like beacons. There also is a preponderance of restaurants, extensive medical offices, and most of the area's collegiate athletic facilities.

Paradise Road itself is the Strip's sister street. On the southern end the Hard Rock Hotel is one of the most popular off-Strip resorts in town, and despite the opening of increasingly over-the-top Strip properties, Paradise has remained popular over the years. A number of other resorts, such as the Platinum and the Rumor Boutique Hotel, qualify as nongaming, but are still within walking distance of larger casinos. This stretch also comprises the heart of the area affectionately known as "Fruit Loop," Vegas's gay-friendly neighborhood. Especially on Friday and Saturday nights, the parties at Gipsy and the Piranha Nightclub are some of the biggest raves in town.

Though there aren't any resorts in the University District, UNLV (University of Las Vegas) and the Thomas and Mack Center provide plenty of things to see and do, from sporting events to (on-campus) museums and more. As is the case with most college towns, the cost of living in this neck of the woods is considerably lower than it is elsewhere in town. In other words, you can usually get dinner and a beer for less than $6. You don't have to be a freshman to know that's a good deal.

GETTING HERE AND AROUND

Public transportation from the Strip to the East Side is actually pretty reliable, so long as you're not traveling in the middle of the night. Taxis know the area well, too, especially if you're heading from the Strip over to the Hard Rock or into the University District. As is the case with most of the Vegas suburbs, the best bet here is to rent a car.

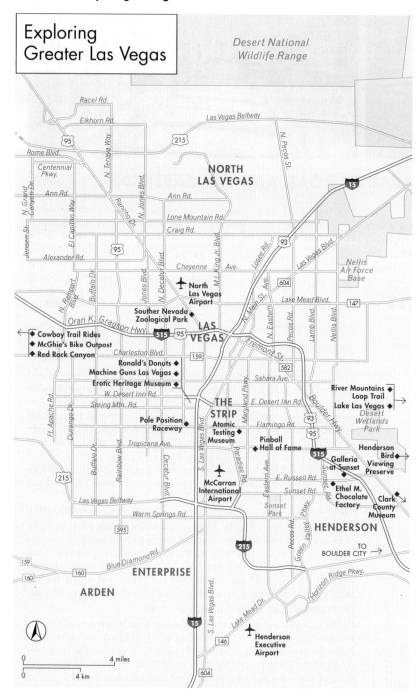

Exploring Greater Las Vegas

Desert National Wildlife Range

Racel Rd.
Elkhorn Rd.
Las Vegas Beltway
Rome Blvd.
Centennial Pkwy.
Ann Rd.
Jensen St.
N. Grand Canyon Dr.
El Capitan Way
Rancho Dr.
N. Tenaya Way
N. Jones Blvd.
N. Decatur Blvd.

NORTH LAS VEGAS

N. Pecos St.
Ann Rd.
Lone Mountain Rd.
Craig Rd.
Alexander Rd.
Cheyenne Ave.
M.L. King Jr. Blvd.
Losee Rd.
Las Vegas Blvd.

Nellis Air Force Base

North Las Vegas Airport
Souther Nevada Zoological Park
N. Rampart Blvd.
Buffalo Dr.
Jones Blvd.
Oran K. Gragson Hwy.

LAS VEGAS

N. Main St.
N. Eastern Ave.
Lake Mead Blvd.
Pecos Rd.
Lamb Blvd.
Nellis Blvd.

◆ Cowboy Trail Rides
◆ McGhie's Bike Outpost
◆ Red Rock Canyon
Charleston Blvd.
Fremont St.
Ronald's Donuts ◆
Machine Guns Las Vegas ◆
Erotic Heritage Museum ◆
W. Desert Inn Rd.
Spring Mtn. Rd.
Ft. Apache Rd.
Durango Dr.
Sahara Ave.
E. Desert Inn Rd.
Boulder Hwy.

River Mountains Loop Trail ◆
Lake Las Vegas ◆
Desert Wetlands Park

THE STRIP
Pole Position Raceway ◆
Atomic Testing Museum ◆
Pinball Hall of Fame ◆
Flamingo Rd.
Maryland Pkwy.
S. Las Vegas Blvd.
Paradise Rd.
Galleria at Sunset ◆
Henderson Bird ◆ Viewing Preserve
Buffalo Dr.
Rainbow Blvd.
Decatur Blvd.
Tropicana Ave.
Eastern Ave.
E. Russell Rd.
Sunset Rd.
Ethel M. Chocolate Factory ◆
Clark County Museum ◆
McCarran International Airport
Sunset Park
Las Vegas Beltway
Warm Springs Rd.
Pecos Rd.
Green Valley Pkwy.
Sunset Rd.

HENDERSON

TO BOULDER CITY →

Blue Diamond Rd.
ENTERPRISE
ARDEN

Lake Mead Dr.
Horizon Ridge Pkwy.

Henderson Executive Airport

0 ___ 4 miles
0 ___ 4 km

WHAT TO SEE

Haunted Vegas Tours. As you ride through the streets of Las Vegas on this 2½-hour tour, your guide, dressed as a mortician, tells the tales of Sin City's notorious murders, suicides, and ghosts (including Bugsy Siegel, Elvis, and Tupac Shakur). A 30-minute *Rocky Horror*–like sideshow, called Haunted Vegas, runs prior to the 21-stop tour. Make reservations in advance and note that kids have to be 13 for the Haunted tour and 16 for the Mob tour. ⊠ *Royal Resort, 99 Convention Center Dr.* ☎ *702/339–8744, 866/218–4935* ⊕ *www.hauntedvegastours.com* ▨ *$66.25* ⊗ *Daily, 9:30 pm.*

National Atomic Testing Museum. Today's Las Vegas is lighted by neon, but during the Cold War, uranium and plutonium illuminated the area from time to time as well in the form of a roiling mushroom cloud in the distance. This museum, in association with the Smithsonian, commemorates southern Nevada's long and fascinating history of nuclear weapons research and testing with film footage and photographs of mushroom clouds; testimonials; and artifacts (including a deactivated bomb, twisted chunks of steel, and bomb-testing machinery from the Nevada Test Site). Alien lovers will love the newest exhibit, which debuted in early 2012 and spotlights the top-secret suspected alien landing ground dubbed Area 51. ⊠ *755 E. Flamingo Rd., Desert Research Institute, East Side* ☎ *702/794–5151* ⊕ *www.nationaltomictestingmuseum.org* ▨ *$14 adults, $11 kids 7–17* ⊗ *Mon.–Sat. 10–5, Sun. noon–5.*

Pinball Hall of Fame. In late 2009 the Las Vegas Pinball Museum moved into a dedicated facility with more than 140 games from all eras, including the old wood-rail models of the 1950s and modern games with fancy effects and complex play. Though this may sound more like an arcade than a museum, the local club is a nonprofit organization whose goal is to preserve this piece of Americana and share the joy of the silver ball with as many folks as possible. There's even an on-site Pinball Hall of Fame. All quarters get donated to the local Salvation Army. ⊠ *1610 E. Tropicana Ave., East Side* ⊕ *www.pinballmuseum. org* ▨ *Free entry, 25¢ or 50¢ per game* ⊗ *Sun.–Thurs. 11–11, Fri. and Sat. 11 am–midnight.*

HENDERSON AND LAKE LAS VEGAS

Dining
★★☆☆☆

Sightseeing
★★★★☆

Shopping
★★☆☆☆

Nightlife
★★☆☆☆

Suburbia spreads quickly to the southeast of the Las Vegas Strip, and it continues to spread; Henderson is one of the fastest growing cities in the entire nation. Much of this area is residential, with only a smattering of casinos.

One of those casinos—the M Resort—has arguably the most commanding views of the Strip; because the property is uphill from town, it literally looks down on the rest of the Valley. Another casino resort, Green Valley Ranch, is adjacent to one of the best shopping malls in the area. Both are worthwhile destinations for either a weekend or an afternoon.

Out near Lake Las Vegas, the vibe is much more luxurious; resorts such as the Westin Lake Las Vegas Resort & Spa and Ravella dot the shoreline of a man-made lake, providing the perfect backdrop for golf and a variety of other outdoor activities. Bicyclists, joggers, roller-bladers, and good-old walkers will love the River Mountains Trail, a 35-mile loop that links Henderson, Lake Las Vegas, and Boulder City to the south. Pedaling over the sometimes-formidable mountains, it's hard to believe this deserted region is just a dozen miles from a major city.

Farther afield are the main attractions in this part of the Valley: Lake Mead National Recreation Area and Hoover Dam (⇨ *see also Side Trips chapter*). If you've got the time, rent a houseboat for a multiday vacation on the lake; it's the best way to explore the body of water at your own pace. At the dam, take the tour for an inside look (literally) at one of humankind's greatest engineering feats. These icons are packed in summer, so it's best to plan your trip for a shoulder season such as spring or fall.

GETTING HERE AND AROUND

From the Strip, both Interstate 515 and Boulder Highway wind southeast toward Henderson, while Lake Mead Drive cuts due east toward Lake Mead. Public transportation serves this area, but the easiest way to get around is to rent a car. Once you're out by Lake Mead, bicycles actually are a great method of transportation. If you're philosophically opposed to exercise in Las Vegas, fear not—taxis are always just a phone call away.

KEEP YOUR MIND IN THE GUTTER

Bowling in Vegas will give you a new appreciation for the sport most of us associate with bad haircuts and ugly shoes. You'll find elements of casinos, bars, and nightclubs here; with lively crowds to match. Locals take their leagues seriously, so spare yourself some heartache and call ahead to make a lane reservation.

The Orleans Bowling Center. The Orleans Resort and Casino is in a working-class neighborhood just off the Strip, and its 70-lane bowling center is a popular spot for locals and tourists alike. ⊠ *4500 W. Tropicana Rd., West Side* ☎ *702/365–7111* ⊕ *www.orleanscasino.com* ☼ *24/7.*

Red Rock Lanes. This 72-lane bowling alley has all the amenities, including Cosmic Bowling—glow-in-the-dark bowling with a deejay—until 2 am on Friday and Saturday nights. Roll on through until morning—it's open 24 hours a day. If you've got the bankroll, you can live the full nightclub-plus-bowling dream with bottle service at your own VIP Lanes. ⊠ *Red Rock Casino Resort Spa, 11011 W. Charleston Blvd., Summerlin* ☎ *702/797–7467, 866/767–7773* ⊕ *www.redrocklanes. com* ☼ *Mon.–Thurs. 8 am–2 am, Fri.–Sun. 24 hrs.*

Sam's Town Bowling Center. This is a 56-lane locals' alley where leagues and tournaments are taken seriously. Tourists come for the cocktail lounge, connecting casino, and "Xtreme Bowling Experience" starting at 9 pm on Friday and Saturday nights that will allow you to "strike out" in a nightclub like never before. The scoring system includes Spare Maker, so rookies know where to aim. ⊠ *5111 Boulder Hwy., Boulder Strip* ☎ *702/456–7777* ⊕ *www. samstownlv.com* ☼ *24/7.*

Santa Fe Station Bowling Center. This 60-lane facility at Santa Fe Station Casino is a traditional bowling center, with video arcade, bar, and the top-of-the-line Brunswick electronic scoring system. ⊠ *4949 N. Rancho Dr., West Side* ☎ *702/658–4900* ⊕ *www.santafestationlasvegas. com* ☼ *Sun.–Thurs. 7 am–midnight, Fri. and Sat. 7 am–1 am.*

Silver Nugget Bowling. This alley has 24 lanes and new equipment, a pro shop, and a modern automatic scoring system. Its version of Cosmic Bowling, which includes fancy lights and a booming sound system, goes 7 pm–midnight on Friday and Saturday. Weekend days you can rent lanes by the hour, instead of paying per person per game. ⊠ *2140 Las Vegas Blvd. N, North Side* ☎ *702/399–1111* ⊕ *www. silvernuggetcasino.net* ☼ *Sun.–Thurs. 9 am–9 pm, Fri. and Sat. 9 am–midnight.*

Suncoast Bowling Center. Reflecting its upscale Summerlin neighborhood, the bowling center at the Suncoast, with 64 lanes, is designed to provide every high-tech toy for bowlers. The alley has "Cosmic Bowling" on Saturday and hosts a number of different leagues throughout the week. ⊠ *9090 Alta Dr., Summerlin* ☎ *702/636–7111, 877/677–7111* ⊕ *www. suncoastcasino.com* ☼ *24/7.*

2

Green Valley Ranch, an elegant resort that rivals many big Strip properties, is a great spot to explore in Henderson.

WHAT TO SEE

Clark County Museum. Step into the past (quite literally) at this modest museum, a 30-acre site that features a modern exhibit hall with a time-line exhibit about southern Nevada from prehistoric to modern times. The facility also offers a collection of restored historic buildings that depict daily life from different decades in Las Vegas, Boulder City, Henderson, and Goldfield. Other attractions include a replica of a 19th-century frontier print shop; and a 1960s wedding chapel that once stood on the Las Vegas Strip. There are also buildings and machinery dating from the turn of the 20th century, a nature trail, and a small ghost town. If you can't get to the Las Vegas Springs Preserve, on the North Side of town, this is a worthwhile substitute. ⊠ *1830 S. Boulder Hwy.* ☎ *702/455–7955* ⊕ *www.clarkcountynv.gov* ⊡ *Adults $2, seniors and children $1.*

♺ **Galleria at Sunset.** This open-air mall, Henderson's largest, boasts dozens of stores and boutiques, restaurants (in a food court), and seasonal carnivals. There's also a Kid's Club that provides sitting services for parents who wish to be child-free while they shop. ⊠ *1300 W. Sunset Rd.* ☎ *702/434–0202* ⊕ *www.galleriaatsunset.com.*

♺ **Ethel M Chocolate Factory.** Watching gourmet chocolates being made will make your mouth water; fortunately the tour is brief and there are free samples at the end. You can buy more of your favorites in the store. This is a self-guided tour, so if your youngsters start to get impatient, pick up the pace (or not). ⊠ *1 Sunset Way* ☎ *702/458–8864.*

2

☾ **Henderson Bird Viewing Preserve.** More than 200 bird species have been spotted among the system of nine ponds at the 100-acre Henderson Bird Viewing Preserve. The preserve's ponds, located at the Kurt R. Segler Water Reclamation Facility, are a stop along the Pacific flyway for migratory waterbirds, and the best viewing times are spring and fall. The earlier you get there the better if you want to fill your bird checklist. The ponds also harbor hummingbirds, raptors, peregrine falcons, tundra swans, cormorants, ducks, hawks, and herons. The office will loan out a pair of binoculars if you ask. Keep the bags of bread crumbs at home. The preserve doesn't allow the feeding of wildlife, and bikes and domestic pets are not allowed. ✉ *350 E. Galleria Dr.* ☎ *702/267–4180* ⊕ *www.cityofhenderson.com/parks/parks/bird_preserve.php* 🖃 *Free* ☉ *Daily, hrs vary according to season.*

Lake Las Vegas. This 320-acre, man-made lake outside of Henderson is regarded for its golf courses, boating, fishing, and hotels. Three resorts sit on the lakeshore, including Ravella at Lake Las Vegas and the new Westin Lake Las Vegas Resort & Spa. There's also a (less-than-notable) casino on-site. The lake was created by an earthen dam in 1991. ⊕ *www.lakelasvegas.com.*

☾ **River Mountains Loop Trail.** Running 35 miles around the River Mountains, this multi-use paved trail is perfect for hiking, biking, running, jogging, and horseback riding. For a stretch, the trail parallels the shores of Lake Mead, and connects with a historic spur that leads from the Lake Mead National Recreation Area to a parking lot just north of the Hoover Dam. The route runs through Boulder City, Henderson, and Lake Las Vegas; bike rentals are available in all three areas. ⊕ *www.rivermountainstrail.com.*

WEST SIDE

Dining
★★★☆☆

Sightseeing
★★☆☆☆

Shopping
★☆☆☆☆

Nightlife
★★★☆☆

The West Side of Las Vegas technically isn't a suburb (it's actually part of Las Vegas proper), but it sure feels like one. Big-box stores and fast-food chains abound. Housing developments sit on just about every major corner. Sure, resorts such as the Palms and the Rio do double-duty as locals' joints and major tourist draws with vibes just as swanky as Strip properties. But for the most part, malls and tract houses in this stretch give way to a small number of locals' casinos here such as the long-standing Gold Coast.

There are hidden gems in this area, and most of them exist in the industrial section a stone's throw (west) from the Strip. Number one on the list: Machine Guns Vegas, a decidedly upscale shooting range. The Erotic Heritage Museum, practically around the corner, fires up a different kind of excitement.

The West Side also has a small but thriving Chinatown. This three-block area has everything from ramen to vegan donuts and world-class Thai food. In particular, restaurants in a stretch of strip malls along Spring Mountain Road are known for their unpretentious and authentic experience. Not surprisingly, this is where many Strip chefs come to eat when they're not on the clock.

The West Side is where many of Vegas's celebrity residents call home. Penn Jillette had his "Slammer" built here. Former tennis stars Andre Agassi and Steffi Graf live here, as well as Sacramento Kings (and Palms Las Vegas) owners George and Gavin Maloof. In the olden days, when Mobsters ruled Sin City, they all lived here, too.

GETTING HERE AND AROUND

Transportation on the West Side depends exclusively on where you're headed. The Palms and the Rio are within easy taxicab distance from the Strip. The Rio is even walkable from the Center Strip—about 20 minutes west on Flamingo. Beyond the Palms, and you're back in rental-car territory. Because the West Side is home to thousands of casino employees, public transportation blankets the area.

WHAT TO SEE

Erotic Heritage Museum. It's makes sense that a museum devoted to erotic art and pornography resides in Sin City. Exhibits feature everything from lingerie to old porno ads, including erotic "artifacts," films, and fine art. The museum is open until 10 pm on weekends and hosts a busy events calendar, offering weekly and monthly seminars on sex and sexuality. ⊠ *3275 Industrial Rd.* ☎ *702/369–6442* ⊕ *www. eroticheritagemuseumlasvegas.com* ☉ *Closed Mon.*

Machine Guns Vegas. Swanky nightclub meets gun range in this only-in-Vegas addition to the scene. In an industrial neighborhood just west of the Interstate, "MGV" (as it's known) offers 10 shooting lanes, including two in an ultra-exclusive VIP area. Visitors have dozens of firearms to choose from, everything from .22-caliber handguns up to an M-60 fully automatic machine gun. Package deals include multiple guns. All target practice enables guests to select their targets; among the options are evil clowns and Osama bin Laden. ⊠ *3501 Aldebaran Ave.* ☎ *800/757–4668, 702/476–9228* ⊕ *www.machinegunsvegas.com* 🖃 *at $25 for handguns, $50 for machine guns* ☉ *Daily 10–8.*

Ⓒ ★ **Pole Position Raceway.** These are no putt-putting lawnmower-engine go-karts. These miniature racers are electric (think: souped-up golf carts) and reach up to 45 mph. You and 12 competitors zip around a ¼-mile indoor track full of twists and turns. The Pole Position computers track your overall performance from race to race, and over multiple visits. A free shuttle service is available from the big Strip hotels. Adults must be 56 inches tall to ride; kids must be 48 inches. ⊠ *4175 S. Arville* ☎ *702/227–7233* ⊕ *www.polepositionraceway.com/vegas* 🖃 *$50 for 2 races* ☉ *Sun.–Thurs. 11–11, Fri. and Sat. 11–midnight.*

NEED A BREAK?

Ⓒ **Ronald's Donuts.** The best donuts in Vegas are sold at this tiny Chinatown storefront tucked in a strip mall along Spring Mountain Road. Surprisingly, all of the offerings are vegan, a quirk that has put the hole-in-the-wall on the national map in recent years. Whenever you go, expect a line. ⊠ *4600 Spring Mountain Rd.* ☎ *702/873–1032* ☉ *Weekdays. 4–4, Sat. 5–4, Sun. 5–2.*

Ⓒ **Southern Nevada Zoological–Botanical Park.** About a five-minute drive northwest of Downtown, you'll find a diverse collection of animals, including a chimpanzee, eagles, ostriches, emus, parrots, wallabies, flamingos, endangered cats (including lions and tigers), and every species of venomous reptile native to southern Nevada—150 species in all. ⊠ *1775 N. Rancho Dr.* ☎ *702/647–4685* ⊕ *www.lasvegaszoo.org* 🖃 *$9 adults, $7 kids 2–12* ☉ *Daily 9–5.*

SUMMERLIN AND RED ROCK CANYON

Dining
★★★☆☆
Sightseeing
★★★★☆
Shopping
★★☆☆☆
Nightlife
★★☆☆☆

There's a master plan behind the Western suburb of Summerlin, and it shows. The town—which was founded by movie legend Howard Hughes—has been developed and built out according to a written-on-paper strategy, a "planned community" through and through. Today the neighborhood comprises dozens of gated communities, as well as a handful of epic golf courses and casino resorts such as the J.W. Marriott and Red Rock Casino Resort & Spa.

While the Red Rock Casino is hip and fun, the highlight of the region is the casino's namesake, the Red Rock National Conservation Area. This area, managed by the Bureau of Land Management, is an expansive open space that heads from civilization into the ocher-rock wilderness of the Spring Mountains beyond. Canyon walls boast some of the best rock climbing in the world. There also are petroglyphs, drawings from Native-Americans who first inhabited this area more than 1,000 years ago.

One of the best ways to explore the wilderness outside Summerlin is, without question, on horseback. A number of outfitters run half- and full-day guided trips; some even include dinner. Just about every ride brings visitors up-close-and-personal with native flora and fauna, including Joshua trees, jackrabbits, and more. If possible, ask your guide to lead you to the top of the canyon for a one-of-a-kind glimpse of the Strip.

GETTING HERE AND AROUND

Public transportation to Summerlin exists from the Strip, but considering how long it'd take you to get out there, the best bet is to rent a car. Interstate 215 winds around the outskirts of the Las Vegas Valley and ends in Summerlin; other options are taking surface roads such as Charleston Boulevard and Spring Mountain Road.

The West Side of Las Vegas is the gateway to the Red Rock Canyon National Conservation Area at the base of the Spring Mountains.

Visitor Info Red Rock Canyon Visitor Center. This modest visitor center, operated by the Red Rock Canyon Interpretive Association, contains an informative history of the region, as well as a number of exhibits on local flora and fauna. ☎ 702/515–5350 ⊕ *www.redrockcanyonlv.org* ✉ *$7 per vehicle ($3 for bikes and pedestrians), $30 annual pass* ⊘ *Weekdays 8–4:30; Scenic Loop year-round, 6 am–dusk.*

WHAT TO SEE

Cowboy Trail Rides. The best way to explore the mountains of Red Rock National Conservation Area is by horseback, and Cowboy Trail Rides has it covered. The outfitter runs one-hour, half-, and full-day trips from a location just east of the Red Rock Visitor Center. Some of the trips include lunch or dinner. Scenic packages include the Sunset BBQ Ride (1 hour, 45 minutes; $169 per person) and the WOW ride (5 hours; $329 per person). Beautiful views of the Strip give way to desert wilderness. Keep your eyes peeled for jackrabbits, Joshua trees, and other notable desert life. The view of the Strip isn't too shabby either. ✉ *Red Rock Canyon Stables* ☎ *702/387–2457* ⊕ *www.cowboytrailrides.com.*

McGhie's Bike Outpost. One of the largest outfitters in the Las Vegas Valley, McGhie's rents equipment for skiing, bicycling, and sandboarding. This location, in Downtown Blue Diamond, specializes in bikes—convenient, since it's right on the doorstep of 125 miles of hard-core mountain-biking. The company rents bikes individually, and also offers a host of guided tours around the Red Rock National Conservation Area and beyond. Unlike other outfitters in the area, McGhie's also rents bikes specifically for kids. ✉ *16 Cottonwood #B, Blue Diamond* ☎ *702/875-4820* ⊕ *mcghies.com.*

     C◔　**Red Rock Canyon National Conservation Area.** Red sandstone cliffs and
Fodor'sChoice　dramatic desert landscapes await day-trippers and outdoors enthusi-
    ★　asts at Red Rock Canyon National Conservation Area. Operated by
the Bureau of Land Management (BLM), the 195,819-acre national
conservation area features narrow canyons, fantastic rock formations,
seasonal waterfalls, desert wildlife, and rock art sites. The elevated Red
Rock Overlook provides a fabulous view of the cream and red sandstone cliffs. For a closer look at the stunning scenery, take the 13-mile,
one-way scenic drive through the canyon. The backcountry byway's
open from dawn to dusk. Other activities including hiking, mountain
biking, rock climbing, canyoneering, picnicking, and wildlife-watching.
A developed campground, located 2 miles from the visitor center, has
71 campsites ($15 per night; $30 for group sites), pit toilets, and drinking water for visitors wanting to extend their stay. ⊕ *www.blm.gov/nv.*

Where to Stay

WORD OF MOUTH

"We love Bellagio—but now will stay at the Wynn if we can get similiary priced rooms, and try to get a Strip/mountain view room higher up. Both are great. And in any event, don't miss the great fountains at the Bellagio, and the Arboretum and the largest chocolate waterfall in the world—at the Patissere just behind the Arboretum."

—Tomsd

Updated by
Matt Villano

The world of Vegas-area casino hotels changes constantly. In the early 2000s just about every resort was investing heavily in family-friendly accommodations and activities. Today, however, most places have refocused squarely on decadence and indulgence.

Just about every property now has a special pool for topless (they call it "European-style") sunbathing. Many resorts also have expanded their cocktail programs (the fancy word for this is now "mixology").

Some of these efforts have been more successful than others. The posh new Encore Beach Club, at Encore, exemplifies the new notion of a "dayclub" in that it creates a nightclub vibe during the day. Developments at The Cosmopolitan Las Vegas have had a similar impact; the property has three on-staff mixology gurus, and a special kitchen where these cocktail whizzes whip up recipes all day long.

Other properties have established new benchmarks in amenities. When CityCenter opened in 2010, the $8.5-billion complex included Crystals, a new-era shopping mall with flagship stores of Prada, Tiffany & Co, and some of the spendiest boutiques in America. Also in 2010, the Palazzo launched "Prestige," an optional $100 reservation upgrade that grants guests access to a concierge level including daily snack service, drink service, and a business center.

Despite competition from these up-and-comers, the established properties still pack em in. Bellagio's rooms still carry cachet, and the Mirage—the hotel that started the megaresort trend more than 20 years ago—continues to sell out. At Wynn Las Vegas and the Venetian, guests rave about everything from comfy beds to exquisite restaurants and great shopping. At Caesars Palace the constantly evolving Qua Baths & Spa might be one of the top spas in town. And for overall experience, the Four Seasons–Las Vegas, which occupies top floors of the tower at Mandalay Bay Resort & Casino, is still one of the best.

LAS VEGAS LODGING PLANNER

TIMING YOUR TRIP

Though a sagging economy hit the city hard in 2011, accommodations still fill up fast. When it's time for a big convention—or a big sporting event—it's not unusual for all of Las Vegas's roughly 150,000 hotel rooms to sell out completely. Combine those with three-day weekends and holidays, and you can see why it's wise to make lodging arrangements for busy weekends as far ahead as possible.

On the other hand, 2010 and 2011 marked the era of the last-minute deals. Many hotels, eager to fill rooms, were offering rock-bottom prices and tempting packages for as low as $79 per night (most offered these deals on their Twitter accounts). What does this mean for you? If you're not traveling during a busy weekend and have the luxury of waiting until the last minute, you probably can find a room somewhere in town—for dirt cheap. Look around.

If your original room isn't to your liking, you can usually upgrade it around checkout time the next day.

GETTING THE BEST ROOM

There's no surefire way to ensure that you'll get the room you want, when you want it, and for the lowest price possible. But here are a few tips for increasing your chances:

Book early. This town's almost always busy, so book as early as possible. Generally, if you book a room for $125 and later find out that the hotel is offering the same category of room for $99, the hotel will match the lower price, so keep checking back to see if the rates have dropped. Of course, this won't work if you prepay for a room on Expedia, Orbitz, Kayak, or Priceline. It also won't work if you buy in for a prepaid package deal. Once you go this route, you either can't get out of the reservation or you may have to pay a hefty cancellation fee.

Getting the room you want. Actual room assignments aren't determined at most Vegas hotels until the day before, or the day of, arrival. If you're hoping for a particular room (for example, a room with a view of the Strip), phone the hotel a day before you arrive and speak with somebody at the front desk. This applies whether you booked originally through the hotel or some other website. Don't be pushy or presumptuous. Just explain that although you realize the hotel can't guarantee a specific room, you'd appreciate it if they'd honor your preference.

Your second-best bet. Simply check in as early as possible on the day of arrival—even if no rooms are yet available (and you have to wait in the casino), you're likely to get first preference on the type of room you're seeking when it opens up.

What about upgrades? It's virtually never inappropriate to request a nicer room than the one you've booked. At the same time, it's virtually always inappropriate to expect that you'll receive the upgrade. The front-desk clerk has all the power and discretion when it comes to upgrades, and is unlikely to help you out if you act pushy or haughty. Gracious humility, smiles, and warmth go a long way.

WHERE SHOULD I STAY?

	Vibe	Pros	Cons
South Strip	Fun! Resorts here are glamorous, but not as serious as Center and North Strip properties. With roller coasters, arcades, shows, and beaches, properties are also the most kid-friendly.	Close to airport; plenty of diversions for the whole family; bargains at top Strip properties can be found here	Need to take a taxi or monorail to hit Center Strip. Fewer shopping options than Center and North Strip.
Center Strip	Happening, hip section of Strip has the newest resorts with all of the latest and greatest amenities. Shopping in this part of town also is second to none.	Many rooms are new or recently renovated; spas are among the largest and most popular in town.	Traffic congestion, both on sidewalks and off; rooms generally pricier than they are elsewhere in town.
North Strip	Glitz and glamour rule. Rooms are among the largest and most ornate, and on-property amenities are all top-of-the-line.	Most (but not all) rooms are suites; incredible restaurant options; golf course at Wynn Las Vegas.	Highest prices on-site; long (and spendy) cab ride from the airport.
Downtown	Vegas as it used to be—back when rooms were an afterthought and everything was about the casino downstairs.	Affordable lodging; classic casinos; proximity to other diversions in the area.	Rooms are bare-bones; streets aren't entirely safe after dark; expensive taxi ride to big resorts on the Strip.
West Side & Summerlin	Smaller, more amenity-heavy resorts sit west of the Strip, with the most lavish of the bunch offering glamorous pools and golf courses nearby. Many resorts appeal to locals.	Quieter and away from hustle of Strip. Lower room rates; incredible views of the Spring Mountains and the Strip.	Summerlin is a half hour from the Strip.
East Side & Henderson	Resorts here (and along Paradise Road) are functional; instead of offering the latest and greatest in amenities, rooms are on the small side.	Lower prices than the Strip; on-site diversions such as bowling; proximity to local services.	Long taxi ride to Strip (half hour from Henderson); doesn't have the excitement of the Strip

Do I tip for an upgrade? It's not customary to tip hotel clerks for upgrades, especially at nicer properties. If you wave some cash around discreetly, it might not hurt, but it won't necessarily help either.

THE LOWDOWN ON RATES

In general, at an average of about $95 per night, rates for Las Vegas accommodations are lower than those in most other American resort and vacation cities. Still, the situation is changing; though rack rates for fancy properties are higher than ever, the sluggish economy has forced

Many rooms in the Cosmopolitan have large, comfortable seating areas that make a great place to relax with friends.

many hotels to offer fantastic deals. There are about a hundred variables that impact price, depending on who's selling the rooms (reservations, marketing, casino, conventions, wholesalers, packagers), what rooms you're talking about (standard, deluxe, minisuites, standard suites, deluxe suites, high-roller suites, penthouses, bungalows), and demand (weekday, weekend, holiday, conventions or sporting events in town).

When business is slow, many hotels reduce rates on rooms in their least desirable sections, sometimes with a buffet breakfast or even a show included. Most "sales" occur from early December to mid-February and in July and August, the coldest and hottest times of the year, and you can often find rooms for 50% to 75% less midweek than on weekends. Members of casino players clubs often get offers of discounted or even free rooms, and they can almost always reserve a room even when the rest of the hotel is "sold out."

HOTEL-RESORT PRICES
Prices in the hotel-resort reviews are the lowest cost of a standard double room in high season, excluding taxes, service charges, and meal plans (except at all-inclusives).

BEST BETS FOR LAS VEGAS HOTELS

Fodor's offers a selective listing of quality lodging experiences in every price range, from the city's best budget beds to its most sophisticated luxury hotels. Here are our top recommendations by price and experience. The very best properties—those that provide a particularly remarkable experience in their price range—are designated in the listings with the Fodor's Choice logo.

Fodor's Choice ★

Aria, p. 77
Bellagio, p. 79
Cosmopolitan Las Vegas, p. 83
Encore, p. 93
Four Seasons–Las Vegas, p. 100
Green Valley Ranch, p. 104
Mandarin Oriental, Las Vegas, p. 102
The Platinum, p. 110
The Venetian, p. 97
Wynn Las Vegas, p. 99

Best By Price

$

Flamingo Las Vegas, p. 102
Harrah's Las Vegas, p. 102
Monte Carlo, p. 100
New York–New York, p. 73

$$

Aria, p. 77
Caesars Palace, p. 81
Green Valley Ranch, p. 104
Hard Rock, p. 110
The LVH, p. 110
Luxor Las Vegas, p. 67
MGM Grand Hotel & Casino, p. 71
The Palms Las Vegas, p. 111
Paris Las Vegas, p. 87
Planet Hollywood, p. 89
The Platinum, p. 110
Red Rock, p. 111
Rio All-Suite, p. 112
Treasure Island, p. 103
Tropicana, p. 101
Trump International Hotel, p. 104
Vdara, p. 102

$$$

Bellagio, p. 79
Cosmopolitan Las Vegas, p. 83
Mandalay Bay, p. 69
The Palazzo, p. 95
THEhotel, p. 100
The Venetian, p. 97
Wynn Las Vegas, p. 99

$$$$

Encore, p. 93
Four Seasons–Las Vegas, p. 100
Mandarin Oriental, Las Vegas, p. 102

Best By Experience

BEST CONCIERGE

Bellagio, p. 79
Caesars Palace, p. 81
Encore, p. 93
Four Seasons-Las Vegas, p. 100
Mandarin Oriental, Las Vegas, p. 102

BEST HOTEL BAR

Aria, p. 77
Bellagio, p. 79
Cosmopolitan Las Vegas, p. 83
Mandarin Oriental, Las Vegas, p. 102
New York–New York, p. 73
The Venetian, p. 97
Wynn Las Vegas, p. 99

BEST GYM

Aria, p. 77
Caesars Palace, p. 81
Encore, p. 93
Mandarin Oriental, Las Vegas, p. 102
Red Rock, p. 111
The Venetian, p. 97

BEST FOR ROMANCE

Caesars Palace, p. 81
Encore, p. 93
Mandarin Oriental, Las Vegas, p. 102
Paris Las Vegas, p. 87
Red Rock, p. 111

3

BEST BUILDING ARCHITECTURE

Aria, p. 77
Caesars Palace, p. 81
Luxor Las Vegas, p. 67
Paris Las Vegas, p. 87
Red Rock, p. 111
The Venetian, p. 97

BEST LOCATION

Aria, p. 77
Bellagio, p. 79
Caesars Palace, p. 81
Flamingo Las Vegas, p. 102
Mirage Las Vegas, p. 85
Paris Las Vegas, p. 87
Planet Hollywood, p. 89

BEST-KEPT SECRET

Monte Carlo, p. 100
Planet Hollywood, p. 89
The Platinum, p. 110
Red Rock, p. 111
Rio All-Suite, p. 112

BEST BEDS

Caesars Palace, p. 81
Cosmopolitan Las Vegas, p. 83
Encore, p. 93
The Palazzo, p. 95
Red Rock, p. 111
Wynn Las Vegas, p. 99

BEST FOR BUSINESS

Bellagio, p. 79
Four Seasons–Las Vegas, p. 100
Mandarin Oriental, Las Vegas, p. 102
MGM Grand Hotel & Casino, p. 71
THEhotel, p. 100
The Venetian, p. 97

BEST VIEWS

Cosmopolitan Las Vegas, p. 83
The Palms Las Vegas, p. 111
Paris Las Vegas, p. 87
Red Rock, p. 111

BEST HIPSTER HOTELS

Aria, p. 77
Cosmopolitan Las Vegas, p. 83
Hard Rock, p. 110
The Palms Las Vegas, p. 111
The Platinum, p. 110
THEhotel, p. 100

BIGGEST (BY ROOM COUNT) HOTELS

Aria, p. 77
Caesars Palace, p. 81
Cosmopolitan Las Vegas, p. 83
Mandalay Bay, p. 69
MGM Grand Hotel & Casino, p. 71
Planet Hollywood, p. 89
The Venetian, p. 97

BEST LOBBY

Bellagio, p. 79
Caesars Palace, p. 81
Cosmopolitan Las Vegas, p. 83
Four Seasons–Las Vegas, p. 100
The Palazzo, p. 95
Wynn Las Vegas, p. 99

BEST POOL

Caesars Palace, p. 81
Encore, p. 93
Flamingo Las Vegas, p. 102
Hard Rock, p. 110

Mandalay Bay, p. 69
MGM Grand Hotel & Casino, p. 71
The Palms Las Vegas, p. 111
Wynn Las Vegas, p. 99

BEST SERVICE

Bellagio, p. 79
Caesars Palace, p. 81
Four Seasons–Las Vegas, p. 100
Mandarin Oriental, Las Vegas, p. 102
Trump International Hotel, p. 104
Wynn Las Vegas, p. 99

BEST NEW HOTELS

Aria, p. 77
Cosmopolitan Las Vegas, p. 83
Encore, p. 93
M Resort, p. 110
Mandarin Oriental, Las Vegas, p. 102
Vdara, p. 102

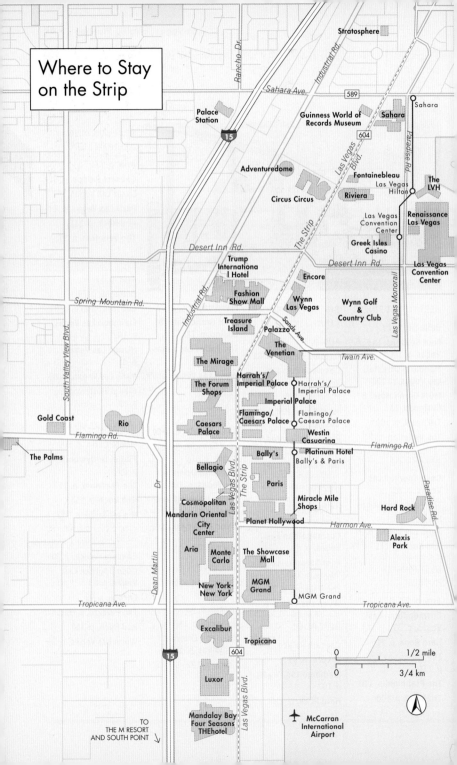

3

THE SOUTH STRIP

With an Oz-like structure that stretches forever, a pyramid with a light you can see from space, and a replica of the New York City skyline, the southern third of the Strip between CityCenter and the iconic "Welcome to Las Vegas" sign could be considered the entertainment hub of Vegas.

Resorts in this area include the Tropicana, Mandalay Bay, Luxor, Excalibur, MGM Grand, New York–New York, and Monte Carlo. Rooms on this side of town generally are within 10 to 15 minutes of the airport and are slightly more affordable than their Center and North Strip counterparts. After major renovations at the Tropicana and New York–New York in 2010 and 2011, the South Strip is among the most recently updated sections of Sin City's most famous street.

SOUTH STRIP TOP PICKS
Luxor Las Vegas
Mandalay Bay/THEhotel
MGM Grand
New York–New York

This part of town has a small claim on Strip history as well; the Tropicana dates back 50 years, and the MGM, Mandalay Bay, and the Luxor were early entrants in the megaresort race of the 90s. And with every fight night at the MGM Grand, concert at Mandalay Bay, and annual event such as the Country Music Awards, entertainment history is written and rewritten from this side of Las Vegas Boulevard.

Another trend here: Ultraexclusive hotels within the ordinary hotels. Mandalay has the Four Seasons; MGM has Skylofts; Monte Carlo has Hotel 32. You don't have to splurge to have a great time on the South Strip, but enjoying sumptuous linens, exclusive amenities, and unparalleled service every once in a while sure is special.

DID YOU KNOW?

New York–New York's towers, which include replicas of the Empire State Building, the Chrysler Building, and the CBS Building, are approximately one-third the actual size of the real buildings.

LUXOR LAS VEGAS AT A GLANCE

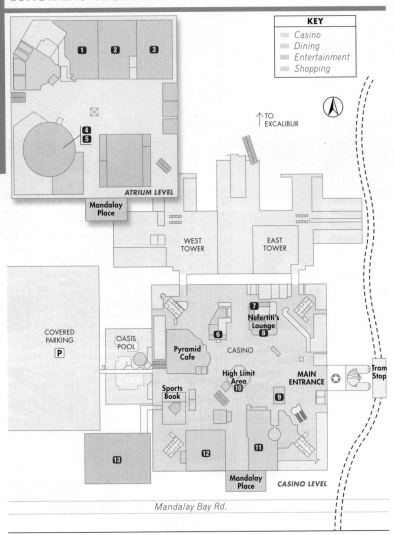

KEY
- Casino
- Dining
- Entertainment
- Shopping

↑ TO EXCALIBUR

ATRIUM LEVEL

Mandalay Place

WEST TOWER

EAST TOWER

COVERED PARKING **P**

OASIS POOL

Pyramid Cafe

CASINO

Nefertiti's Lounge

High Limit Area

Sports Book

MAIN ENTRANCE

Tram Stop

Mandalay Place

CASINO LEVEL

Mandalay Bay Rd.

LUXOR LAS VEGAS

$ *Rooms from: $189* ⊠ *3900 Las Vegas Blvd. S* ☎ *702/262-4444, 877/386-4658* ⊕ *www.luxor.com* ⇗ *3,958 rooms, 442 suites.*

AMENITIES

■ The Luxor has one of the largest pools on the Strip. For a truly indulgent treat, an exclusive poolside VIP oasis offers services such as hand-delivered treats, iced aroma-therapy towels, and margarita popsicles, to name a few.

■ At Nurture, the resort's spa, enjoy a eucalyptus steam bath, dry sauna, and whirl-pools as preparation for any number of rejuvenating massage treatments.

■ Women (or couples) eager to take sexy (but tasteful) photos can schedule an in-room boudoir photo session with a local photographer.

Welcome to the land of the Egyptians—Vegas style. This modern-world wonder is topped with a xenon light beam that burns brighter than any other in the world and can be seen from anywhere in the Valley at night; for that matter, it's supposedly even visible from space. The exterior is made with 13 acres of black glass. Forget elevators; climbing the slanted walls of the Luxor pyramid requires four "inclinators" to reach guest rooms. On each floor, open-air hallways overlook the world's largest atrium. Pyramid rooms are large but otherwise nondescript. One wall slopes because of the building's design—an interesting effect, but it makes these rooms feel cramped. We prefer the twin 22-story towers next door: they're newer and have brighter rooms with large windows, many that offer killer views of the pyramid. Bathrooms are spacious and have separate showers and tubs. Spa suites in the pyramid have plenty of extra space and deep whirlpool tubs with brilliant views of the skyline. **Pros:** decent value; hip casino; expansive pool. **Cons:** slanted room walls; removed from main Strip action. **TripAdvisor:** "would stay again," "amazing must stay," "good value for the price."

HIGHLIGHTS

The Atrium: Inside is the world's largest atrium—you get the full impact of the space from the second floor, where "Bodies... The Exhibition" gives guests an eerie view of the human body.

*Fantasy***:** This seductive adult revue is fun to share with your significant other.

The...um...archaeology: For something entirely unique, head outside the casino, walk past the porte cochere, and follow the sidewalk inside a replica of the Great Sphinx of Giza. Only in Vegas.

MANDALAY BAY AT A GLANCE

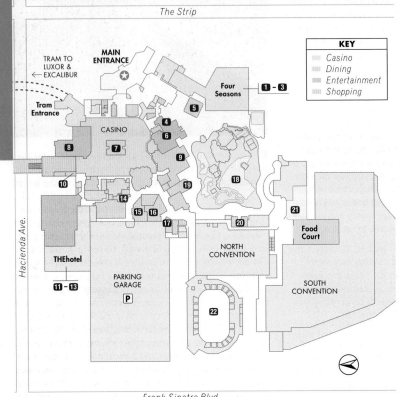

The Strip

TRAM TO LUXOR & ← EXCALIBUR

MAIN ENTRANCE

Tram Entrance

Four Seasons

KEY

Casino
Dining
Entertainment
Shopping

1 – 3

5

CASINO

4

6

8

7

9

Hacienda Ave.

10

14

18

19

15 16

17

20

21

Food Court

THEhotel

11 – 13

PARKING GARAGE

P

NORTH CONVENTION

SOUTH CONVENTION

22

Frank Sinatra Blvd.

MANDALAY BAY

$ *Rooms from: $279* ✉ *3950 Las Vegas Blvd. S* ☎ *702/632–7777, 877/632–7800* ⊕ *www. mandalaybay.com* ⇗ *2,775 rooms, 436 suites.*

AMENITIES

■ Located on 11 acres, the Mandalay Beach offers guests a wave pool, lazy river, three swimming pools, a jogging track, and 2,700 tons of real sand that's trucked in regularly. The Beach has premium seating and the exclusive new Beachside Casino. If that weren't enough, the Moorea Beach Club also offers raft and tube rentals, as well as cabanas, daybeds, and bungalows and villas that include personalized service.

■ Two on-site spas–the Spa at Mandalay Bay and the bathhouse at THEHotel–offer a variety of relaxation chambers and dozens of signature treatments. Men love the gentlemen's facial at the Spa at Mandalay; women swear by the crème brûle treatment at the bathhouse.

■ Mandalay Place, a shopping corridor that connects Mandalay Bay to the Luxor next door, offers a number of shops, including Nike Golf, Urban Outfitters, and more.

This resort is actually three hotels in one—the namesake Mandalay Bay, THEhotel, and the Four Seasons–Las Vegas. Each brand is distinct, and each has a separate entrance. *(For individual reviews of THE-Hotel and the Four Seasons see Other Highly Recommended Hotels.)* Mandalay itself is decked out like a South Seas beach resort, complete with the scent of coconut oil drifting through the casino and pagodas rising out of the vast casino floor. It's the most affordable and least fabulous lodging component of the overall resort, but it's still a first-rate property with cavernous rooms. Bathrooms have stone floors and counters, as well as deep soaking tubs with separate showers. Guests also receive full access to the Beach, the Beachside Casino, and the Moorea Beach Club, which offers topless sunbathing. Perhaps the only downside to staying at Mandalay Bay is the spacious layout of the property itself; without a map, it could take you five or six tries to get your bearings when you come and go. **Pros:** large rooms; ample options; the Beach. **Cons:** concerts can be loud. **TripAdvisor:** "okay hotel but way too far from everything else," "great choice," "excellent from top to bottom."

HIGHLIGHTS

The sharks: The Shark Reef aquarium features a 1.6-million-gallon saltwater tank with more than 2,000 different animals.

The concerts: Between an outdoor pavilion and the House of Blues, there's never a shortage of good live music.

The views: Two ultralounges, MIX and the Foundation Room, provide amazing views of the Vegas Valley.

The eats: Celebrity chefs such as Charlie Palmer, Hubert Keller, Rick Moonen, and Mary Sue Milliken have restaurants here.

MGM GRAND AT A GLANCE

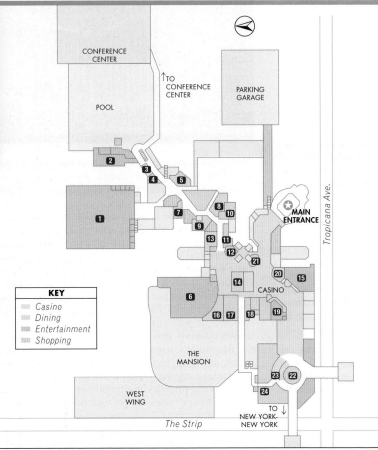

KEY
- Casino
- Dining
- Entertainment
- Shopping

SHOPPING
CBS Television City 3

SPAS
MGM Grand Spa 2

SHOWS
Crazy Horse, *Theater* 19
Hollywood Theatre,
Arts Centers 15
KÀ, Cirque du Soleil, *Theater* 6
MGM Grand Garden,
Arts Centers 1

NIGHTLIFE
Centrifuge, *Lounge* 22
Rouge, *Lounge* 12
Tabú, *Lounge* 20
Zuri, *Lounge* 21

EXPENSIVE DINING
Craftsteak, *Steakhouse* 10
Emeril's New Orleans Fish House,
Cajun–Creole 8
Fiamma, *Italian* 13
Joël Robuchon at
the Mansion, *French* 16
L'Atelier, *French* 17

Nobhill Bistro, *American* 18
SeaBlue, *Seafood* 7
Shibuya, *Japanese* 11

MODERATE DINING
Diego, *Mexican* 5
Pearl, *Chinese* 9
Rainforest Cafe, *American* 24
Wolfgang Puck
Bar & Grill, *American* 14

INEXPENSIVE DINING
Stage Deli, *Deli* 23
'wichcraft, *American* 4

MGM GRAND HOTEL & CASINO

$ *Rooms from: $219*
✉ *3799 Las Vegas Blvd. S*
☎ *702/891–7777, 877/880–0880, 877/646–5638 Skylofts*
🌐 *www.mgmgrand.com*
🛏 *4,293 rooms, 751 suites.*

AMENITIES

- MGM has one of the largest pools in the world. Dubbed the Grand Pool Complex, the area features five separate pools, three separate whirlpools, and a lazy river for meandering in giant inner tubes. There's even a waterfall, and a European-style (read: topless) sunbathing area called the "Wet Republic Ultra Pool."
- Airport check-in from 9 am to 11 pm.
- The MGM Grand Spa & Health Club has a bevy of treatment rooms and a state-of-the-art fitness center; and Cristophe Salon, one of the best on the Strip, is adjacent to the spa.
- In-room "entertainment hubs" allow guests to connect to the Internet, project presentations on the flat-screen television, charge multiple Smartphones, and play MP3 players.

A regal, solid bronze MGM lion mascot fronts the four emerald-green, fortress-like towers of the MGM Grand, one of the largest hotels in the world. The self-proclaimed "City of Entertainment" is loosely based on Oz, but it tries just a little too hard to be something for everyone. Rooms in the five 30-story towers that comprise this property come in nine different varieties. Standard accommodations are masculine and modern; all were updated in 2012. Further up the line, the various types of suites are more stylish and striking, and offer many fun perks. The best of the bunch include the 650-square-foot Bungalow suites, which are fitted with black-and-white Italian-marble bathrooms; the corner Premiere suites, which come with four-person dining areas and two TVs; and the two-story Terrace suites, which have 14-foot vaulted ceilings. At the very high end, the super-posh **Skylofts at MGM Grand** occupy the hotel's top two floors. There also are 29 villas located within the **Mansion at MGM Grand**, the resort's high-roller palace. **Pros:** something for everyone; great concerts and fights; fantastic restaurants. **Cons:** easy to get lost; schlep to parking. **TripAdvisor:** "awesome Vegas experience," "pleased with our stay," "good value except for the resort fee."

HIGHLIGHTS

Joël Robuchon: The Mansion houses the ultraluxe (and expensive) restaurant from the French superchef.

The "City of Entertainment:" MGM delivers on their self-proclamation with the impressive MGM Grand Garden Arena—which hosts big-name concerts and championship boxing matches, and "CSI: The Experience," an attraction based on the popular television show.

Family fun: Kids enjoy the Rainforest Cafe; there's also a complete day-care facility.

3

NEW YORK–NEW YORK AT A GLANCE

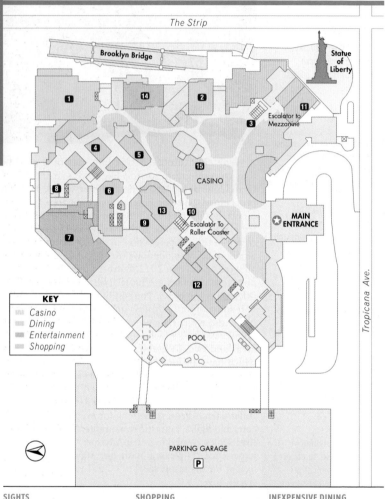

The Strip

Brooklyn Bridge

Statue of Liberty

1   **14**   **2**

11

Escalator to Mezzanine   **3**

4   **5**

15

CASINO

8   **6**

13   **10**

MAIN ENTRANCE

9

Escalator To Roller Coaster

7

12

Tropicana Ave.

KEY
- Casino
- Dining
- Entertainment
- Shopping

POOL

PARKING GARAGE
P

NEW YORK–NEW YORK HOTEL & CASINO

💲 Rooms from: $139 ✉ 3790 Las Vegas Blvd. S ☎ 702/740–6969, 800/689–1797 ⊕ www.newyorknewyork.com 🛏 1,920 rooms, 104 suites.

AMENITIES

■ At the Spa at New York–New York, therapists perform a variety of treatments, including Swedish and deep-tissue massages, hydrotherapy, and facials.

■ The Regis Signature Salon is a great place for haircuts and mani-pedis.

■ Though the pool always draws a crowd, it pales in comparison to some of the other pools on the Strip—unless you splurge $65 for the VIP package that includes guaranteed seating, two raft rentals, and a snack basket.

■ The SoHo Village shopping area, designed to look just like SoHo in the Big Apple, features brands such as Ed Hardy.

Vegas takes on Manhattan in this fantasy version of Gotham City. The mini-Manhattan skyline is one of our favorite parts of the Strip with third-size to half-size re-creations of the Empire State Building, the Statue of Liberty, the Chrysler building, and other iconic NYC structures. Rooms in this sprawling compound are quite a bit larger than the typically tiny hotel rooms in the *real* Gotham. Beyond all the legroom, they're not particularly fancy, but the hotel has made some improvements in recent years. Also, the trek from the front desk to some of the towers can feel longer than the New York City Marathon, and the Manhattan Express roller coaster that loops around the hotel can be intrusively loud if your room is near the tracks. Several grades of room are available, and as you pay more, you get plush amenities such as separate sitting areas with sofas, marble bathroom counters, and separate glass showers. **Pros:** admirable New York facsimile; art deco lobby; new casino floor. **Cons:** layout is somewhat confusing; cramped sports book; mediocre pool. **TripAdvisor:** "fun hotel, awesome location," "great stay," "nice vacation hotel."

HIGHLIGHTS

The Manhattan Express: The roller coaster darts between the "buildings" of the hotel's skyline and is hands down the best ride on the Strip.

Big Apple flavor: Walk through an art deco lobby, play virtual-reality games at an arcade reminiscent of Coney Island, chow down at a surprisingly good food court patterned after Greenwich Village. While you explore, keep your eye out for details such as names on mailboxes and brownstone apartment facades with air-conditioners in the windows.

Zumanity: The risqué, entertaining performance has become one of the most popular (and provocative) Cirque du Soleil shows of all time.

3

THE CENTER STRIP

Things tend to be larger than life in the heart of the Strip. Consider the scale replica of the Eiffel Tower—half the size of the original. Or wander into CityCenter, the $8.5-billion city-within-the-city.

This part of the Strip stretches from CityCenter and Planet Hollywood to the Mirage, including Mandarin Oriental, The Cosmopolitan, Paris, Bally's, Caesars Palace, the Flamingo, and Harrah's along the way. Taken as a group, these properties represent some of the most storied on the Strip (Caesars Palace) and the newest (The Cosmopolitan).

The Center Strip can be characterized by shopping. Lots, and lots of shopping. The highest of the high-end stores are inside Crystals, the gateway to CityCenter. At Planet Hollywood, reputable brands dominate the Miracle Mile. Stores inside the astonishing Forum Shops, next to Caesars, fall somewhere in between. The Center Strip even is home to one of the largest Walgreens in the world. Another commonality among hotels here: great spas. Treatment options at Mandarin Oriental, Aria, The Cosmopolitan, and Caesars Palace, could keep visitors busy (or is it relaxed?) for months. Some spas also offer hammams.

Rooms themselves in this area are all over the lot; some, like standard rooms at Bally's, are affordable and bare-bones; others, such as those inside The Cosmopolitan, make all others appear to be so yesterday. It pays to shop around.

CENTER STRIP TOP PICKS

Aria

Bellagio

Caesars Palace

The Cosmopolitan

The Mirage

Paris

Planet Hollywood

ARIA AT A GLANCE

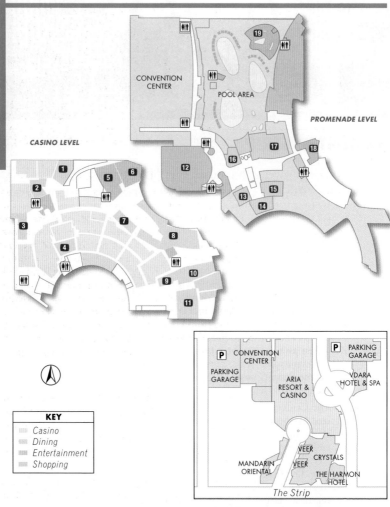

KEY

Casino
Dining
Entertainment
Shopping

ARIA

$ *Rooms from: $219* ⊠ *3730 Las Vegas Blvd. S* ☎ *702/590–7757, 866/359–7757* ⊕ *www.arialasvegas.com* ➳ *3,436 rooms, 568 suites.*

3

AMENITIES

■ While first-time visitors to Aria rave about the lake-like pool and on-site restaurants, the real attraction is the spa, which, when it opened, was the largest in town. The facility is the only spa in the country to offer Japanese stone sauna "Ganbanyoku" beds, and boasts three private spa "suites," each of which serves up to eight people at a time.

■ The pools: Take a dip in (or just people-watch near) one of three ellipse-shaped pools on the secluded pool deck. Inquire about deals for cabanas; especially midweek, they can be surprisingly affordable.

■ The room service: Most of the on-site restaurants will deliver to your room; all you have to do is ask.

■ The property features the world's first fleet of stretch limousines powered by compressed natural gas.

★ Fodor's Choice Lauded across town as the "new kid on the block," Aria truly deserves most of the attention it receives. The lobby is a soaring, three-story atrium bathed in natural light (a novel concept in this town). There's even more natural light upstairs, where every guest room boasts floor-to-ceiling windows. Tech-geeks will love the touch-screen control pad that operates everything from curtains to television, music, and lights. Bathrooms are spacious, though it's challenging to use the connected-but-separate shower and whirlpool tub combo without making a mess. Nightly turndown service and laptop-size safes are nice touches. **Pros:** high-tech rooms; natural light; service. **Cons:** confusing technology for Luddites; weird shower setup. **TripAdvisor:** "perfect location, pure luxury," "great rooms," "great hotel/resort/casino."

HIGHLIGHTS

The art: Aria is home to many of the pieces that comprise CityCenter's $40 million fine-art collection—Maya Lin's "Colorado River," an 84-foot sculpture of reclaimed silver that mirrors the route of the eponymous waterway, hangs in the lobby behind the check-in desk.

The green: As of spring 2012, Aria was the largest building in the world to achieve LEED Gold certification from the U.S. Building Council.

Crystals: The adjacent shopping and entertainment complex offers some of the most high-end boutiques in the nation, including Gucci, Prada, Mikimoto, Tom Ford, and Harry Winston (to name a few).

BELLAGIO AT A GLANCE

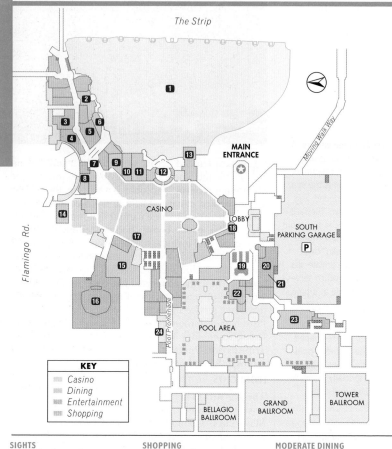

BELLAGIO LAS VEGAS

$ Rooms from: $249 ⊠ 3600 Las Vegas Blvd. S ☎ 702/693–7111, 888/987–6667 ⊕ www. bellagio.com ⇆ 3,421 rooms, 512 suites.

3

AMENITIES

■ Marvel at the Mediterranean-infused alfresco pool complex, which comprises five pools, a café, and a pool bar. Book a chair inside one of the ultraexclusive Cypress Premier Lounges and enjoy chilled towels and smoothie shots throughout the day.

■ Spa Bellagio, where traditional treatments such as Swedish and deep-tissue massages are complemented by innovative hydrotherapy and hot-stone options. Five definitive pool-courtyard settings invite you to splash into serenity; cabana rentals also are available.

■ The Via Bellagio contains luxe boutiques, with names like Chanel, Dior, and Gucci.

★ **Fodor's Choice** Bellagio is impressive more for its refined elegance than for gimmicks. If it's pampering you're after, stay in the Spa Tower, which has impressive rooms and suites (with steam showers and soaking tubs), as well as an expanded full-service spa and salon. Rooms in the original hotel tower are snazzy, with Italian marble and luxurious fabrics that were refreshed in 2011. Elegant, faux Italian provincial furniture surrounds either a single king-size bed or two queen-size beds. Bellagio has one of the higher staff-to-guest ratios in town, which results in visibly more solicitous service than you might expect at such an enormous property. This service is best in the Executive Suite Lounge, which opened in January 2009 and offers complimentary business center services. **Pros:** centrally located; posh suites; classy amenities. **Cons:** not kid-friendly; pricey; pretentious attitude among some guests. **TripAdvisor:** "beautiful, clean, and relaxing," "location great," "worth it for the building and location."

HIGHLIGHTS

Top-tier meals: With eateries from Michael Mina, Jean-Gorges Vongerichten, and Julian Serrano, Bellagio has one of the best restaurant-rosters in town.

The Bellagio fountains: More than 1,200 fountains erupt in a choreographed water ballet across the man-made Bellagio lake.

The lobby: Here you're dazzled with a fantastic and colorful glass sculpture called *Fiori di Como*, by famed artist Dale Chihuly.

The Conservatory: This indoor botanical conservatory is gorgeous. The gardens are particularly stunning during Christmas and Chinese New Year.

CAESARS PALACE AT A GLANCE

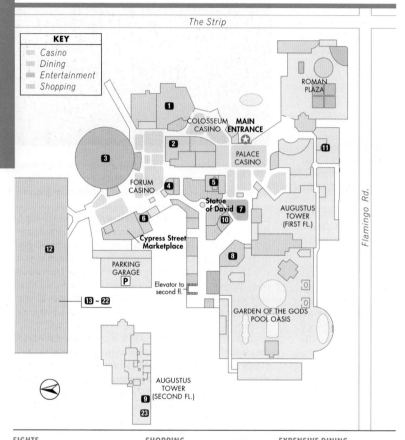

The Strip

KEY
Casino
Dining
Entertainment
Shopping

ROMAN PLAZA

1

COLOSSEUM CASINO **MAIN ENTRANCE**

2

PALACE CASINO

11

3

FORUM CASINO

4

5

Statue of David **7**

10

AUGUSTUS TOWER (FIRST FL.)

6

Cypress Street Marketplace

8

12

PARKING GARAGE **P**

Elevator to second fl.

GARDEN OF THE GODS POOL OASIS

13 – 22

Flamingo Rd.

AUGUSTUS TOWER (SECOND FL.)

9

23

CAESARS PALACE

$ *Rooms from: $189* ✉ *3570 Las Vegas Blvd. S* ☎ *702/731–7110, 866/227–5938* ⊕ *www.caesarspalace.com* 🛏 *3,495 rooms, 465 suites* 🍴 *No meals.*

AMENITIES

■ Qua Baths & Spa is a dream. For massages, the facility offers 51 treatment rooms, including wet rooms with Vichy showers and an herbal steam room. Both the men's and women's areas have Arctic ice rooms—a cold sauna where it's always 55°F.

■ As the name suggests, hair highlights are the specialty at the on-site salon, Color—a Salon by Michael Boychuck.

■ At the Men's Zone barber Sal Jeppi administers old-school flat-razor shaves with lather from a latherizer machine that's probably older than you.

■ Dogs that weigh 50 pounds or less are welcome in certain rooms through the hotel's PetStay program. Amenities for these guests include food dishes, disposable waste bags, and dog treats.

The opulent entrance, fountains, Roman statuary, bas-reliefs, and roaming centurions all add up to the iconic, over-the-top Las Vegas hotel. You can get your picture taken with Caesar, Cleopatra, and the centurion guard; find the full-size reproduction of Michelangelo's *David*; or amble along Roman streetscapes in the Forum Shops to see the robotic Fall of Atlantis show. Caesars was one of the first properties to create lavish rooms that guests might actually want to spend time in; today the rooms are as sumptuous as any on the Strip. For an additional $70 to $100 or more per night, guests can book a Deluxe Room in the new Octavius or Augustus towers; these rooms have marble-and-brass bathrooms with oversize whirlpool tubs. A number of fancier and more expensive "Fantasy" suites also are offered. The second floor of the Augustus Tower features Qua Baths & Spa and Guy Savoy, the famous French chef's first restaurant outside Paris. **Pros:** Arctic ice rooms at Qua; Garden of the Gods Pool Oasis; storied property. **Cons:** complex floorplan is difficult to get your bearings; small casino; limited on-site parking. **TripAdvisor:** "one of the coolest places in Vegas," "can't wait to go back," "this place just keeps getting better."

HIGHLIGHTS

The shopping: Some of the best shopping of any Vegas casino resort, with more than 160 stores at the Forum and Appian Way shops.

The pools: The lavish Garden of the Gods Pool Oasis, a series of Roman-style gardens, baths, and fitness areas anchored by the Temple pool, is one of the best pool spots in town.

The entertainment: Shows at the new Colosseum are second to none, attracting headliners such as Celine Dion, Cher, and Jerry Seinfeld.

The technology: Rooms in the circa-2012 Octavius Tower have their own app for guests to connect with hotel services via Smartphone.

3

COSMOPOLITAN LAS VEGAS AT A GLANCE

NIGHTLIFE

Book and Stage, *Lounge* **1**

The Chandelier, *Lounge* **3**

Marquee, *Nightclub* **2**

SHOPPING

AllSaints, *Vintage Clothing* **7**

Beckley, *Women's Clothing* **5**

DNA2050, *Women's Clothing* **4**

Stitched, *Men's Clothing* **6**

EXPENSIVE DINING

Estiatorio, *Greek* **8**

Jaleo, *Spanish Tapas* **9**

MODERATE DINING

Comme ça,
French Brasserie **11**

Scarpetta, *Italian* **10**

THE COSMOPOLITAN OF LAS VEGAS

[$] *Rooms from: $280*
✉ *3708 Las Vegas Blvd. S*
☎ *702/698–7000* 🌐 *www.cosmopolitanlasvegas.com*
🛏 *2,436 rooms, 559 suites.*

AMENITIES

- A slate of restaurants that includes offerings from Scott Conant (Scarpetta, D.O.C.G.), Jose Andreas (Jaleo, China Poblano), and Costas Spilidas (Estiatorio Milos) will excite even the most jaded diner.
- The on-site spa, Sahra, offers dozens of unique skin and body treatments, and boasts one of the only open-to-the-public hammams in town.
- Three different pools on the mezzanine offer three different daytime experiences; there's also an outdoor living room that is a great spot to watch a big game.
- Violet Hour Salon, the on-site beauty parlor, specializes in hair, nails and makeup.
- World-class shopping includes a number of one-of-a-kind boutiques, including Stitched (men's clothes), Retrospecs & Co. (eyewear), and Kid Robot (toys).

★ Fodor's Choice The Cosmopolitan is truly different Las Vegas resort experience—a blend of arty sophistication and comfortable elegance. Everything about accommodations starts with the open-air private terraces. The vast majority the hotel's 2,995 rooms and suites boast them, and they're the only standard outdoor balconies on the Strip (north-facing terraces are the best, as they look out on the Fountains at Bellagio next door). The other distinguishing characteristic in most Cosmo rooms is the kitchenette; a mini-fridge and microwave are available for guest use. Rooms also feature plush and comfortable couches, coffee-table art books and a spacious work desk. Bathrooms are enormous, and most feature a soaking tub, standalone shower, and ample counter space. All rooms boast state-of-the-art technology that allows guests to preset ambiences including lighting, music, and temperature, and book dining and spa reservations through the TV. **Pros:** terraces; in-room technology; Yoo-Hoo in minibar! **Cons:** kitchenette seems random; walls paper-thin. **TripAdvisor:** "perfect for bachelorette party," "glad we took a chance," "perfect hotel for Las Vegas."

HIGHLIGHTS

The nightlife: The main attractions are Marquee nightclub and The Chandelier—a three-story bar that exists in a giant light fixture—and the future never has looked as bright.

The creativity: Consider the vending machine with wood-block paintings from local artists and the limited-edition sneakers at CRSVR Sneaker Boutique.

The Talon Club: More than just a high-limit gaming salon, the Talon is a speakeasy and a place to unwind from the hubbub of the casino floor.

MIRAGE AT A GLANCE

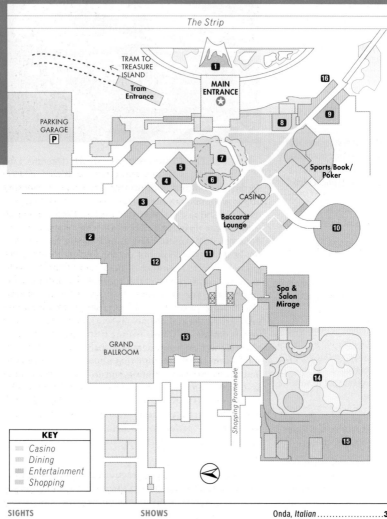

The Strip

TRAM TO
TREASURE
ISLAND

**Tram
Entrance**

**MAIN
ENTRANCE**

PARKING
GARAGE
P

**Sports Book/
Poker**

CASINO

**Baccarat
Lounge**

**Spa &
Salon
Mirage**

GRAND
BALLROOM

Shopping Promenade

KEY
- Casino
- Dining
- Entertainment
- Shopping

SIGHTS

Mirage Pool **14**
Siegfried & Roy's Secret Garden
and Dolphin Habitat **15**
Tropical Lobby Rainforest **7**
Volcano at Mirage **1**

SHOWS

Love,
Cirque du Soleil Theater **10**
The Terry Fator Theater **13**

NIGHTLIFE

1 Oak, *Dance Club* **2**
Rhumbar, *Lounge* **16**

EXPENSIVE DINING

Fin, *Seafood* **4**
Japonais, *Pan Asian* **6**

Onda, *Italian* **3**
Samba, *Brazilian* **11**
STACK, *Contemporary* **5**

INEXPENSIVE DINING

BLT Burger, *Bistro* **9**
Carnegie Deli, *Deli* **8**
Cravings Buffet, *Buffet* **12**

MIRAGE LAS VEGAS

$ *Rooms from: $189* ✉ *3400 Las Vegas Blvd. S* ☎ *702/791–7111, 800/374–9000* ⊕ *www.mirage.com* ⇥ *2,763 rooms, 281 suites.*

AMENITIES

■ No, it's not a mirage—the pools at the Mirage really are as beautiful as they seem. Surrounded by lush tropical landscaping, the pools interconnect through lagoons and link around a magnificent cascading waterfall. At BARE, the newest addition to the pool complex, DJ-spun music sets a lively mood as guests enjoy European-style sunbathing secluded by towering palms.

■ Kim Vo, he of Beverly Hills fame, operates the salon and specializes in hair coloring. If you're seeking a blow-out, be sure to ask about discount packages.

■ The Spa offers challenging (but almost offensively expensive) pool- and dolphin-side yoga classes on weekends.

When Steve Wynn opened the Mirage in 1989, the $630-million property was the most expensive resort-casino in history. The hotel's distinctive gold windows get their color from actual gold used in the tinting process. Once it started to look a little *too* 1989, compared to modern hotel trends, the Mirage's casino and restaurants received an end-to-end makeover. Rooms were renovated in 2009 to reflect a more modern theme. Gone is the South Seas tableau; in is a cosmopolitan look with blacks, dark browns, and deep reds. Bathrooms have marble accents and sumptuous appointments but tend to be on the smaller side. Rooms with incredible views of the Strip and the volcano cost a bit more, but you can sometimes get a free upgrade if you request one at check-in. Several upscale restaurants, including STACK and BLT Burger, give the Mirage an impressive slate of both high-end and casual eateries. **Pros:** classic Vegas; incredible views; one of the best pools in town. **Cons:** smoky casino; rooms hard to get to. **TripAdvisor:** "good deal," "what we had hoped for," "very enjoyable vacation."

HIGHLIGHTS

The Love: The Beatles-inspired show from Cirque du Soleil is astounding.

The tropics: There's a 20,000-gallon aquarium behind the hotel's front desk, an indoor tropical rain forest, and the wondrous Siegfried & Roy's Secret Garden and Dolphin Habitat

The volcano: Renovated in 2009 this Vegas icon features breathtaking fire effects and music composed by Grateful Dead drummer Mickey Hart.

The dolphins: Say hello to Flipper at Siegfried & Roy's Secret Garden & Dolphin Habitat. Guests willing to burn a few c-notes can don a wet suit and act as "trainer" for a day.

PARIS LAS VEGAS AT A GLANCE

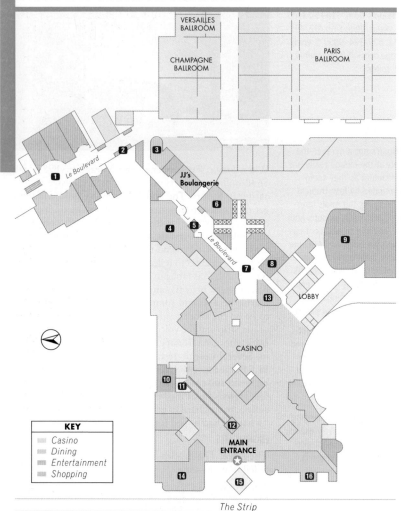

SIGHTS

Eiffel Tower Experience ... **11, 15**

SHOWS

Anthony Cools, *Theater* **10**

Jersey Boys, *Theater* **9**

NIGHTLIFE

Chateau, *Nightclub* **16**

Le Central, *Lounge* **13**

Napoleon's, *Lounge* **3**

SHOPPING

Bally's–Paris Promenade, *Mall* ... **1**

La Cave, *Food* **5**

Le Boulevard, *Mall* **7**

Les Mémories,
Gifts & Souvenirs **8**

Paris Line,
Women's Clothing **2**

EXPENSIVE DINING

Eiffel Tower Restaurant,
French **12**

Mon Ami Gabi, *French* **14**

MODERATE DINING

Le Provençal, *French* **6**

Le Village Buffet, *Buffet* **4**

PARIS LAS VEGAS

$ *Rooms from: $169* ✉ *3655 Las Vegas Blvd. S* ☎ *702/946–7000* ⊕ *www.parislasvegas. com* ⤴ *2,621 rooms, 295 suites.*

This homage to the City of Light aims to conjure up all the charm of the French capital, and while it isn't quite as glamorous as the Strip's other Euro-themed wonder (the Venetian), it's still good fun. Paris' standard units have marble baths with separate tubs and showers. Still, some find the heavy-handed decor a little busy. West-facing rooms overlook the magnificent fountains and lagoon across the street at Bellagio. A handful of rooms, dubbed "Red Rooms," have 42-inch plasma TVs and custom-designed furniture with French-inspired decorative elements and artwork. Suites add not only more space, but also considerably more dashing red, beige, and gold furniture and rich fabrics. Downstairs, the fabulous buffet serves dishes from five French regions. Other dining options are mostly mediocre, save perhaps for Mon Ami Gabi bistro. A massive octagonal pool sits in the shadows of the Eiffel Tower on the hotel rooftop. **Pros:** campy decor; spacious rooms; views. **Cons:** some rooms are tired; lack of standout restaurants. **TripAdvisor:** "going back," "surreal," "rocky start, then perfection."

AMENITIES

■ The resort's 2-acre, octagonal rooftop pool and exquisitely manicured French gardens are a great place to spend the afternoon.

■ Paris Spa by Mandara offers the latest in body treatments and fitness regimens.

■ Shopping at Paris Las Vegas is limited but noteworthy: the shops on Le Boulevard feature boutiques, gift shops, and a gourmet food shop, while the Bally's-Paris Promenade shops sell exclusive French jewelry and women's accessories.

■ Le Rendezvous Lounge, on the 31st floor, provides continental breakfast, afternoon hors d'ouevres, and free drinks. It's well worth the surcharge at check-in.

HIGHLIGHTS

The faux France: Replicas of The Arc de Triomphe, the Paris Opera House, the Hôtel de Ville, and the Louvre, along with an *Around the World in Eighty Days* balloon marquee are magnifique!

The Eiffel Tower: The crowning achievement is the 50-story, half-scale replica of the Eiffel Tower where guests are whisked 460 feet to the top for spectacular views of the Valley.

The musical: Tap your feet to the music of *Jersey Boys*, the acclaimed Broadway hit about Frankie Valli and the Four Seasons. The show moved here from Palazzo in March 2012. Paris is also the new home of Barry Manilow.

PLANET HOLLYWOOD AT A GLANCE

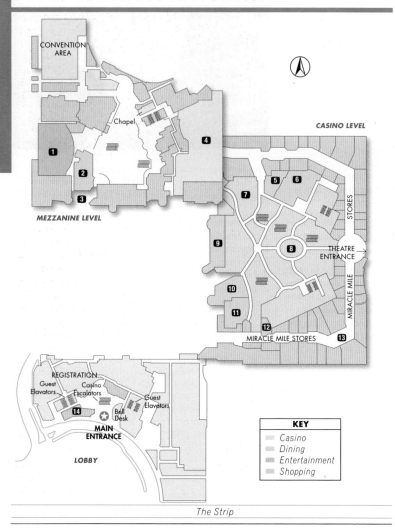

CONVENTION AREA

Chapel

CASINO LEVEL

1

2

3

4

MEZZANINE LEVEL

5 **6**

7

STORES

9

8

THEATRE ENTRANCE

10

MIRACLE MILE

11

12

MIRACLE MILE STORES

13

REGISTRATION

Guest Elevators

Casino Escalators

Guest Elevators

14

Bell Desk

MAIN ENTRANCE

LOBBY

KEY
- Casino
- Dining
- Entertainment
- Shopping

The Strip

SHOPPING	**NIGHTLIFE**	**MODERATE DINING**
Miracle Mile Stores **13**	Extra Lounge, *Lounge* **7**	P.F. Chang's, *Asian* **9**
ph Stuff, *Gifts* **14**	Heart Bar, *Bar* **8**	Planet Dailies, *Café* **6**
SPAS	The Playing Field, *Lounge* **11**	Yolos, *Mexican* **10**
Mandara **4**	**EXPENSIVE DINING**	**INEXPENSIVE DINING**
SHOWS	Koi, *Asian* **3**	Earl of Sandwich, *Café* **12**
Peepshow **1**	Strip House, *Steakhouse* **2**	Starbucks, *Café* **5**

PLANET HOLLYWOOD RESORT & CASINO

$ Rooms from: $199 ✉ 3667
Las Vegas Blvd. S ☎ 702/785–
5555, 866/919–7472 ⊕ www.
planethollywoodresort.com
↪ 2,486 rooms, 1,335 suites.

3

AMENITIES

■ The Spa by Mandara still has a vestigial Arabian theme, but female guests rave about the in-house nail salon.

■ The pool deck offers limited bar and food service, and the better-late-than-never Pleasure Pool VIP section is swanky.

■ For a shopping fix, hit the on-site mall, the Miracle Mile Shops, which include a new H&M department store and Urban Outfitters, to name a few.

Everything at Planet Hollywood is designed to make ordinary people feel like stars, and the lodging accommodations are no exception. The modern standard rooms are a spacious 450 square feet, and feature a king or queen bed, a 27-inch flat-screen television, iPod docking stations, plush chairs, and warm, fuzzy robes. On higher floors, some of the hotel's pricier suites come with butler service—the "PHabulous" suites feature six plasma televisions, as well as foosball and pool tables, and stripper poles in the showers (of course). Each of these suites also comes with its own private butler. The adjacent Planet Hollywood Towers Westgate offers 1,201 apartment-like rooms and a separate pool. **Pros:** classic Hollywood vibe; incredible views; posh suites. **Cons:** relatively small casino; in-room bath products are nothing special. **TripAdvisor:** "hip spot to stay," "great location, needs updating," "in the center of the Strip."

HIGHLIGHTS

The tease: Planet Hollywood's main attraction has become PEEPSHOW, a theatrical striptease starring Holly Madison, she of reality television fame.

The premieres: Because Planet Hollywood is obsessed with celebrities, the property often hosts world-premiere events that attract stars from all over the world.

The restaurants: At the upscale Koi and Strip House, paparazzi are a common sight. Yolo's is good, too, not as much for celeb-sightings, but more for its fresh Mexican food.

The dancers: On the casino floor, inside "The Pleasure Pit," scantily clad dancers hug the poles while men play blackjack and stare.

THE NORTH STRIP

Luxury reigns supreme in the top third of the Las Vegas Strip. There aren't as many resorts here but spacious rooms, exquisite details, and deep-sleep-inducing beds make four of them among the most luxurious in the world. This part of town is about a 30-minute ride from the airport and at least 20 minutes to the South Strip, so visitors often stay put. But when you're staying at resorts that have just about everything, who wants to leave?

The cluster of hotels that make up this section include the Venetian, Palazzo, Treasure Island, Wynn, Encore, and Trump Hotel Las Vegas. Of particular interest: pools. Swanky, ultraexclusive day-lounge areas surround the pools at North Strip properties; the Palazzo's Azure Pool is the newest and Encore Beach Club is by far the most popular. As with most pools in Vegas, these offer European-style sunbathing sections, too. Bikini tops optional.

NORTH STRIP TOP PICKS
Encore
Palazzo
Venetian
Wynn

Other amenities are worth raves, as well. Wynn, for instance, houses a master barber. Venetian has one of only two Canyon Ranch spas in the country. Factor in additional amenities such as golf courses, shopping, indoor gardens, and breathtaking design, and it's no wonder the North Strip is seen as the spot where Vegas meets high fashion, year after year.

ENCORE LAS VEGAS AT A GLANCE

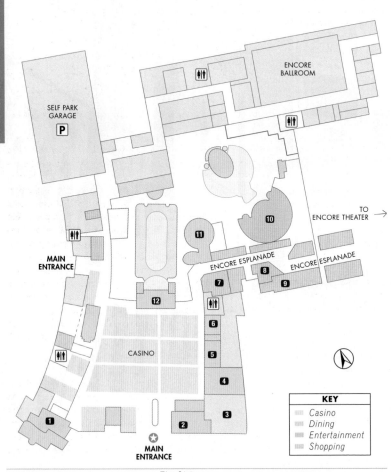

KEY
- Casino
- Dining
- Entertainment
- Shopping

The Strip

NIGHTLIFE

Eastside Lounge, *Lounge* **12**
Southside Bar, *Bar* **5**
Surrender, *Dance Club* **2**
XS Nightclub, *Dance Club* **10**

SHOPPING

CHANEL, *Women's Clothing* **8**
Ensemble, *Women's Clothing* **9**
Hermés, *Women's Clothing* **7**

EXPENSIVE DINING

Botero, *Steakhouse* **11**
Sinatra, *Italian* **1**

MODERATE DINING

Society Cafe Encore,
American **4**
Switch, *Steak & Seafood* **3**
Wazuzu, *Asian* **6**

ENCORE

$ Rooms from: $329 ✉ 3121 Las Vegas Blvd. S ☎ 702/770–7171, 888/320–7125 ⊕ www.encorelasvegas.com ↘ 2,034 suites.

AMENITIES

■ The main hotel pools are surrounded by sculpted gardens, mosaic tiling, and feature Jacuzzi spas and 29 luxurious cabanas.

■ Todd-Avery Lenahan designed the Moroccan-themed Spa and the Salon, which features 37 treatment rooms, 14 naturally lighted garden rooms, a number of oversize couples' suites for massage, body treatments, and facials, as well as daily spin and yoga classes.

■ Society Cafe serves up dim sum on weekends and is famous for whimsical dishes such as pretzel bread and mac-and-cheese nuggets.

■ The beautiful Esplanade at Encore features Hermès, Chanel, and the first-ever Rock & Republic store.

■ In-room televisions include a channel that lists up-to-the-minute betting lines in the Wynn Las Vegas sports book.

★ **Fodor's Choice** Though smaller than its neighbor, Wynn Las Vegas, Encore combines the very best of all of Wynn's masterpieces. As far as luxury is concerned, Las Vegas simply doesn't get much better. Encore redefines the typical Vegas casino-resort experience with new levels of extravagance. All of the rooms are suites, and measure a minimum of 700 square feet (up to a maximum of 5,800 square feet). These accommodations come standard with spacious sitting areas, flat-panel televisions, floor-to-ceiling windows, and electronic curtain controls. Bathrooms feature Italian marble and Wynn's Bambu signature bath products. Bedside control panels enable guests to operate nearly everything in the room. **Pros:** huge suites; glorious pools; fun (but intimate) casino. **Cons:** cab ride to other casinos; pricey. **TripAdvisor:** "lovely stay," "first class," "worth every cent."

HIGHLIGHTS

The details: A wall at Wazuzu Asian restaurant is decorated with a large dragon made from 90,000 Swarovski crystals; Sinatra, the Italian restaurant, displays Frank Sinatra's 1953 Oscar for the film *From Here to Eternity*. And designer Roger Thomas invested in authentic antiques from all over the world to adorn common areas.

The sunlight: Sunlit corridors with flower-filled atriums and sprawling pools are visible from throughout the property; there also are a number of signature mosaics.

The clubs: XS, a Vegas legend on the nightclub circuit, combines an outdoor pool environment with a sizzling club atmosphere. Encore Beach Club and Surrender offer more of the same (though these two are heavier on the pool part).

THE PALAZZO AT A GLANCE

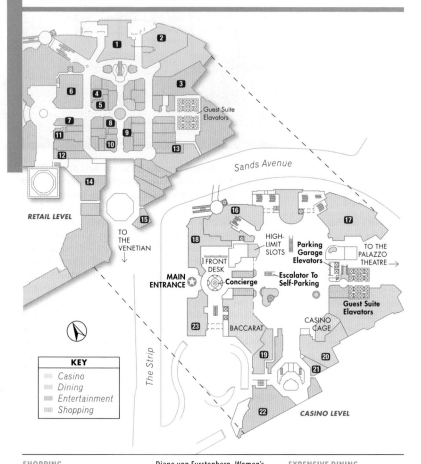

SHOPPING

Barneys New York, *Men's and Women's Clothing* **22**

Bottega Veneta, *Women's Clothing* **5**

Burberry, *Men's and Women's Clothing* **14**

Catherine Malandrino, *Women's Clothing* **11**

Chloe, *Women's Clothing* **10**

Christian Louboutin, *Women's Accessories* **8**

Cole Haan, *Accessories* **13**

Diane von Furstenberg, *Women's Clothing* **9**

Ferragamo, *Men's and Women's Clothing* **12**

Jimmy Choo, *Women's Accessories* **7**

Michael Kors, *Men's and Women's Clothing* **15**

Ralph Lauren, *Men's and Women's Clothing* **6**

Tory Burch, *Women's Clothing* ...**4**

Victoria's Secret, *Women's Clothing* **3**

EXPENSIVE DINING

CarneVino, *Steakhouse* **16**

Cut, *Steakhouse* **20**

Lavo, *Mediterranean* **23**

Morels, *French* **18**

SushiSamba, *Asian* **2**

Table 10, *American* **1**

MODERATE DINING

Zine Noodles Dim Sum, *Asian* .. **19**

INEXPENSIVE DINING

Espressamente, *Café* **21**

Grand Lux, *Café* **17**

THE PALAZZO

$ *Rooms from: $229* ⊠ *3325 Las Vegas Blvd. S* ☎ *702/607–7777, 866/263–3001* ⊕ *www. palazzo.com* ⤳ *3,066 suites.*

AMENITIES

■ Each suite comes standard with a sunken living room, marble bathroom, and linens from Anichini. Rooms also boast a printer/fax/scanner, DVD player, and iPod adapter.

■ A walkway connects the property to the Venetian.

■ The Canyon Ranch Spa-Club includes a 40-foot high climbing wall and Aquavana, the first complete suite of European-inspired thermal spa cabins, tubs, and aqua-thermal bathing in the United States.

■ The rooftop pool deck showcases an ornate pool complex with an almost-overwhelming number of cabanas and VIP areas.

■ On-site parking sits beneath the casino and is among the most accessible on the Strip.

"Palazzo" means "palace" in Italian, and the $1.8-billion, all-suites resort aims to bring new meaning to the word, ushering even more luxury to the north end of the Las Vegas Strip. Though it has struggled to keep restaurants, the hotel's an understated blend of style and sophistication. The floor plan for the Palazzo suites are almost exactly the same as the Venetian's. Each suite comes standard with a sunken living room, two plasma TVs, a dining area, sectional couch, and desk. Remote-controlled Roman shades and curtains add to the modern conveniences; let the sun in without getting out of bed! Bathrooms are appointed with marble and feature a separate shower and soaking tub. For $100 more per night, concierge-level rooms (known as "Prestige") include breakfast, afternoon snacks, hors d'oeuvres, and business center services. **Pros:** state-of-the-art amenities; spacious suites; sumptuous linens. **Cons:** thin walls; deserted on weekdays. **TripAdvisor:** "great location and beautiful rooms," "great place for a girl's weekend getaway," "wonderful experience."

HIGHLIGHTS

The Shoppes: With 50 international boutiques, including Barneys New York, Christian Louboutin, and Diane von Furstenberg, The Shoppes at The Palazzo are perhaps the No. 1 nongaming attraction at this palatial resort.

The pool: Palazzo has one of the Strip's newest pool decks, a humongous complex with private whirlpools, statues, and gardens galore.

The waterfall: A three-story waterfall graces the outskirts of the casino.

The green: With a top-quality energy conservation program and other green amenities, Palazzo has received LEED-Gold distinction from the U.S. Green Building Council.

THE VENETIAN AT A GLANCE

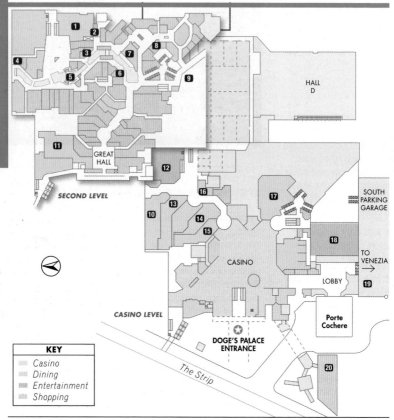

KEY
- Casino
- Dining
- Entertainment
- Shopping

THE VENETIAN RESORT CASINO

$ *Rooms from: $239* ⊠ *3355 Las Vegas Blvd. S* ☎ *702/414– 1000, 866/659–9643* ⊕ *www. venetian.com* ⇨ *4,027 suites.*

3

AMENITIES

■ The Canyon Ranch Spa Club offers the same lavish treatments as the spa resort's main campuses in Arizona and Massachusetts, and features a three-story climbing wall that guests can use for free. It's also open late on most weeknights, meaning you can spend more time at the tables before that workout.

■ The combination copier/ scanner/fax/printer in every suite is perfect for business travelers who hope to get work done during their stay.

■ One of the best-kept secrets of Venetian's room-service: They'll bring you food from any restaurant on property, for a price.

★ **Fodor's Choice** This theme hotel re-creates Italy's most romantic city with meticulous reproductions of Venetian landmarks—including the Grand Canal. Some of the Strip's largest and plushest accommodations are found at this gilded resort that's a hit with foodies, shoppers, and high rollers alike. It's all about glitz and "wow" effect here, which makes it a popular property if you're celebrating a special occasion or looking for a quintessential over-the-top Vegas experience. Each 700-plus-square-feet suite offers a sunken living room with a coffee table and convertible sofa, walk-in closets, a separate shower and tub, three telephones (including one in the bathroom), two flat-screen TVs, and remote-controlled curtains. The even posher Venezia Tower has a garden, private entrance, fountains, and gargantuan suites. **Pros:** exquisite artwork; modern amenities; those remote-controlled curtains. **Cons:** sprawling property; unpredictable service. **TripAdvisor:** "decent but not incredible," "loved it all," "better than expected."

HIGHLIGHTS

The scenery: From the Strip you enter through the Doge's Palace, set on a walkway over a large lagoon. Inside, Renaissance characters roam the public areas, singing opera, performing mime, jesting, even kissing hands. Walking from the hotel lobby into the casino is one of the great experiences in Las Vegas: overhead, reproductions of famous frescoes—highlighted by 24-karat-gold frames—adorn the ceiling; underfoot, the geometric design of the flat marble floor provides an Escher-like optical illusion of climbing stairs.

The gondolas: On a lake in front of the casino visitors can take gondola rides and look out on the Strip. Inside, climb aboard with a gondolier who'll sing opera as he paddles you through canals that line the Grand Canal Shoppes.

WYNN AT A GLANCE

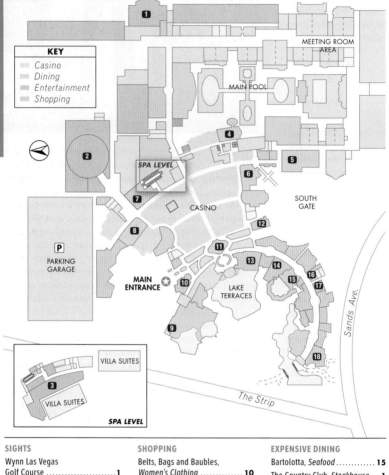

KEY
- ▥ Casino
- ▥ Dining
- ▥ Entertainment
- ▥ Shopping

MEETING ROOM AREA

MAIN POOL

SPA LEVEL

SOUTH GATE

CASINO

PARKING GARAGE

MAIN ENTRANCE ★

LAKE TERRACES

Sands Ave.

VILLA SUITES

VILLA SUITES

SPA LEVEL

The Strip

SIGHTS

Wynn Las Vegas
Golf Course **1**

SPAS

The Spa Wynn Las Vegas **3**

SHOWS

Le Rêve, *Theater* **2**

NIGHTLIFE

Parasol Up and Parasol Down,
Lounge **11**

Tryst, *Dance Club* **9**

SHOPPING

Belts, Bags and Baubles,
Women's Clothing **10**

Brioni, *Men's Clothing* **18**

Cartier, *Jewelry* **12**

Chanel, *Women's Clothing* **13**

Louis Vuitton,
Luggage and Accessories **14**

Manolo Blahnik, *Shoes* **17**

Oscar de la Renta,
Women's Clothing **16**

EXPENSIVE DINING

Bartolotta, *Seafood* **15**

The Country Club, *Steakhouse* ...**1**

Tableau, *Contemporary* **4**

Wing Lei, *Chinese* **5**

MODERATE DINING

Red 8, *Chinese* **6**

Stratta, Italian **8**

INEXPENSIVE DINING

The Drugstore Café, *Café* **7**

WYNN LAS VEGAS

$ *Rooms from: $299* ⊠ *3131 Las Vegas Blvd. S* ☎ *702/770–7000, 877/321–9966* ⊕ *www.wynnlasvegas.com* ⥋ *2,359 rooms, 357 suites.*

AMENITIES

■ One of the most highly regarded spas in town, the Wynn Spa offers dozens of signature treatments, as well as relaxation and hydrotherapy rooms to while away a day. The spa specializes in facials, and therapists incorporate a number of Asian oils and herbs into each experience.

■ Men's barbershop services–including flat-razor shaves–are available in the salon. They incorporate products from Paris and New York's famous Hommage Atelier.

■ Relatively minor touches, such as richly appointed armchairs with ottomans and giant, fluffy Turkish towels, speak to the sheer sumptuousness of this place.

★ **Fodor's Choice** In a city that keeps raising the bar for sheer luxury, the Wynn—monolithic in both name and appearance—offers a discreet turn for the tasteful. The resort is a best-of-everything experience—a playground for jet-setters, high rollers, or anyone who wants to feel like one. Decked out with replicas of Steve Wynn's acclaimed art collection, the princely rooms, averaging a whopping 650 square feet, offer spectacular views through wall-to-wall, floor-to-ceiling windows. Rest your head on custom pillow-top beds with 320-thread-count linens, and call room service from the cordless phone. Bedside drapery and climate controls are another nice touch. The super-posh Tower Suites units have use of a separate pool and lanai, and some have opulent amenities such as granite wet bars, separate powder rooms, 42-inch flat-screen TVs, and walk-in closets. Downstairs, restaurants such as Wing Lei, Bartolotta Ristorante di Mare, and Stratta provide endless culinary delights. **Pros:** signature Bambu bath products; access to gorgeous pool; on-site golf course. **Cons:** cramped casino walkways; slow elevators. **TripAdvisor:** "simply the best," "Wynn = quality," "like no place else...."

HIGHLIGHTS

The Esplanade: the Wynn Esplanade Shoppes are second to none, including stores such as Louis Vuitton and Dior.

The golf course: The outstanding course incorporates 11 water hazards, including a 37-foot waterfall.

The chefs: Famous chefs don't just lend their name to Wynn's restaurants, they often take residence there, including Alex Stratta, legendary Italian chef Paul Bartolotta, and rising star David Spero.

The talent: Garth Brooks's intimate show remains one of the most highly rated on the Strip. Also on property, Le Reve is a dance show in the vein of Cirque du Soleil.

OTHER HIGHLY RECOMMENDED HOTELS

For expanded reviews, facilities, and current deals, visit Fodors.com.

SOUTH STRIP

$ ⬚ **Excalibur Hotel and Casino.** The giant Lego-like castle is popular
HOTEL   with families—child-oriented attractions include the basement arcade
☾   (dubbed the "Fun Dungeon") and the medieval-themed Tournament
of Kings dinner show—but recent makeovers in all of the property's
rooms make much of the property look more grown-up. **Pros:** fun
place for kids; low table minimums make for more accessible gambling; easy access to Luxor and Mandalay Bay. **Cons:** low table minimums also attract huge crowds; most on-site dining options are not
good. **TripAdvisor:** "value for money but not special," "excellent stay,"
"a bit old fashioned." [$] *Rooms from: $109* ⊠ *3850 Las Vegas Blvd.
S* ☎ *702/597–7777, 877/750–5464* ⊕ *www.excalibur.com* ⇱ *3,940
rooms, 41 suites* ⦿| *No meals.*

$$$$ ⬚ **Four Seasons Hotel Las Vegas.** After checking in at a separate ground-
RESORT   level lobby, guests are whisked up to the top floors of the main hotel
Fodor's Choice   tower at Mandalay Bay, cushioned from the general casino ruckus.
★   If peace and quiet are what you're after, this is your spot. **Pros:** kid-
☾   friendly; ultraposh; hotel-within-a-hotel vibe. **Cons:** pricey; far from
rest of Vegas action; stuffy at times. **TripAdvisor:** "wonderful escape
from the strip," "an oasis in the desert," "always our first choice for
Las Vegas." [$] *Rooms from: $399* ⊠ *Mandalay Bay Resort, 3960 Las
Vegas Blvd. S* ☎ *702/632–5000* ⊕ *www.fourseasons.com/lasvegas*
⇱ *424 rooms.*

$ ⬚ **Monte Carlo Resort and Casino.** The Strip could use more places like
RESORT   this—handsome but not ostentatious, elegant rooms outfitted with cher-
☾   rywood furnishings. **Pros:** exceptional rooms; easy to navigate casino.
Cons: taxi entrance in the middle of nowhere. **TripAdvisor:** "another
great stay," "more than pleasantly surprised," "couldn't be in a better
position." [$] *Rooms from: $129* ⊠ *3770 Las Vegas Blvd. S* ☎ *702/730–
7777, 888/529–4828* ⊕ *www.montecarlo.com* ⇱ *2,768 rooms, 224
suites* ⦿| *No meals.*

$$ ⬚ **Signature Suites at MGM Grand.** The three towers that comprise this
RESORT   spacious and well-appointed luxury resort adjacent to the MGM Grand
are perhaps most notable for what they lack: a casino. **Pros:** relatively
inexpensive room rates. **Cons:** inconvenient off-Strip entrance; a trek
to nearest casino (at MGM Grand). **TripAdvisor:** "some sanity in Las
Vegas," "quiet place to stay," "elegant oasis." [$] *Rooms from: $189*
⊠ *145 E. Harmon Ave.* ☎ *702/797–6000, 877/612–2121* ⊕ *www.
signaturemgmgrand.com* ⇱ *1,728 suites* ⦿| *No meals.*

$$$ ⬚ **THEhotel at Mandalay Bay.** If James Bond were staying on the Strip,
RESORT   something tells us he'd book a suite here: Elaborate wet bars, giant
42-inch plasma TVs, plush carpeting, dark wooden desks, floor-to-
ceiling windows, and mirrored wardrobes at the foot of the most comfortable beds on the Strip all add up to the perfect bachelor pad. **Pros:**
lavish suites; great views; separate and swanky entrance. **Cons:** long
walk to main casino; dark elevator lobbies; hard-to-find entrance.

CLOSE UP

What's New and Next

Las Vegas doesn't have much on tap in terms of new construction. After the completion of The Cosmopolitan in early 2011, future projects struggled. At the north end of the Strip, the tower that was supposed to be **Fontainebleau Las Vegas** sits unfinished; at CityCenter, the tower that was to be the Harmon Hotel is nothing more than an empty shell. Plans for the **Echelon**, a $4.8-billion project on the site of the former Stardust hotel (near Trump International), were shelved in 2010, and owners Boyd Gaming won't comment on whether the place will ever get built. Still, at least one project appears to be moving forward—**The Nobu Hotel** at Caesars Palace. This property, at this writing expected to be completed in early 2013, will transform the Centurion Tower at Caesars into a Japanese-themed micro-resort complete with 180 rooms, 16 suites, and a penthouse. The resort will operate as a hotel-within-a-hotel, featuring private check-in and decor that showcases natural materials. Of course the new tower will feature a **Nobu Restaurant and Lounge**. The eatery will be Chef Nobu Matsuhisa's first on the Strip; currently his only other Vegas restaurant is inside the Hard Rock Casino Hotel.

Then, of course, there are (potentially) imminent changes at the former site of the Sahara. This iconic hotel, which opened in 1952, shuttered its doors in May 2011 and has remained closed to the public. SBE Entertainment Group, the company that owns the Sahara, appears to be optimistic. Sam Nazarian, CEO of SBE, was quoted in the *Las Vegas Sun* as saying, "We are confident that we ultimately will find a creative and comprehensive new solution for this historic property."

Finally, following in the footsteps of the Smith Center and the Mob Museum, continued improvements are expected Downtown. By the end of 2012, Fitzgeralds Casino & Hotel was anticipating extensive renovations associated with rebranding itself as **The D Las Vegas Hotel & Casino**. Farther down the road, **Zappos.com** is expected to move into the building that formerly served as City Hall (and bankroll major improvements in the process).

TheHotel: [$] *Rooms from: $289* ✉ *3950 Las Vegas Blvd. S* ☎ *877/632–7800, 702/632–7777* 🌐 *www.mandalaybay.com/thehotel* 🛏 *1,117 suites* 🍴 *No meals.*

$$ RESORT 🏨 **Tropicana Las Vegas.** Considering it was one of the original Strip casinos (dating back more than 50 years), the "Trop," was desperate for the exhaustive multi-billion renovation it had in 2010 and 2011. **Pros:** Bagatelle Beach Club; swim-up blackjack; easy-breezy style. **Cons:** casino still tiny; not easy to find your way inside. **TripAdvisor:** "exceeded expectations," "awesome pool," "excellent remodel and location." [$] *Rooms from: $149* ✉ *3801 Las Vegas Blvd. S* ☎ *702/739–2222, 800/462–8767* 🌐 *www.troplv.com* 🛏 *1,279 rooms, 96 suites* 🍴 *No meals.*

CENTER STRIP

$$ RESORT 🏨 **Bally's Las Vegas.** Bally's isn't as new or swanky as some other Vegas resorts, but it's definitely an underrated choice for a Strip stay. **Pros:** affordable rooms on the Strip; perfect Center Strip location. **Cons:** rooms and pool need updates. **TripAdvisor:** "right in the thick of it," "awesome view," "good location." [$] *Rooms from: $159* ✉ *3645 Las Vegas Blvd. S* ☎ *702/967–4111, 877/603–4390* 🌐 *www.ballyslasvegas.com* 🛏 *2,570 rooms, 244 suites* 🍴 *No meals.*

$ RESORT 🏨 **Flamingo Las Vegas.** Bugsy Siegel's ill-fated foray into Vegas real estate is massive, pink, and smack dab in the middle of the Strip. **Pros:** Margaritaville; heart-of-the Strip location; the pool lives up to its reputation. **Cons:** Hard to reach by car or taxi; regular rooms are pretty old. **TripAdvisor:** "totally surprised," "very well located," "great pool." [$] *Rooms from: $119* ✉ *3555 Las Vegas Blvd. S* ☎ *702/733–3111, 888/902–9929* 🌐 *www.flamingolasvegas.com* 🛏 *3,192 rooms, 268 suites* 🍴 *No meals.*

$ RESORT 🏨 **Harrah's Las Vegas.** Old-school Vegas is alive and well at this Center Strip property. **Pros:** old-school Vegas vibe; affordable, reliable rooms; ideal location. **Cons:** casino hard to navigate; small pool. **TripAdvisor:** "perfect location," "pleasant stay," "great value." [$] *Rooms from: $119* ✉ *3475 Las Vegas Blvd. S* ☎ *800/214–9110* 🌐 *www.harrahslasvegas.com* 🛏 *2,293 rooms, 233 suites* 🍴 *No meals.*

$ RESORT 🏨 **Imperial Palace.** The Far East is the theme at this budget-minded resort owned by Caesars; a number of wacky attractions on the casino floor tend to distract visitors from remembering the Orient. **Cons:** no-frills; "Dealertainers"; karaoke bar. [$] *Rooms from: $89* ✉ *3535 Las Vegas Blvd. S* ☎ *702/731–3311, 800/351–7400* 🌐 *www.imperialpalace.com* 🛏 *2,640 rooms, 286 suites* 🍴 *No meals.*

$$$$ RESORT Fodor's Choice ★ 🏨 **Mandarin Oriental, Las Vegas.** As a brand, Mandarin Oriental pledges to provide everything for the business traveler; rooms are on the small side, though sumptuous sheets and soothing Asian-inspired artwork make you forget relieve any closed-in feelings you might have. **Pros:** efficiency; valet closet. **Cons:** smallish rooms; almost overly formal. [$] *Rooms from: $349* ✉ *3752 Las Vegas Blvd. S* ☎ *702/590–8888, 888/881–9578* 🌐 *www.mandarinoriental.com/lasvegas* 🛏 *335 rooms, 57 suites* 🍴 *No meals.*

$$ RESORT 🏨 **Vdara.** This boutique (read: low-key) property is actually a hotel-condo, with beautiful independently owned suites that are arranged like efficiency apartments, with efficiency kitchens, pull-out sofas, and lots of extra space. **Pros:** Quiet retreat right in the middle of the action; efficiency kitchens; spa. **Cons:** trek to Strip by foot; Market Cafe restaurant is ho-hum. **TripAdvisor:** "a unique experience," "great rooms," "a lovely non smoking hotel." [$] *Rooms from: $209* ✉ *2600 W. Harmon Ave.* ☎ *702/590–2767, 866/745–7111* 🌐 *www.vdara.com* 🛏 *1,495 suites* 🍴 *No meals.*

Stroll beneath the soaring glass canyons of CityCenter and experience a serene streetscape insulated from the bustle of the surrounding Strip.

NORTH STRIP

$ RESORT **Circus Circus.** The hotel at the "Big Top" has renovated all of its rooms since 2009, giving some much-needed TLC to some of the oldest rooms on the Strip (the resort opened in 1968). **Pros:** Adventure Dome Theme Park; pet-friendly. **Cons:** Gaming atmosphere isn't nearly as elegant as most Strip properties. **TripAdvisor:** "very child friendly," "great value," "indulged." [$] *Rooms from: $89* ✉ *2880 Las Vegas Blvd. S* ☎ *702/734–0410, 800/634–3450* 🌐 *www.circuscircus.com* 🛏 *3,632 rooms, 135 suites* 🍴 *No meals.*

$ RESORT **Stratosphere.** The Stratosphere's 1,149-foot observation tower soars over every other building in town, and it's an iconic part of the Las Vegas skyline. **Pros:** the Tower (of course); singer/songwriter Frankie Moreno; value for the rooms. **Cons:** surrounding neighborhood; ho-hum casino. **TripAdvisor:** "definitely coming back," "little gem," "clean rooms." [$] *Rooms from: $119* ✉ *2000 Las Vegas Blvd. S* ☎ *702/380–7777* 🌐 *www.stratospherehotel.com* 🛏 *2,294 rooms, 133 suites* 🍴 *No meals.*

$$ RESORT **Treasure Island.** Once a bastion of pirate-hood on the Las Vegas Strip, the "T.I.," has lost its way since Phil Ruffin purchased it from MGM Resorts at the end of 2009. **Pros:** price point; location; *Mystere*. **Cons:** no real nightlife; needs a stronger identity and some TLC. **TripAdvisor:** "very comfortable," "great location," "huge rooms." [$] *Rooms from: $169* ✉ *3300 Las Vegas Blvd. S* ☎ *702/894–7111, 800/288–7206* 🌐 *www.treasureisland.com* 🛏 *2,665 rooms, 220 suites* 🍴 *No meals.*

$$ RESORT **Trump International Hotel Las Vegas.** It took him a while, but Donald Trump finally broke into the Las Vegas market in early 2008 with this lavish, 64-story condo-hotel. **Pros:** apartment-style rooms make you feel right at home; Spa rivals best on the Strip. **Cons:** long walk through Fashion Island Mall to the nearest casino, especially at night. **TripAdvisor:** "good rooms," "classy," "first class accommodations and service." [$] *Rooms from: $189* ✉ *2000 Fashion Show Dr.* ☎ *702/982–0000, 866/939–8786* 🌐 *www.trumplasvegashotel.com* 🛏 *1,282 rooms* 🍴 *No meals.*

DOWNTOWN

$ HOTEL **Four Queens.** Named after former owner Ben Goffstein's four daughters, the Four Queens is what Vegas regulars would consider an "oldie but goodie," one of the most iconic casinos on all of Fremont Street. **Pros:** kitsch factor; Hugo's. **Cons:** needs a better makeover; pool off-site. **TripAdvisor:** "a smoker's paradise," "lots of fun," "the best in customer service." [$] *Rooms from: $59* ✉ *202 Fremont St.* ☎ *702/385–4011, 800/634–6045* 🌐 *www.fourqueens.com* 🛏 *650 rooms, 44 suites* 🍴 *No meals.*

$ RESORT **Golden Nugget Hotel & Casino.** The Golden Nugget has pretty much reigned as Downtown's top property since the mid 1970s, evolving with the times, but maintaining classic appeal. **Pros:** legendary Vegas property; one-of-a-kind pool. **Cons:** small sports book; despite its charm, Downtown Vegas can be sketchy. **TripAdvisor:** "beautiful clean rooms," "cool," "fun filled time." [$] *Rooms from: $99* ✉ *129 E. Fremont St.* ☎ *702/385–7111, 800/634–3454* 🌐 *www.goldennugget.com* 🛏 *2,148 rooms, 197 suites* 🍴 *No meals.*

$ HOTEL **Main Street Station Casino Brewery Hotel.** It's worth a visit to this pint-size property for the Victorian era-aesthetics alone, displaying stained glass, marble; and an antiques collection that includes Buffalo Bill Cody's private railcar, a fireplace from Scotland's Preswick Castle, and lamps that graced the streets of 18th-century Brussels. **Pros:** decor and quirky antiques; prices of rooms. **Cons:** no pool; no gym; no Internet in rooms (only Wi-Fi in lobby). **TripAdvisor:** "great place to eat and gamble," "will come back," "best bang for the buck." [$] *Rooms from: $59* ✉ *200 N. Main St.* ☎ *702/387–1896, 800/713–8933* 🌐 *www.mainstreetcasino.com* 🛏 *392 rooms, 14 suites* 🍴 *No meals.*

PARADISE ROAD, EAST SIDE, AND HENDERSON

$$ RESORT Fodor's Choice ★ **Green Valley Ranch Resort & Spa.** Locals have long known that Green Valley is a low-key, refined resort for the high-end crowd that prefers style over bustle (the Strip is a 25-minute drive away). **Pros:** gorgeous, airy casino; proximity to malls that offer great shopping. **Cons:** located about 25 minutes from the Strip. **TripAdvisor:** "awesome property," "excellent alternative to the Strip," "beat my expectations." [$] *Rooms from: $149* ✉ *2300 Paseo Verde Pkwy., Henderson* ☎ *702/617–7777* 🌐 *www.greenvalleyranchresort.com* 🛏 *417 rooms, 79 suites.*

Continued on page 110

THE POOL SCENE

You, a lounge chair, and a tropical drink with an umbrella. Sound like paradise? Then plant yourself poolside in Sin City.

Las Vegas might just be America's coolest landlocked beach resort. Swimming pools can be just as over-the-top as the Strip sidewalk shows: fringed with lush landscaping and tricked out with wave machines, swim-up bars, ultraquiet misting machines, and wild water slides. Or they can be snazzy affairs—think private cabanas (satellite TV, Wi-Fi, and private misting machines), which range in price from about $40 a day for a basic one at the Monte Carlo to $500 a day (on weekends) for one of the four cabanas at Mandalay Bay's Moorea Beach Club, which offers European-style (read: topless) sunbathing for guests 21 and older.

PLANNING YOUR TAN

Alas, unless you're a guest of the hotel, you're generally not allowed to use the pool facilities. If swimming and sunning are important to you, book your stay at a hotel with a great pool.

Updated by Matt Villano

TOP PICKS

THE PALMS

As part of The Palms' tower—dubbed Palms Place—the resort recently dumped $40 million into its pool area to make it bigger and better. The new three-acre complex, which is open to the public (weekdays 9 am to 6 pm), has three separate pools, all of which are fed by waterfalls and boast colorful underwater lighting. Hands down, the best feature is the triangular Glass Bar, set cleverly under a glass-bottomed pool deck. In this area, modern spins on traditional tropical drinks like margaritas and mojitos are popular, and the menu features delectable high-end poolside fare such as rock-shrimp quesadillas and Waygu beef hamburgers. If you want to go all out, book one of the 27 cabanas or bungalows, which are outfitted with high-end sound systems, plasma TVs, and swank furnishings. A handful of bungalows have their own lap pool, double-sided fireplace, bedroom, and lawn. For some, it seems, decadence knows no bounds.

PERKS WE LOVE: Poolside massages, swim-up blackjack, Astroturf, live concerts on weekends, views of the Spring Mountains. ✉ 4321 W. Flamingo Rd., West Side ☎ 702/942–7777 ⊕ www.palms.com

ENCORE BEACH CLUB

Building off the success of the opulent pool next door at Wynn Las Vegas, Encore has introduced the Encore Beach Club, a two-tier pool and dayclub. The complex is open to hotel guests and the general public (generally beautiful, that is). Inside, the semicircular spectacle revolves around a main pool with daybed-style cushions that appear to float like lily pads. Twenty-six cabanas ring the perimeter and eight bungalows offer the most indulgent accommodations (private hot tubs and bathrooms and individual air-conditioning). There's a gaming pavilion with craps and blackjack. During the summer, premier DJs spin house every Sunday. The dayclub, naturally, becomes a happening nightclub after dark when the pool complex becomes an extension of Surrender Nightclub.

PERKS WE LOVE: Chilled towels, poolside gambling, "shower poles," dayclub vibe.

✉ 3121 Las Vegas Blvd., S. North Strip ☎ 702/770–7171 ⊕ www.encorelasvegas.com

TOP PICKS

HARD ROCK

No pool in town, especially after expansions in 2008 and 2009, has a more happening scene than this one. The Hard Rock throws fabulous pool parties and bears an uncanny resemblance to that Polynesian beach hideaway you've always dreamed about. The Hard Rock has buckets of soft sand, both in the two pools and in its lushly landscaped Beach Club. And lest you miss the pulse of the music while you're swimming laps, there's even a high-quality underwater sound system. Grab a colorful cocktail at Palapa Lounge, with its Indonesian vibe and tropical waterfalls. Feeling lucky? Hit the swim-up blackjack and craps bar. The cabanas are in keeping with the Polynesian vibe— they're gussied up to resemble Tahitian huts, with thatch roofs and rattan chairs. Predictably, the Hard Rock caters to a young-adult crowd of hipsters and bon vivants in their 20s and 30s. If you're outside this demographic, you may feel a bit like a fish out of water.

PERKS WE LOVE: Underwater music, four Jacuzzis (more than most properties), swim-up gaming, the Palapa Lounge. ✉ 4455 Paradise Rd., Paradise Road ☎ 702/693-5000 🌐 www.hardrockhotel.com

MANDALAY BAY

Pardon us if we sound like we're gushing, but we can't get over this place. Hands down, this is the mother of all Vegas pools. The experience includes an 11-acre beach spread with a huge wave pool (where else in town can you surf waves that rise as high as 6 feet?), a Euro-inspired topless pool with plush daybeds called the Moorea Beach club, a meandering river, and some of the cushiest cabanas in town. The beach is piled high with a couple thousand tons of California-imported golden sand, which feels just perfect between the toes. You can raft along the river, admiring the verdant foliage. After the sun sets, the beach becomes one of the city's hottest nightspots, attracting buffed and bronzed partyers for cocktails, music, and mingling. There are also two casual restaurants and a casino right by the beach. A huge soundstage overlooks the wave pool, hosting concerts by a wide range of rock and pop acts all summer long. The one complaint we have? It's relatively short on personal service and amenities.

PERKS WE LOVE: The comfy daybeds at Moorea Beach, sand—lots of it, the lazy river, the best outdoor concert venue on the Strip. ✉ 3950 Las Vegas Blvd. S, South Strip ☎ 702/632-7777 🌐 www.mandalaybay.com

HONORABLE MENTIONS

CAESARS PALACE

The ancient Romans revered water for its healing powers, and they built sumptuous public baths amid fragrant gardens, exercise areas and playing fields. Caesars Palace has recreated those glorious havens with its 4.5-acre Garden of the Gods Pool Oasis, which is comprised of six pools and two whirlpool spas. Surrounding each pool are 40 posh rental cabanas and ample room for sunbathing. A poolside bar serves up cold treats, as well as a full food menu.

PERKS WE LOVE: Topless sunbathing at the Venus Pool, handheld face spritzers, swim-up blackjack at the Fortune Pool, all those Corinthian columns. ✉ 3570 Las Vegas Blvd., Center Strip ☎ 702/731-7110 ⊕ www.caesarspalace.com

MIRAGE

If you prefer a shaded, tropical spread, check out the verdant pool area at the classy Mirage. The two main pools are connected through a series of dramatic lagoons and waterfalls. The Mirage won't wow you with nonstop activities or goofy gimmicks—it's just a handsome, well-maintained pool that's ideal whether you're a serious aficionado or a toe-dipping dabbler. Lounge chairs are outfitted with comfy mesh sailcloth. The cabanas are chichi here, with teak chairs and high-end entertainment systems.

PERKS WE LOVE: Chaise lounge reservations, flat-screen TVs and BOSE Wave stereos in the cabanas, ample misting coverage, above-average chow in the poolside café and bar. ✉ 3400 Las Vegas Blvd. S, Center Strip ☎ 702/791-7111 ⊕ www.mirage.com

TOPLESS POOLS

Listen up girls: sunbathing with tops is so yesterday. European (read: topless) sunbathing was all the rage in Vegas during the summer of 2009, and many of the biggest hotels have renovated their pool areas to build super-swanky private areas in which women can tan without their tops. The Bare Pool Lounge at The Mirage started this trend and still offers it from late May to early September. Everything about this special area is more upscale, with a menu that includes lobster tacos and ahi tuna. Caesars Palace has its own "adult" pool: the Venus Pool Club. Here, servers regularly distribute ice-cold towels and frozen grapes—a blatant shout out to the resort's Roman theme. At Mandalay Bay, the Moorea Beach Club also offers European sunbathing. In all places, cover charges apply. And in case you were wondering, yes, bottoms are required.

Moorea Beach, Mandalay Bay

3

IN FOCUS THE POOL SCENE

ALSO WORTH NOTING

M Resort

FLAMINGO LAS VEGAS

The Flamingo may have lost its luster, but its pool is one of the best around. Take a dip in Bugsy Siegel's original oval-shaped pool, play swim-up blackjack, explore waterfalls in the lagoon pool or swim beneath stone grottoes not unlike those at the Playboy Mansion (sorry, no naked women here). Throughout the entire pool area, real penguins, swans, and pink flamingoes roam free. Average pool furniture is on the cheap side, but it's Vegas—you can always pay to upgrade.

PERKS WE LOVE: Ample supply of rafts and pool toys, separate kiddy pool with waterslides, exclusive cabanas.

✉ 3555 Las Vegas Blvd., S, Center Strip
☎ 702/733–3111
⊕ www.flamingolasvegas.com

Vegas's perennial favorite with locals and savvy visitors, **Red Rock Casino Resort & Spa** (✉ 11011 W. Charleston Blvd., Summerlin ☎ 702/797–7777 ⊕ www.redrocklasvegas.com) has a beautiful swimming complex with a giant circular pool, a glamorous and contemporary design and comfy rattan chairs. The best of the Downtown pools, the **Golden Nugget Hotel and Casino** (✉ 129 E. Fremont St., Downtown ☎ 702/385–7111 ⊕ www.goldennugget.com), built a new pool in early 2007. Be sure to try the water slide that tunnels through the middle of the new 200,000-gallon aquarium before depositing riders back into the pool. At the posh **M Resort** (✉ 12300 Las Vegas Blvd., South Henderson ☎ 702/797–1000 ⊕ www.themresort.com), the entire Villagio del Sol pool complex (including the exclusive Daydream Pool Club) offers sweeping views of desert mountains and the entire Strip. It's one time we can say without being trite that you'll feel as if you're in a desert oaisis.

POOL PARTIES

Head to the festive beach at **Mandalay Bay** to watch rockin' summer concerts—they've hosted such festive acts as the Go-Go's and the B-52's. **Hard Rock Hotel and Casino** has become famous for Rehab, an all day Saturday and Sunday party that draws scads of good-looking scenesters. Not to be outdone, **Palms Hotel & Casino** offers Ditch Fridays, a weekly bash that includes live DJs, yard-long drink specials and lots of scantily clad humans, frolicking in the water.

$$ ⌂ **Hard Rock Hotel & Casino.** This sprawling resort is a living tribute to
RESORT   rock and roll—with rock tributes and exhibits everywhere, it's impos-
sible to forget you're in the Hard Rock: even the carpeting's decorated
with musical notes. **Pros:** party central; great restaurants (Pink Taco
and Ago) and pool; lively casino. **Cons:** rowdy crowd; minuscule sports
book. **TripAdvisor:** "the most fun you can have," "a great getaway,"
"go if you're hip." $ *Rooms from: $189* ✉ *4455 Paradise Rd., Para-
dise Road* ☎ *702/693–5000, 800/693–7625* ⊕ *www.hardrockhotel.com*
↩ *1,055 rooms, 384 suites* ⧚ *No meals.*

$$ ⌂ **The LVH.** Convention attendees have loved this hotel for decades; it's
RESORT   connected to the Las Vegas Convention Center. **Pros:** great location for
convention-goers; classic sports book. **Cons:** no poker room. **TripAdvisor:** "great reception with superb service," "incredible spa," "very
friendly." $ *Rooms from: $149* ✉ *3000 Paradise Rd., Paradise Road*
☎ *702/732–5111, 888/732–7117* ⊕ *www.thelvh.com* ↩ *2,700 rooms,
300 suites* ⧚ *No meals.*

$$ ⌂ **The M Resort.** Built in 2009 by the Marnells, the same family that
RESORT   created the Rio, this resort is 6 miles south of McCarran Airport and
is a destination onto itself. **Pros:** huge rooms; convenient yet removed
from hubbub. **Cons:** cab ride to other casinos; planes roaring over-
head. **TripAdvisor:** "very nice," "very chic," "good place to eat and
view." $ *Rooms from: $149* ✉ *12300 Las Vegas Blvd. S, Hender-
son* ☎ *702/797–1000, 877/673–7678* ⊕ *www.themresort.com* ↩ *351
rooms, 39 suites* ⧚ *No meals.*

$$ ⌂ **The Platinum Hotel and Spa.** This swank, nongaming, condo-hotel has
HOTEL   become a fashionable hideaway for Vegas regulars who prefer top-notch
Fodor'sChoice   amenities but don't need to stay on the Strip. **Pros:** cocktail menu at
★   STIR Lounge; lavish rooms with comfy sofas and beds. **Cons:** no casino;
location off the Strip makes it challenging to find a cab on busy nights.
TripAdvisor: "more than wonderful," "excellent service," "relaxing
stay." $ *Rooms from: $159* ✉ *211 E. Flamingo Rd., Paradise Road*
☎ *702/365–5000, 877/211–9211* ⊕ *www.theplatinumhotel.com* ↩ *255
suites* ⧚ *No meals.*

$$$ ⌂ **Ravella.** Formerly the Ritz-Carlton, Lake Las Vegas, this luxury
RESORT   resort reopened in early 2011 as Ravella, retaining its Mediterranean
vibe and resplendent pool complex. **Pros:** relaxing; desert-oasis set-
ting; golf nearby. **Cons:** marginal casino; far from Strip. **TripAdvisor:**
"respite from the Strip," "staff was great," "Tuscan resort feel with
lovely room." $ *Rooms from: $229* ✉ *1610 Lake Las Vegas Pkwy.,
Henderson* ☎ *888/810–0440, 702/567–4700* ⊕ *www.ravellavegas.com*
↩ *314 rooms, 35 suites* ⧚ *No meals.*

$$ ⌂ **Renaissance Las Vegas Hotel.** With "merely" 578 rooms and suites,
HOTEL   this nongaming Rat Pack–inspired hotel feels downright intimate when
compared to some of the megaresorts in town. **Pros:** the steak house
really is something to envy; fresh rooms. **Cons:** rooms a bit small; pool
can get overcrowded. **TripAdvisor:** "unexpected luxury," "excellent
Vegas non-gaming hotel," "hotel employees rock." $ *Rooms from:
$149* ✉ *3400 Paradise Rd., Paradise Road* ☎ *702/784–5700, 800/750–
0980* ⊕ *www.renaissancelasvegas.com* ↩ *518 rooms, 30 suites.*

$ HOTEL **Silverton Hotel and Casino.** Don't overlook this Rocky Mountain lodge–themed hotel with popular attractions such as a huge Bass Pro Shop, a 117,000-gallon saltwater aquarium (complete with mermaid shows), and the Shady Grove Lounge, complete with plasma-screen televisions and a mini-bowling alley. **Pros:** Bass Pro Shop is a fisherman's heaven; bowling alley is a nice diversion; great value not too far from Strip. **Cons:** casino underwhelms, mediocre dining options. **TripAdvisor:** "very fun," "nice room," "great food." [$] *Rooms from: $89 ✉ 3333 Blue Diamond Rd., Outskirts ☎ 702/263–7777, 866/722–4608 🌐 www.silvertoncasino.com 🛏 288 rooms, 19 suites 🍴 No meals.*

$$$ RESORT **Westin Lake Las Vegas Resort & Spa.** This lavish resort on the shore of Lake Las Vegas has richly appointed rooms, with arched windows that offer sweeping views of the glittering lake and desert. **Pros:** lake vistas; Marssa restaurant; activity center on beach rents kayaks and paddleboats. **Cons:** casino is not for avid gamblers.**TripAdvisor:** "beautiful property," "nice and quiet," "breathtaking views." [$] *Rooms from: $229 ✉ 101 Montelago Blvd., Lake Las Vegas, Henderson ☎ 702/567–6000 🌐 www.starwoodhotels.com/westin 🛏 447 rooms, 46 suites 🍴 No meals.*

WEST SIDE AND SUMMERLIN

$$$ RESORT **JW Marriott Las Vegas Resort & Spa.** If you have a penchant for pampering and personal service—or if your plans include golfing or hiking—this stunner in Summerlin is for you. **Pros:** proximity to golf and Red Rock National Conservation Area; terrific spa. **Cons:** a bit pricey for a Marriott; casino sports book can fill up quickly during big events. **TripAdvisor:** "large rooms," "got a full week of relaxation," "very nice property." [$] *Rooms from: $229 ✉ 221 N. Rampart Blvd., Summerlin ☎ 702/869–7777, 877/869–8777 🌐 www.marriott.com 🛏 391 rooms, 77 suites 🍴 No meals.*

$$ RESORT **The Palms Las Vegas.** Standard rooms at the Palms are large, opulent, and modern, with some unusual amenities for Las Vegas, such as beds with ultrafirm mattresses, duvets, and ample minibars. **Pros:** renowned, three-story spa; excellent coin games; low table-game minimums. **Cons:** it's taxi-distance from the Strip; doesn't quite have the of-the-moment hipness it had as recently as five years ago. **TripAdvisor:** "casino was great," "amazing staff and pool," "perfect luxury room stay." [$] *Rooms from: $159 ✉ 4321 W. Flamingo Rd., West Side ☎ 702/942–7777 🌐 www.palms.com 🛏 1,303 rooms, 266 suites.*

$$ RESORT ★ **Red Rock Casino Resort & Spa.** Way out on the western edge of the Las Vegas suburbs, this swanky golden-age Vegas throwback is a delight. **Pros:** movies; bowling; VIP section of sports book; access to Red Rock canyon. **Cons:** waitress service in gaming areas can be slow; distance from Strip. **TripAdvisor:** "beautiful," "first class all the way," "very nice room." [$] *Rooms from: $129 ✉ 11011 W. Charleston Blvd., West Side ☎ 702/797–7777, 866/767–7773 🌐 www.redrocklasvegas.com 🛏 735 rooms, 81 suites 🍴 No meals.*

$$ HOTEL [icon] **Rio All-Suite Hotel & Casino.** In Brazil, Rio is party central, and in Las Vegas so is this sprawling resort just west of the Strip. **Pros:** mecca for poker fans; large rooms; festive atmosphere. **Cons:** just off-Strip enough to be inconvenient; terrible house advantage for gaming. **TripAdvisor:** "great customer service," "I'll be back," "great value." [$] *Rooms from: $139* ✉ *3700 W. Flamingo Rd., West Side* ☎ *702/777–7777, 866/746–7671* 🌐 *www.riolasvegas.com* 🛏 *2,522 suites* 🍴 *No meals.*

Gamble

WORD OF MOUTH

"Every casino offers classes on how to play many of the table games so definitely take advantage of those. Plus they often teach you on the hotel TV channel in your room."

—melissaki5

Updated by Dante Drago and Matt Villano

If the sum total of your gambling experience is a penny-ante neighborhood poker game or your company's casino night holiday party, you may feel a little intimidated by the Vegas gambling scene. We're here to tell you that you don't need to be a gambling expert to sit and play.

All you need is a little knowledge of the games you plan on playing, the gumption to step up to the table, a bankroll, and the desire to have a great time. It would also be wise to remember that other than a very few extreme cases, the odds are always with the house. There are no foolproof ways or methods, miracle betting systems, lucky charms, or magic spells or incantations, that will change this fact. So if you feel as though you can brave the risk, and handle the action, roll up your sleeves and pull up a chair—it's gambling time.

GAMBLING PLANNER

CASINO RULES

Keep IDs handy. Dealers strictly enforce the minimum gambling age, which is 21 years everywhere in Nevada.

No kids. Children are only allowed in gaming areas if they're passing through on their way to another part of the resort.

No electronic distractions. As a general rule, casinos forbid anything that distracts gamblers at the tables, like a phone, iPad, or MP3 player. When you sit down at a table make sure to remove any listening devices from your ears and set phones on silent mode. If you must take a call, the dealer will hold your place while you step away from the table to take the call. Cell phones and any two-way communication devices are also strictly prohibited in the sports books. Period.

Smoking. Smoke only in designated areas. Signs on the tables and around the casino will inform you whether it is okay to smoke in a specific area. If you are unsure, ask someone before lighting up.

CASINO STRATEGY

The Right Mind-set. There's nothing quite like the excitement you feel when you step into a Vegas casino for the first time. The larger-than-life sights and sounds draw you in and inspire fantasies of life-changing jackpots and breaking the bank at a blackjack table. There's nothing wrong with dreaming about hitting it big. Plenty of folks win money every single day in Las Vegas, but most do not. Gambling should be entertainment, a pastime, a bonding activity with friends or family, and occasionally an intellectual challenge. It should never be an investment, job, or a way of making a quick buck. If you think of it that way, you may be leaving Las Vegas without a shirt.

The Best Approach. Learn enough about the games so that you aren't simply giving away your money. A little education will prevent you from making terrible bets or playing out of control. The bad bets (i.e. high-risk, high payout) can be some of the most exciting to play at the tables, and great fun if you like the action. With luck, you may come out ahead. But understand that higher-risk games are much less likely to pay out over time.

Have fun! If you have reasonable expectations, set and keep to your financial goals, and play with proper strategy, you are bound to have a successful trip, and leave Las Vegas with your sanity, dignity, and your shirt.

■ TIP→ Notice how bets are advertised. A good rule of thumb for discerning good bets from bad bets at the tables is to look how/if the bet is advertised. Good bets generally aren't posted (e.g. odds in craps aren't even on the table). Bad bets will be in flashing lights, and their big payouts will be prominently shown on the table or on large printed cards. Or they will be "sold" by the dealer (like insurance in blackjack, and Proposition bets in craps).

HOW NOT TO GO BROKE

■ Create solid goals on what you are willing to lose, and what would be a satisfying amount to win.

■ Consider what you can afford to lose and stick to this number, *no matter what.*

■ Pace yourself when you play, so you don't spend all your money too early in your trip.

■ Break your play into sessions.

■ If you lose your allotted goal during a session, quit playing and accept the loss. Many gamblers get deep into debt trying to "chase" a loss, and end up betting more than they can afford.

■ Make sure your winnings goal is realistic. If you wager $10 a hand at blackjack, it is not reasonable to think you will win $5,000 in a session—$50–$100 would be a more obtainable goal. If you're fortunate enough to reach your realistic goal during one of your sessions, end that session immediately. You can put half of your winnings away, and gamble with the profit during another session.

■ The most important thing is to exercise discipline and not exceed your goals. Sticking to sessions, regardless of whether you are up or down, will contain your losses and preserve your winnings.

THE GOOD, THE BAD, AND THE UGLY

Games you can actually beat under the right circumstances: poker, sports betting, video poker.

Games where you can lose money slowly: baccarat (bank), blackjack, craps (Pass/Don't Pass, Come/Don't Come), Pai Gow Poker, tiles, Single Zero Roulette, Three-Card Poker, and some slot machines.

Games with terrible odds: Basically the rest of the games you don't see above can hold a medium to large house edge, keno and the Big Six Wheel being the worst. Avoid these two like the plague.

PLASTIC PITFALLS

Never gamble with money borrowed on your credit card! Check out this sobering math: Say you want a $500 cash advance. The casino will charge a fee (it varies but for our example, 5%), which makes the total $525. Then the (credit card) bank will charge you for the cash advance (usually 3%). You're now $45.75 in the hole before you even start playing! Don't *even* get us started on the long-term costs of finance charges on that advance, if you carry a previous balance. ATM instead? The casino could still charge you up to a $10 fee, and the bank could also charge a fee, and even more if you use an ATM that is not owned by your bank.

THE HOUSE EDGE

Think of a coin-flip game paying you $1 on heads and taking $1 on tails. Over time, you'd win about as much as you'd lose. But the *casino*-hosted game would only pay $0.98 on heads while still taking your $1 on tails. This difference is the "house edge." Two cents doesn't seem like much, but if enough people play, the casino earns millions over an extended period of time; it's a mathematical certainty. Another example: The "true odds" of rolling double sixes in craps is 1 in 36, but they only pay you 30 to 1, instead of $36 on a $1 bet. The extra $6 that should be paid to you is, in essence, kept by the house, making it a very bad bet. The house edge varies from game to game, so knowing the odds for each game can help minimize your losses.

COMPS, CLUBS, AND COUPONS

Nearly every establishment has a rewards program, or Players Club, used to identify and reward its loyal gamblers. Members of the casino's Players Club will get regular mailings advertising specials, discounts, contests, and other information. When you sign up you receive a card to present whenever you play. You may also get a pin number so you can check your comp totals at one of the kiosks (a comp ATM) on the casino floor. The card is used to track your play at table games and slot machines. The amount of comps you're entitled to is based on factors such as the amount you buy in for, overall time played, average bet, and expected losses. Comps can be used for restaurants, gifts, rooms, or even cash in some places. In many cases one card is accepted at multiple casinos with the same owner. Sign up for a card at the Bellagio, and use it at all of the MGM-owned properties. Present your card every single time you play at a table or slot machine, and every time you move to a new one. Remember that comps are based on play, so don't expect to get a free meal if you only sit at a game for 15 minutes, and bet $10 a hand.

If you don't want casinos tracking you or sending you junk mail, ask about "fun books" when you check in. These coupon books have free-bies and discounts that offer some real value. The best fun books can be found at places like Casino Royale and Stratosphere. Be sure to scan for coupons in the back of those free magazines available in hotel gift shops, poker rooms, or in your room.

TIPS TO GETTING AND HANDLING COMPS

Get a Players Club Card. You *might* get a comp without a club card, but it's not very likely.

Don't forget to ask. No one is going to come up and offer you a comp. Even if you are not sure you have played enough for a comp, you should ask the floorperson, or Pit Boss. The worst they can do is politely say no.

Buy in often, buy in big. Your initial cash stake at a table is often what gets you noticed by the casino comp-masters. When you're finished at one table, cash in your chips at the cashier, and use those bills to buy in at the next table.

Consider the value of the comp. Never increase what you intended to gamble just to earn comps. It will cost you *much* less to pay for dinner than to lose enough money in order to get a comp for that same dinner.

BETTER BETTOR ETIQUETTE

Know a little before you play. Dealers are available for questions, but you should learn the basics. Watch for a while, or ask the casino host about beginner's classes. Even better, find an empty table and ask the dealer if he or she would be willing to walk you through the game.

Understand betting minimums before you sit down. Each table has a plaque or digital display with table minimums, maximums, and specific gaming rules.

Sympathy for the dealer. Dealers can't take cash directly from your hand, so lay it down on the table when you buy in. Place your bet in the proper area, and stack your entire bet in one pile, with the largest denomination chips on the bottom, and the smallest on the top.

Ask for change as you need it. Dealers prefer to give you enough small chips for 10 to 20 minimum bets at a time. If you're at a $10 table and you buy in with $300; they'll give you twenty $5 chips and eight $25 chips. If you run out of $5 chips, just ask them to change your $25 chips as needed.

THE GAMES

BEST FOR BEGINNERS

The whole gambling scene can seem intimidating for the first-timer. But casinos have worked hard to help newbies feel comfortable playing the games, in the hopes that once they get a taste of the excitement, they will be back for more.

BEST BEGINNER CLASSES

Free lessons in Vegas are widely available. One place to look is in your hotel room; many resorts play a running loop of gaming lessons on TV. If you prefer the in-person format, most resorts offer free group lessons where would-be gamblers gather around a real table game while a dealer or supervisor explains how it works. Classes usually take place at scheduled times during low-traffic hours (just ask the casino host or one of the supervisors). Venues we like include:

Excalibur offers poker lessons at 11 am, roulette at 11 am and 7 pm, blackjack at 11:30 am and 7:30 pm, and craps at noon and 8 pm.

Golden Nugget has lessons every weekday for the most popular games: Three-Card Poker at 10 am, Pai Gow at 10:30 am, craps at 10 am and noon, Texas Hold'em at 11 am, roulette at 11:30 am, and blackjack at noon.

HELPFUL WEBSITES

Perhaps the best time and place to learn how the games are played is before you leave for Las Vegas, on your home computer. There are tons of websites that not only teach you how to play the games, but also provide simulations of the gaming experience in the casino. And unlike the brief lessons given at the casino, you can learn at your own pace, and practice playing as much as you like, whenever you like.

To practice without having to register, or download any software, try **Linesmaker** (⊕ *casino.betlm.eu/free-casino*) for craps, baccarat, and Pai Gow poker

For roulette: ⊕ *www.freeroulette.com*

For blackjack and video poker: **Wizard of Vegas** (⊕ *www.wizardofvegas. com/games*).

BEST DEALERS

Dealers on the Strip keep the games moving fast and aren't prone to many mistakes, but they often don't go in for a lot of small talk. Many beginners feel more comfortable at tables that are social and lively. For that, try the folksy atmospheres of the locals' casinos off the Strip and away from Downtown, like Gold Coast or Sunset Station. Vegas is about fun, so consider Paris and Bally's if you want a lighthearted atmosphere with some musical accompaniment while you play. For sheer brainpower and experience, try the classics: Golden Nugget, Caesars Palace, and Mirage; watch and learn.

Before you sit down, make sure the game's moving at a speed you're comfortable with. Do the dealer and players look happy? Do the players have big stacks of chips? If you're feeling especially chatty, locate

CLOSE UP

Las Vegas Lingo

Bank. A row or group of similar gaming machines.

Bankroll. The amount of money you have to gamble with.

Buy-in. The amount of cash you exchange for chips during a gaming session.

Cage. The casino cashier, where you can exchange your chips for cash.

Cheques (or Checks). The chips with money-equivalent values, used to place wagers at the tables.

Color Up. To exchange a stack of lower denomination chips for a few high-denomination chips. Dealers will ask if they can "color you up" before you leave their table. Say yes.

Comp. Short for complimentary (i.e., a freebie). Can be a drink, room, dinner, or show tickets from the casino.

Cut. A ritual splitting of a deck or cards performed after shuffling.

Eye-in-the-sky. The overhead video surveillance system and its human monitors in a casino.

Fill. When chips are brought to a table from the casino cage to refill a money rack that is low.

House. Another name for the casino's side of any bet, as in this sentence: "the house wins on any tie."

Layout. The printed felt covering of a particular table game, which states the game being offered, betting area, payout odds, and other pertinent information related to the playing of the game.

Marker. A player's IOU to the casino. Rather than buy in with cash, players who register for casino credit can sign a marker in exchange for chips at the table.

Match Play. A onetime bet voucher for a table game, often given as a perk by casinos.

Pit. A subdivision of the casino floor, with several adjacent gaming tables.

Pit Boss. A senior casino employee who supervises the gaming tables in a casino pit, settles player disputes, and authorizes comps. The pit boss can usually be found at a computer console in the middle of the pit, or patrolling the entire pit he is assigned to.

Players Club Card. A card with a magnetic stripe on it used to track a gambler's activities in a casino.

Progressive. A special kind of jackpot, often available to multiple tables or game machines that continues to grow until it's won.

Push. A Tie bet, where you neither win nor lose.

Rake. In poker, it's an amount the casino takes out of each pot as compensation for running the game. Usually it is 10% of the total pot, or a flat fee per hour, depending on the game or casino.

Shoe. A small box in a table game from which cards are dealt.

Sports Book. The casino area for sports betting.

Table Games. All games of chance such as blackjack and craps played against the casino with a dealer.

Toke. A tip (short for token, or token of your esteem). Usually given to dealers during play, to reward outstanding service, or celebrate a player's good fortune.

4

a dealer from a familiar or interesting city (their hometowns are often printed on their name tags) and strike up some friendly banter. But remember: choose a dealer like you'd choose a doctor. If you don't like the vibe or you don't feel comfortable—for whatever reason—move on. Don't ask permission, and don't apologize; just pick up your remaining chips and leave. Conversely, don't hesitate to throw the dealer a toke (tip), if he enhances your overall experience.

EASIEST GAMES TO PLAY

Roulette is considered the easiest table game, but it's also one with a high house edge. That's not a coincidence; players typically pay for easier games in the form of a larger advantage for the house. ■TIP→ Play a single-zero wheel. It will cut the house edge almost in half.

LEARN BEFORE YOU GO

The Internet has resources galore: The Las Vegas Advisor (⊕ *lasvegasadvisor.com*) and Gaming Today (⊕ *gamingtoday.com*) are two publications that keep the rest of the world up to speed on the gaming industry, including where to find the best deals, promotions, and events. To find an in-depth discussion of game rules and odds, check out the Wizard of Odds (⊕ *wizardofodds.com*). Vegas visitors stay up to speed on the latest news, including great tourism information from the two local newspapers' websites: *The Las Vegas Review-Journal* (⊕ *lvrj.com*) and *Las Vegas Sun* (⊕ *lasvegassun.com*).

You can play **keno** while you eat in many casino coffee shops. Keno carries the worst odds in the whole casino, but it is extremely easy to play. You just mark numbers on a betting slip, give it to the keno runner with a buck or two, and watch the board on the wall to see if your numbers come up.

Bingo is also a fun, simple casino game. It's played in specialized parlors, mostly in the Downtown casinos, with a crowd of people sitting at tables in a large room listening for their lucky numbers to line up. The people you run into are often locals and casino workers, who like bingo's humble aesthetic after a long day filled with glitz and kitsch.

Newer **slot machines** are a little more complicated than traditional slots, but they still remain the easiest to play in the casino—put the money in (or bet your credits) and touch a button (or pull the handle if it's an older machine) and wait for the reels to stop spinning to see if you won or lost.

BLACKJACK

4

Blackjack, aka "21," anchors virtually every casino in America. It's the most popular table game because it's easy to learn, fun to play, and has excellent odds for the player.

The object of this classic card game is simple. You want to build a higher hand than the dealer without going over 21—a *bust*. Two-card hands, from one deck of cards up to eight decks of cards, are dealt to everyone at the table, including the dealer, who gets one card facedown (the "hole" card) and one card faceup for all to see. Play then proceeds from gambler to gambler. You play out your hand by taking additional cards ("hitting") or standing pat ("staying"). When all the players have finished playing out their hands, the dealer then plays the house hand following preset rules. Once that's complete, the dealer pays winning players and rakes the chips of the losers.

PLAYING THE GAME

The value of a blackjack hand is the sum of all the cards; aces count as 1 or 11 (whichever is more advantageous to your hand), and face cards (jacks, queens, and kings) count as 10. Suit plays no role in blackjack. If you bust, you lose your bet immediately, no matter what happens with the dealer's cards. The dealer can also bust by going over 21, in which case all players remaining in the hand get paid off. If you're dealt a combination of a 10-valued card (a 10 or any face card) and an ace on your first two cards, it's a *natural* blackjack. If this is the case, you're paid a bonus on your bet, unless the house also has a blackjack. The payout is either 3 to 2 on your original bet, or 6 to 5, depending on the house rules where you're playing. The dealers use a little mirror or other device at the table to check their hidden card for blackjacks prior to dealing out extra cards.

For those who aren't lucky enough to be dealt 21, play starts with the person sitting to the dealer's left. Everyone plays out his or her hand by motioning to the dealer whether they want to hit or stand. Players *must* make specific motions to the dealer about their intentions:

■ If the cards have been dealt faceup, which is the case at most casinos these days, you're not supposed to touch your cards, so you hit by tapping on the table with your finger(s) in front of your cards. To stand, you simply wave your hand side to side over your cards.

■ If the cards have been dealt facedown, pick them up and hold them (with one hand only!). To hit, you "scratch" on the table toward yourself with the corner of your cards. To stand, you slide the cards facedown under your chips. Don't fret if you knock over your chips in the process. The dealer will restack them for you if necessary. As long as your hand is less than 21, you can continue hitting and taking cards. If you bust, you must expose your cards immediately (if you are holding them), and the dealer will rake your bet and remove your cards. At that point the dealer turns to the next player who repeats the same hit/stand process.

> **AT A GLANCE**
>
> **Format:** Single-dealer card game played with up to seven players
>
> **Goal:** Players compete against the dealer for highest hand without going over 21
>
> **Pays:** Even-money on winning bets 3 to 2, or 6 to 5 if player receives 21 on first two cards
>
> **House Advantage:** Varies
>
> **Best Bet:** Learn basic blackjack strategy. 3-to-2 payout on 21.
>
> **Worst Bet:** Insurance side bet, games with limited split/double-down rules, 6-to-5 payout on blackjack.

■ Once every player has a chance to act on his/her hand, the dealer reveals his hidden card and plays out the hand according to the following rules:

■ Dealer shows 16 or less: dealer must hit

■ Dealer shows 17 or more: dealer must stand (in most casinos)

Once the dealer's hand is complete, the bets are either paid (if the player's hand is higher than the dealer's) or raked (if the dealer's hand is higher than the player's). If the dealer has busted, all players remaining in the hand win their bets. In the event a player's hand value is equal to that of the dealer, it's a *push* (the dealer will knock on the table in front of the bet); the bet is neither paid nor raked.

DOUBLING-DOWN

If your first two cards total 10 or 11, your chances of hitting and drawing a 10-value card to create a great hand are very good. To take full advantage of that, you can double-down. It's a special bet you place after the hand has started, whose value can be up to your initial bet. The upside is you put more money in play for an advantageous situation. The downside is that you receive only a single card in lieu of the normal hit/stand sequence. A few casinos rules vary on which starting hands you can double-down on, so ask the dealer before you slide a matching stack of chips beside your first bet. The most common rule variation says you can double-down on any two cards.

SPLITTING

Splitting is another good way to raise your bet in a favorable situation. If your first two cards are of equal value, you can split them apart and form two separate hands, then play each hand out separately as if it were a brand-new hand. When you want to split, push a stack of chips equal to your original bet into the betting circle, and tell the dealer your intentions. Never touch the cards yourself, unless you are playing a game that calls for it (like single deck), in which case you will lay your cards down and place the extra bet. In some casinos you can re-split if you get another matching card for three or even four separate hands. You can draw as many cards as you want to make a hand when you split. In many casinos, you can't re-split aces and are only allowed to draw one card on each ace.

INSURANCE

When the dealer's up card is an ace, she'll ask if anyone wants to buy insurance. You can take insurance for up to half of your original wager. If the dealer makes blackjack, the insurance bet pays off at 2-to-1 odds; if she doesn't, the insurance bet is lost, and the hand is played normally. Experts consider this a bad bet. Always pass on it.

> ### BLACKJACK SWITCH
>
> Two is better than one right? That's the thinking behind Blackjack Switch, a ShuffleMaster-owned game that started at Casino Royale but can now be found at just about every gambling hall in town. Instead of playing one hand, players are required to play two. Players can switch the second cards of their two hands to make two totally new hands. Standard splitting and doubling rules apply. Think the switcheroo favors the players? Think again. Blackjack only pays even money, and when the dealer breaks with 22, all bets push.

STRATEGY

Although it's easy to learn, blackjack has varying layers of complexity that can be tackled, depending on your interest level. With practice and the perfection of **basic strategy**, you can reduce the house edge to about .5% (as opposed to about 2.5% for the average uninformed gambler), making blackjack one of the best bets of table games.

Basic strategy is simply the optimal way for a player to play his cards, based on the dealer's exposed card, and a particular set of casino rules. We will discuss these rules below (⇨ *The House Hedges*), because basic strategy changes as certain rules change.

At its *most* basic, basic strategy is the assumption that the dealer's hole card is a 10. If the dealer's up card is a 9, he or she likely has a 10 underneath to make 19. If the dealer shows a 4, he or she likely has a 14. You then act accordingly, standing pat or hitting depending on whether you can beat the dealer's hand. Learning and memorizing basic strategy is a must for professional gamblers, who can't afford to give up anything more to the house edge. For the casual or beginning gambler, the rules are printed on small charts (⇨ *example chart in this chapter*) that you can buy in any casino gift shop. You are allowed to use these cards at

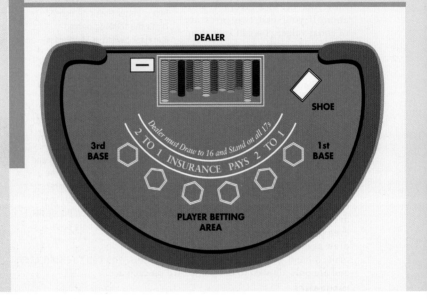

the table for reference at any time, and you should every time you're not sure of whether to hit, stand, split, or double-down on any given hand. You should however try to come with some basic knowledge of the game and strategy before you start playing, so you don't have to consult the card on *every* hand, which considerably slows down the game for other players.

■ **TIP→** To practice basic strategy, try ⊕ www.hitorstand.net. If you make the wrong decision on a hand, the program will tell you.

If you don't have the patience to practice or memorize, or don't want to refer to a chart, you can always ask the dealer, who should have knowledge of basic strategy from his experience, or follow these basic rules-of-thumb based on the dealer's up card:

■ Ace, 10, 9, 8, 7—assume the dealer has a made hand (i.e., a hand totaling between 17 and 21 and will therefore not need to draw). If your hand is 17 or higher, stand. If your hand is 16 or lower, you should hit.

■ 2, 3, 4, 5, 6—assume that the dealer has an easily busted hand, so there's no need to take any risks. If your hand is 13 or higher, stand and hope the dealer busts. If your cards total 11 or lower, take a hit and then reevaluate using the same set of rules. If your hand totals 12 only hit against a dealer's 2 or 3.

■ If you have a "soft" hand (an ace with a value card; for example A,7) that totals less than 8 (or 18), you should always hit. If it totals 18 only hit against a dealer's 9, 10, or ace, and always stand on a soft total of 19 or 20.

BLACKJACK BASIC STRATEGY CHART

Your Hand	Dealer's Up Card									
	2	3	4	5	6	7	8	9	10	A
5–8	H	H	H	H	H	H	H	H	H	H
9	D	D	D	D	D	H	H	H	H	H
10	D	D	D	D	D	D	D	D	H	H
11	D	D	D	D	D	D	D	D	D	D
12	H	H	S	S	S	H	H	H	H	H
13	S	S	S	S	S	H	H	H	H	H
14	S	S	S	S	S	H	H	H	H	H
15	S	S	S	S	S	H	H	H	H	H
16	S	S	S	S	S	H	H	H	H	H
17	S	S	S	S	S	S	S	S	S	S
18	S	S	S	S	S	S	S	S	S	S
19	S	S	S	S	S	S	S	S	S	S
20	S	S	S	S	S	S	S	S	S	S
21	S	S	S	S	S	S	S	S	S	S
A,2	H	H	D	D	D	H	H	H	H	H
A,3	H	H	D	D	D	H	H	H	H	H
A,4	H	H	D	D	D	H	H	H	H	H
A,5	H	H	D	D	D	H	H	H	H	H
A,6	D	D	D	D	D	H	H	H	H	H
A,7	S	D	D	D	D	S	S	H	H	H
A,8	S	S	S	S	S	S	S	S	S	S
A,9	S	S	S	S	S	S	S	S	S	S
A,A	SP	SP	SP	SP	SP	SP	SP	SP	SP	SP
2,2	H	SP	SP	SP	SP	SP	H	H	H	H
3,3	H	H	SP	SP	SP	SP	H	H	H	H
4,4	H	H	H	D	D	H	H	H	H	H
5,5	D	D	D	D	D	D	D	D	D	H
6,6	SP	SP	SP	SP	SP	H	H	H	H	H
7,7	SP	SP	SP	SP	SP	SP	H	H	H	H
8,8	SP	SP	SP	SP	SP	SP	SP	SP	SP	SP
9,9	SP	SP	SP	SP	SP	S	SP	SP	S	S
10,10	S	S	S	S	S	S	S	S	S	S
H-Hit, S-Stand, D-Double Down, SP-Split										

DID YOU KNOW?

With a bit of knowledge and the use of basic strategy *(see chart)*, blackjack players can reduce the house's edge to less than 1%.

■ If your hand total equals 11, you should consider doubling-down against everything but a dealer ace. If your hand totals 10, you should consider doubling-down against everything but a dealer 10 or ace.

■ Always split 8,8, and A,A, and never split 5,5, or 10,10.

THE HOUSE HEDGES

The casinos know that their edge in blackjack is very small, especially against those who employ basic strategy, so they have come up with ways to hedge their bets by adding certain rules, side bets, or restrictions to the once-standard rules. These things not only increase the house edge against you, but they can distort the odds for basic strategy decisions, and make your chart much less effective by changing some variables of the games. Because the variables change from game to game, and casino to casino, you must be sure your basic strategy card matches the game you are playing. Here are some general rules for choosing a good blackjack table and keeping the house edge low. Choose a table that:

■ Pays blackjack at 3 to 2, not 6 to 5 or anything else

■ Uses a smaller number of decks in the game. The fewer decks, the better for you

■ The dealer must stand on a soft 17 (A,6), instead of hitting

■ Allows you to double-down on any hand. Some casinos will only let you double on 10 or 11

■ Allows you to re-split aces. The more times they let you split aces in one hand, the better

■ Allows you to split aces, and receive more than one card if you choose

■ Allows you to double-down after splitting

■ Has surrender. This allows you to surrender a bad hand before drawing extra cards. The casino will charge you half your wager for this privilege. Sometimes it is a good idea, and basic strategy will let you know when.

Now, chances are you won't find a game with all of these things in your favor. The trick is to find one that uses a combination of as many as possible.

SIDE BETS AND VARIATIONS GAMES

Other strategies used by the casino to separate you from your money involve side bets and variation games. A side bet is a high-paying bet that is based on getting three 7s, a pair, a two-card 20, etc. This bet is usually placed before the cards are dealt, and is not tied to the results

> ### SHOE BREAK
>
> If you see a sign on a table that reads, "No mid-shoe entry," you can't enter play in the middle of the shoe. You have to wait until the shoe ends to start play. Some players have the belief (unsupported by mathematics) that new people can bring bad luck or change the cards. Or they feel it just ruins the flow of the game. Casinos mostly put these signs at high-limit tables to keep their highest-betting customers happy.

4

of the main game. Like the bonus bets in poker table games *(⇨ below)*, these bets carry a hefty house edge and should be avoided.

Variation games like Double Attack Blackjack, Double Exposure Blackjack, or Spanish 21 are games that use the rules of blackjack but change the dynamics of the game to stimulate more action, and entice high-house-edge bets. For example, in Spanish 21, one of the more popular variations, the deck has only 48 cards, because the 10s have been removed. Because of this fact player 21s are paid immediately, and the rules allow players to do common blackjack things at strange times— you can surrender after your first two cards are dealt, or double-down on any number of cards. Plus, hands like 6-7-8 and 7-7-7 pay automatic bonuses. There are so many different variation games these days, and new ones popping up all the time, that we will not describe them all here. The rules and bets are posted on the individual games. If you are interested in learning them, you can take a course or ask the dealer if he is not busy. You should have a good understanding of how to play standard blackjack before attempting these games though. Of course basic strategy does not apply for these games, and occasionally, neither does common sense.

WHERE TO PLAY

In a bathing suit: Many hotels offer swim-up blackjack, but we like the game at Caesars, Flamingo, or the Hard Rock Hotel.

For the best odds: Head Downtown to El Cortez or Binion's and you'll find 3-to-2 payoffs on 21 at low table minimums. Strip hotels like Monte Carlo and Tropicana have 3-to-2 (single-deck) games if you're willing to play $15 or $25 per hand.

On a tight schedule: Cosmopolitan, where you can reserve table seats ahead of time. Of course, you have to buy in with a certain amount of money, and bet according to the table minimums.

To learn the game: Circus Circus, which still has $1 and $2 games.

POKER

4

Folks can't seem to get enough of poker. The top players are celebrities, and poker's on TV more than hockey. If you've played, you know why: it's an intellectual challenge to suit any size brain. And it has an egalitarian quality that beginners love; sometimes the cards fall just right for rookies and they win a tournament, or take home a huge pot.

BASIC RULES

In poker you win by being the last player standing at the end of the hand. That happens one of two ways: by betting more than anyone else is willing to bet and forcing other players to "fold" (drop out until the next hand), or by having the best hand of all players remaining in the game after the final round of betting. The two twists that make poker great are that the players' hands evolve as the game continues and more cards are dealt or revealed, and that some or all of the cards are hidden from view, so you can only speculate on other players' hand values.

The variations played in casinos—Seven-Card Stud, Texas Hold'em, Omaha, and a smattering of others like Razz and Pineapple—all demand that the player create the best five-card hand from a deal that originates from a single standard deck of 52 cards. Five-card hands are valued in order of their statistical rarity:

■ Straight Flush: Five cards of the same suit in consecutive rank. A Ten-to-Ace straight flush is called a "royal flush," the rarest and highest of all hands.

■ Four of a Kind: Four cards of the same rank plus one nonmatching card

■ Full House: Three cards of the same rank, and two of a different equal rank (e.g. 7-7-7-5-5). This hand is declared as "sevens full of fives." The value of the full house is dependent on the three equal cards, not the two. If two players both have full houses, the player whose three equal cards are higher value, will win (e.g. A-A-A-2-2 is better than K-K-K-7-7)

■ Flush: Five cards of the same suit, regardless of order

■ Straight: Five cards in consecutive order regardless of suit

■ Three of a Kind: Three cards of the same rank and two other non-matching cards

■ Two Pair: Two cards of one rank, two cards of a second rank, with a fifth nonmatching card. Similar to the Full House, the value of the highest ranking pair wins (e.g. 10-10-4-4 beats 7-7-6-6).

■ Pair: Two cards of one rank, and three other nonmatching cards

■ High Card: Any five cards that don't fit into one of the *above* categories

The high card will also determine a winner when pair-hands have the same value. For example, if two players have a pair of 9s, the player with the highest value of the remaining three cards wins (which is referred to as a "kicker, as in "I have a pair of 9s with an Ace kicker"). Aces are the highest ranked card with one exception: they can act as the low end of a straight (Ace, 2, 3, 4, 5). The 5 card is considered the highest ranked card for such a straight, and in a final round showdown that hand would lose to a 6-high straight (2, 3, 4, 5, 6). The suits are all equal in poker and totally identical hands split the pot.

The game starts when cards are dealt to all players at the table, who then take turns putting casino chips into a central "pot" during a pre-determined number of betting rounds. When it's your turn to bet, you can decide to *fold*, which means you no longer participate in the hand. Any money you've already bet stays in the pot after you fold and will go to the winner of the hand. To stay in the game, each player must match, or *call*, the highest bet of that round to stay in the game. Players can also *raise*, which means that they are betting more than the round's current highest bet. After a raise, the betting round continues until everyone who wishes to stay in the game has contributed an equal amount to the pot.

Once all the betting rounds are over, if more than one player remains in the game there's a *showdown* where all cards are revealed. In most games the highest-value hand wins, although some poker games pay players for having the lowest hand, as you will soon see.

RULES FOR THE MOST POPULAR GAMES
TEXAS HOLD'EM

Hold'em is *the* most popular form of poker. Each player (up to 10 can play one game) is dealt two cards facedown, followed by a betting round. Then five community cards are dealt on the table in three groups, each followed by a betting round. First is a group of three cards (the *flop*), and then there are two more rounds of one card each (the *turn* and the *river*). You can use any combination of your cards and community cards to create your best five-card hand.

Position is very important in Hold'em. The deal rotates around the table after every hand, and with it, the *blinds* (minimum opening bets used to stimulate the betting action). Depending on house rules, either one or two players must automatically bet in the first betting round, regardless of their cards (that's why they're called blinds; you have to bet without even seeing your cards). To stay in and see the three cards of the flop, the other players must match (or raise) the blind bet. This ensures that no player sees the flop for free, and adds heft to the pot. The later your position, the better—players have an advantage if they can see what the players before them decided to do, and can better judge whether the size of the pot justifies the risk of betting and staying in the game.

■ TIP→ The dealer will hold your seat at a poker table for up to a half hour (for bathroom breaks, smoking, or just fresh air). Upon returning, you will have to post the small and big blinds if you want to play immediately, or wait until the deal comes around to you naturally. If you do not return in the allotted time, you will lose your seat at the table and your cheques will be collected, and stored in the cashier cage until you claim them.

4

OMAHA
Omaha is dealt, and played exactly like Hold'em except the player is given four cards instead of two, and *must* use two, and *only* two of the four cards, plus three of the community cards, to make his final hand. This adds another dimension to the game, as you must base your strategy on using only two of the four cards in your hand, and this strategy may change drastically from flop to river, because of the extra cards you are holding. You should have some experience playing Hold'em before taking on Omaha, in which reading hands is more complicated.

SEVEN-CARD STUD
In Seven-Card Stud there are no community cards; you're dealt your own set of seven cards over the course of five betting rounds: an initial batch of three cards (two down, one up); three more single up-cards; and a final down-card. By the showdown, every player remaining in the game has three down cards and four up cards from which to make his best five-card hand.

HI-LOW GAMES
Sometimes you will see Omaha and Seven-Card Stud listed with Hi-Low. These games are played with the same rules as their relatives with one big exception. To win the entire pot, you must have the best high hand *and* the best low hand. A low hand is basically the lowest value

POKER BETTING LIMITS

Casino poker rooms list ongoing games and soon-to-start tournaments on a large video monitor at their entrance. Before you get into a game, you should understand the betting limit nomenclature. Here are the basics:

Limit Games. Also known as a "Fixed Limit" game, the amount you can bet is listed with two numbers, like "$3-$6". This means you must bet and raise $3 in the first two rounds of play and $6 in the third and fourth rounds. The amount of the "big" blind bet is equal to the low limit ($3).

Spread Limit. This type of game gives the player a range for betting and raising. An example would be a "$1-$4-$8" game, where your bets must be at least $1 and at most $4 for the first two rounds, and between $1 and $8 in the later rounds.

Pot Limit. Players are allowed to wager any amount up to the total of what's currently in the pot.

No Limit. These games are exactly what they sound like; they usually have low betting minimums (they're listed as "$1-$2NL"). If you've got the chips on the table, you can bet them. This is the style of play you see on television, where players go "All In." Don't get involved in a No Limit game if you don't know what you're doing.

you can make for your 5 cards. For example 5,4,3,2,A (or "wheel" as it is referred to) is the lowest possible hand. In a regular game of Omaha, this would be a straight, and a fairly high-ranked hand. In Hi-Low the straight rank used for the high hand is not also assumed when determining the low hand. If one player has the high hand, and another has the low hand, the pot is split between them. If more than one player has an identical winning low, or high hand, then half of the pot is split between them and so forth.

STRATEGY

If you're a beginner, focus on learning how to play the game at low-stakes tables or tournaments before you invest any serious bankroll. The old adage "if you aren't sure who the sucker is at the table, it's you" is never more true than at a Las Vegas poker table. Online poker is a valuable tool for players who are trying to learn the game prior to a Vegas trip, but the style of play is different. Playing online ignores a lot of the subtleties of playing live, including the all-important *tells,* outward quirks that reveal the contents of your hand to observant opponents. Also, remember that you are not betting real money when you play online, and may be inclined to play bad hands that you would be ill-advised to play in real money games.

Although bluffing and big showdowns are part and parcel of the TV poker phenomenon, casino poker success in limit games and small tournaments comes with a steady, conservative approach. The most important thing to learn is how to calculate *pot odds.* You compare the amount of money likely to be in the pot—your potential win—with the relative odds that your hand will be improved as more cards are dealt or revealed. As with everything in life, if the payoff is big enough, the price you pay to stay in the game is worth the risk.

There are no shortcuts to learning poker strategy. Each variation of the game has its nuances. Part of learning the game is understanding how good your hand has to become to win a hand, given a certain pot size and number of opponents. You can get lucky, but it takes study and repetition to become consistently good at poker over the long haul.

POPULAR POKER VARIATIONS

All of the following games are played like traditional casino table games that use the elements of poker at their core. These games are found in the main casino area with the other table games instead of the poker room. Although there are other variations of poker games around Vegas, these five are the most common. Most of these games carry high house advantages, but move at a slower, more relaxed pace, so you won't lose as quickly as you might at blackjack or craps. Most of them also have a jackpot or bonus bet that can carry a very high payout for rarer hands, which makes the hefty house advantage worth it to many players. The bonus hands and payouts are always clearly listed at the table, and you can always ask the dealer how to play these bets if you are feeling frisky.

THREE-CARD AND FOUR-CARD POKER

Three- and Four-Card Poker are two of the most popular poker table games, and at least one table of either can be found in virtually every casino in Vegas. Because you have fewer than the standard five cards to make your final poker hand in both of these games, the odds of making certain hands changes. As a result, the ranking system of hands is adjusted. For example, in Three-Card Poker, a straight beats a flush. The hand rankings will be listed clearly right on the table layout in front of you for your convenience. As always, if you are not sure of something, ask the dealer.

Three-Card Poker. First place a bet in the Ante spot. You and the dealer get three cards facedown. After seeing your cards, you have the option to fold and surrender your Ante, or to play and make the "Raise" wager (located directly beneath the Ante). The Raise will always be equal to your Ante. The dealer will then reveal his cards. If the dealer doesn't have a total hand value of Queen-High or better, he does not *qualify*. If this is the case he will return your "Raise" bet to you, and you will get paid even money on your Ante. If you have a straight or better, you will also get a bonus on your Ante for having a rare hand. If the dealer qualifies for the hand with a Queen-High or better, and has a hand that is better than yours, he collects your Ante and Raise bets. If he qualifies and your hand is better, you will be paid even money on both your Raise and Ante bets (and an ante bonus if your hand qualifies).

Four-Card Poker. You start with an aAnte wager and are dealt five cards, which you must use to make your best four-card hand. The dealer, however, will be dealt six cards to make his best four-card hand. Because of this extra card, there is no minimum hand needed for the dealer to qualify, as in Three-Card, so you will always have to beat the dealer to get paid. If you fold, you lose your Ante. If you decide to play you can wager from 1 to 3 times your Ante wager in the spot marked "Play" (directly beneath Ante). If your hand beats the dealer's when it is revealed, you will be paid even money on both Ante and Play bets. You will be paid a bonus on your aAnte if your hand is three of a kind or better. If your hand isn't better than the dealer's, you lose both bets. Because the house has a large advantage by receiving an extra card in this game, it will pay you if you push, or tie, the dealer's hand.

BONUS BETS

Both of these games have a stand-alone bet that has nothing to do with whether you win the hand or not. These bets are the real reason that these games are so popular, and even though they are optional, they are placed by most people who play the game. They pay high odds for rare hands, adding the excitement of potentially hitting a small jackpot. In Three-Card Poker it is called Pairs Plus (located above the Ante). If you choose this bet, and get any hand that has a rank value of a pair or better, you get paid a bonus of up to 40 to 1 on your initial bet, depending on what the hand is. In Four-Card Poker the same bet is called Aces Up (also above the Ante). It pays if you get a hand that is at least a pair of Aces or better, and like the Pairs Plus bet in Three-Card, it is paid at increasing odds depending on how rare your hand is, up to 50 to 1. In both games the bonus hands, and what they pay, will be clearly marked on the table layout.

CARIBBEAN STUD

Caribbean Stud has been around for many years, but recently has waned in popularity, as more exciting games like Three-Card Poker have taken its place. To start, each player places an initial Ante bet. You and the dealer are then dealt five cards facedown. The dealer will expose one of his cards to entice you to play. You must then decide whether to remain in the game, in which case you place an additional wager in the "Bet" square equal to double your Ante, or fold, in which case you lose your Ante.

After you have placed your additional bet, or folded, the dealer reveals the rest of his hand. If the dealer's hand is not better than a minimum value of Ace-King high, he does not *qualify*, and you are paid even money on your Ante wager, and push on your Bet wager, even if the dealer's nonqualifying hand is better than yours. If the dealer has a hand that is better than a value of Ace-King high, it qualifies. If it's better than your hand, you lose both bets. If your hand is better than the dealers *qualifying* hand, you are paid even money on your Ante wager, and your additional wager will get paid at even money, or at increasing odds, depending on what the hand is (e.g., two pair pays 2 to 1, a straight pays 4 to 1, etc.). This game also offers a hard-to-resist $1 side bet for a progressive jackpot that pays bonuses for any hand better than a straight, and the jackpot (advertised in flashing lights) for a royal flush. This bet offers terrible odds, but adds to the excitement factor.

PAI GOW TILES

Many Vegas casinos offer Pai Gow Tiles, a distant cousin to poker. You'll recognize it right away because it's the only game in the house that uses a set of 32 dominoes (or "tiles") along with three dice. The goal of the game is to assemble a hand that beats the banker.

The dice are used to determine order of play, which begins with each player being given a stack of four tiles. The player then arranges them into two hands of two. Once everyone has set their pairs, the banker reveals the house hands and the players who beat both hands win even money, the players who win one and lose the other push, and the players who lose both hands lose their wager. There is also a 5% commission involved and a bank option for the players.

The twist, and what makes Pai Gow so addictive according to its adherents, is that there are different approaches to arranging your pairs. Because of this, and whether or not you bank the hand, the house edge can vary. What makes it a difficult game to learn is that the tile pairs have a specific—and nonintuitive—ranking system which determines when hands win and lose.

4

LET IT RIDE

You're dealt three cards, and the dealer presents two community cards. If your three cards, plus his two cards make a five-card hand that's a pair of tens or better, you win. You start by placing three bets of equal size. On the first two bets you have the option to take them back or let them ride, as the community cards are revealed one by one. When the last community card is revealed the dealer turns over your cards. If you don't have tens or better, you lose your remaining bets. If you have the tens or a better hand, you're paid even money or at increasing odds based on what hand you have, on all the bets you let ride during the betting rounds. Like Caribbean Stud, there is a $1 bonus bet that will pay out if you get a hand that is three of a kind or better.

PAI GOW POKER

You're dealt seven cards from which you make one five-card and one two-card poker hand. The two-card hand can *never* have a better rank value than the five-card hand, so make sure you set your cards carefully. There's a joker in the mix, which can be used as an ace in either hand, or a wild card to complete a straight or flush in your five-card hand. You play against the dealer, who also makes two hands from seven cards, and will always set them according to a strict set of "house rules." If both of your hands are beat by the dealer's hands, you lose. If you lose one and win one, you push. If you win both hands, you win even money on your bet, minus a 5% commission to the casino.

WHERE TO PLAY

Where the big boys play: Aria, which is now home to Phil Ivey's "Ivey Room"; and **Bellagio,** the jewel in the poker-room crown on the Strip.

Best all-around poker room: The **Caesars Palace** poker room is huge, well run, and offers a great variety of games and stakes.

SLOTS

Slot machines are the lifeblood of Vegas, earning the casinos mountains of cash. Remember, there's a reason why there are what seems like zillions of slot machines compared to table games—the odds are worse for you. But some gamblers can't get enough of the one-armed bandits, and if you're one of them (a gambler, not a bandit), set yourself a budget and pray for those three 7s to line up.

BASIC SLOT PLAY

Playing slots is basically the same as it's always been. Players insert money, start the game, and watch to see what happens. But the look and feel of the games has changed dramatically. Machines that dispense a noisy waterfall of coins have all but given way to machines that pay with printed, coded tickets. If you're a historian, or sentimental, you can still find a few coin-dispensing relics in some of the Downtown or off-Strip casinos, but they have been replaced in virtually all of the larger Strip casinos by ticket machines. The tickets can be inserted like cash into other slot machines, or redeemed at the Cage or at ATM-like machines that dispense cash. Most of the games are digital, with touch screens, and play like video games. But the underlying concept is still the same: you're looking for the reels—real or virtual—to match a winning pattern of shapes.

Each reel may have a few dozen shapes, creating an enormous number of possible patterns. The payout varies, depending on how rare the pattern is. The payout tables for each shape are usually posted above or below the "play" area of the machine. On some of the newer digital machines, there's a button marked "Payout Table." Prizes range from merely returning the bettor's initial stake, to multimillion-dollar *progressive* prizes.

STRATEGY

All slot machines, including every mechanical reel game, are run by on-board computers. The machine's computer brain generates a new random number thousands of times a second, which then determines where each reel will come to rest.

Although the casino can set the percentage an individual machine will retain for the house over the long term, each individual spin is an independent, random event. That means that if a jackpot reel pattern appears and pays a huge amount, the next jackpot is equally likely (or unlikely) to appear the very next spin. There is no such thing as an overdue machine, or a machine that's "tapped out."

Slot payout ranges can vary between 70% and 98%. A machine that pays out at 98% will, in the long run, pay back 98 cents out of every dollar you put in, as opposed to the paltry 70 cents you'll get back on the 70% machine. Picking the right machine can make the biggest difference in how fast you lose. Of course, information on which slot machines are the loosest (the ones that pay out the most) is hard to obtain, and can change often. Play the games you enjoy, but never lose sight of the fact that the payout percentage of that machine will usually determine how much you win or lose.

AT A GLANCE

Format: Bill- and ticket-operated electronic/mechanical machines

Goal: Line up winning symbols on machine's reels according to payout schedule

Pays: Varies by machine and casino

House Advantage: Varies widely; depends on many factors

Best Bet: Playing "loose" machines close to the change booth or coffee shop

Worst Bet: Playing "tight" machines at non-casino locations (e.g., the airport or service stations)

■TIP➔ Make sure you always insert your player card into the appropriate slot before you insert cash or tickets. Slot players often enjoy lucrative promotions and comps that table games players do not.

CHOOSING A MACHINE

■ Higher denomination machines tend to have higher payback percentages.

■ Look for machines that advertise a higher payout, but beware of the fine print. The machines with the high progressive jackpots are usually the tightest. Resist the temptation, and avoid them.

■ If you want to take a shot at the jackpot, you need to play the *maximum* coins with *every play*. If that means stepping down to a lower denomination machine (e.g., from dollars to quarters) so you can afford it, then do it. After all, we know that hitting the jackpot is the "reel" reason you are in Vegas.

DID YOU KNOW?

Chips are the currency of table games, but you can stroll up to a blackjack table and lay down cash for a single hand. This is referred to as "money plays." To continue playing hands, however, the dealer will insist that you purchase chips.

VIDEO POKER

4

Video poker attracts a large following. Many gamblers enjoy the solo play of a slot machine, but prefer a slightly more complex set of rules, like to have a say in the outcome, and can't get enough of that feeling when the fifth card of a full house falls into place. Make no mistake, video poker is not "live poker on training wheels." People love video poker because it's fun, convenient, and mostly because the house advantage can be relatively low (even none) under the right circumstances.

BASIC RULES

Casino visitors will find video poker in long rows of machines just like slot machines. And many casino bars feature video-poker consoles for patrons to play as they sip. To play, just feed in bills, or tickets to buy credits, then play the game until those credits run out or you decide to take the money and run.

Unlike regular poker, with its multiple betting rounds, bluffs, and competing players, video poker is all about you making the best possible five-card hand as the computer deals. Video poker comes in many different flavors like "Jacks or Better," "Double Bonus," and "Deuces Wild." Each game has a slightly different gimmick but follows the same basic sequence. After your bet (usually from one to five credits), you get dealt five cards, faceup. You then have to choose which of the five cards to keep by either touching the card on the screen or by activating the appropriate button underneath each card. The cards you didn't keep are replaced with new cards to complete your final hand. If it contains a winning combination, you get paid. It's that simple.

Or is it? Imagine you've bet one coin on a Jacks or Better game and you're dealt four hearts and one spade. Holding your four hearts and discarding your spade gives you a decent chance at making a flush (five cards of the same suit) which pays six coins. But before you throw it away, you realize the spade you hold is an ace, which matches your ace of hearts to make a pair. A pair only pays one coin but it's a guaranteed payout versus the possible payout of the flush. That dilemma—and others like it—is at the heart of video poker, and is what makes it so much fun for so many.

UNSPOKEN RULES

Be aware that veteran slot players can be territorial about their machines and may even play several at one time. If there's any doubt about whether a machine is currently "occupied," politely ask before you sit down. If in doubt, casino slots personnel can direct you to open machines.

STRATEGY

The first priority for any video-poker player is finding the best machines. That's because even though two machines may be identical in the game or games they offer, slight variations in the payoff table make one far more advantageous to play than the other.

PAYOUTS

Video-poker enthusiasts identify games by certain key amounts in their payout tables (displayed on the machine). For example, with Jacks or Better games, the important values to look for are those for the payout on a full house and flush. Put simply, what you want are what's known affectionately as full-pay machines, and for Jacks or Better that means a 9/6 payout. If your game pays nine coins on a Full House and six coins on a flush, you've found a 9/6 machine (that is "nine six" machine, not "nine-sixths" machine) and it's the most advantageous you'll find. So if the Jacks or Better game you just bellied up to pays less than 9/6 on a full house and flush, you should take your coins elsewhere.

Full pay for Double Bonus games are 10 coins to 1 on a full house and 6 coins on a flush. So if that's your game, look for 10/6 machines (if you're very lucky you might find a rare 10/7 machine). Full pay for a Deuces Wild game is 9/5, but these numbers actually refer to the single coin payout for a straight flush and a four-of-a-kind. If that seems low for such stellar poker hands, remember that the presence of wild cards makes the likelihood of an outstanding hand quite a bit higher. In fact, some experts go so far as to list the five-of-a-kind payout and define

VIDEO POKER RULES

You'll find a many video-poker variations in Vegas casinos; and a single machine can sometimes host several different game types, allowing the player to pick his poison from a menu. Here's a quick primer on the most popular:

Jacks or Better: The most common video-poker game, and the basis for many variations. The player must have at least a pair of jacks to be in the money.

Deuces Wild: Player must have a three-of-a-kind to be in the money, but 2s are wild; that is, they become whatever card you need them to be to make your poker hand. Got two jacks, two queens, and a 2? The 2 can act as a jack or queen, so you've got a full house!

Double Bonus: Requires a pair of jacks or better to be in the money, but offers varied payouts on four-of-a-kind hands, with a bonus for getting four aces.

full-pay Deuces Wild as 15/9/5. Such machines are rare these days on the Strip, and when they're found, it's often for low-bet denominations. Why? Read on.

Certain video-poker games are considered positive advantage games, meaning the potential exists for players to actually win money over the long term (unlike just about every other game in the casino). ■ TIP➔ To make the house edge negative though, the player must bet the maximum coins and make the statistically optimum choice during every single hand. In a 25¢ game, you can choose to play any multiple of 25¢ up to five times that amount (five quarters or $1.25) per hand. If you examine the payout schedule for most video-poker games, you'll see that the payout on the highest-value hands is inflated for maximum bet games. This is the casino urging you to bet more per hand.

For example, if you get a royal flush with four quarters in a common Jacks or Better game, the payout is 1,000 quarters. Bump your bet up to five quarters per hand and your royal flush is worth 4,000 quarters. The occasional windfall of a royal flush can boost the game's return up over 100%. The casino is betting on human behavior here—expecting many royal flush winners will have inserted less than the full bet. Nevertheless, the positive payout expectation is what makes video poker such an attractive game. However, the time and bankroll necessary to invest before hitting the full-pay royal flush can be prohibitive, so don't count on paying for your kid's college with video-poker proceeds.

WHERE TO PLAY

For the most full-pay machines: The Gold Coast (✉ *4000 W. Flamingo Rd., West Side* ☎ *702/367–7111 or 800/331–5334* ⊕ *www.goldcoastcasino. com*) has an abundance of full-pay machines, as do the **Red Rock Casino, Resort & Spa,** and **M Resort.**

For low-limit video poker: Fremont (✉ *200 Fremont St., Downtown* ☎ *800/634–6460* ⊕ *www.fremontcasino.com*) has a great array of full-pay 25¢ machines.

ROULETTE

Roulette's an easy way to cut your teeth on the whole table-game experience. You select and bet on numbers, groups of numbers, or a color (red or black); watch the dealer drop a ball on a spinning wheel; and hope that the ball lands on your space. It doesn't get more straightforward than this.

BASIC RULES

The wheel's divided into red and black slots numbered 1 through 36 along with two green slots labeled 0 and 00 (zero and double-zero). The dealer (or croupier) drops a little white ball onto the spinning wheel, and as it loses momentum, it falls onto a series of randomizing obstacles until it settles into one of the numbered slots. You place your bet on a layout filled with numbers; the main betting area has 12 rows of three squares each, alternating red and black and covering numbers 1 through 36. There are also two green spaces for betting on 0 or 00. You can put chips on single numbers, or the lines that connect two, four, five (if 0/00 is involved), or six numbers together. You can also bet on entire categories of numbers, such as red/black, odd/even, and 1 through 18/19 through 36, or one of six different ways to bet on one-third of the numbers at one time.

INSIDE AND OUT

When you buy into roulette you're issued specialty chips so that each player at the table has his own color. When you want to stop, trade your roulette chips for regular casino chips. As in any other game, you have to meet the table minimums when you're betting, but it gets a little confusing with roulette because the rules are different depending on what you want to bet on. Outside bets and inside bets are separate, and if you choose to bet on either or both, the table minimum rules apply independently. An "outside" bet is made anywhere but on the actual area of the layout that contains the numbers 0, 00, and 1–36. Even, Odd, Black, and Red would be outside bets. An "inside" bet is any bet

Roulette Table

	Bet	Payoff
A	Single number	35 to 1
B	Two numbers	17 to 1
C	Three numbers	11 to 1
D	Four numbers	8 to 1
E	Five numbers	6 to 1
F	Six numbers	5 to 1
G	12 numbers (column)	2 to 1
G	1st 12, 2nd 12, 3rd 12	2 to 1
H	1-18 or 19-36	1 to 1
H	Odd or Even	1 to 1
H	Red or black	1 to 1

placed within the numbered area. Betting the 1, 22, 36 would be considered inside bets. A $5 minimum roulette table means you must bet $5 *per bet* if you bet on the outside, and $5 *total* if you bet inside. You may bet in smaller denominations on inside bets, but all inside bets must add up to the minimum (even if you placed outside bets that make your total amount wagered over the table minimum).

So $5 on a single outside bet (like "Red") is legal, while five different $1 bets on the outside aren't. And regardless of whether you've placed an outside bet or not, a $1 inside bet is legal only if there are other inside bets that bring the total amount wagered inside to $5. So you could place $2 on your birth month, $2 on your birthday, then $1 on No. 24 in honor of your favorite TV show.

AT A GLANCE

Format: Sit-down table game with specialized spinning wheel

Goal: Place bet on the number or group of numbers that come up on the wheel

Pays: Varies by type of bet. From 35 to 1 on single numbers to even money on odd/even and red/ black bets

House Advantage: 5.26% for almost every bet on double-zero tables

Best Bet: Play at a single-zero table

Worst Bet: The Five-way bet (0, 00, 1, 2, 3) that has an 8% house advantage

Once betting is closed and the ball lands in its spot, the croupier places a marker on the winning number, on top of the stack of winning chips (if there are any). All the losing chip areas, inside and outside, are raked, and the croupier pays out each winning bet. *Never* reach for your winnings, or start to make new bets until *all* the winning bets have been paid, and the dealer has removed the marker from the table.

STRATEGY

Roulette is as simple a game as you'll find in the casino. The only complexity is in learning exactly where to place bets to cover the numbers you like. The odds, though, aren't good. The casino keeps over 5% of the total amount wagered on American (or double-zero) roulette.

Though the odds make this game one to avoid, we think it's too much fun to give up playing. The best plan, if you're going to get serious about it, is to seek out the handful of single-zero wheels in Las Vegas—most of them are Downtown; the few on the Strip reside behind the velvet ropes of the high-limit areas. Without the dreaded double-zero, your odds improve to a respectable 2.5% house advantage. A European Wheel is even better yet, because it only has one 0, and if the ball lands in 0, all even money bets only lose half. This brings the house edge on even money bets to a very good 1.3%.

RAPID ROULETTE

Rapid Roulette is an automated version of Roulette. Instead of standing around a table, you sit at your own video terminal. Players give live dealers cash for credits, and make bets via the video screen. The ball is then spun on a live wheel, and the winning number is input into the machine. You are paid by credits for your winnings at your own terminal. When you cash out, the live dealer will give you chips for your winnings. You can find Rapid Roulette at Strip casinos like Luxor and MGM Grand.

WHERE TO PLAY

For low-limit games: Try Sam's Town (✉ *5111 Boulder Hwy., Boulder Strip* ☎ *800/897-8696* ⊕ *www.samstownlv.com*).

For single-zero games: Try Mandalay Bay on the weekends, and Caesar's Palace. Venetian offers single-zero roulette at low betting minimums with its handheld electronic gaming device.

To go all night: Golden Nugget's croupiers will hold your spot while you run to the 24-hour Starbucks in the South Tower for a jolt of gambling gasoline.

4

CRAPS

Even if you've never played this game, you may have heard the roar of a delighted crowd of players from across the casino floor. Craps is a fun and fast-paced game, in which fortunes can be made, or lost very quickly, depending on how smart you play.

It can look intimidating or complicated to the beginner, because there are so many bets that can be placed on every roll, but this should not deter you from stepping up to the table to play. Craps offers a couple of the best Odds bets in the casino for the player.

BASIC RULES

At its core, craps is a dice game. A dice thrower—"shooter"—tosses two dice to the opposite end of a table, and people bet on what they think the outcome or future outcome of the dice will be. It's the job of the "stickman" (the dealer with the stick) to keep the game moving, and to call out the dice totals so everyone knows them no matter what their vantage point at the table is. Two other dealers place bets for you, pay the winners, and collect from the losers. A "boxman" sits in the middle and supervises the action. The main layout is duplicated on the right and left sides of the table, although the middle section (the Proposition area in front of the stickman) is common to both wings of the craps table.

To play, step up to the table wherever you can find an open space. You can start betting casino chips immediately, but you have to wait your turn to be the shooter. If you don't want to "roll the bones" (throw the dice) when it's your turn, motion your refusal to the stickman, and he'll skip you. To roll the dice, you must place a bet first. Then choose only two of the five dice offered by the stickman.

DO'S AND DON'TS OF SHOOTING
Do: Use one hand to pick up the two dice you have chosen. Use the same hand to throw them.

Don't: Move the dice from one hand to the other before you shoot. It arouses suspicion of cheating.

Do: Throw both dice at the same time, and be sure to hit the far wall. A roll that doesn't hit the far wall will not count, and the boxman will make you retry.

Don't: Slide the dice during your toss.

Do: Follow table etiquette when someone else is shooting.

Don't: Put your hands down into the table when someone else is shooting. If the dice hit your hand, it's considered bad luck. If a 7 "loser" is rolled after touching your hand, you may be blamed.

> ## AT A GLANCE
>
> **Format:** Dice game played around a long, high-walled table
>
> **Goal:** Players bet that certain numbers or sequences of numbers will be rolled
>
> **Pays:** Even money on Pass/Don't Pass, Come/Don't Come, various for other bets
>
> **House Advantage:** Varies
>
> **Best Bets:** Pass/Don't pass with full odds
>
> **Worst Bet:** Field bet, any Proposition bet

4

PASS-LINE BETS

The game starts with the "come out" roll. This is the first roll after someone rolls a 7, or if you happen to be the first one that comes to the table. The most common bet on the come-out roll is the Pass/Don't Pass Line, which can only be placed on the come-out roll, and which serves to illustrate the basic pattern the game follows.

RIGHT-WAY

Pass Line bettors bet *with* the shooter, or *right way*. If the come-out roll turns up a 7 or 11, it's an automatic win and they will be paid even money on their Pass Line bet. If a total of 2, 3, or 12 (aka "craps") comes up on the come-out roll, they lose. The exact opposite applies for the Don't Pass bettor, who bets *against* shooter, or *wrong way*. For learning purposes, we'll focus more on Right-way bets, which is the majority of bettors. Wrong-way bets are covered below.

If a shooter rolls a total of 4, 5, 6, 8, 9, or 10 on the come-out roll, it is known as hitting a "point." The point (5 for example) will be marked with a puck so everyone knows what it is. Once a point has been established, the players have the option to back up their Pass Line bets with "odds." The Odds bet is probably the hardest bet for the beginner to understand. This is unfortunate, because it is one of the best bets in the casino for the player, and it is not marked on the layout for this reason. The Odds bet is placed directly behind the Pass Line bet, and the maximum amount of odds you can take will be listed on the table, and varies by casino. "5x odds" means you can bet up to 5 times your Pass Line bet. *The Odds bet is so great because it is the only bet that has a 0% house edge.* Because of this, you should always play maximum odds, if you can afford to. Many other bets can be made at this point as well, but we'll cover them separately. Once all Odds bets, and any other bets are placed, the shooter keeps rolling the dice until he rolls the point again, or a 7. Any other rolls in the meantime will not affect the Line bets from winning or losing. If a point is hit before a roll of 7, it is called a *winner,* and anyone who bet Pass will get paid even money on their Line bet, and the "true odds" on their Odds bet. These are 2 to 1 for a roll of 4 or 10, 3 to 2 for a roll of 5 or 9, and 6 to 5 for a roll of 6 or 8. If the shooter rolls a 7 before he rolls the point, it is called a *loser,* and all Pass Line bets, and the odds are lost. Once that happens, the dice are passed to the next player to "come out" and the sequence starts all over again.

OTHER BETS

In addition to Pass and Don't Pass bets, you can also make the following important wagers at craps:

COME BETS

Come bets can also be confusing for beginners, but if you understand how the Pass Line works, it's just as easy. The Come bet pays exactly the same as a Line bet, and has the same great odds, so you should take the time to learn how to bet it. The main difference between a Line bet, and a Come bet is, that the Come bet is placed *after* the come-out roll, once a point has been established. Try to think of a Come bet as being just like its own little private Pass Line bet for you only, that you can place at any time during the roll (which you can't do with a Pass Line bet). Put your Come bet in the area marked "Come." The next roll is now the come-out roll for your Come bet only, which will win on 7 or 11, or lose on 2, 3, or 12. If the next roll is any other number, the dealer will put your Come bet on that number, and that number will now be the point for your Come bet only, not the Pass Line point (which has already been established). Now that the point has been established for your Come bet, you can take odds on it, just like the Line bet. This is done by placing your chips in the "Come" area and stating to the dealer that you want odds on your Come bet. The dealer will stack your Come odds, on top of your Come point bet and a little offset, so he knows the amount of your original Come bet as opposed to your Odds bet. Now that your Come bet has a point it is subject to the same rules as the Pass Line. If your Come point is rolled before a 7 you win, and the dealer will pay you in the "Come" area. If a 7 is rolled before your Come point, you lose.

PLACE BETS

If you want to bet on a number without subjecting to the rules of the Pass Line or Come. you can "place" it. The casino pays reduced odds for this bet, as opposed to true odds on the Line, or Come. A Place bet can be wagered at any time on any number in the squared boxes. If that number is rolled before the 7 you win, otherwise you lose. If you place the 4 or 10 it will pay 9 to 5; the numbers 5 or 9 pay 7 to 5, and the numbers 6 or 8 pay 7 to 6. If you win the Place bet the dealer will pay you your winnings only, and leave your original bet on the number. Unlike a Come, or Line bet, you can take down this bet at any time if you want. To make it easier for the dealers to figure the payouts, you must bet in multiples of $5 for the numbers 4, 5, 9, and 10, and multiples of $6 for the 6 or 8. The house edge is a very reasonable 1.52% for a Place bet on the 6 or 8, and a good option, but this is not true for the other numbers. If you must place the 4 and 10, then "buy" them, and you will reduce the house edge on those bets. A "Buy" bet is a Place

Craps Table

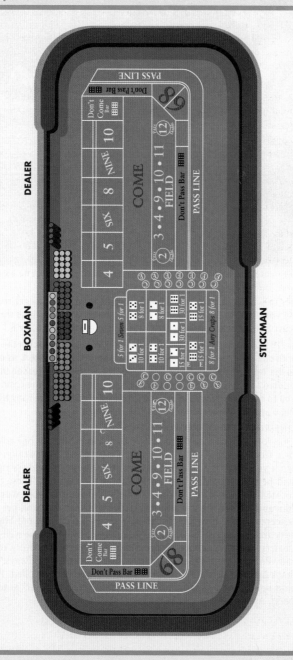

Las Vegas casinos never use dice with round corners. Check them out the next time you roll the bones in Sin City.

bet in which you pay a 5% commission to the house to get true odds on your money (in the case of 4 or 10, that is 2 to 1). Make this bet at least $20, or it won't be worth it. Never buy the 5, 9, 6, or 8.

■ TIP→ Betting the Big 6 and 8, is exactly the same as placing the 6 and 8 with one important difference. Big 6 and 8 only pays you 1 to 1, as opposed to the 7 to 6 you will get when you place them. This is the reason this bet is printed so huge, and is closer to you on the table layout. The casino wants you to bet here, instead of making the better Place bet. Just say NO to the Big 6 and 8.

ONE-ROLL BETS OR PROPOSITION BETS

One-roll bets are exactly that, bets that win or lose on one roll of the dice (for example, Field, Eleven, or Double Sixes). Basically you bet what you think the next roll will be. If you happen to guess right you will be paid the odds listed on the table for that bet. These bets are located in front of you or the stickman, and you toss your wager in to him and tell him what you want. He'll place your One-roll bet for you (except the Field, which you place yourself). One-roll and Hard-way bets are considered "Proposition bets," so named because well-trained dealers will try to entice you to make these bets after every roll. The only Proposition bet that is not a One-roll bet is the "hardways," which stays up until the "soft" number you bet on, or a 7 is rolled. Proposition bets carry an abysmal house edge (as much as 16.67% for some bets). Avoid these at all costs.

CRAPS SAMPLE BETTING SEQUENCE

Here's a sample sequence of bets, starting with a new shooter coming out. You begin by placing a $10 chip directly in front of you on the Pass Line:

Roll 1. Come out: shooter throws a 7, a winner for the Pass Line. The dealer pays you $10. Since no point was established by this roll, the dice are still in the come-out phase.

Roll 2. Come out: shooter throws a 2—craps. Dealer takes your $10 Pass Line chip, which you must replace to keep playing. There's still no point, so the dice are still "coming out."

Roll 3. Come out: shooter throws a 4—a point. Pass Line bets now win only if another 4 is thrown before a 7 is thrown. You take $10 odds behind your Pass Line bet, and decide to place a $10 chip in the "Come" betting area.

Roll 4. Shooter throws a 12—craps. Your Pass Line bet is unaffected, but your Come bet loses because it's still in the come-out phase. You replace it with another $10 Come bet.

Roll 5. Shooter throws a 9. Your Pass Line bet is unaffected. Dealer moves your Come bet chips onto the 9 square. You take $10 odds on your Come bet, and the dealer stacks it on top of your original $10 Come bet that is now in square 9, so you are now rooting for either a 4 (Pass Line bet) or a 9 (Come bet) to appear before any 7.

Roll 6. Shooter throws a 3—craps. Both of your bets are unaffected.

Roll 7. Shooter throws a 9. Your Come bet is a winner. The dealer will pay you $10 for your original bet, and $15 (3 to 2) for your Odds bet, and place your winnings, original bet, and odds in the "Come" area for you to pick up. You now have no more Come bet.

Roll 8. Shooter throws a 7. Your remaining bet—on the Pass Line—loses.

DON'T PASS BETTORS
WRONG WAY

Don't bettors, or Wrong-way bettors as they are called, are betting against the shooter. They win when the shooter rolls a 7 (once the point is established), when everyone else at the table will lose. The Wrong-way bets are the Don't Pass and Don't Come, and they work exactly opposite to the Pass and Come. You can "lay" odds on the don't bets also, but since you have the advantage once the point has been established (because 7 is the most common roll), the casino will compensate for this by making you bet $6 to get $5 on the point of 6 or 8, $7 to get $5, on the 5 or 9, and $2 to get $1 on the 4 or 10. Many people avoid Wrong-way betting because they don't like the idea of betting more to get paid less, or they don't like to "go against" everyone else at the table. This is understandable, but Wrong-way betting carries slightly better odds than Right-way betting, and should be considered once you feel comfortable playing the game.

STRATEGY

Getting an education first is a good strategy for all the games, but it is essential for craps. Before you step up to a craps table, learn and understand the rules and mathematics of the game, as well as table etiquette, betting procedures and placement, and which bets to stay away from. Craps is by far the most complicated game to learn in the casino, and if you throw money blindly into it without understanding how it works, you will lose fast. Our advice is to use the basics we have given you as a starting point, then build on that by getting a more advanced book, taking a lesson at a casino, or learning and playing online for free. Playing craps offers too much fun and excitement to be ignored, so take the next step and do your homework. You won't regret it.

For those who don't mind playing "without a net" (you know who you are), or don't have the time or patience to sit for a class, you can enjoy the game using the basics *above*. Keep in mind that only a few bets carry a low house edge. They are:

- Pass/Don't Pass Line with maximum table odds
- Come/Don't Come bet with maximum table odds
- Place bet on the 6 or 8.

Stick to these bets. If you can't afford to bet maximum odds, then bet as much as you can comfortably. If you feel you must bet Proposition bets for some extra action, limit the amount you bet to single dollars. Even if you get lucky and hit some of these on occasion, rest assured that over time these bad bets will eat a big chunk of your potential winnings.

WHERE
TO PLAY

For the highest odds: Main Street Station Downtown offers up to 20-times odds and several $5 craps tables. On the strip, Casino Royale (⊠ 3411 Las Vegas Blvd. S. Center Strip ☏ 702/737-3500 ⊕ www.casinoroyalehotel. com) has low minimums, and a generous 100x odds on certain craps bets.

For the friendliest dealers: The crews at Treasure Island or Mirage will help you learn and keep your bets on track.

BACCARAT

4

Baccarat (pronounced bah-kah-rah) is a centuries-old card game played with an aristocratic feel at a patient rhythm. It's not an American favorite, but it's popular around the world in varied forms.

Although it's an easy game to play, baccarat has an air of mystery about it—perceived by many as a game played only by James Bond and powerful tycoons, behind closed doors with special access. Not so. It may be the game of choice for many wealthy gamblers, and it's usually in a roped-off or enclosed area, but anyone who can afford the minimum bet, usually $100 and up, can play.

PLAYING THE "BIG BAC"

Up to 14 players can squeeze into a baccarat table, but the game is played out with just two hands. Before play starts, you place your bet on one of three possible outcomes: the Player hand will win, the Bank hand will win, or that play will result in a Tie. The Tie bet can be placed along with a Bank or Player bet, or by itself. When it's your turn, you can either accept the responsibility of representing the Bank, or you can pass the shoe on to the next player in line.

The dealers, with an assist from the Bank player holding the shoe, start the game by dealing two two-card hands facedown. The Player hand is dealt first, and is traditionally placed in front of the gambler with the largest Player bet, who then turns them over and slides them back to the dealer. The player holding the shoe does the same with the Bank hand. These rituals are really only for ceremony, and to keep the game lively. Everyone at the table is tied to these two hands, regardless of how they're dealt and who gets to turn them over.

MISSING NUMBERS

You may notice that some of the baccarat layouts are missing numbers (usually 4 and 14). This is because they are considered unlucky numbers in Asian and European cultures, and are omitted so they do not offend players from these countries.

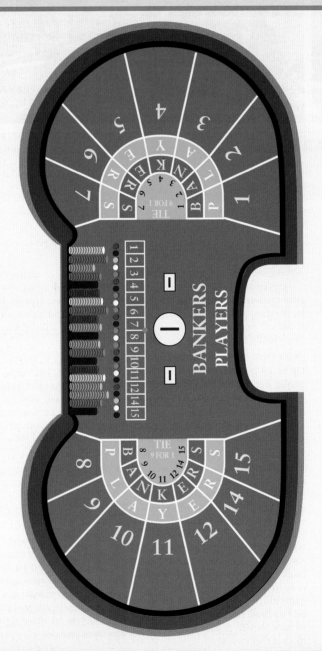

Depending on the value of the initial two-card hands, an extra card may be added to each hand according to a complicated set of drawing rules. Ask your dealer where you can get a copy of the rules when you sit down so you can follow the action. The winner of the hand is determined by which side has the higher total after all cards have been drawn. If you win on the Bank side, you must pay the house a 5% commission. The dealers keep track of this in the numbered boxes in front of them, which correspond to the numbered seats the players are sitting in. You can pay down this commission at any time during the shoe, but must pay any remaining balance after the last hand of the shoe has been played.

UNDERSTANDING THE HANDS.

■ Face cards and 10s equal zero.

■ For any total more than 9, the first digit is ignored.

So if the cards are 7, 7, and Jack, the total would be 14: 7 + 7 + 0 = 14. The first digit [1] in 14 is ignored, so the final total is 4.

If you draw a total of 9 (a 10 + 9 for example) on the first two cards, it is called a "natural" and is an automatic winner, unless the other side draws a natural 9 for a tie. A total of 8 is also called a natural, and can only be beaten by a natural 9 or tied with another natural 8. If a tie does occur, the Bank and Player bets push and the Tie wagers are paid at 8 to 1.

STRATEGY

There's no play strategy in the North American version of baccarat; the game is carried out according to immutable rules. In essence it is like choosing heads or tails, and flipping a coin to see who wins. Baccarat players enjoy looking for patterns in previously dealt hands that might give them a clue what will win next, by keeping track of them on little scorecards. But in the end your guess is as good as theirs as to who will win the next hand. ■TIP→ The Bank bet, at a 1.06% house advantage, has good odds for such a simple game. Always avoid the Tie bet, because it has an excessive house advantage.

MINI-BACCARAT AND EZ-BACCARAT

A more accessible version of baccarat is called mini-baccarat. If you have a taste for baccarat but can't handle the high minimum bets, the glacial pace, and the odd, superstitious rituals, look for a mini-bac table. They're in the main pit of any casino with the rest of the table games, or sometimes in an Asian-themed room. Mini-bac follows the same rules as its blue-blooded cousin, but it is played at a much smaller blackjack-style table. The minimums are low, and a single dealer dispenses the hands, without the players ever touching the cards. Midi-bac, or Macau-style Mini-bac, is a hybrid of the big and mini-bac games. It is played at a mini-bac table, with one dealer, but the players handle the cards as in the big game. These games sometimes employ an extra bet called "Dragon Bonus" or "Emperor Bonus." As with most side bets on table games, this one has a high house edge, and should be ignored.

EZ-Baccarat is a relatively new version of Mini-bac, that plays the same, except there is no commission charged for winning Bank bets. In this game the casino makes its money on the "Dragon" bet. If the bank wins the hand with a three-card 7 total, it is called a "Dragon." When this occurs, the Player hand and Tie lose, and all Bank bets are pushes. If you bet on the "Dragon," you will be paid 40 to 1 if it hits.

WHERE TO PLAY

Baccarat on a budget: Harrah's, M Resort, and the Golden Nugget have tables with reasonable minimums.

With the whales: Try the new Aria at CityCenter; it's baccarat Nirvana.

To be alone: Try wireless handheld electronic baccarat at the Venetian. Find a comfortable chair and play for stakes so low it makes the high rollers giggle.

SPORTS BETTING

4

Nevada is the only place in America where you can physically, legally, bet on sporting events. The betting takes place in a sports book, a dedicated area of a casino that accepts wagers on upcoming games. Here you can try your luck on all the major team sports in America, plus a few individual sports. You can place a wide variety of wagers—from the outcome of a single game to a combination of events. You can even place "futures" wagers on a game that won't kick off for several months.

Sports books make money by taking a small percentage of the total amount bet on both sides of a game; this is called Vigorish, Vig for short. Casinos adjust the odds they offer on a game to attract a similar amount to be bet on both teams. That ensures that they get their cut risk-free, regardless of who actually wins the game.

BASIC RULES

Placing a bet in a sports book is simple. Pick a game where you like the betting odds, either in the form of a "point spread" or a "money line," *both of which will be explained below*. The sports book will have a betting window or counter with a cashier who will take your wager (you have to pay up front) and issue you a ticket that states the details of your bet. Don't lose that ticket! If your wager is a winner, return to the betting window after the game, turn in your ticket, and you'll get your initial bet plus your winnings.

The most common bet in a sports book are 11-to-10 bets and involve a point spread. That means for every $11 you risk (or lay), you win a profit of $10. Place an $11 sports bet, and you get back $21 if your team beats the spread.

Nevada is the only state where you can legally bet on sporting events. Bets must be placed in sports books, which you'll find in almost every casino on the Strip.

POINT SPREADS

An 11-to-10 bet indicates a nearly even-money bet. But if the two teams aren't evenly matched, the casino needs some way to prevent the public from betting heavily on the superior team. That's what a point spread is for; it provides a scoring "handicap" to make both teams equally attractive to a bettor.

When you read a point spread listing, one team is usually the favorite (denoted with a negative number), and one is the underdog (with a positive number). Consider this point spread listing:

Sooners

Longhorns -6.5

The spread on this game is 6½. They sometimes use half points to eliminate the possibility of ties. The sports books have determined that the public believes the Longhorns are more likely to win the game. To lure bettors to wager on the Sooners, the casino is effectively agreeing to *take away 6½ points* from the Longhorns' final score (or add 6½ points to the Sooners' score, depending on which way you look at it) when it evaluates bets placed on that game. Sports bettors will say that the spread on this game is "the Longhorns minus 6½" or "the Sooners plus 6½"—the two phrases mean the same thing. If you bet on the Longhorns, they'll have to have won by a margin greater than the point spread for you to win your bet. If you bet on the Sooners, your bet wins if the Longhorns win by less than the spread (e.g., Longhorns win 21–17, a margin of victory less than the point spread) or lose the game outright. If your point spread wager ends in a tie, the sports book will return your original bet, minus the Vig, which it always takes.

OVER/UNDER

Here you're betting on whether the combined final score of the game will be either over or under a designated total. The total is determined by the sports book and usually appears in the point spread listing like this:

Giants 42.5

Eagles -7

The negative number is the point spread, and it has no effect on Over/Under bets. The other number, 42.5, is the total for this game. Bettors are welcome to bet on the point spread, the Over/Under, or both. Over/Under bettors would try to predict whether the combined score of the Giants and Eagles will

> ### AT A GLANCE
>
> **Format:** Wagering against the house at a dedicated betting counter
>
> **Goal:** Correctly predict the outcome of sporting events
>
> **Pays:** Varies by type of bet and casino. Standard is $10 won for every $11 bet
>
> **House Advantage:** 4.55% on 11-to-10 bets, varies with other types of bets
>
> **Best Bet:** NCAA basketball; NFL Over/Unders
>
> **Worst Bet:** Proposition bets; Futures bets; Teasers

be higher or lower than the total (in this case, 42.5). If the Giants won 24–20, the combined score would be 44, so the over bets win and the under bets lose. An Over/Under bettor wouldn't care who won the game, as long as either lots of points were scored (over bettors) or few points were scored (under bettors).

■TIP→ Betting odds vary from sports book to sports book, and they can change over time, right up to the moment a sporting event starts. But once you place your bet, the point spread, money line, and/or payout odds are locked in place for that wager. Your bet is evaluated and paid according to the odds on your betting ticket.

THE MONEY LINE

Money Line bets have no scoring handicap attached to them (such as a point spread). The bet wins if the team wins on the field. Sports books use money lines to entice you to bet on the underdog by increasing the payout in the event that team wins. And they discourage bettors from taking the better team by reducing the payout if they win. Let's take a look at an example:

Astros +150

Cubs -170

The two numbers represent money lines. The underdog has a positive number and the favorite has a negative number. For underdogs, the amount shown is the amount (in dollars) you'd win on a $100 bet. In this case, if the underdog Astros won and you bet $100, you'd win $150. On the other hand, the Cubs money line represents the amount you have to risk to win $100. Because the Cubs are seen to be more likely to win, the sports book asks a bettor to pay a premium to bet on them—to win $100, you'd have to bet $170.

NUMBER OF TEAMS	PARLAY BETTING ODDS	PAYOUT ODDS
2	13–5	3–1
3	6–1	7–1
4	10–1	15–1
5	20–1	31–1
6	40–1	63–1
7	75–1	127–1
8	140–1	225–1
9	200–1	511–1
10	400–1	1,023–1

Note: you don't have to bet $100-plus at a time. The money line just represents the proportions of amount risked to amount won (and vice versa). Most casinos require a $5 or $10 minimum bet.

PARLAYS

A Parlay bet is a combination bet where two or more bets must win in order for your wager to pay off. A single Parlay bet might include several different sports, as well as Point Spread, Money Line, and Over/Under bets. You can even Parlay two games being played simultaneously. Standard Parlay odds vary by casino, *but the above table is a good example of what to expect*:

If you get all wins plus a tie on your Parlay, the bet will still pay, just at the next lowest level of odds. For example, if you bet a four-team Parlay and three of the bets beat the spread but the final game tied against the spread, you'd be paid 6 to 1 as if it were a three-teamer. If you get a win and a tie on a two-team Parlay it pays as if it were a straight 11-to-10 bet.

⚠ Parlay cards are a quick way to bet on multiple games, but they sometimes have reduced payouts relative to normal Parlay bets; sports books do not take Vigs on Parlay bets.

STRATEGY

Sports betting is harder than it looks. Just because you're a fan of a sport doesn't mean you can pick winners against the spread. The best tips for smart sports betting are:

Betting against a team is just as valid—and profitable—as betting for a team.

Pick a few teams, become intimately acquainted with them, and be prepared to bet for and against them based on your expertise. Don't try to learn the habits of the entire league.

Be realistic. Sporting events include innumerable random events, so even the best sports bettors are thrilled to win 60% of their 11-to-10 bets over the long haul.

Avoid exotic bets. Casinos let you bet on almost anything; don't take them up on it. *Stick with the bets listed in this chapter.*

Beware of hype. It's often wrong. Do your own homework and draw your own conclusions and take joy in being a contrarian. The sports media have a way of making certain teams look utterly unbeatable. No team ever is. History is littered with examples.

Become an NCAA hoops fan. With so many teams in play leading up to March Madness, it's easy for odds-makers to get a point spread wrong, especially when smaller schools are playing each other.

Take a pass sometimes. Remember that a losing bet not placed is a win.

WHERE TO PLAY

With an empty stomach: Every casino has plenty of eateries, but at Lagasse's Stadium, inside The Palazzo, the snacks are all gourmet, and they're made by Emeril Lagasse. Reservations are required (usually with a $200 food-and-beverage minimum) for big events.

To watch the big game with your buddies: Hands-down its Caesars Palace, followed by the Mirage and the Wynn. If you are in the hinterlands, head to the Red Rock.

WHERE TO PLAY

SOUTH STRIP

Luxor Las Vegas. After a major, multi-year renovation, Luxor's casino has become one of the most exciting gaming floors in town. Brand-new tables and slots abound, and the sports book offers comfortable seats to cheer your bets. A new drinking establishment, Highbar, looks out over the casino's refurbished high-limit area, offering guests the opportunity to bet with the big boys or just watch. In the regular-limit area, table minimums are usually around $15 on weekends, but during the week you might find $10 tables. If poker's your game, heads up: the Luxor's room has received awards from local newspapers and offers special retroactive room rates for players who spend more than five hours at the tables. ⊠ *3900 Las Vegas Blvd. S* ☎ *702/262–4444, 877/386–4658* ⊕ *www.luxor.com* ⊅ *3,958 rooms, 442 suites.*

Mandalay Bay Casino. It's easy to drool at the hordes of fabulous beautiful people and millionaires crowding this casino's tables. Table limits start around $15, and on Friday and Saturday nights you'll be hard-pressed to find a table for less than $25 a pop. Pits of table games are spread out across 135,000 square feet, and with rows and rows of slot machines, the casino seems to stretch on forever. The high-limit Crystal Room is one of the fanciest high-roller parlors on the Strip, but offers little other than baccarat. Toward the entrance to THEhotel, the sports book has high ceilings but a noticeable dearth of seats. The poker room occupies a corner of the sports book with great views of the big screens. For those who wish to gamble in bathing suits, check out the Beachside Casino, which offers three stories of open-air gaming that overlooks the Beach. ⊠ *3950 Las Vegas Blvd. S* ☎ *702/632–7777, 877/632–7800* ⊕ *www.mandalaybay.com.*

MGM Grand Hotel & Casino. The biggest of the Las Vegas casinos, the MGM has a staggering amount of gaming space, which includes more than 3,500 slot machines and 165 different table games. Table minimums on blackjack, craps, and roulette mostly start at $10; on weekends nearly all jump to $25. The Strip entrance is slot heavy, and at night takes on a fun atmosphere, with videos and music blaring from monitors overhead. The casino bar, Centrifuge, occupies the center of a giant rotunda room in the rear of the casino, with a poker room and a remodeled sports book nearby. The Mansion, the casino's high-roller area (with mostly baccarat), exists in a separate wing with its own bar, kitchen, and entrance. ⊠ *3799 Las Vegas Blvd. S* ☎ *702/891–7777, 877/880–0880, 877/646–5638 Skylofts* ⊕ *www.mgmgrand.com.*

New York–New York Hotel & Casino. The casino at New York–New York is just like New York City itself: loud, boisterous, and incessant. The gaming floor was completely redone in 2009, and its decor can now be described as art deco meets neon-futuristic. Table limits are on the higher side, with most minimums starting at $15. Keep an eye out for Sic Bo, a high-low game played with dice that you won't find in many other places on the Strip. Table games fan out from the Center Bar, while slot machines line the periphery of the casino. The new, oval-shaped high-limit table games and slots area feature ornate Murano crystal chandeliers and wood paneling. Sports bettors will be disappointed by New York–New York's race and sports book—the area sits in a corner by The Sporting House, and barely has enough seats for a professional basketball team. ⊠ *3790 Las Vegas Blvd. S* ☎ *702/740–6969, 800/689–1797* ⊕ *www.newyorknewyork.com.*

CENTER STRIP

Aria. CityCenter's lone casino is located at Aria. Oddly, however, while the rest of the hotel is bathed in sunlight, the main gaming floor (especially the middle pits) can at times feel too dark. Brighter gaming experiences can be had in the high-limit salons; there are separate rooms for American games (blackjack and roulette) and Asian games (mostly baccarat). Another popular spot to throw down cash is The Deuce Lounge, a part-nightclub, part high-roller room that also serves appetizers. Poker fans rave about Aria's spacious poker room, which has the private "Ivey Room" (named after Phil Ivey) for professionals. Perhaps the only disappointment is the sports book, which is oddly shaped and has sequestered horse betting in a closet-sized satellite. ⊠ *3730 Las Vegas Blvd. S* ☎ *702/590–7757* ⊕ *www.arialasvegas.com.*

Bellagio Las Vegas. This roomy casino is luxurious and always packed. Under its hushed orange canopies you can sometimes spot high rollers betting stacks of black chips ($100 apiece) per hand. In Club Privé, the high-roller's area, wagers climb even higher. There are games for more typical budgets, too. Low-denomination slots are tucked in the back corners for low-rollers and excellent blackjack games are offered for mid- to high-level players (table minimums usually start at $15). If you can find them, the $10-minimum craps tables also can get lively. The casino's epicenter remains its now-famous poker room, which rose to national notoriety as a key element of the TV poker fad. Players such as Daniel Negreanu and Phil Ivey are regulars here, though they frequently hit Bobby's Poker Room, a private room behind a closed door. Elsewhere in the casino, the race and sports book is small but cozy; each leather seat is equipped with its own TV monitor. ⊠ *3600 Las Vegas Blvd. S* ☎ *702/693–7111, 888/987–6667* ⊕ *www.bellagio.com.*

Caesars Palace. Considering how huge Caesars Palace really is, the actual gaming area feels remarkably small. The Palace Casino retains its 1966 intimacy, with low ceilings and high stakes. The Colosseum Casino offers a Pussycat Dolls–themed gaming pit and new ShuffleMaster automated table games. The Forum Casino boasts high ceilings, soaring marble columns, graceful rooftop arches, and embraces the middle market with 5¢ and 25¢ slots and lower limits (but more stringent rules) on table games. Across the board, video-poker pay schedules are liberal. The best place to gamble in Caesars Palace is in the race and sports book. With 6 12-foot-by-15-foot oversize screens, a 20-by-50-foot LED board, and 12 50-inch plasma screens, the Caesars book is like an IMAX theater for sports. The spacious, adjacent poker room is pretty nice, too. ⊠ *3570 Las Vegas Blvd. S* ☎ *702/731–7110, 866/227–5938* ⊕ *www.caesarspalace.com.*

The Cosmopolitan of Las Vegas. Even with windows that look out onto the Strip, the gaming floor at Cosmopolitan feels cozy. Unlike the cavernous casinos in most Strip resorts, this one is long and narrow, creating a feeling of intimacy. Bettors can request and reserve semiprivate "casino cabanas," single-table gambling pods separated from the rest of the casino by beaded curtains. Most slot banks have their own television monitors. Perhaps the only drawbacks are the light-up roulette tables and the cramped sports book, which is located on the second floor, near where clubbers line up for Marquee. If you venture up there, you're better off hitting The Chandelier for a drink. ⊠ *3708 Las Vegas Blvd S.* ⊕ *www.cosmopolitanlasvegas.com.*

Mirage Las Vegas. The casino at the Mirage can be described as old-school fun. Blackjack and craps tables with $10 minimums are along side tables with $500 minimums, bringing low rollers and high rollers together on the same gaming floor. A roulette pit overlooks the crowded poker room, which has some of the most active games in all of Vegas. Slots abound in just about every direction on the gaming floor. There's a high-limit gaming area that offers blackjack, baccarat, and video poker. True gamblers come to the Mirage for its race and sports book. The book, to your left when you enter from the Caesars Palace side of the Strip, brags about 10,000 square feet of big-screen action and, well, it should—it resembles NASA's mission control. ⊠ *3400 Las Vegas Blvd. S* ☎ *702/791–7111, 800/374–9000* ⊕ *www.mirage.com.*

Paris Las Vegas. Dealers in this casino are trained to wish players *bonne chance,* which loosely translates into "good luck" in English. This catchphrase, coupled with the psychedelic sky-painted ceiling, conveys a dreamlike feeling that might distract you from the fact that some table rules are poor for the player (Hint: stay away from those single-deck blackjack tables; they only pay 6-to-5 for natural blackjacks). Livelier pits include the craps and baccarat sections; roulette is prevalent here, too—perhaps in keeping with the French theme. Slot machines are plentiful, though waitress service away from the tables can be spotty at best. The race and sports book is quaint but smoky. ✉ *3655 Las Vegas Blvd. S* ☎ *800/722–5597* ⊕ *www.parislasvegas.com.*

Planet Hollywood Resort & Casino. Slots abound in the casino at Planet Hollywood; fittingly it's one of the few casinos on the Strip with Elvis-themed one-arm bandits. Table-game pits are clustered under Swarovski crystal chandeliers in the center of the main casino floor, and some feature scantily clad go-go dancers at night. On weekends the low-limit blackjack and Pai Gow tables stay busy for hours on end. The poker room, which comprises a full gaming pit on the main casino floor, is clean and spacious, and is outfitted with plenty of TVs to catch the big game when you're not staked in a pot. Nearby, a modest race and sports book is swanky and state-of-the-art. ✉ *3667 Las Vegas Blvd. S* ☎ *702/785–5555, 866/919–7472* ⊕ *www.planethollywoodresort.com.*

NORTH STRIP

Encore. Instead of occupying one giant space, Encore's gaming floor is broken up into tiny salons, separated by columns and exquisite red curtains. Thanks to floor-to-ceiling windows, each of the parlor-style casino areas has a garden or pool view. The gaming is surprisingly diverse, with a variety of low-minimum tables and slots (yes, you can play $10 blackjack here). The main-floor high-limit room features mostly baccarat; upstairs, an even more exclusive area named the Sky Casino features tables with betting limits in the stratosphere. Noticeably absent from Encore's gaming operation are a sports book and poker room; to place these bets, head to Wynn Las Vegas. Guest room keys double as players' cards and track play over the duration of each stay. ✉ *3131 Las Vegas Blvd. S* ☎ *702/770–7171, 888/320–7125* ⊕ *www.encorelasvegas.com.*

Palazzo Resort-Casino. While the Venetian's casino can be described as busy and buzzing, the Palazzo's has a more composed vibe. Higher ceilings and wider walkways create a much slower pace on the casino floor; people are always gambling, but there's just more space to absorb their exuberance. The most prevalent table games include blackjack, roulette, Pai Gow poker, and Caribbean Stud; a separate high-limit room houses baccarat tables, assuming the biggest bettors will go here. Dealers at all of these tables are friendly (you'll just have to look past their garish vests). There are thousands of slot machines, some that accept pennies, nickels, and quarters. The sports book, part of Lagasse's Stadium (which also serves food), provides mobile devices that enable bettors to wager from just about anywhere in the casino. ✉ *3325 Las Vegas Blvd. S* ☎ *702/607–7777, 866/263–3001* ⊕ *www.palazzo.com.*

Treasure Island. Treasure Island has a reputation for being one of the best places to learn table games. Dealers are patient and kind, and just about every table game has an hour of free lessons every day. The best tutorials are in craps, where some pit bosses will go so far as to explain odds on certain bets. When you consider that most midweek table minimums are no more than $10 a bet, there's great incentive to stay put. TI's slot machines aren't nearly as enticing; the mix is oddly generic.

If you're heading to the sports book, beware; crowds from the *Sirens of TI* show create traffic-flow problems each time a performance ends. Look for a pedestrian bridge to the Fashion Show Mall at the north end for a faster escape. ✉ *3300 Las Vegas Blvd. S* ☎ *702/894–7111, 800/288–7206* ⊕ *www.treasureisland.com.*

The Venetian Resort Casino. The Venetian's casino is a sprawling, bustling nexus of energy at just about every time of day. All told, the gaming floor contains more than 120 games. Most table limits are higher than the other casinos', though on weeknights you might find some with minimums of $15. The blackjack tables in particular have very good odds for high-level players; it's hard to find a single-deck game, but the double-deck games come with the once-standard, but now rare, pay-offs and rules. If you like slots, you're in luck—progressive machines abound. The Venetian has kept up with the poker craze with two huge rooms, expanded and renovated in 2008 and again in 2011. With more than 50 tables and daily deep-stack tournaments, it's currently the largest poker spot in town. ✉ *3355 Las Vegas Blvd. S* ☎ *702/414–1000, 866/659–9643* ⊕ *www.venetian.com.*

Wynn Las Vegas. Wynn's casino is a gorgeous, inviting place to play (and a great place to spot celebrities). Many table limits in the main casino are dauntingly high. Sure, you might find a $15 or $25 table during the day, but it's not uncommon to spot $500-minimum blackjack tables on the regular casino floor. Lest you dismiss Wynn Las Vegas as exclusively opulent, rest assured that a healthy number of 1¢ slots are out in a prominent area, rather than relegated to some remote corner. It may also surprise you that the coin games have some of the best pay schedules in town. The poker room unfolds near the exotic car dealership, and there's a nice bar area next to the sports book, where plush chairs line individual viewing cubicles. ✉ *3131 Las Vegas Blvd. S* ☎ *702/770–7100, 877/321–9966* ⊕ *www.wynnlasvegas.com.*

DOWNTOWN

Four Queens Hotel & Casino. This isn't the fanciest casino in town, but locals and tourists alike love it for its approachable style and low table limits. At certain times of day, this means $3 blackjack (with single-deck games that pay 3 to 2 for blackjack), and 5x odds on craps. The casino also is home to the world's largest slot machine, as well as a host of video poker options that pay out at 100%. The modest sports book is rarely crowded, making it a better option than some of the others in town. ✉ *202 Fremont St.* ☎ *702/385–4011, 800/634–6045* ⊕ *www.fourqueens.com.*

Golden Nugget. This might be one of the oldest casinos in Downtown Vegas, but the place is as lively as ever. The biggest crowds tend to congregate in the older rooms, which are teeming with slot machines and lower-limit table games. For higher-limit table games (and decent rules on blackjack), head to the newest part of the casino, on the ground floor of the new Rush Tower. The poker room, located in a corner of the main casino floor, holds regular daily tournaments, and offers free lessons daily at 10 am. It also hosts "Poker After Dark," a popular late-night poker show on NBC. Perhaps the only disappointment is

4

the sports book, which is small and cramped. ✉ *129 E. Fremont St.* ☎ *702/385–7111, 800/634–3454* ⊕ *www.goldennugget.com/lasvegas.*

PARADISE ROAD

Hard Rock Hotel & Casino. A favorite among the young and wealthy crowd, this hip casino revolves around table games, offering limits that are generally lower than elsewhere in town (which means you can stretch bankrolls longer). The result, however, is that slot machine offerings are pretty slim; if this is your game, it's best to gamble elsewhere. Hard Rock has spent gobs of money in recent years on a cavernous poker room and a new mobile system that enables bettors to wager on sports anywhere on property. If you've got the cash, the swanky high-limit rooms are worth exploring, too. ✉ *4455 Paradise Rd.,* ☎ *702/693–5000, 800/693–7625* ⊕ *www.hardrockhotel.com.*

WEST SIDE

Palms Casino Resort. This casino is geared toward locals, with regular and generous promotions for those who sign up for the Club Palms gaming rewards program. Still, especially when visitors descend on the property for partying on weekend nights, the casino floor takes on a Strip-like vibe (and table limits rise accordingly). The best values on this floor are craps (with standard $10 minimums) and poker, where there's almost always a low-limit game of Hold'em being spread. For an exclusive gambling experience (and high-limit gaming), head upstairs to the world-famous Playboy Club and Mint Lounge. ✉ *4321 W. Flamingo Rd.* ☎ *704/942–7777* ⊕ *www.palms.com.*

Rio Las Vegas Hotel & Casino. Slots and table games seem almost secondary on this lively casino floor, where dealers (they're actually called "dealertainers") get up and perform, and music is almost always blasting. The casino is perhaps best known for its role as the home of the annual World Series of Poker, six weeks' worth of poker tournaments that culminate with the "Main Event" in which one pro takes home millions of dollars in cash. Elsewhere, the gaming floor offers table games with some of the worst odds in town (it's one of the few Vegas casinos to spread a game dubbed "Asia Poker"), and more than 1,200 slot machines, including dozens of different statewide progressives. ✉ *3700 W. Flamingo Rd.* ☎ *702/777–7777, 866/746–7671* ⊕ *www.riolasvegas.com.*

SUMMERLIN

Red Rock Casino Resort & Spa. Without question, this locals' casino in Summerlin is one of the best-kept secrets in the entire Las Vegas Valley. Swarovski crystals sparkle over gamblers who wander around the circular gambling hall, creating a vibe of opulence and swank. However, betting minimums are low; it's not uncommon to stumble upon $5 craps and blackjack tables at peak hours. The gem of the casino is the sports book, with its comfy chairs and giant big-screens. A cozy poker room and ornate high-limit room also are worth a look. ✉ *11011 W. Charleston Blvd.* ☎ *702/797–7777, 866/767–7773* ⊕ *www.redrocklasvegas.com.*

Where to Eat

WORD OF MOUTH

"Las Vegas is truly a foodie heaven these days. My most recent great meals have been at the Cosmopolitan. I don't think it has a badly reviewed restaurant. I loved Comme Ca and Milos, and hope to go to Scarpetta soon."

—frankie

THE SCENE

Updated by
Matt Villano

Las Vegas is America's hottest restaurant market. Celebrity chefs have opened clones of famous signature restaurants as well as newborn establishments in the Strip's top casino resorts. Away from the Strip, the unprecedented population growth in the city's suburbs has brought with it a separate and continuous wave of new eateries, both familiar chains and increasing numbers of legitimate destination restaurants.

Casino-resort dining basically falls into one of three categories. In the top echelon are the several properties that now have a half dozen or more bona fide star-status restaurants: Aria, Bellagio, Caesars, Encore, Mandalay Bay, MGM Grand, Venetian/Palazzo, and Wynn Las Vegas, plus the nearby Palms and Hard Rock properties. At the next level are those resorts with one or two stellar restaurants and a smaller range of worthwhile but not quite top-of-the-line options. On the Strip, these include The Cosmopolitan, Mandarin Oriental, Mirage, Monte Carlo, New York–New York, Paris, Planet Hollywood, and Treasure Island. Off the Strip, you can add M Resort, the Rio All-Suite Hotel, Green Valley Ranch, the JW Marriott, Red Rock Resort, and some of the Lake Las Vegas properties to this mix. And then there's everybody else: casino-resorts with maybe a decent eatery or two but that simply aren't known for great food.

Outside of casino properties, Las Vegas has a number of marquee restaurants with increasing cachet among foodies from out of town—places such as Origin India Restaurant & Bar, ENVY Steakhouse, Rosemary's, Marché Bacchus, and Lotus of Siam. There's great food to be had off the beaten path in Las Vegas, and you'll pay a lot less in these areas, too.

If you haven't been to Vegas in three or four years, you'll notice some major changes. While names like Wolfgang Puck, Michael Mina, and Emeril Lagasse still have plenty of pull in this town, the Vegas chefs commanding the most attention are French imports such as Pierre Gagnaire, Joël Robuchon, and Guy Savoy, along with vaunted U.S. chefs like Charlie Palmer and Mario Batali.

There's also a trend toward high-minded restaurants with exclusive-nightclub vibes. Note the success of see-and-be-seen Pan-Asian hot spots KOI and Tao, the youthful late-night haunts LAVO and FIX, and bordello-chic establishments such as Strip House—to name just a few. Elsewhere in town, Las Vegas's growing international, and especially Asian, population has created a market for some of the best Chinese, Thai, Vietnamese, and Pan-Asian restaurants in the country.

LAS VEGAS DINING PLANNER

RESERVATIONS

As the Vegas dining landscape has become rife with showstopping, one-of-a-kind restaurants, reservations at dinner (and occasionally even at lunch) have become a necessity in many cases. Generally, if you have your heart set on dinner at any of the celeb-helmed joints at the bigger

Strip casinos, you should book several days, or even a couple of weeks, ahead. On weekends and during other busy times, even at restaurants where reservations aren't absolutely essential, it's still prudent to phone ahead for a table.

WHAT TO WEAR

Although virtually no Vegas restaurants (with the exception of Joël Robuchon at the Mansion inside MGM Grand) require formal attire, men will likely feel a bit out of place at some of the top eateries on the Strip if not wearing a jacket—at the very least, avoid jeans in these spots. Dressing according to the mood of the restaurant (smart, stylish threads at the better ones) will generally help you out in terms of how you're treated and where you're seated. Casual attire is the norm at lunch, at less fancy venues, and virtually anywhere off the Strip or outside upmarket resorts.

HOURS

The majority of the top restaurants on the Strip are dinner only, although there are plenty of exceptions to this rule—unless otherwise noted, the restaurants *listed in this guide* are open daily for lunch and dinner. Hours vary greatly from place to place, with 5 to 10 pm typical for dinner hours, but many of the more nightlife-driven venues serve until after midnight or even round the clock. Las Vegas is definitely a city where it's best to phone ahead and confirm hours.

TIPPING AND TAXES

In most restaurants, tip the waiter 16%–20%. (To figure the amount quickly, just double the tax noted on the check and add a bit more.) Bills for parties of six or more sometimes include the tip already. Tip at least $1 per drink at the bar.

CHILDREN

Although it's unusual to see children in the dining rooms of Las Vegas's most elite restaurants, dining with youngsters does not have to mean culinary exile. *Some of the restaurants reviewed in this chapter are excellent choices for families, and are marked with a symbol.*

PRICES

Las Vegas's status as a bargain-food town has evaporated steadily, even rapidly, as the restaurant scene has evolved and the city has been thrust into the gastronomic spotlight. Now at top restaurants in town it's unusual to experience a three-course meal (including a bottle of wine, tips, and tax) for less than $100 per person, and prices can be two to three times that at many establishments. You can save money by trying lunch at some of the top eateries, and by checking out the increasingly noteworthy crop of restaurants that have developed off of the Strip. Credit cards are widely accepted, but some restaurants (particularly smaller ones off the Strip) accept only cash. If you plan to use a credit card, it's a good idea to double-check its acceptability when making reservations or before sitting down to eat.

Prices in the restaurant reviews are the average cost of a main course at dinner or, if dinner is not served, at lunch; taxes and service charges are generally included.

BEST BETS FOR LAS VEGAS DINING

With hundreds of restaurants to choose from, how will you decide where to eat? Fodor's writers and editors have selected their favorite restaurants by price, cuisine, and experience in the Best Bets lists below. In the first column, Fodor's Choice properties represent the "best of the best" in every price category.

Fodor'sChoice★

Burger Bar, p. 171
Ichiza, p. 212
Jean Philippe Patisserie, p. 181
Joël Robuchon, p. 176
KOI, p. 196
Lotus of Siam, p. 208
Nobhill Tavern, p. 176
Sensi, p. 182

Best by Price

$

Hash House A Go Go, p. 212
Ichiza, p. 212
LBS, p. 214
SuperMex, p. 219

$$

BLT Burger, p. 195
Burger Bar, p. 171
Lotus of Siam, p. 208
Tides Oyster Bar, p. 214

$$$

Diego, p. 173
ENVY, p. 206
Marché Bacchus, p. 212
Mon Ami Gabi, p. 196
Stratta, p. 202
Sushi Roku, p. 185

$$$$

Aureole, p. 171
B&B Ristorante, p. 200
BOA, p. 182
Border Grill, p. 171
Estiatorio Milos, p. 194
Joël Robuchon, p. 176
KOI, p. 196
Mastro's Ocean Club, p. 186
Nobhill Tavern, p. 176
Sage, p. 193
Sensi, p. 182
Spago, p. 185
Twist, p. 193

Best by Cuisine

AMERICAN

American Fish, p. 186
Aureole, p. 171
Mastro's Ocean Club, p. 186
Nobhill Tavern, p. 176

ASIAN

Ichiza, p. 212
KOI, p. 196
Lotus of Siam, p. 208
Sushi Roku, p. 185
Wing Lei, p. 202

FRENCH

Comme Ca, p. 193
Joël Robuchon, p. 176
Le Cirque, p. 181
Mon Ami Gabi, p. 196
Restaurant Guy Savoy, p. 185
Twist, p. 193

ITALIAN

B&B Ristorante, p. 200
Nove Italiano, p. 211
Sinatra, p. 197

LATIN AMERICAN

Border Grill, p. 171
Diego, p. 173
Doña Maria, p. 203
Isla Mexican Kitchen, p. 200
Jaleo, p. 194

SEAFOOD

American Fish, p. 186
Bartolotta, p. 201
Joe's Seafood, Prime Steak, and Stone Crab, p. 183
Mastro's Ocean Club, p. 186
RM Seafood, p. 173
SeaBlue, p. 176

SOUTH STRIP

FOUR SEASONS HOTEL

$$$$ STEAKHOUSE

🍴 **Charlie Palmer Steak.** The whole concept of putting a Four Seasons hotel inside Mandalay Bay was to have a quiet enclave "hidden" within a busy hotel-casino complex. Charlie Palmer got the idea right away. Although his Aureole at Mandalay Bay can be something of a scene, this nearby steak house is easygoing and understated—it's also a comparative bargain in a city of ultrapricey steak joints. The mahogany-paneled room off the Four Seasons lobby serves only Black Angus that's been dry-aged for a minimum of 28 days. There's commendable seafood, too; options might include pan-roasted Shetland Island salmon or stuffed Maine lobster. Among the several first-rate desserts, try the house-made crème brûlée, the flavors of which change seasonally. The lounge presents live entertainment on weekends. [$] *Average main: $49* ✉ *Four Seasons Hotel, 3960 Las Vegas Blvd. S* ☎ *702/632–5120* 🌐 *www.charliepalmer.com* 🕒 *Closed Sun. No lunch.*

MANDALAY BAY RESORT & CASINO

$$$$ AMERICAN

🍴 **Aureole.** Celebrity-chef Charlie Palmer re-created his famed New York restaurant for Mandalay Bay. He and designer Adam Tihany added a few playful, Vegas twists: a four-story wine tower, for example, holds 10,000 bottles that are reached by "wine fairies," who are hoisted up and down via a system of electronically activated pulleys. Seasonal specialties on the fixed-price ($95) menu might include roasted guinea fowl with sautéed foie gras, ravioli, and natural juices, or roasted rack of venison with glazed chestnuts, parsnip-potato puree, and orange-rosemary sauce. For dessert, try innovative offerings such as warm blue cheese-and-poached pear tart with port-wine vinaigrette or citrus tea–infused crème brûlée. [$] *Average main: $95* ✉ *Mandalay Bay Resort & Casino, 3950 Las Vegas Blvd. S* ☎ *702/632–7401* 🌐 *www.mandalaybay.com/dining* ✍ *Reservations essential* 🕒 *No lunch.*

$$$$ SOUTHWESTERN

🍴 **Border Grill.** Mary Sue Milliken and Susan Feniger, the popular cooking personalities who made a name for themselves on the Food Network, created this cheery, sophisticated outpost of their fantastic Santa Monica restaurant. Appetizers include green-corn tamales, ceviches, and plantain empanadas; for lunch, options might include an excellent turkey tostada or grilled skirt steak. For dinner, opt for dishes such as sautéed jumbo shrimp, beef brisket taquitos with guajillo chili sauce, or Kobe beef tacos with grilled pineapple salsa. Oaxacan mocha cake and Key lime pie are solid dessert choices. You'd be hard-pressed to find a tastier margarita in town—the pomegranate and honeydew versions are particularly delicious. Open daily for lunch. [$] *Average main: $45* ✉ *Mandalay Bay Resort & Casino, 3950 Las Vegas Blvd. S* ☎ *702/632–7403* 🌐 *www.mandalaybay.com/dining.*

$$ BURGER
Fodor's Choice ★

🍴 **Burger Bar.** You build your own burger at this jovial joint with marble tables and wood-paneled walls—it's a creation of Hubert Keller from the esteemed Fleur (and Fleur de Lys in San Francisco). First, start with your meat; selections include Colorado lamb, buffalo, Black Angus beef, and Kobe beef, just to name a few (there are also a few vegetarian alternatives). Then pile on the toppings, such as prosciutto, pan-seared

You can find this decadent dessert, as well as the world's largest chocolate fountain, at Jean Philippe Patisserie in the Bellagio (there's also a new one at Aria).

foie gras, jalapeños, fried egg, sliced zucchini, smoked salmon, or grilled lobster. Desserts continue the burger theme with choices such as the peanut butter–and–jelly burger (a warm doughnut with peanut butter mousse and raspberry jelly). You can even get a spiked milk shake. $ *Average main: $19* ✉ *Mandalay Place, 39350 Las Vegas Blvd. S* ☎ *702/632-9364* ⊕ *www.mandalaybay.com/dining.*

$$$$ ✕ **Fleur.** Formerly the Vegas outpost of Chef Hubert Keller's famous
MODERN Fleur de Lys restaurant, this eatery received a new concept and shorter
AMERICAN name at the end of 2010. The result: a fun and open atmosphere, along with a globally inspired menu that features a host of small plates. Many of these items change regularly, but stalwarts include crab-and-avocado "spheres" and "In the Shower" macaroni and cheese (a play on mac-and-cheese that Keller cooked in a dorm room shower on the television show, "Top Chef"). Then there's the Fleur Burger 5000, a Waygu beef hamburger with foie gras, truffles, and a bottle of 1995 Chateau Petrus (the price tag for this one is—hold your breath—$5,000). Deserts are varied, but the chocolate soufflé with Tabasco ice cream is certainly worth a try. Open for lunch daily. $ *Average main: $50* ✉ *Mandalay Bay Resort & Casino, 3950 Las Vegas Blvd. S* ☎ *702/632-9400* ⊕ *www.mandalaybay.com/dining.*

$$$$ ✕ **MIX.** Look out over Las Vegas from Chef Alain Ducasse's 64th-floor
FRENCH perch atop THEhotel at Mandalay Bay. Stylish and sexy diners seated at small tables or in egg-shape pods tuck into French-influenced fare, such as bigeye tuna tartare; seared scallops with sweet corn fricassee; and beef tenderloin au poivre. Portions are on the small side, but you're also paying for the view, which is one of the best among Vegas restaurants; every seat in the house has great sightlines through the floor-to-ceiling

windows. An attentive staff can help you navigate the more than 1,300 nightly wine options, but don't overlook the list of eye-catching cocktails. A 24-foot-tall Murano blown-glass chandelier made up of some 15,000 handblown spheres never fails to amaze newcomers. $ *Average main: $90* ⊠ *THEHotel at Mandalay Bay, 3950 Las Vegas Blvd. S* ☎ *702/632–9500* ⊕ *www.mandalaybay.com/dining* ☽ *No lunch.*

$$$$ ✕ **RM Seafood.** This bi-level space at Mandalay Place is operated by one
SEAFOOD of the culinary world's leading proponents of the sustainable seafood movement. Executive Chef Rick Moonen refuses to serve Chilean sea bass and other overfished species. Fear not—you'll find plenty of delicious treats from the sea. On the upper level the more formal restaurant, with its sleek mahogany decor, feels a bit like a luxury yacht. Here you might dine on smoked sturgeon with osetra caviar, sauternes-poached pear, and lemon crème fraîche, or slow-roasted Arctic char with purple-potato puree and truffle vinaigrette. At the less pricey Rbar Café, on the lower level, you'll find a bustling raw bar with oysters from throughout North America and simpler treats like New England clam chowder, lobster rolls, and salt-and-pepper calamari with a Thai chili dipping sauce. $ *Average main: $75* ⊠ *Mandalay Bay Resort & Casino, 3950 Las Vegas Blvd. S* ☎ *702/632–9300* ⊕ *www.mandalaybay.com/dining* ☽ *No lunch Upper Level.*

MGM GRAND HOTEL AND CASINO

$$$ ✕ **Diego.** This isn't your typical Americanized Mexican food, but rather
MEXICAN authentic regional cooking served in a whimsically decorated space decked out with hammered-tin mirrors, bright red walls, and a well-dressed crowd. Sink into the *Cochinita Pibil*, Yucatecan-style pork marinated in achiote and orange, then slow-cooked in banana leaves; or opt for the Diego carne asada, a beef rib eye marinated in red-chili adobo, then grilled over a wood fire and topped with black beans and a salsa made with tequila, roasted cactus, and onion. Diego serves only 100% blue agave tequilas and mescals and offers more than 125 varieties to choose from. Our favorite drink pick? The frozen-fruit margarita on a stick. There's a handy to-go window to grab a bite on the run. And late on weekend evenings, the restaurant morphs into Vida! nightclub, with dancing into the wee hours. $ *Average main: $35* ⊠ *MGM Grand Hotel & Casino, 3799 Las Vegas Blvd. S* ☎ *702/891–3200* ⊕ *www. mgmgrand.com/restaurants* ☽ *No lunch.*

$$$ ✕ **Emeril's.** Enter this boisterous spot, chef Emeril Lagasse's first Vegas
SOUTHERN restaurant (one of the city's earlier celeb-helmed eateries), under an arch of water spouting from a wrought-iron fish. Menu highlights might include Creole-mustard glazed Texas redfish, pepper-crusted prime sirloin, or sweet barbecued Scottish salmon with andouille sausage and Brabant potatoes. Be sure to order a side of mac-and-cheese with Serrano ham. A sommelier will guide you through the selection of some 2,000 wine bottles in the wine tower. Finish with a slice of banana cream pie. ■TIP➔ Emeril's is one of the better lunch options in MGM Grand, as many fine-dining options are dinner-only. $ *Average main: $40* ⊠ *MGM Grand Hotel & Casino, 3799 Las Vegas Blvd. S* ☎ *702/891– 7374* ⊕ *www.mgmgrand.com/restaurants.*

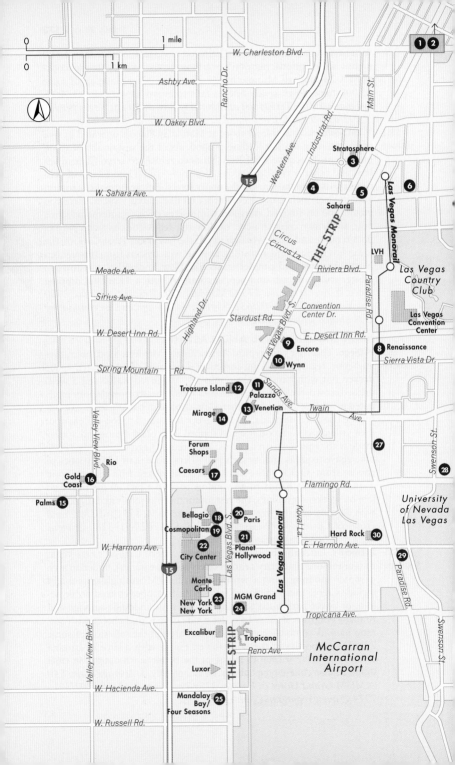

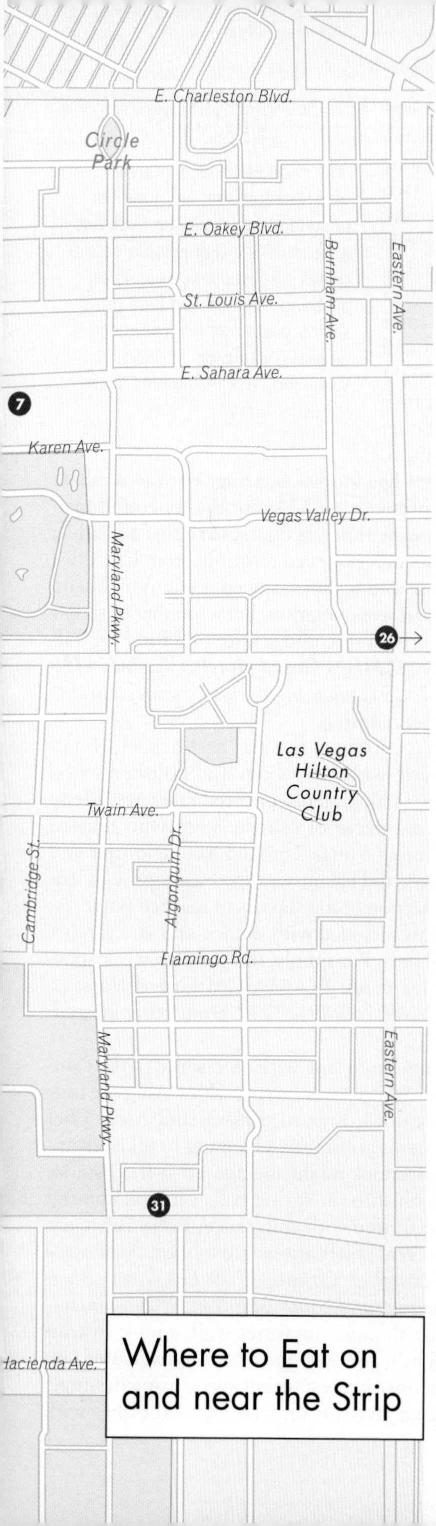

E. Charleston Blvd.
Circle Park
E. Oakey Blvd.
St. Louis Ave.
Burnham Ave.
Eastern Ave.
E. Sahara Ave.
7
Karen Ave.
Vegas Valley Dr.
Maryland Pkwy.
26
Las Vegas Hilton Country Club
Twain Ave.
Cambridge St.
Algonquin Dr.
Flamingo Rd.
Maryland Pkwy.
Eastern Ave.
31
Hacienda Ave.

Where to Eat on and near the Strip

35 Steaks **30**
Alizé **15**
American Fish **22**
Aureole **25**
Bartolotta **10**
B&B Ristorante **13**
BLT Burger **14**
BOA Steakhouse **17**
Border Grill **25**
Botero **9**
Bouchon **13**
Bradley Ogden **17**
Burger Bar **25**
Canter's Deli **12**
CarneVino **11**
Charlie Palmer Steak **25**
Comme Ca **19**
Country Club Grill **10**
Crown & Anchor British Pub **31**
Diego **24**
Dona Maria **2**
Eiffel Tower **20**
Emeril's **24**
ENVY Steakhouse **8**
Estiatorio Milos **19**
Firefly Tapas Kitchen **27**
FIX **18**
FLEUR **25**
Gallagher's **23**
Golden Steer **4**
Grand Lux Cafe **13**
Hofbräuhaus **29**
I Love Burgers **11**
Il Fornaio **23**
India Oven **5**
Isla Mexican Kitchen **12**
Jaleo **19**
Jean Georges Steakhouse **22**
Jean Philippe Patisserie **18**
Joël Robuchon **24**
Joe's Stone Crab **17**
Julian Serrano **22**
KOI **21**
La Cave **10**
Lavo **11**
Le Cirque **18**
Lindo Michoacán **26**
Little Buddha **15**
Lotus of Siam **7**
Marrakech **27**
Mastro's Ocean Club **22**
Mesa Grill **17**
MIX **25**
Mon Ami Gabi **20**
Morels **11**
Mr. Lucky's 24-7 .... **30**
Nine Fine Irishmen **23**
Nobhill Tavern **24**
Nobu **30**
Nove Italiano **15**
Onda **14**
Osteria del Circo **18**
Pamplemousse **6**
Payard Patisserie **17**
Pearl **24**
Picasso **18**
Ping Pang Pong **16**
Pink Taco **30**
Prime Steakhouse **18**
Rao's **17**
Restaurant Guy Savoy **17**
RM Seafood **25**
Roy's **28**
Sage **22**
Scarpetta **19**
SeaBlue **24**
Sensi **18**
Shibuya **24**
Simon **15**
Sinatra **9**
Society Cafe **10**
Spago **17**
STACK **14**
Stratta **10**
Sushi Roku **17**
SUSHISAMBA **11**
Tableau **10**
TAO **13**
Todd English P.U.B. **22**
Top of the World **3**
Triple George Grill **1**
Twist **22**
Valentino **13**
Village Eateries at New York-New York **23**
Wing Lei **10**
'Wichcraft **24**

$$$$ FRENCH Fodor's Choice ★ 🍴 **Joël Robuchon.** Arguably the biggest name in contemporary French cuisine, chef Joël Robuchon came out of retirement to open two massively hyped (and some say criminally overpriced) side-by-side restaurants at the MGM Grand in 2005. L'Atelier, less formal though still highly refined, offers à la carte entrées plus a long list of small "tasting" portions (which might include steak tartar or free-range quail stuffed with foie gras) that let you create your own fantasy meal. But it's the main restaurant that has foodies buzzing. For the ultimate gastronomical rush, you can spring nearly $240 for the six-course tasting menu; less expensive versions with fewer courses are also available. The cuisine changes daily and includes rarefied creations from Executive Chef Claude Le Tohic, such as seared scallops, spiced coconut milk, and fresh coriander. This is one impressive operation, but a number of stellar restaurants in town deliver nearly as splendid service and food for half the price. [$] *Average main: $240* ✉ *MGM Grand Hotel & Casino, 3799 Las Vegas Blvd. S* ☎ *702/891–7925* 🌐 *www.mgmgrand.com/restaurants* ✍ *Reservations essential. Jacket required.*

WORD OF MOUTH

"The MGM will have a number of restaurants that are good but unpretentious. Wolfgang Puck has a Bar and Grill that is more on the casual side where you can order anything from a wood fired pizza, salads, pasta and fish and meat entrees. I've always had luck at Wolfgang Puck restaurants in Las Vegas." —tom42 .

$$$$ AMERICAN Fodor's Choice ★ 🍴 **Nobhill Tavern.** San Francisco cuisine is the star at Michael Mina's handsome, understated brasserie with clean lines and polished-wood floors. Emphasis here is on seasonal, globally inspired favorites. Menu items might include caramelized-puree of celeriac soup with toasted walnuts, lobster potpie (containing a huge 2-pound Maine lobster and baby vegetables in truffle cream), and bacon-wrapped scallops with lentil stew and baby carrots. A selection of five flavors of mashed potatoes, such as lobster, curry, or basil, is included with dinner, and you can bet the sourdough bread's the real deal. Put simply, there are no weak spots in Mina's repertoire. [$] *Average main: $53* ✉ *MGM Grand Hotel & Casino, 3799 Las Vegas Blvd. S* ☎ *702/891–7337* 🌐 *www.mgmgrand.com/restaurants* ⏲ *No lunch.*

$$$$ CHINESE 🍴 **Pearl.** Serving traditional Chinese cuisine with an essence of the Canton and Shanghai provinces, Pearl prepares its specialties using the four Chinese cooking methods: steamed, braised, baked, and fried. Chef Kai-Wa Yau creates a menu that is constantly changing to take advantage of seasonal offerings. Selections might include crisp-fried spider prawn dumplings and Asian mushroom spring rolls on wok-charred Mongolian beef, or wok-fried shrimp with chili sauce. Every February, the restaurant's Chinese New Year celebrations are a blast. [$] *Average main: $45* ✉ *MGM Grand Hotel & Casino, 3799 Las Vegas Blvd. S* ☎ *702/891–7380* 🌐 *www.mgmgrand.com/restaurants* ⏲ *No lunch.*

$$$$ SEAFOOD 🍴 **SeaBlue.** Faux-brick floors, a shimmering water wall, a tank swarming with hundreds of colorful fish, and two open kitchens welcome you into Michael Mina's dynamic, über-hip restaurant specializing in simple but sensational seafood. The emphasis is on wood-grilled dishes with

DINING WITH KIDS

Sin City dining has never been geared especially toward families, and the increasing numbers of high-end, ultrafancy restaurants at Strip casino resorts further the "adult" mentality. But you'll still find plenty of spots around town—both on and off the Strip—that happily welcome kids, from ubiquitous fast-food chains and something-for-everyone buffets to quite a few distinctive choices. Here's a look at several restaurants worth a special trip if you have kids in tow.

Jean Philippe Patisserie, Aria and Bellagio, Center Strip.

The draw: beautifully displayed cakes, cookies, gelati, and dessert crepes, and a fanciful Wonka-esque ambience.

Village Eateries, New York–New York, South Strip.

The draw: an outdoor food court that's designed to resemble the Big Apple's Greenwich Village—pizza, hot dogs, cheese steak

s, and ice cream are among the many offerings.

LBS: A Burger Joint, Red Rock Casino, Summerlin.

The draw: classic burgers and fries, set in a funky space with a ceiling made of pressed license plates.

Hofbräuhaus Las Vegas, Paradise Road.

The draw: kitschy Bavarian decor, German bands playing oompah music, and decadent desserts, including a knockout Black Forest chocolate cake.

J.C. Wooloughan's Irish Pub, JW Marriott, Summerlin.

The draw: it's a genuine recon-structed Irish pub, and the hearty Irish fare pleases even picky palates.

Grimaldi's, Palazzo, North Strip; Henderson.

The draw: exceptionally tasty pizza and a casual dining room with a cheery little patio that's good fun on a nice day.

Mediterranean-inspired preparations, and the fish is flown in from all over the world—pink dorade from Senegal, striped bass from Nantucket, barramundi from Australia. You might start off with the lobster bisque with tarragon oil, or the fried lobster corn dogs served with whole-grain mustard. Moroccan-style tagines are a specialty here, as well—consider the one with Atlantic cod, almonds, couscous, lemon broth, and artichokes. There's an inspired list of desserts, including a chocolate molten cake. $ *Average main: $49* ✉ *MGM Grand Hotel & Casino, 3799 Las Vegas Blvd. S* ☎ *702/891–3486* ⊕ *www.mgmgrand. com/restaurants* ⊗ *No lunch.*

$$$$
JAPANESE ✕ **Shibuya.** This hot spot along MGM's Studio Walk has skyrocketed in popularity, as much for the finely prepared Japanese dishes as for the dazzling decor. Items such as the Mifune roll (with soft-shell crab, tobiko caviar, scallion, daikon, and spicy mayo) have made it the Strip's top sushi destination. It also happens to be the only Teppanyaki experi-ence on Las Vegas Boulevard. Sushi alternatives might include Florida rock-shrimp tempura, Japanese wagyu beef with truffle ponzu sauce and maitake mushrooms, and Jidori chicken. Kinaco tiramisu with

Las Vegas Hamburger Roundup

A number of casino resorts have opened eateries dedicated to that most quintessentially American of cuisines—the compact and delicious hamburger. All of these restaurants are casual affairs; most don't even accept reservations.

BLT Burger. Burger choices in this Laurent Tourondel restaurant near the Mirage sports book include American Kobe, lamb, and turkey. Spiked milk shakes—including "Grandma's Treat" with Maker's Mark, caramel, and vanilla ice cream—make a great accompaniment. ⊠ *Mirage Las Vegas, 3400 Las Vegas Blvd. S, Center Strip* ☎ *702/792-7888.*

Burger Bar. Chef Hubert Keller started the burger trend with this modest restaurant in 2004; the simple build-your-own-burger menu features a variety of different meats (beef, buffalo, turkey) and toppings. As a treat, sample the Peanut Butter and Jelly Burger. The name says it all. ⊠ *The Palazzo, 3950 Las Vegas Blvd. S, South Strip* ☎ *702/632-9364.*

Holstein's. Chef Anthony Meidenbauer concocted the concept of

this burger joint specifically for The Cosmopolitan with an emphasis on organic ingredients. Everything on the menu—from burgers to house-made sausages, buns, and sides—is made in-house. ⊠ *The Cosmopolitan, 3708 Las Vegas Blvd. S, Center Strip* ☎ *702/698-7000*

I Love Burgers. This expansive burger joint inside the Palazzo features dozens of different gourmet burgers (including buffalo, ahi tuna, and vegan varieties), as well as the largest fry menu in town (try the truffle butter–tossed fried Yukon Golds). Executive Chef Errol LeBlanc has put together a great beer selection, too. ⊠ *The Palazzo, 3325 Las Vegas Blvd. S, North Strip* ☎ *702/242-2747.*

LBS. Happy Hour is indeed happy at this Anthony Meidenbauer burger joint inside Summerlin's Red Rock Resort; the eatery offers half-price snacks, sliders, and salads on weekdays from 3 to 6. Gourmet burgers of beef, turkey, and other meats are available all the time. ⊠ *Red Rock Casino Resort, 1101 W. Charleston Blvd., Summerlin* ☎ *702/797-7777.*

5

Kuromitsu syrup and Kinaco ice cream ranks among the top desserts. Also, with more than 125 labels, the restaurant claims the biggest selection of sake in North America. $ *Average main: $65* ⊠ *MGM Grand Hotel & Casino, 3799 Las Vegas Blvd. S* ☎ *702/891-3001* ⊕ *www. mgmgrand.com/restaurants* ⊙ *No lunch.*

$ ✕ **'Wichcraft.** Skip the drab fast-food court at MGM and grab a bite
AMERICAN at this futuristic space with marble-top café tables, vibrant lime-green walls, and blond-wood floors. The creative sandwiches (all the brain-children of Tom Colicchio) might include Sicilian tuna with fennel, black olives, and lemon juice on a baguette, and meat loaf with bacon, cheddar, and tomato relish on a roll. The eatery is a great option for (late) breakfast, too—try a roll stuffed with a fried egg, bacon, Gorgonzola cheese, and (optional) frisée. Although it's possible to stop here for an early dinner, keep in mind that it closes at 5 nightly. $ *Average main: $15* ⊠ *MGM Grand Hotel & Casino, 3799 Las Vegas Blvd. S*

☎ *702/891–7777* ⊕ *www.mgmgrand.com/restaurants* ⌱ *Reservations not accepted.*

NEW YORK–NEW YORK HOTEL & CASINO

$$$$
STEAKHOUSE

✕ **Gallagher's Steakhouse.** This credible remake of the famed 1927 Manhattan original offers an old-school carnivore experience inside the cleverly decorated New York–New York Casino. This convivial tavern's walls are lined with black-and-white photos of sports stars, actors, and politicos, and the hardwood floors and tray ceilings transport guests directly to Gotham. You can admire the aged steaks in a big cooler visible from the cobblestone promenade near the entrance. The menu's refreshingly simple: pick your main dish (Colorado lamb chop, center-cut filet mignon, and so on) and then one of the four sauces (béarnaise, brandied peppercorn, caramelized shallot, and Beaujolais) to accompany it. Gallagher's is open until midnight on Friday and Saturday, and serves lunch at the bar. ⓢ *Average main: $65* ⊠ *New York–New York Hotel & Casino, 3790 Las Vegas Blvd. S* ☎ *702/740–6450* ⊕ *www. newyorknewyork.com/restaurants.*

$$
ITALIAN

✕ **Il Fornaio.** Cross the Central Park footbridge and you come to Il Fornaio, a cheery and bright Italian café. You can dine "outdoors" beneath old-fashioned street lamps, on a terrace by the meandering "lagoon," or at a table inside. From an exhibition kitchen cooks prepare fresh fish, wood-oven pizzas, spinach linguine with shrimp, and traditional Italian dishes such as gnocchi and angel-hair pasta with marinara sauce. There's also tasty rotisserie fare like rosemary chicken. Breads (including the delicious ciabatta) are baked twice daily, and you can buy loaves to go at the on-site Panetteria. For breakfast or brunch, choose from French toast, a selection of omelets, and cholesterol-free eggs. ⓢ *Average main: $29* ⊠ *New York–New York Hotel & Casino, 3790 Las Vegas Blvd. S* ☎ *702/740–6403* ⊕ *www.newyorknewyork. com/restaurants.*

$
ECLECTIC

✕ **Village Eateries at New York–New York.** Just about every big casino on the Strip has an inexpensive food court, but most feature common fast-food chain restaurants. New York–New York stands out from the pack on several fronts. There are numerous dining options in this faux–Greenwich Village setting where the resort's wild roller coaster whizzes overhead. You can nosh on pizza, burgers, bratwurst, cheese steaks, fish-and-chips, ice cream, and plenty of other treats. Almost all of the restaurants are open until 3 am. ⓢ *Average main: $8* ⊠ *New York–New York Hotel & Casino, 3790 Las Vegas Blvd. S* ⊕ *www. newyorknewyork.com/restaurants* ⌱ *Reservations not accepted.*

CENTER STRIP

BELLAGIO LAS VEGAS

$$$
AMERICAN

✕ **FIX.** The ceiling, constructed almost entirely of Costa Rican padouk wood, curves like a breaking wave at this upscale comfort-food restaurant. A-list celebrities frequent this spot, and for good reason: all of your favorite childhood foods are prepared with a twist for your grown-up taste buds. Take the mac-and-cheese side dish—it's croquettes and a cheese sauce for dipping. Craving carbs? Indulge in lobster mashed potatoes. Entrées have included a delicious "drunken" lobster with prosciutto, gnocchi, and truffle cream, and sea bass with baby shrimp in a lobster broth. House-made doughnuts served with two dipping sauces are a perfect ending to your meal. The kitchen serves until 11 pm most evenings, and until 1 am on Friday and Saturday. [$] *Average main: $45* ✉ *Bellagio Las Vegas, 3600 Las Vegas Blvd. S* ☎ *702/693–8865* 🌐 *www.bellagio.com/restaurants* 🕒 *No lunch.*

$ CAFÉ Fodor's Choice ★ 👶 🍴 **Jean Philippe Patisserie.** You can always order a fresh-fruit smoothie at this Wonka-esque sweet shop at Bellagio, but why would you commit a healthy act like that? This artful homage to chocolate has so many decadently *devilish* desserts, including cakes, cookies, gelato, hand-dipped chocolate candies, and particularly memorable crepes (try the one filled with mango, coconut, passion-fruit, and pineapple sorbets). Café tables are set around a gorgeous circular bar, and some face a towering fountain of liquid chocolate. It's open late, until midnight on Friday and Saturday and 11 pm the rest of the week. A sister sweet-shop under the same name opened next door, at Aria, in late 2009. [$] *Average main: $8* ✉ *Bellagio, Las Vegas, 3600 Las Vegas Blvd. S* ☎ *702/693–7111* 🌐 *www.bellagio.com/restaurants/jean-philippe.aspx* [$] *Average main: $8* ✉ *Aria, 3730 S. Las Vegas Blvd.* ☎ *702/590–7111.*

$$$$ FRENCH 🍴 **Le Cirque.** This sumptuous restaurant, a branch of the New York City landmark, remains one of the city's true temples of haute cuisine, despite increased heavy-hitting competition. The mahogany-lined room is all the more opulent for its size: in a city of mega-everything, Le Cirque seats only 80 under its drooping silk-tent ceiling. Even with a view of the hotel's lake and its mesmerizing fountain show, you'll only have eyes for your plate when your server presents dishes such as the "Rabbit Symphony," which comprises rabbit cooked three different ways (ravioli, roasted loin, and braised with spaetzle). The menu offers a prix-fixe option or dining à la carte, while the wine cellar contains about 900 selections representing the major wine-producing regions of the world. One little-known secret: Le Cirque offers a reduced-price prix-fixe pre-theater dinner menu. [$] *Average main: $89* ✉ *Bellagio Las Vegas, 3600 Las Vegas Blvd. S* ☎ *702/693–8865* 🌐 *www.bellagio.com/restaurants* ✍ *Reservations essential* 🕒 *Closed Mon. No lunch.*

$$$$ ITALIAN 🍴 **Osteria del Circo.** With its expansive view of the lake, this is one of Bellagio's prime dining spots. The colorful Circo sports velveteen harlequin-pattern seats and whimsically decorated chandeliers, and serves home-style Tuscan food. Appetizers might include house-cured beef carpaccio with roasted radicchio and frisée salad, or ahi tuna tartare with a prosecco gelée and paddlefish caviar. The homemade pastas might include ravioli with spinach and sheep's milk ricotta in a butter-sage sauce. Caviar of various types is offered by the ounce for dinner, and the extensive wine cellar has selections from many of the major wine-producing regions of the world. It's the casual sister restaurant of next-door Le Cirque; food from Circo also can be purchased in Hyde Lounge. [$] *Average main: $52* ✉ *Bellagio Las Vegas, 3600 Las Vegas Blvd. S* ☎ *702/693–8865* 🌐 *www.bellagio.com/restaurants* 🕒 *No lunch.*

5

$$$$
SPANISH

✕ **Picasso.** This restaurant, adorned with some of the artist's original works, raised the city's dining scene a notch when it opened. Although it's still much adored, detractors insist it may be resting a bit on its laurels, and that Executive Chef Julian Serrano doesn't change his menu often enough. The artful, innovative cuisine has plenty of fans, however—it's based on French classics but also has strong Spanish influences. Appetizers on the seasonal menu might include boudin sausage of lobster, shrimp, and scallops with a simple but sublime tomato coulis, or poached oysters with osetra caviar and vermouth sauce. Sautéed fillet of halibut with a ragout of corona beans, Serrano ham, vegetables and mushrooms; or roasted-almond-and-honey-crusted pigeon might appear as entrée choices. Dinners are prix-fixe, with four- or five-course menus. $ *Average main: $123* ⊠ *Bellagio Las Vegas, 3600 Las Vegas Blvd. S* ☎ *702/693–8865* ⊕ *www.bellagio.com/restaurants* ⚄ *Reservations essential* ⊗ *Closed Tues. No lunch.*

$$$$
STEAKHOUSE

✕ **Prime Steakhouse.** Even among celebrity chefs, Jean-Georges Vongerichten has established a "can't touch this" reputation. Prime—with its gorgeous view of the fountains—is a place to see and be seen at Bellagio. In a velvet-draped gold, dark brown, and blue room that recalls a Prohibition-era speakeasy, choice cuts of beef are presented with mustards and sauces, from classic béarnaise to kumquat-pineapple chutney. You can also try signature dishes such as Dungeness crab cakes with celeriac rémoulade, ruby grapefruit, and ginger, and grilled foie gras with glazed chestnuts and brandy. Men are encouraged, but not required, to wear jackets. $ *Average main: $59* ⊠ *Bellagio Las Vegas, 3600 Las Vegas Blvd. S* ☎ *702/693–8865* ⊕ *www.bellagio.com/restaurants* ⚄ *Reservations essential* ⊗ *No lunch.*

$$$$
ECLECTIC
Fodor's Choice
★

✕ **Sensi.** It's no easy feat coming up with a truly original restaurant in Vegas that offers more than just a gimmicky theme or celebrity-chef pedigree. Sensi, a casual but cosmopolitan spot that's secluded from Bellagio's noisy gaming areas, succeeds on all counts. Executive Chef Royden Ellamar presents a menu that's divided into four distinct culinary realms: Asian dishes, Italian fare, raw and seafood specialties, and grilled meat. Specials on a given night might include spice-rubbed butter-curry chicken prepared in an authentic tandoori oven, ahi tuna ceviche, and wood-fired focaccia topped with Vacherin cheese and black truffles. Quench your thirst with a glass of house-made ginger ale. If you have a couple of friends with you, try the showy dessert sampler, which offers a taste of several sugary creations. The dining room, with its sandstone and glass walls and flowing waterfalls, is as dramatic as the food. $ *Average main: $49* ⊠ *Bellagio Las Vegas, 3600 Las Vegas Blvd. S* ☎ *702/693–8865* ⊕ *www.bellagio.com/restaurants* ⊗ *No lunch.*

CAESARS PALACE

$$$$
STEAKHOUSE

✕ **BOA Steakhouse.** This bold space brightened with massive red lanterns overlooks the immense atrium of the Forum Shops at Caesars—the tables up front offer the best people-watching, but the space in the back is quieter and more secluded. Choose from the long list of meats, such as bone-in Kansas City filet mignon or free-range veal chop, and then match your selection with any number of rubs, sauces, and mustards (blue cheese, chimichurri, or horseradish, to name a few). Surf-and-turf is taken to new levels here with the Australian lobster tail, Kobe filet mignon, and Hudson Valley foie gras. The service is outstanding from the moment you set foot inside, and the prices fairly reasonable by Vegas steak-house standards. The best part? The restaurant is open for lunch. [$] *Average main: $49* ✉ *Forum Shops at Caesars, 3500 Las Vegas Blvd. S* ☎ *702/733–7373* 🌐 *www.boasteak.com.*

$$$ AMERICAN 🍴 **Bradley Ogden.** San Francisco culinary wizard Bradley Ogden brought his magic touch to Vegas with this sleek, modern room at Caesars. As a keen proponent of the farm-to-table movement, Odgen uses only fresh ingredients (many of them organic). Depending on the season, menu items might include a cream of garlic soup with marinated jicama and basil oil, or a pan-roasted halibut with a cauliflower fritter and fennel-orange hash. For dessert, save room for the divine passion-fruit and chocolate cake. Go formal in the main dining room, flanked by a fireplace and waterfall, or take it down a notch in the lounge (which offers a separate menu, as well). A special three-course prixe-fixe menu for 2012 was $65. [$] *Average main: $40* ✉ *Caesars Palace, 3570 Las Vegas Blvd. S* ☎ *877/346–4642* 🌐 *www.caesarspalace.com* 🕒 *No lunch.*

$$$ SEAFOOD 🍴 **Joe's Seafood, Prime Steak & Stone Crab.** Drop by this bustling branch of the famed South Miami Beach restaurant for, at the very least, a pile of fresh stone crabs and a beer. But Joe's is worth a try whether for a light lunch or snack (the bar menu features a nice range of raw-bar items, salads, and sandwiches) or a full meal to remember. Carnivores won't go hungry here, considering the leviathan bone-in New York strip steak or Colorado lamb chops. Waiters finish many dishes table-side. For dessert, save room for Key lime pie or banana-cream pie with Foster sauce. [$] *Average main: $39* ✉ *Forum Shops at Caesars, 3500 Las Vegas Blvd. S* ☎ *702/792–9222* 🌐 *www.joes.net/las-vegas.*

$$$ SOUTHWESTERN 🍴 **Mesa Grill.** Playful splashes of bright green, blue, red, and yellow offset the swanky curved banquettes and earth tones at Iron Chef and grill-meister Bobby Flay's first restaurant outside New York City. The menu's decidedly Southwestern, but with plenty of contemporary twists. Options might include a starter of barbecued duck with habanero chili–star anise sauce over blue-corn pancakes, and main dishes like mango-and-spice-encrusted tuna steak with green peppercorn and green chili sauce or ancho-chili honey-glazed salmon with spicy black-bean sauce and roasted jalapeño crema. Some tables have views of the casino sports book. There's also an impressive weekend brunch. [$] *Average main: $39* ✉ *Caesars Palace, 3570 Las Vegas Blvd. S* ☎ *877/346–4642* 🌐 *www.caesarspalace.com.*

$ CAFÉ 🍴 **Payard Patisserie & Bistro.** Dessert is king at the Las Vegas outpost of this New York–based restaurant from celebrated chef François Payard. Tourists and business travelers queue during lunch at the counter for made-to-order crepes and treats that might include a raspberry-rhubarb Napoleon with vanilla mascarpone cheese. The 46-seat dining room (dinner is served Wednesday through Sunday) offers the city's only all-dessert tasting menu, as well as a lengthy wine list and savory items such as classic croque monsieur (grilled ham-and-cheese sandwich) and eggs Florentine. Best of all is the Continental buffet breakfast, which offers unlimited lox and whitefish. There's no dinner, but desserts are served

at the counter until 11 nightly. $ *Average main: $12* ⊠ *Caesars Palace, 3570 Las Vegas Blvd. S* ☎ *877/346–4642* ⊕ *www.caesarspalace.com.*

$$$
ITALIAN
✕ **Rao's.** While its 10-table New York counterpart is notorious for a jam-packed reservation list, this 200-seat outpost at Caesars Palace offers greater availability. Hearty portions of family-style, rustic, southern Italian cuisine are featured on the menu, including traditional dishes of baked clams, shrimp fra diavolo, and meatballs as well as the signature dish, lemon chicken. The red walls are crammed with framed celebrity photos—many of them digital replicas of originals back East. On warm nights, diners can end their meal with friendly games of bocce on the in-house (and first-come, first-served) court that overlooks the redone Garden of the Gods pool oasis. $ *Average main: $39* ⊠ *Caesars Palace, 3570 Las Vegas Blvd. S* ☎ *877/346–4642* ⊕ *www.caesarspalace.com* ⊙ *No lunch Mon. and Tues.*

$$$$
FRENCH
✕ **Restaurant Guy Savoy.** In an ultraswank dining room on the second floor of the Augustus Tower, Michelin three-star chef Guy Savoy introduces Vegas gourmands to his masterful creations, such as artichoke and black truffle soup, crispy veal sweetbreads, and John Dory fish à la plancha with grilled ginger and sunchokes. The 10-course Menu Prestige is the restaurant's crown jewel, featuring signature dishes such as artichoke and black truffle soup, and the delicately spiced crispy sea bass. Prices creep into the upper stratosphere (unless you dine in the less expensive Bites & Bubbles, or the Krug Room), but the restaurant has earned high marks from all, and not just for its stellar modern French cuisine. The selections from the Savoy's 15,000-bottle wine cellar only add to its mystique. $ *Average main: $150* ⊠ *Caesars Palace, 3570 Las Vegas Blvd. S* ☎ *877/346–4642* ⊕ *www.caesarspalace.com* ⊙ *Closed Mon. and Tues. No lunch.*

$$$$
AMERICAN
✕ **Spago Las Vegas.** Fellow chefs raised eyebrows in wonder when Wolfgang Puck opened this branch of his famous Beverly Hills eatery in the culinary wasteland that was Las Vegas in 1992, but Spago Las Vegas has become a fixture in this ever-fickle city, and it remains consistently superb. The less expensive café, which overlooks the busy Forum Shops at Caesars, is great for people-watching (and it's open for lunch); inside, the dinner-only dining room is more intimate. Both menus are classic Puck. In the café, sample dishes such as pancetta-wrapped meat loaf or Thai-style chicken salad. Options for the dining room might include stir-fried Maine lobster with egg noodles and confit pork belly, and red wine–braised beef short ribs with roasted vegetables and homemade gnocchi. $ *Average main: $49* ⊠ *Forum Shops at Caesars, 3500 Las Vegas Blvd. S* ☎ *702/369–6300* ⊕ *www.wolfgangpuck.com/restaurants.*

$$$
JAPANESE
✕ **Sushi Roku.** On the top floor of the towering atrium at the entrance to the Forum Shops, Roku occupies an airy dining room lined with bamboo stalks and tall windows facing the Strip. Sushi is the main draw, and you can't go wrong with the bluefin tuna or oyster nigiri, or the baked lobster roll with creamy miso sauce. But greater rewards come to those who venture deeper into the extensive menu. Seasonal items worth considering: popcorn rock shrimp tempura in spicy miso glaze, katana lamb chops marinated in soy garlic, or Hakata ramen with pork Cha-shu. Roku has the same management as BOA Steakhouse,

5

next door—you're welcome to order food from either menu in either space. $ *Average main: $30* ⊠ *Forum Shops at Caesars, 3500 Las Vegas Blvd. S* ☎ *702/733–7373* ⊕ *www.sushiroku.com/sushiroku/index.htm.*

CITYCENTER

$$$$
SEAFOOD

✕ **American Fish.** As the name suggests, Michael Mina's newest Vegas restaurant pays homage to fish of all shapes and sizes. The eatery is designed to look like a lodge, and diners can select fish entrées from a list that includes branzino, rainbow trout, diver scallops, and big-eye tuna (yes, there's a selection of meat, as well). All fish orders are prepared in one of four different cooking methods: salt-baking, wood-grilling, cast-iron griddling, and ocean-water poaching. Still, some of the menu's biggest treasures are in the appetizers section: stuff like fried geoduck clam, smoked salmon BLT and New Bedford mussels and chorizo. Also pay attention to the side-dishes; the collard greens, ham hock, and maple syrup is addicting. $ *Average main: $49* ⊠ *Aria, 3730 Las Vegas Blvd. S* ☎ *877/230–2742* ⊕ *www.arialasvegas.com/dining* ⌂ *Reservations essential* ⊘ *Closed Mon. No lunch.*

$$$$
STEAKHOUSE

✕ **Jean Georges Steakhouse.** This steak house, named after Executive Chef Jean Georges Vongerichten, serves up a modern spin on the traditional meat-and-potatoes type of place. To wit: dishes such as the Soy-Glazed Short Rib with apple jalapeño puree and rosemary crumbs, and the Broiled Bone Marrow with parsley-lemon gremolata. The eatery also spotlights an extensive bar program that focuses on classic cocktails. During particularly busy weekends at the resort, dine at the bar and look for poker pros on break from the nearby poker room; "J.G.," as it's known, has become one of the favorites of players such as Daniel Negreanu, Phil Ivey, and Phil Hellmuth. $ *Average main: $69* ⊠ *Aria, 3730 Las Vegas Blvd. S.* ☎ *877/230–2742* ⊕ *www.arialasvegas. com/dining.*

$$$
SPANISH

✕ **Julian Serrano.** Most of the food at Executive Chef Julian Serrano's eponymous restaurant is served tapas-style, so prepare to order a bunch of small plates. Some of Serrano's signature dishes: lobster-pineapple skewers with wasabi, goat-cheese stuffed Piquillo peppers, fresh oysters with gazpacho foam, and *escalibada* (essentially, a roasted eggplant). The menu also features ceviche options and numerous different kinds of paella. For dessert, try the almond-flavored Santiago's Cake. There's even a special three-course prix fixe pre-theater dinner menu for $39, as well as a signature $59 tasting menu. And during lunchtime, seats on the edge of the "patio" that face hotel registration and the casino are great spots from which to people-watch. $ *Average main: $39* ⊠ *Aria, 3730 Las Vegas Blvd.,* ☎ *877/230–2742* ⊕ *www.arialasvegas.com/dining.*

$$$$
SEAFOOD

✕ **Mastro's Ocean Club.** Sure, the food is upscale and tasty at the Las Vegas outpost of Mastro's Ocean Club inside the Crystals retail and entertainment complex at CityCenter. But the restaurant's two biggest draws are its piano lounge, which serves stellar martinis and is open nightly until 2 am, and the "Tree House," a two-story wooden sculpture that rises from the ground level of the shopping complex and houses the main dining room 30 feet above the ground. Menu items range from tempura lobster tails and ahi tuna tartare to New York strip steak and rack of lamb. Side dishes tend to be boring; the lone exception: the

Continued on page 193

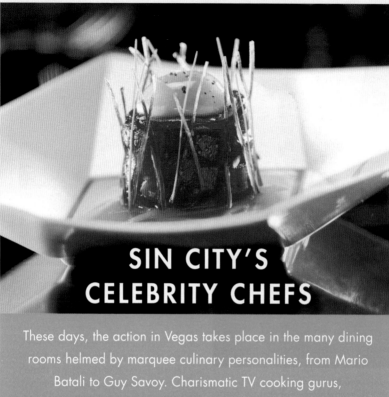

SIN CITY'S CELEBRITY CHEFS

These days, the action in Vegas takes place in the many dining rooms helmed by marquee culinary personalities, from Mario Batali to Guy Savoy. Charismatic TV cooking gurus, Michelin-knighted French chefs, dynamic cookbook authors— these are Las Vegas' hottest celebrities.

It's hard to grasp at times how quickly—and dramatically—Las Vegas has emerged as America's most exciting restaurant destination. High-rollers happily plunk down $500 per person to partake of Joël Robuchon's seven-course "white truffle" menu, or $200 for a 6-ounce A5 (the highest grade) Kobe filet mignon at Michael Mina's Stripsteak. Sure, plenty of critics and food purists ridicule the glitzy dining rooms, gaudy prices, and sometimes absentee chefs. But, there is something magical about vaunted kitchen wizards like Tom Colicchio, Hubert Keller, Pierre Gagnaire, and Alain Ducasse all conjuring up the most decadent and delicious meals possible along a single 3-mile stretch.

Showmanship has always been the draw to this mirage in the Nevada desert. It makes perfect sense that as Americans demand increasingly stellar restaurant experiences, Las Vegas responds with some of the most jaw-dropping, elaborate culinary options possible. (Yes that *is* edible gold leaf gleaming radiantly atop the risotto-style farro grains). It's all just part of a culinary equivalent of Cirque du Soleil.

By Andrew Collins

(above) Joël Robuchon's tuna tartare with bergamot-red pepper confit and quail egg

JOËL ROBUCHON

(clockwise from top left) Chef Joël Robuchon; orange and mascarpone custard in a sugar bubble with cinnamon ice cream; dining at the bar at L'Atelier de Joël Robuchon

Widely celebrated Parisian chef Joël Robuchon emerged exuberantly from retirement in 2005 to lead the French culinary charge into Las Vegas, opening a pair of restaurants at the MGM Grand. The man the French restaurant guide *Gault Millau* dubbed "the chef of the century" in 1989 was born in 1945 in Poitiers, France, and cut his teeth at age 15 working at the celebrated Relais of Poitiers hotel. His restaurant empire spans three continents (Paris–Hong Kong–Las Vegas), and it wouldn't be gilding the lily to describe him as the most influential chef of the past two decades.

In Vegas

At MGM, **Joël Robuchon** is the chef's over-the-top fine-dining destination, while the small-plate-driven **L'Atelier de Joël Robuchon** gives diners a less formal, more accessible dining experience (here, for instance, you might dine on a classic steak tartare with crispy french fries). Robuchon's Mansion—where the standard 6-course menu is $230—has lived up to the hype, becoming the only restaurant in town to garner three Michelin stars.

Culinary Trademarks

Robuchon's cuisine is characterized by an intense respect for the finest ingredients and a technical precision that is without peer. He's become synonymous with the foams and emulsions that are a hallmark of modern molecular gastronomy. Arguably no dining experience in Las Vegas commands more respect than the 16-course tasting menu available at his main restaurant. A crustacean trio of king crab with aromatic emulsion, sea urchin with potato puree and flecks of coffee, and lobster in a pasta shell with coral butter and chives might just be that meal's masterpiece.

GUY SAVOY

(clockwise from top left) Chef Guy Savoy; crispy seabass with "delicate spices"; jelly of raw peas, pea puree, and soft-poached egg

Like Joel Robuchon, Guy Savoy is one of the great culinary masters of Paris. He was born in Bourgoin-Jallieu in 1955 and developed his astounding talent by apprenticing at the famed Maison Troisgros in Roanne in his late teens. By 1980, he'd opened his own Parisian restaurant, which drew instant acclaim. In 2002, Savoy earned the elusive three stars from the *Michelin Red Guide* for his Restaurant Guy Savoy in Paris, a stunning space designed by cutting-edge architect Jean-Michel Wilmotte. The chef's broad grin, twinkly eyes, and silver hair suggest a *joie de vivre* that keeps his signature Las Vegas restaurant from ever feeling stilted or pretentious.

In Vegas

Guy Savoy opened his eponymous restaurant in the exclusive Augustus Tower at Caesars Palace in 2006. His only U.S. restaurant is relatively accessible compared with rival Joël Robuchon's, but prepare to pay $200 to $300 per person (plus wine) to dine in this hallowed culinary ground. The space is deliberately free of clutter or gimmicky decor—the focus here is squarely on the ethereal food.

Culinary Trademarks

The best way to understand Savoy's rarified cuisine is to book the 10-course Menu Prestige, an elaborate tasting menu that lets you sample famed masterworks like a silky artichoke and black truffle soup with toasted mushroom brioche or ethereal butter-roasted veal sweetbreads. The restaurant also regularly dreams up special thematic menus, such as the recent "white truffle and wild game" feast that included scallop carpaccio with white truffle pasta and poached quail egg.

MARIO BATALI

Mario Batali grew up in Washington state, where his dad now runs the exalted cured-meat shop, Salumi. Batali is recognized by American foodies far and wide because of his many years at the Food Network hosting the Italian cooking show *Molto Mario* and appearing regularly on *Iron Chef America*. He has refined the home-style Italian cooking inspired by his grandmother at such venerable restaurants as Babbo in New York City and Pizzeria Mozza in Los Angeles. Today, there are more than a dozen establishments in his portfolio.

In Vegas

Batali and business partner (and wine expert) Joseph Bastianich took quite a few years building their extensive restaurant empire before conquering Vegas with **B&B Ristorante** and **Enoteca San Marco;** both opened at the Venetian in 2007. Batali's latest Las Vegas venture, **Carnevino Italian Steakhouse,** opened inside the Venetian's adjacent sister property, the Palazzo, in 2008—it's a credible effort, but serious adherents of Batali's gift for faithfully prepared, head-to-hoof Italian cooking should stick with B&B, which has both a handsome yet unfussy dining room and a stylish little bar where the full menu is available. For a casual brush with Batali-Bastianich delicacy, partake in the surprisingly affordable cheese and charcuterie selection at Enoteca, which has a superb (but spendy) selection of Italian wines.

Culinary Trademarks

Batali is, in some respects, the antithesis of a Vegas showman. He favors a rustic, unfussy approach to old-world cooking, and he and partner Bastianich also present authentic wine lists that emphasize Italian varietals. Batali uses local market ingredients at Enoteca San Marco, where he elevates such quintessentially modest Italian fare as cauliflower fritters and veal-and-ricotta meatballs to lofty gustatory heights. At B&B, the antipasti selection is exemplary, including warm lamb's tongue with chanterelles and grilled octopus with spicy limoncello vinaigrette. But serious fans of country Italian fare shouldn't miss the Pasta Tasting Menu, which shows off five sublime varieties of this hearty treat.

TOM COLICCHIO

(clockwise from top left) Chef Tom Colicchio; 'Wichcraft's BLT sandwich; Craftsteak's grilled rib eye for two

Aspiring chefs quake under their toques on TV's *Top Chef*, as they await the often brutally honest verdicts of head judge Tom Colicchio. Even tempered but tough, the New Jersey native taught himself to cook by studying the books of French chef Jacques Pepin. He worked his way up through the Manhattan restaurant ranks, earning accolades as one of *Food & Wine*'s 10 "Best New Chefs" in 1991 for his work at Mondrian. He later dazzled hard-to-please critic Ruth Reichl at Gramercy Tavern, and has since 2001 been steadily expanding his Craft Restaurant Group with Craft, Craftsteak, and Craftbar eateries in Atlanta, Connecticut, Dallas, Los Angeles, and New York. With his small fleet of 'Wichcraft restaurants, he's also lent gravitas to the humble art of sandwich-making.

In Vegas

Colicchio runs outposts of **Craftsteak** and **'Wichcraft** at the MGM Grand in Las Vegas. In his signature Vegas dining room, Craftsteak, Colicchio ushers classic steakhouse cooking into the modern age. 'Wichcraft is the perfect spot for a bargain-priced, light snack before a show at MGM Grand. In this petite sandwich shop that's open only until 5 pm on weekdays and 8 pm on weekends, order at the counter and dine in at one of the small tables or carry out.

Culinary Trademarks

At Craftsteak, Colicchio utilizes stellar ingredients (sublime Wagyu beef for his tartare, precious Kumamoto oysters in the raw bar) and offers up enticing sides (soft polenta with blue cheese, sautéed hen-of-the-woods mushrooms) with his prodigious steaks—that tender 32-ounce Porterhouse is meant to be shared. Desserts are a big part of the Colicchio show—consider the bourbon-pecan tart with sweet potato-spiced ice cream and pomegranate caramel. Looking for hit-the-spot lunchtime fare? Try 'Wichcraft's pole-caught tuna with fennel, black olives, aïoli, and lemon on a crisp baguette.

MICHAEL MINA

(from left) Chef Michael Mina; Seablue's Maine lobster with olive oil smashed potatoes and asparagus

Among celebrity chefs Michael Mina is more of a behind-the-scenes chef than some of his peers; fans know his name and coo over his urbane, creative cooking, but relatively few could spot him in a crowd. Born in Egypt in 1969 but raised in Washington state, Mina didn't release his first cookbook until 2006, and he's appeared very little on TV. He has, however, generated plenty of buzz through sheer talent, and by developing a series of first-rate restaurants in a partnership with tennis star Andre Agassi—four are in Las Vegas, and the rest are scattered around the country.

In Vegas

MGM Grand has a pair of Mina's venues: the airy and bustling **Seablue**—with its backlit blue walls and high ceilings—and the dressier and more refined **Nobhill Tavern**, an homage to the city that brought him the greatest culinary acclaim, San Francisco. Inside the lavish Bellagio, you'll find the only self-titled **Michael Mina** restaurant outside San Francisco. It's considered the premier Mina destination, with its tasting menus, posh interior, and slightly formal air. The youngest in the quartet, **Stripsteak,** opened in Mandalay Bay in 2006 and might just be the real showstopper. Then, of course, there's **American Fish**, which opened to rave reviews inside Aria in 2009.

Culinary Trademarks

Mina seems most in his element when preparing seafood—Seablue has become renowned for market-fresh fish flown in daily. The real common denominator with his cuisine is the innovative use of often disparate international ingredients. At Michael Mina, he's known to pair sashimi of kampachi with sweet coconut gelee and fiery vindaloo curry, but he also nods to traditional flavors with his organic pheasant set against wild mushroom risotto, salsify, and chestnut foam. Or consider the juicy Kobe beef burger brought out with a portion of perfectly crisp duck-fat fries (a favorite at Stripsteak). Seablue's paella is another standout; it's prepared Moroccan-style in a clay pot and studded with clams, shrimp, mussels, chorizo, rabbit, and quail.

Gorgonzola macaroni and cheese, which is reason enough to return. [$] *Average main: $69* ✉ *Crystals, 3270 Las Vegas Blvd. S, Suite 244* ☎ *702/798–7115* 🌐 *www.mastrosrestaurants.com* ✍ *Reservations essential* 🕓 *No lunch.*

$$$$ MEDITERRANEAN 🍴 **Sage.** The farm-to-table produce and artisanal meats incorporate flavors and concepts from the Mediterranean in new and exciting ways at Executive Chef Shawn McClain's swanky eatery. Exciting fare includes charred baby octopus salad with grilled Shishito peppers, oven-dried tomatoes, and a basil aioli. Depending on when you visit, entrée options might include braised short rib with spring onions and roasted day boat scallops with a salted caramel reduction. Still, the main attraction at this popular restaurant is the bar program. Mixologists incorporate fresh-fruit purees, boutique liquors, and homemade bitters into cocktails, and the bar offers more absinthe than any other spot in Vegas. They've also put together a beer-pairing list to maximally complement your entree. [$] *Average main: $49* ✉ *Aria, 3730 Las Vegas Blvd.* ☎ *877/230–2742* 🌐 *www.arialasvegas.com/dining* ✍ *Reservations essential* 🕓 *Closed Sun.*

$$ BRITISH 🍴 **Todd English P.U.B.** That crunching you hear underfoot at this rollicking bar? Why, they're peanut shells, of course. This eatery represents three-time James Beard Award-winner Todd English's first pub concept, and it was well worth the wait. The menu takes playful approaches to traditional bar food; try the cocktail-size corn dogs or the kettle chips with bacon bits and fried chicken livers. The curved wooden bar features two carving stations and an area for raw shellfish, while bartenders serve more than 30 beers on draught (if you chug your beer in less than seven seconds, it's free). Throughout the room, plasma televisions are plentiful but not obtrusive; there's also a spacious patio overlooking one of Aria's "pocket parks" for outdoor dining. [$] *Average main: $24* ✉ *Crystals, 3720 Las Vegas Blvd. S.* ☎ *702/489–8080* 🌐 *www.toddenglishpub.com.*

$$$$ FRENCH 🍴 **Twist.** The 23rd floor of the Mandarin Oriental is the only place in the United States to experience food from internationally renowned Chef Pierre Gagnaire. The French chef pioneered the "fusion" movement in cooking, and every dish blends together flavor and texture in surprising ways. To wit: appetizers such as the sea bream tartlette with mozzarella ice cream; or the entrée of beef sirloin with burgundy escargots sauce. Desserts are just as appealing—consider the baba cake with limoncello and citrus gelée. Items can be ordered à la carte or as part of three- or six-course tasting menus ($105 or $189, respectively). The restaurant is sexy and sophisticated, with an expansive wine loft (reached by a glass staircase) and nearly 300 illuminated globe-like spheres that float above the dining room like tiny moons. [$] *Average main: $105* ✉ *Mandarin Oriental, 3752 Las Vegas Blvd. S* ☎ *888/881–9367* 🌐 *www.mandarinoriental.com/lasvegas* ✍ *Reservations essential* 🕓 *Closed Mon. No lunch.*

COSMOPOLITAN LAS VEGAS

$$$ FRENCH 🍴 **Comme Ca.** French food is often pretentious, yet the menu at this popular and comfy-casual David Myers restaurant is approachable and innovative. There's a house special every night of the week (the

pillow-soft Parisian gnocchi on Tuesday reigns supreme). Other dishes include cutting-edge options such as roasted beef marrow and oxtail jam with toast and fleur de sel, and traditional offerings such as a bouillabaisse teeming with shellfish and other goodies from the sea. With part of the dining room cantilevered over the sidewalk below, the restaurant has a commanding third-floor view of the Strip. It's also one of Cosmopolitan's few eateries open for lunch. [$] *Average main: $39* ✉ *The Cosmopolitan, 3708 Las Vegas Blvd. S* ☎ *702/698–7000* 🌐 *www.cosmopolitanlasvegas.com* ✍ *Reservations essential.*

$$$$ MEDITERRANEAN 🍴 **Estiatorio Milos.** So long as you've just cleaned up at a craps table somewhere, the first Greek restaurant on the Las Vegas Strip certainly doesn't disappoint. Chef Costas Spiliadis is the mastermind behind a relatively simple concept: The eatery flies in fresh fish from New York and Montreal daily, diners pick out the piece of fish they desire, then select how they'd like it prepared. Side dishes such as Milos Special (paper-thin slices of fried zucchini and eggplant) are a nice compliment to the main course. Also worth sampling: grilled octopus with chick-peas and capers. The real treat at Estiatorio Milos comes in the dining experience itself—the dining room is stark white, and the glass-enclosed terrace looks out on the Strip. Perhaps the only downside to this eatery is the prices; it's virtually impossible to escape without paying $150 per person. [$] *Average main: $150* ✉ *The Cosmopolitan, 3708 Las Vegas Blvd. S* ☎ *702/698–7000* 🌐 *www.cosmopolitanlasvegas.com* ✍ *Reservations essential* 🕑 *No lunch weekdays.*

$$$ SPANISH 🍴 **Jaleo.** Chef Jose Andres was one of the first to capitalize on the tapas concept in the United States (at the Washington, D.C. version of Jaleo), and small plates are the highlights of the menu here, too. With choices such as *jamon iberico* (Spanish ham) and *gambas al ajillo* (shrimp in oil), you haven't thoroughly explored the menu until there are stacks of plates on your table. Another highlight: paella, which changes daily. Bring a sense of humor to the main dining room, as some tables are fashioned out of foosball tables that still function perfectly (balls available upon request). For a more formal and intimate experience, try dining in the private room—an intimate, prix fixe experience with seats that overlook a separate kitchen. [$] *Average main: $39* ✉ *The Cosmopolitan, 3708 Las Vegas Blvd. S* ☎ *702/698–7000* 🌐 *www.cosmopolitanlasvegas.com* ✍ *Reservations essential* 🕑 *No lunch.*

$$$ ITALIAN 🍴 **Scarpetta.** In Italian, "scarpetta" refers to the shape bread takes when it is used to soak up every last morsel of a dish. Chef Scott Conant hopes diners will do just that when they eat at his casual and festive modern Italian eatery. Conant makes all his own pasta, which takes front-and-center on the eclectic menu (the simple spaghetti with tomato and basil is, in a word, divine). Also worth trying: Sicilian-spiced duck breast with preserved orange, root vegetables, and caramelized endive; or Mediterranean Branzino with salsa verde. Floor-to-ceiling windows that look out on the Bellagio and the Strip provide memorable views. For a more casual experience, try D.O.C.G., Conant's wine bar and light-bite eatery next door. [$] *Average main: $39* ✉ *The Cosmopolitan, 3708 Las Vegas Blvd. S* ☎ *702/698–7000* 🌐 *www.cosmopolitanlasvegas.com.*

MIRAGE LAS VEGAS

$$ BURGER — 🍴 **BLT Burger.** In the same space where Siegfried & Roy's white tigers once roamed, diners, not tigers, are now on display at BLT Burger, which serves up the traditional burger, fries, and a shake—but with some tasty twists. For a sugar rush, start with a Twinkie Boy milk shake made with vanilla ice cream, caramel syrup, and real Twinkies. Or, spike that shake with bourbon (Maker's Mark, no less). Bite into a Kobe beef burger, or choose one made from lamb, turkey, or salmon. Sweet-potato fries are the perfect carbo sideshow for all this protein. BLT is open until 4 am on weekends. [$] *Average main: $22* ✉ *The Mirage, 3400 Las Vegas Blvd. S* ☎ *702/792–7888* 🌐 *www.mirage.com/restaurants.*

$$$$ ITALIAN — 🍴 **Onda.** You enter this restaurant through a piano bar opening onto the casino. Beyond the lounge, with its arched, stained-glass ceiling and marble floor, is the restaurant, tucked behind one-way glass. The menu offers seafood choices such as garlic-crusted sea bass and Osso Bucco as well as traditional pasta dishes such as lasagna, fettuccine Alfredo, and tagliatelle with garlic shrimp and zucchini. House specials have included soft-shell crab with corn relish and red pepper aioli, and braised veal shank served osso buco style. ■ **TIP→ Bargain hunters should check out Onda's $20 all-you-can-eat mussels promotion from Sunday–Thursday.** There's also a free wine-tasting at 5 pm every Friday. [$] *Average main: $49* ✉ *The Mirage, 3400 Las Vegas Blvd. S* ☎ *866/339–4566* 🌐 *www.mirage.com/restaurants* ⏲ *Closed Tues. and Wed. No lunch.*

$$$$ AMERICAN — 🍴 **STACK.** Curvy strips of exotic wood form the "stacked" walls of this beautiful restaurant, owned by nightclub impresarios The Light Group. Happy Hour comprises drink specials and a host of small plates, available seven days a week. For dinner, inventively prepared comfort classics dominate the menu—start with the (totally modern) pigs in a blanket or the miso black cod before tucking into the lamb shank with lentils and watercress or the bone-in 24-ounce cowboy steak. Be sure to order a side of "Adult Tater Tots" with bacon and Brie. A new prix-fixe menu for 2012 was $49. The lounge is open until midnight on Monday, Friday, and Saturday, 11 pm the rest of the week. [$] *Average main: $50* ✉ *The Mirage, 3400 Las Vegas Blvd. S* ☎ *866/339–4566* 🌐 *www.mirage.com/restaurants.*

PARIS LAS VEGAS

$$$$ FRENCH — 🍴 **Eiffel Tower Restaurant.** The must-do restaurant of Paris Las Vegas is a room with a view, all right—it's about a third of the way up the hotel's half-scale Eiffel Tower replica, with views from all four glassed-in sides (request a Strip view when booking for the biggest wow factor—it overlooks the fountains at Bellagio, across the street). But patrons are often pleasantly surprised that the food here measures up to the setting. The French-accented menu usually includes appetizers of roasted foie gras with marinated grapes and Julianne crepes. On the entrée list, you might find Atlantic salmon in pinot noir sauce, sautéed semi-boneless quail, roasted rack of lamb Provençale, and filet mignon topped with porcini butter. [$] *Average main: $59* ✉ *Paris Las Vegas, 3655 Las Vegas Blvd. S* ☎ *702/948–6937* 🌐 *www.eiffeltowerrestaurant.com* ✍ *Reservations essential.*

$$$
FRENCH

✕ **Mon Ami Gabi.** This French bistro and steak house that first earned acclaim in Chicago has become much beloved here in Vegas. It's the rare restaurant with sidewalk dining on the Strip—though renovations in early 2011 partially blocked views of Bellagio and CityCenter. For those who prefer a lower traffic environment, a glassed-in conservatory just off the street conveys an outdoor feel, and

WORD OF MOUTH

"If you get a good table with view of the Bellagio Fountains—Mon Ami Gabi across the street at Paris is hard to beat—and for an appertif or post dinner treat. They also used to have a nice piano bar in the hallway toward the buffet."
—Tomsd

still-quieter dining rooms are inside, adorned with chandeliers dramatically suspended three stories above. The specialty of the house is steak frites, offered four ways: classic, au poivre, bordelaise, and Roquefort. The skate with garlic fries and caper-lemon butter is also excellent, and the prices are, on the whole, quite reasonable for first-rate French fare on the Strip. ■ TIP→ This place is a favorite for Sunday brunch. [$] *Average main: $39* ⊠ *Paris Las Vegas, 3655 Las Vegas Blvd. S* ☎ *702/944–4224* ⊕ *www.monamigabi.com.*

PLANET HOLLYWOOD RESORT & CASINO

$$$$
ASIAN
Fodor'sChoice
★

✕ **KOI Las Vegas.** KOI has garnered a reputation as a see-and-be-seen restaurant in New York, Bangkok, Los Angeles, and Vegas. The cavernous 220-seat eatery continues to attract A- and B-list celebrities who line up for sublime Asian-fusion fare that might include baked lobster roll with creamy sauce, yellowtail carpaccio with soy-citrus and truffle essence, and Kobe-beef filet mignon. The main dining room can get noisy, so request a table along the back wall. After dinner, hit the swanky lounge to order a cosmo or martini, then head for the open-air patio to enjoy the Bellagio fountains across the street. [$] *Average main: $49* ⊠ *Planet Hollywood Resort & Casino, 3667 Las Vegas Blvd. S* ☎ *702/454–4555* ⊕ *www.planethollywoodresort.com.*

NORTH STRIP

ENCORE LAS VEGAS

$$$$
STEAKHOUSE

✕ **Botero.** Soaring white columns, white napery, and a handful of Botero sculptures convey a sense of luxury inside this ultramodern steak house. This vibe is matched by Chef Mark LoRusso's contemporary preparations of chops and seafood. Enticing starters might include crispy frogs' legs with Meyer lemon butter and fennel salad, or a sampling of crudo that includes hamachi cured in tangerine juice. Old-style classics like chateaubriand for two compete among the entrées with other options that might include such rarefied dishes as olive oil–poached halibut with crab Brandade, and Japanese Kobe beef topped with Hudson foie gras. Sides run the gamut from playful (tater tots or vanilla-scented yams with marshmallows) to sublime (roasted bone marrow with onion jam). For dessert consider Valrhona chocolate soufflé with a dollop of coffee-flavored crème anglaise. [$] *Average main: $89* ⊠ *Encore Las*

CLOSE UP

Dining Rooms with a View

Bombastic, curious, and gaudy, the Las Vegas Strip has one of the most dramatic and recognizable skylines in the world. One memorable way to take in the incredible views is to dine at one of the city's sky-scraping restaurants. Keep in mind that the best views are often had from settings off the Strip, rather than right in the middle of it. You'll probably need to make a reservation early at these literally high-profile dining rooms.

Alizé. A fine French restaurant set high atop the Palms Casino, Alizé lies far enough west of the Strip to offer amazing views of the skyline. André Rochat, of André's Las Vegas fame, runs this remarkable (yet in-need-of-a-makeover) eatery. [$] *Average main: $59* ✉ *The Palms, 4321 W. Flamingo Rd., West Side* ☎ *702/951–7000* 🌐 *www.palms.com/dining* ✍ *Reservations essential.*

Eiffel Tower Restaurant. Sheer height isn't everything. This restaurant atop a half-scale replica of the Eiffel Tower rises 11 stories—nothing special in this town. But this beautifully decorated dining room with its glassed-in walls sits in the middle of the Strip, offering great views of Bellagio, Caesars Palace, CityCenter, and several other landmarks. [$] *Average main: $59* ✉ *Paris Las Vegas, 3655 Las Vegas Blvd. S, Center Strip* ☎ *702/948–6937* 🌐 *www.eiffeltowerrestaurant.com* ✍ *Reservations essential.*

MIX. You can enjoy the remarkable contemporary French cuisine of world-renowned chef Alain Ducasse in this ultrahip restaurant on the 64th floor of THEhotel at Mandalay Bay. The floor-to-ceiling windows afford unobstructed views all the way up the Strip. [$] *Average main: $90* ✉ *Mandalay Bay Resort & Casino, 3950 Las Vegas Blvd. S, South Strip* ☎ *702/632–9500* 🌐 *www.mandalaybay.com/dining* ✍ *Reservations essential.*

Top of the World. The name here says it all. The Top of the World serves decent food, but the main attraction is the revolving dining room, which sits some 800 feet above the Strip and offers positively mesmerizing views. [$] *Average main: $69* ✉ *Stratosphere Las Vegas Hotel & Casino, 2000 Las Vegas Blvd. S, North Strip* ☎ *702/380–7777* 🌐 *www.topoftheworldlv.com* ✍ *Reservations essential.*

5

Vegas, 3131 Las Vegas Blvd. S ☎ *702/248–3463* 🌐 *www.wynnlasvegas.com* ✍ *Reservations essential* 🕒 *No lunch.*

$$$$ ITALIAN 🍴 **Sinatra.** The swish Encore resort aims to recall the pure panache of Vegas through the years—and what better way to accomplish this than to dedicate one of the hotel's top dining venues to Ol' Blue Eyes? Framed photos of Sinatra (as well as his Academy Award for *From Here to Eternity*) adorn the ivory-and-ruby-hued dining room with a mix of banquettes and high-back chairs set beneath ornate chandeliers. Chef Theo Schoenegger, formerly of L.A.'s celebrated Patina, turns out simple, elegantly presented Italian cuisine. Menu items might include pappardelle tossed with shrimp, scallops, lobster, and clams, or a delectable bone-in rib eye served with eggplant parmigiana, cherry tomatoes, capers, and basil. Have a cocktail in the hip bar adorned

with sparkly antiques; it's a perfect spot to enjoy an after-dinner limoncello or grappa. [$] *Average main: $75* ✉ *Encore Las Vegas, 3131 Las Vegas Blvd. S* ☎ *702/248–3463* 🌐 *www.wynnlasvegas.com/Restaurants* ✍ *Reservations essential* ⏲ *No lunch.*

$$$ CAFÉ 🍴 **Society Cafe.** Whimsy is always available at this imaginative and hip eatery off Encore's main casino. The hostess stand offers departing patrons Swedish fish instead of mints. What's more, with menu items such as frosted-flake French toast, steak-and-egg sliders, and mac-and-cheese "bites," there are surprises at every meal. Sweet-tooths delight in the face-size "XL Sticky Bun" (you'll need a to-go box for this one, trust us). Chef Kim Canteenwalla also prepares a mean Philly cheese steak. Brunch here is big, with five takes on the traditional Bloody Mary (served from a roving cart, natch). Perhaps the restaurant's biggest draw is its late-night "Munchi" menu, available on Friday and Saturday until 1 am. [$] *Average main: $39* ✉ *Encore Las Vegas, 3131 S. Las Vegas Blvd.* ☎ *702/248–3463* 🌐 *www.wynnlasvegas.com/Restaurants.*

THE PALAZZO

$$$$ STEAKHOUSE 🍴 **Carnevino Italian Steakhouse.** The giant bronze steer just inside the front door of Chef Mario Batali's sprawling restaurant attests to the primary offering: beef. Steaks here are dry-aged, grilled until the crust is slightly charred, then carved table-side by knowledgeable, attentive servers. A favorite appetizer is the steak tartare, egg-free and chopped to order. Others include fresh pastas served with everything from guinea hen to Dungeness crab. The fine wines are complimented by an equally impressive list of other spirits, including beers, bourbons, and rums. When the bread arrives, be sure to try the lardo, a savory spread made from pork fat, ginger, allspice, and rosemary. The bar and more casual taverna serve lighter fare daily from noon until midnight. [$] *Average main: $49* ✉ *The Palazzo, 3325 Las Vegas Blvd. S* ☎ *702/789–4141* 🌐 *www.palazzo.com/Las-Vegas-Restaurants* ⏲ *No lunch in main dining room.*

$ BURGER 🍴 **I Love Burgers.** The menu at this cavernous burger joint in The Shoppes at Palazzo is about as straightforward as the name of the place itself; hamburgers, in just about every iteration possible, are a common theme. Chicken, salmon, and vegetarian burgers complement traditional offerings of beef and turkey. Fries are plentiful. Milk shakes are addicting; especially the ones with booze. The restaurant also offers a multitude of domestic, imported, and artisan beers. [$] *Average main: $15* ✉ *The Palazzo, 3325 Las Vegas Blvd. S* ☎ *702/242–2747* 🌐 *www.iloveburgers.com.*

$$$$ MEDITERRANEAN 🍴 **Lavo.** Food at this Moroccan-furnished restaurant/nightclub superplex is top-notch but it often plays second fiddle to the thump-thump from techno music from the dance party upstairs (our advice: Go early to avoid this cacophony). Many dishes are meant to be shared and might include delights such as tuna tartare, veal Milanese, and a lobster scampi pizza. Entrees might feature grilled tuna with roasted artichokes or rack veal chop. For dessert, try a dessert cocktail (we like the Noce with Nocello walnut liqueur) or the Oreo zeppoles served with a malted vanilla milk shake. Chase it all with a cocktail at the hopping lounge. [$] *Average main: $59* ✉ *The Palazzo, 3325 Las Vegas*

Blvd. S ☎ *702/791–1800* 🌐 *www.palazzo.com/Las-Vegas-Restaurants* ⏲ *No lunch.*

$$$ FRENCH 🍴 **Morels French Steakhouse & Bistro.** Relaxed, dapper, and spacious with panoramic views of the Strip and outdoor seating, Morels is Palazzo's upscale yet unfussy all-day dining option. Its specialty is both traditional Parisian-inspired bistro fare and fine steak-house victuals. Except for a couple of ultrapricey wagyu beef dishes, most of the food here is affordable by Strip standards. Our favorites: dishes such as crispy-skin Scottish salmon, chicken Paillard, and cheese fondue with crisp baguettes for dipping. Wine is a big part of the Morels experience, too; more than 60 wines by the glass are available, and the wine list has garnered high praise. Grazers also can choose from a huge selection of raw-bar, artisanal cheese, and cured meat items. [$] *Average main: $39* ✉ *The Palazzo, 3325 Las Vegas Blvd. S* ☎ *702/607–6333* 🌐 *www.palazzo.com/Las-Vegas-Restaurants.*

$$$ ASIAN 🍴 **SUSHISAMBA.** If you're not a lover of sushi, don't despair—there's much more on offer than just raw fish. The eclectic menu is the result of the owner's regular visits to São Paulo, Brazil, and Lima, Peru, both of which have large Japanese communities. The fusion is surprising yet delicious, and guests are encouraged to try a variety of smaller dishes, such miso-marinated Chilean sea bass and seared Kobe beef. There are sushi, hot dishes, and robata, which is basically a Japanese grill. If all these choices prove too daunting, then order the "Omakase," an ever-changing seven-course meal fusing the various cuisines. The decor (heavy on orange, red, and black), the video walls, and the hip music cater to a younger crowd. That also explains why the restaurant is open until 1 or 2 am daily. [$] *Average main: $39* ✉ *The Palazzo, 3325 Las Vegas Blvd. S* ☎ *702/607–0700* 🌐 *www.palazzo.com/Las-Vegas-Restaurants.*

5

STRATOSPHERE LAS VEGAS HOTEL & CASINO

$$$$ EUROPEAN 🍴 **Top of the World.** This high-in-the-sky eatery lacks the celeb-chef cachet of others on the Strip, but rounded floor-to-ceiling windows give 360-degree views of the Vegas Valley. The entire 106th-floor dining room revolves once every 80 minutes. The fare here is Continental and often has some intriguing, contemporary twists that might include lobster ravioli, Kurobuta pork with an apple-apricot compote, or blackened tuna with pink peppercorn vinaigrette. Still, remember that you're paying primarily for the view—were this restaurant at street level, you probably wouldn't be reading about it in this book. The place also has a stationary cocktail lounge on the 107th floor for casual sipping. [$] *Average main: $69* ✉ *Stratosphere, 2000 Las Vegas Blvd. S* ☎ *702/380–7777* 🌐 *www.topoftheworldlv.com* ✍ *Reservations essential.*

TREASURE ISLAND LAS VEGAS (TI)

$ DELI 🍴 **Canter's Delicatessen.** You'll find this noisy, crowded, but festive version of the 1930s Los Angeles institution next to the race and sports book. A stainless-steel counter and dining tables make for a clean, almost futuristic look. Dive into huge sourdough rye sandwiches packed with corned beef or pastrami, as well as generous sandwiches with other deli meats and cheeses, and their famous barley-bean soup. During big games (or March Madness) in the adjacent book, $20 gets you a bucket of four beers, a basket of chicken wings, and fries. The place is open daily until midnight. [$] *Average main: $12* ✉ *Treasure Island, 3300 Las Vegas Blvd. S* ☎ *702/894–7111* 🌐 *www.treasureisland.com/restaurants* ✍ *Reservations not accepted.*

$$$ MEXICAN 🍴 **Isla Mexican Kitchen & Tequila Bar.** The spotlight's on tequila at this loud (close to the slots), brashly decorated, nouveau-Mexican place. Especially during Happy Hour, a circulating Tequila Goddess (the first such expert in Vegas, mind you) teaches you all the specifics of the liquor and offers recommendations on tequila-based specialty drinks (there are more than 100 tequilas here). But before you start on the latest and greatest margarita, place your order and try dishes such as pulled-pork tamales or Mexican meatballs with chipotle tomato sauce. The guacamole is prepared table-side on a roving cart. [$] *Average main: $35* ✉ *Treasure Island, 3300 Las Vegas Blvd. S* ☎ *866/286–3809* 🌐 *www.treasureisland.com/restaurants* 🕒 *No lunch.*

THE VENETIAN

$$$$ ITALIAN 🍴 **B&B Ristorante.** Ubiquitous food personality Mario Batali and his trusty wine pro Joe Bastianich are the owners of this surprisingly unflashy, inviting (and grossly underappreciated) tribute to the simple foods of the Italian countryside. Along the Venetian's "restaurant row," B&B glows from within its dark-wood and leather confines. You can easily make a meal of several antipasti; choices such as winter root carpaccio with ricotta and hazelnuts, or warm lamb's tongue with chanterelles and a fried egg. Top entrées might include fennel-dusted sweetbreads with sweet-and-sour onions, and quail with Kabocha squash and chestnuts. ■ **TIP→ Batali and Bastianich also run the less expensive Otto Enoteca Pizzeria in Venetian's Grand Canal Shoppes (specifically, on St. Mark's Square),** where you can nosh on toothsome antipasti, pizza, cured meats, and artisanal cheeses while sipping on imported Italian wines. [$] *Average main: $59* ✉ *The Venetian, 3355 Las Vegas Blvd. S* ☎ *702/266–9977* 🌐 *www.venetian.com/Las-Vegas-Restaurants* 🕒 *No lunch.*

$$$ FRENCH 🍴 **Bouchon.** Ask many chefs to name their idol, and more than a few will cite French Laundry chef Thomas Keller, the star behind this stunning, capacious French bistro and oyster bar in the Venezia Tower. Soaring Palladian windows, antique lighting, and painted tile lend a sophisticated take on French country design, but the service and overall quality don't always match up to the standards you'd expect. Menu options include classics such as steak frites, mussels with white wine, and an extensive raw bar. Finish with profiteroles, a lemon tart, or crème caramel. Bouchon does turn out a memorable breakfast, where you might try bread pudding–style French toast or a smoked-salmon baguette. [$] *Average main: $39* ✉ *The Venetian, 3355 Las Vegas Blvd. S* ☎ *702/414–6200* 🌐 *www.venetian.com/Las-Vegas-Restaurants.*

$ AMERICAN 🍴 **Grand Lux Cafe.** This 24-hour chain operation at the Venetian (and the Palazzo) is part of the Cheesecake Factory empire. Attractive, expansive, and decked out in bright colors, Grand Lux presents an extensive menu of familiar crowd-pleasers—Asian nachos, Thai chicken pizzas, Jamaican pork tenderloin, skirt steak topped with Mexican ranchero sauce. For dessert, leave room for the molten-chocolate cake, and, of course, the restaurant's signature cheesecake. Neither the food nor the atmosphere here earns raves, but the "Lux" is a perfectly reliable option for a budget-friendly meal. Another benefit: It's right off the main casino floor. $ *Average main: $19* ⊠ *The Venetian, 3355 Las Vegas Blvd. S* ☎ *702/414–3888* ⊕ *www.venetian.com/Las-Vegas-Restaurants.*

$$$

ASIAN

✕ **TAO.** Yet another of the Strip's see-and-be-seen nightclubs that's sometimes overlooked as a dining option, Tao offers all the panache of the Manhattan original with a dark and seductive dining room filled with candles and Buddha statues (including one that's 20 feet tall and seated above a carp-filled pool). The expertly prepared Asian fare includes sushi and sashimi (consider the spicy lobster roll with shiso and black caviar) and might include items such as braised spicy shrimp with chive flowers, corn-and-crab soup, miso-glazed Chilean sea bass with wok vegetables, and wasabi-crusted filet mignon with tempura of onion rings. Stick around after your meal for cocktails, dancing, and celebrity-spotting. $ *Average main: $39* ⊠ *The Venetian, 3355 Las Vegas Blvd. S* ☎ *702/388–8338* ⊕ *www.venetian.com/Las-Vegas-Restaurants.*

$$$$

ITALIAN

✕ **Valentino.** This elegant contemporary Italian eatery on the Venetian's busy "restaurant row" serves the complex, rather rich cuisine of Executive Chef Luciano Pellegrini. Choose either appetizer or entrée portions of pasta, which might include stuffed calamari gratin with marinara sauce or tricolor gnocchi with rabbit sausage and wild mushrooms. Among the main dishes, options can range from broiled fillet of fluke served over white asparagus with a black truffle–olive oil emulsion to buffalo medallions grilled alongside pickled cippollini onions. For lunch, try smaller and lighter portions in The Grill. The wine list that serves both dining rooms has an astounding 2,400 options. $ *Average main: $59* ⊠ *The Venetian, 3355 Las Vegas Blvd. S* ☎ *702/414–3000* ⊕ *www.venetian.com/Las-Vegas-Restaurants* ⚑ *Reservations essential.*

WYNN LAS VEGAS

$$$$

SEAFOOD

✕ **Bartolotta.** Arguably the most romantic choice among the Wynn's many restaurants, Bartolotta specializes in Italian seafood. Set along the resort's chic shopping promenade, it has a curved bar on the upper level, from which a staircase leads down to a dining room and (mostly covered) patio. Chef Paul Bartolotta (a James Beard–award winner) has fish such as sea bream and pink snapper flown in thrice-weekly from the best markets in Europe. The menu changes nightly but could include options such as charcoal-grilled cuttlefish and sautéed Mediterranean turbot in a white wine broth with leeks and clams. There are superb non-seafood entrées, too. $ *Average main: $85* ⊠ *Wynn Las Vegas, 3131 Las Vegas Blvd. S* ☎ *702/248–3463* ⊕ *www.wynnlasvegas.com/Restaurants* ⊘ *No lunch.*

$$$

MEDITERRANEAN

✕ **La Cave.** If you're looking for an intimate meal, this quiet and modest restaurant is the place. Opened in conjunction with restaurant impresario Michael Morton, La Cave is an entirely different concept for Steve Wynn. Instead of large, over-the-top meals, the eatery focuses on wine and Mediterranean-inspired tapas-style dishes. The menu splits the offerings by type of cuisine: From the Sea, Farm, Oven, Garden, Grill, Butcher, and so on. Flatbreads such as ham, egg and cheese with quail eggs, are ideal for sharing, while vegetable dishes including salt-roasted

CLOSE UP

Cheap and Sweet

Looking for a quick sweet-fix that won't break the bank? Check out these two options:

Ethel's Chocolate Lounge. Inside the Fashion Show Mall, as well as other locations around town, this home-grown purveyor of top-notch chocolates serves exquisite hot cocoa, espresso drinks, fine-crafted chocolate bars, and other sweets in a cushy café with comfy sofas. $ *Average main: $6* ✉ *Fashion Show Mall, 3200 Las Vegas Blvd. S, North Strip* ☎ *702/796–6662.*

Luv-it Frozen Custard. Pull up to this tiny take-out stand at the north end of the Strip, on the edge of Downtown, to sample unbelievably delicious, velvety smooth frozen custard. The flavors change daily, and sundaes are a popular offering—try the "Jimmies Scotch Treat," with butterscotch sauce, jimmies, sliced bananas, and a maraschino cherry. It's been goin' strong since 1973, and is open until 11 pm on weekends. $ *Average main: $6* ✉ *505 E. Oakey Blvd., North Strip* ☎ *702/384–6452.*

---

beets with whipped goat cheese and pistachio satisfy those with dietary restrictions. The wine list reflects global selections, with an emphasis on Europe. $ *Average main: $36* ✉ *Wynn Las Vegas, 3131 Las Vegas Blvd. S.* ☎ *702/770–7100, 877/321–9966* ⊕ *www.wynnlasvegas.com/ Restaurants.*

$$$
ITALIAN
✕ **Stratta.** In this intimate space with red leather chairs, a wood-burning hearth oven, an open kitchen, and a long, swanky bar, fans of Italian cooking encounter a menu that mixes the traditional with the innovative. The list of chilled and hot appetizers usually includes clams casino and fried artichoke hearts with lemon-parsley aioli. On the dinner menu, options might comprise striped bass with roasted orange fennel and confit tomato; cavatelli with spicy ground sausage; and veal piccata. This is one of the few upscale Wynn restaurants that won't cost you a king's ransom. What's more, with the 2011 closure of Chef Alex Stratta's eponymous eatery, Alex, this is now the culinary superstar's only toehold in the Vegas scene. $ *Average main: $39* ✉ *Wynn Las Vegas, 3131 Las Vegas Blvd. S* ☎ *702/248–3463* ⊕ *www.wynnlasvegas. com/Restaurants* ☽ *No lunch.*

$$$$
AMERICAN
✕ **Tableau.** Cloistered away from the busier parts of the Wynn, this restaurant overlooks a serene pool and garden off the gleaming Tower Suites lobby. A highlight is the fabulous weekend brunch, where you might try Maine lobster salad with baby beets and winter citrus, or blueberry-buttermilk pancakes. Breakfast is also served daily; all guests leave with a bag of homemade trail mix. For lunch, try items such as the Dungeness crab club sandwich with smoked bacon or the pan-roasted halibut with peas, morel mushrooms, fava beans, and gnocchi. The restaurant is closed for dinner. $ *Average main: $49* ✉ *Wynn Las Vegas, 3131 Las Vegas Blvd. S* ☎ *702/248–3463* ⊕ *www.wynnlasvegas.com/ Restaurants* ⌕ *Reservations essential* ☽ *No dinner.*

$$$$
CHINESE
✕ **Wing Lei.** With all the panache of an Asian royal palace this restaurant serves some of the best Chinese food on the Strip. Chefs present contemporary French-inspired Chinese cuisine that blends the Cantonese,

Shanghai, and Szechuan traditions. The decadent five-course Peking duck dinner for two is one of the restaurant's true showstoppers, but don't overlook options that could include kung pao chicken, crisp prawns with walnuts and a honey-peach sauce, or orange beef with ginger, scallion, bok choy, and a tangerine-peel sauce. Whatever you do, be sure to order a side of the tantalizing abalone fried rice. $ *Average main: $59 ⊠ Wynn Las Vegas, 3131 Las Vegas Blvd. S ☎ 702/248–3463 ⊕ www.wynnlasvegas.com/Restaurants.*

DOWNTOWN

$ ✕**Doña Maria.** You'll forget you're in Las Vegas after a few minutes in
MEXICAN this relaxed and unpretentious (read: no-frills) Downtown cantina with two locations in the area. Stop in at either one on a Wednesday night and you might see a crowd gathered for the *fútbol* game on satellite-provided Mexican TV. All of the combinations and specials are good, but the best play here is to order tamales; in particular, the enchilada-style tamale (with red or green sauce), for which Doña Maria is justly renowned. You also won't go wrong with the *queso fundido con chorizo* (melted cheese with sausage). $ *Average main: $15 ⊠ 910 Las Vegas Blvd. S ☎ 702/382–6538 ⊕ www.donamariatamales.com.*

$$$ ✕**Golden Steer.** In a town where restaurants come and go almost as
STEAKHOUSE quickly as visitors' cash, the longevity of this steak house, opened in 1958, is itself a recommendation. Both locals and visitors adore this San Francisco–theme restaurant with red-leather chairs, polished dark wood, and stained-glass windows for the huge slabs of well-prepared meat. Steak, ribs, blackened swordfish, and Italian classics such as veal marsala and chicken parmigiana are particularly popular. Although you wouldn't know it from the outside, the Steer is cavernous. Lots of small, intimate rooms, however, break up the space. $ *Average main: $39 ⊠ 308 W. Sahara Ave. ☎ 702/384–4470 ⊕ goldensteersteakhouse-lasvegas.com/ ⊘ No lunch.*

$$$ ✕**Triple George Grill.** You won't find too much in the way of nouvelle
AMERICAN flourishes or ultramod decor at this old-school Downtown tavern, and that's just how locals prefer it—the elegant dining room is a favorite haunt for power-lunching and hobnobbing. The Triple George is known for its commendably prepared traditional American fare such as oysters Rockefeller, classic "wedge" salad, and country-fried steaks. Seafood and chops dominate the fancier parts of the menu, from shellfish cioppino and traditional fish-and-chips to osso buco–style beef short ribs and a hefty pan-seared porcini-crusted rib eye. $ *Average main: $32 ⊠ 201 N. 3rd St. ☎ 702/384–2761 ⊕ www.triplegeorgegrill.com ⊘ Closed Sun. No lunch Sat.*

PARADISE ROAD

HARD ROCK HOTEL & CASINO

$$$$ ✕**35 Steaks + Martinis.** The key number at this always-buzzing hot spot
STEAKHOUSE is 35. All steaks are aged for at least 35 days, and the signature dish, the Tomahawk, is a 35-day-aged, 35-ounce prime steak. The menu

CHEAP EATS

Don't forget about Sin City's terrific hole-in-the-wall dives, inexpensive regional chains, and cheap-and-cheerful take-out counters that serve tasty treats at rock-bottom prices.

Blueberry Hill. This local mini-chain feels a bit like Denny's but serves far superior food, including hearty Mexican specialties, fruit-topped pancakes and waffles, and a number of "diet delight"–type platters. Blueberry Hill has seven locales within a short drive of the Strip (some are open 24 hours). $ *Average main: $15* ✉ *1505 E. Flamingo Rd., University District* ☎ *702/696–9666.*

Espressamente Illy. The first U.S. branch of the famed Italian coffee purveyor opened, appropriately, in the swank Palazzo in 2008. Since then, fans of java have gone abuzz over the café's richly brewed lattes and cappuccinos, plus panini sandwiches and heavenly baked goods. There are also more than 50 flavors of seriously good gelato. $ *Average main: $9* ✉ *The Palazzo, 3325 Las Vegas Blvd. S, North Strip* ☎ *702/869–2233* ⊕ *www.palazzo.com/Las-Vegas-Restaurants.*

Fatburger. Billing itself immodestly "the Last Great Hamburger Stand," this fast-food joint across from Monte Carlo (with about a dozen locales elsewhere around town) cooks up toothsome charbroiled burgers, hefty chili dogs, and crispy "fat fries." The Strip location is open 24 hours. $ *Average main: $9* ✉ *3763 Las Vegas Blvd. S, South Strip* ☎ *702/736–4733.*

In-N-Out. The simple menu of fresh burgers, just-cut fries, and milk shakes makes this affordable West Coast fast-food joint a cult fave. If you're extra hungry (and we mean seriously so), go "off menu" and order a "4x4" (four beef patties with four slices of American cheese on a freshly baked bun). $ *Average main: $7* ✉ *4888 Dean Martin Dr., West Side* ☎ *800/786–1000.*

Jason's Deli. Soups, sandwiches—including hero-style muffuletas and po'boys—and salads star on Jason's extensive menu, which focuses on healthful and often organic ingredients. Devotees swear by the "Ciabatta Bing": oven-roasted turkey, roasted tomatoes, purple onions, guacamole, Swiss cheese, and field greens on a ciabatta roll. $ *Average main: $9* ✉ *3910 S. Maryland Pkwy., University District* ☎ *702/893–9799.*

L&L Hawaiian Barbecue. This growing chain of zero-ambience fast-food eateries serves authentic Hawaiian-style barbecue (to the sounds of cheesy piped-in Hawaiian tunes). The plate lunch is the draw here; it comes in many permutations, but always includes macaroni salad and rice. $ *Average main: $7* ✉ *4030 S. Maryland Pkwy., University District* ☎ *702/880–9898.*

includes a bevy of openers such as oysters, crab cake, and surf-and-turf skewers with both béarnaise and bordelaise for dipping. Further along in the meal you might opt for a salmon or organic chicken. Steaks, of course, reign supreme, and you can add lobster tails or shimp to any order. Drinks here are exquisite, and include flavor-infused martinis and a stellar wine list (dubbed "Wines that Rock"). For dessert, try "Buzzed," a coffee-themed concoction with coffee custard, coffee

CLOSE UP

Downtown Dining of Note

Even back during its heyday as the city's casino-gaming hot spot, Downtown was never much of a haven for gourmands. As the Strip and other parts of the city have become renowned for fantastic dining, Downtown's culinary reputation has steadily declined to the point that few set foot in any of the neighborhood's casinos solely in search of a good meal. That being said, if you happen to be staying, playing, or wandering Downtown, you will find a handful of worthwhile restaurants turning out perfectly fine meals. Just don't venture this way with the same expectations you would of the dining scene on the Strip. Here are a few dining options at Downtown casinos of particular note:

Carson Street Cafe. Open 24/7 and serving tasty regional American fare, with particularly good breakfasts, this reliable and expansive option at the Golden Nugget has plenty of adherents. [$] *Average main: $15* ✉ *Golden Nugget Hotel & Casino, 129 E. Fremont St.* ☎ *702/385–7111* 🌐 *www.goldennugget.com/dining.*

Hugo's Cellar. Every woman receives a red rose at this romantic, old-school institution inside the Four Queens Casino that's been popular with Vegas locals since it opened in 1976. [$] *Average main: $36* ✉ *Four Queens Hotel and Casino, 202 Fremont St.* ☎ *702/385–4011* 🌐 *www.hugoscellar.com.*

Lillie's Asian Cuisine. This longtime Golden Nugget favorite draws crowds thanks to its excellent, reasonably priced Chinese food and late hours. The Cantonese dishes might include old familiars such as moo goo gai pan, plus spicier choices such as Szechuan shrimp. [$] *Average main: $18* ✉ *Golden Nugget Hotel & Casino, 129 E. Fremont St.* ☎ *702/386–8131* 🌐 *www.goldennugget.com/lasvegas.*

Second Street Grill. Daily specials at this Pacific Rim–inspired seafood restaurant inside the Fremont Casino are flown in daily from Hawaii. The art deco–style dining room is dark and intimate, with oversize chairs and elegant wood paneling. [$] *Average main: $19* ✉ *Fremont Hotel and Casino, 200 E. Fremont St.* ☎ *702/385–3232* 🌐 *www.fremontcasino.com/dine.*

gelato, and coffee cream. [$] *Average main: $69* ✉ *Hard Rock Hotel & Casino, 4455 Paradise Rd.* ☎ *702/693–5585* 🌐 *www.hardrockhotel.com/las-vegas-restaurants* 🕒 *No lunch.*

$ ECLECTIC 🍴 **Mr. Lucky's.** The hippest casino coffee shop in Las Vegas is still inside the Hard Rock Hotel, overlooking the main gaming area. Light-wood floors and vintage rock-and-roll posters highlight this bubbly, circular café. You can have a vegetable omelet, pizza, burger, or pasta; more filling options include grilled salmon, teriyaki chicken bowls, and baby back ribs. Food from the on-site noodle bar is irresistible. Also, the garlic mashed potatoes are superb. This place is open 24/7. [$] *Average main: $19* ✉ *Hard Rock Hotel & Casino, 4455 Paradise Rd.* ☎ *702/693–5000* 🌐 *www.hardrockhotel.com/las-vegas-restaurants.*

$$$$ JAPANESE 🍴 **Nobu.** Executive Chef Nobu Matsuhisa has replicated the decor and menu of his Manhattan Nobu in this slick restaurant with bamboo

5

pillars, a seaweed wall, and birch trees. Dishes might include spicy Kumamoto oyster sashimi, monkfish pâté with caviar, sea-urchin tempura, and Maine lobster with wasabi-pepper sauce. The menu comprises small or moderate-size plates, making Nobu perfect for sharing, but an easy place to drop a wad of cash (as all those artful food presentations add up). For dessert there's usually a terrific coffee-vanilla panna cotta with cashew brittle, candied orange zest, and an orange-champagne granita. $ *Average main: $49* ⊠ *Hard Rock Hotel & Casino, 4455 Paradise Rd.* ☎ *702/693–5000* ⊕ *www.hardrockhotel.com/las-vegas-restaurants* ⊘ *No lunch.*

$$
MEXICAN

╳**Pink Taco.** Nothing inside the Hard Rock Hotel is boring, and that goes for this over-the-top take on a Mexican cantina, which evokes a playful, even rollicking, vibe. The Tex-Mex food takes a decided backseat to the party scene, which includes a huge four-sided bar, patio doors that open onto the hotel's elaborate pool area, and waitresses in low-cut tops. Still, the grub is good. Fill up on shredded pork tacos, chiles rellenos, slow-roasted pork carnitas, and baby back ribs with tamarind-chipotle sauce. Come during happy hour (weekdays from 4 to 7 at the bar) for half-price appetizers and two-for-one beers and margaritas; there also are late-night food specials after 10. $ *Average main: $22* ⊠ *Hard Rock Hotel & Casino, 4455 Paradise Rd.* ☎ *702/693–5000* ⊕ *www.hardrockhotel.com/las-vegas-restaurants.*

RENAISSANCE LAS VEGAS

$$$
STEAKHOUSE

╳**ENVY Steakhouse.** A hip restaurant at the Rat Pack–inspired Renaissance Las Vegas, ENVY offers an update of the steak-house concept. The glamorous contemporary dining room is bathed in jewel tones, and the young and knowledgeable staff is quick to explain the creative cuisine, or suggest wines from the 1,500-bottle repertoire. Among the sides, consider a bowl of the irresistible potatoes, which you can order mashed with any number of add-ins from lobster to truffles. Pair this with tremendous entrées such as bone-in New York steak, Colorado lamb chops, or red curry-seared ahi tuna. Lunch and breakfast are served, too. $ *Average main: $39* ⊠ *Renaissance Las Vegas, 3400 Paradise Rd.* ☎ *702/784–5716* ⊕ *www.envysteakhouse.com.*

NONCASINO RESTAURANTS

$$
MEDITERRANEAN

╳**Firefly Tapas Kitchen.** A dapper, hip bistro opened by a pair of Mon Ami Gabi alumni, the original Firefly occupies the same shopping center as the popular Paradise Road favorites Marrakech and Yolie's. As the name suggests, the kitchen focuses on Spanish and Mediterranean small plates, none of which cost more than $10. Order a few, and you've got a meal. On any given day, options might include ham-and-cheese croquettes, meatballs in a sherry-tomato sauce, marinated and grilled octopus, and shrimp in lemon-garlic-butter sauce. There are usually a few heartier entrées, such as a rib-eye steak or paella, offered as well. For dessert, order the rich chocolate-and-cherry bread pudding with a port wine reduction. Dine in the colorful and compact dining room or outside on the cheerful patio. Two other locations exist around town. $ *Average main: $29* ⊠ *3900 Paradise Rd.* ☎ *702/369–3971* ⊕ *www.fireflylv.com.*

$ GERMAN 🍴 **Hofbräuhaus Las Vegas.** Enjoy a heavy dose of kitsch at this gargantuan offshoot of Munich's most famous brewery. The interior beer garden is the perfect spot to down a brew in those notorious liter mugs, especially on too-hot Vegas evenings. Pair your beer with hearty Bavarian classics, including Bavarian potato soup with sausage, Wiener schnitzel, goulash, and *Schweinebraten,* or updated dishes such as Caesar salad with pretzel croutons. For dessert, try apple strudel or Black Forest chocolate cake. They've covered the oompah here, too: bands brought in from Germany keep things as lively as they are back in Munich. [$] *Average main: $19* ✉ *4510 Paradise Rd.* ☎ *702/853–2337* 🌐 *www.hofbrauhauslasvegas.com.*

$ INDIAN 🍴 **India Oven.** You have to brave a neighborhood of illicit-looking 24-hour "massage" parlors to find this remarkably natty restaurant that serves surprisingly good food. It's in a shopping center north of the former Sahara Casino, and the space is filled with imported antiquities. Tandoori meats and naan bread are prepared in the tandoor (oven), and other specialties include lamb korma with cashews, almonds, and raisins, as well as Goa-style fish curry with an aromatic coconut sauce. For dessert, try the homemade kulfi, also known as pistachio ice cream. [$] *Average main: $19* ✉ *2218 Paradise Rd.* ☎ *702/366–0222* 🌐 *www.indiaovenlasvegas.com.*

$$$ MOROCCAN 🍴 **Marrakech.** Sprawl out on soft floor cushions and feel like a pampered pasha as belly dancers shake it up in a cozy Middle Eastern–style "tent" with a fabric-covered ceiling and eye-catching mosaics. The $39.95 prix-fixe feast is a six-course affair that you eat with your hands; it usually includes Moroccan-spiced shrimp scampi, vegetable salad, lentil soup, Cornish game hen, lamb shish kebab, and the tasty dessert *B'stilla,* which is baked phyllo dough layered with apples, peaches, and pecans. Algerian wines flow freely in this upbeat spot where servers wear Moroccan robes and patrons are invited to join the belly dancers if they feel the urge. [$] *Average main: $40* ✉ *3900 Paradise Rd.* ☎ *702/737–5611* 🌐 *www.marrakechvegas.com* ⏲ *No lunch.*

$$$ HAWAIIAN 🍴 **Roy's.** A popular import from Hawaii, Roy's is plush without feeling pretentious or overdone—a good bet for a relaxed, elegant meal. You enter the restaurant along a torch-lighted lane, and a highly professional, friendly staff works the bustling dining room. Executive Chef Roy Yamaguchi has become synonymous with creative Hawaiian fusion fare, such as the "Maui Wowie" shrimp salad with avocado, capers, sweet onions, and feta cheese. There's a full sushi bar, as well. The food bar overlooking the action in the kitchen is perfect for those dining alone. On Monday nights in winter, try the three-course price-fixe meal for $35.95. [$] *Average main: $36* ✉ *620 E. Flamingo Rd.* ☎ *702/691–2053* 🌐 *www.roysrestaurant.com* ⏲ *No lunch.*

$$$ ECLECTIC 🍴 **Table 34.** Run by Laurie Kendrick and Stan Carroll, two highly respected Vegas chefs who trained under Wolfgang Puck, this intimate, modern restaurant with clean lines, blond-wood floors, and high ceilings looks like something you'd find in California wine country. Especially good among the reasonably priced, outstanding bistro creations are the fresh pastas and thin-crust pizzas (try the one topped with prosciutto, figs, and blue cheese). Entrees such as herb-roasted chicken with

5

apple-sage dressing and all-beef meat loaf with mashed potatoes and onion gravy each score high marks. An impressive wine list has nearly 100 selections. Note: the restaurant sits just south of where Paradise Road intersects with Interstate 215 (south of the airport), and the constant planes overhead contribute a bit of unpleasant noise. [$] *Average main: $39* ✉ *600 E. Warm Springs Rd.* ☎ *702/263–0034* 🕒 *Closed Sun. No lunch Sat. No dinner Tues.*

EAST SIDE AND UNIVERSITY DISTRICT

$ BRITISH 🍴 **Crown & Anchor British Pub.** With 24-hour service and graveyard specials, Crown & Anchor is uniquely Las Vegas (and a favorite haunt of students from nearby UNLV). Most of the food is British, including the steak-and- kidney pie, bangers and mash, and authentic fish-and-chips. Sandwiches with American and British flavors are plenty, and nightly specials make this spot even more of a bargain proposition. There are beers from all over the world and a "shoppe" selling anglophile favorites like Branston pickle. If you still doubt the authenticity, know that the trifle is made with Bird's English custard. The decor and faux-cottage exterior are decidedly British, and special events add to the fun: on New Year's Eve the celebration starts when it's midnight in the United Kingdom, which is 4 pm in Las Vegas. [$] *Average main: $12* ✉ *1350 E. Tropicana Ave., University District* ☎ *702/739–8676* 🌐 *www.crownandanchorlv.com.*

$ MEXICAN 🍴 **Lindo Michoacán.** Javier Barajas, the congenial owner and host of this colorful cantina chain, named it for his home in Mexico. He presents outstanding specialties that he learned to cook while growing up in the culinary capital of Michoacán. Many menu items are named for his relatives, including *flautas Mama Chelo* (corn tortillas filled with chicken). Michoacán is known for its carnitas, so don't miss them. Or try the *cabrito birria de chivo* (roasted goat with red mole sauce). Guacamole is made table-side. Finish with the flan, a silken wonder. Barajas has three other locations around the city, and has had a hand in two other similar restaurants—Bonito Michoacán and Viva Michoacán—on Decatur Boulevard and Sunset Road, respectively. [$] *Average main: $19* ✉ *2655 E. Desert Inn Rd., East Side* ☎ *702/735–6828* 🌐 *www.lindomichoacan.com.*

$$ THAI Fodor's Choice ★ 🍴 **Lotus of Siam.** This simple Thai restaurant has attained near-fanatical cult status, with some critics hailing it the best in North America. What's all the fuss? Consider the starter of marinated prawns, which are wrapped with bacon and rice-paper crepes, then deep-fried and served with a tangy sweet-and-sour sauce. For a main course, try dishes such as charbroiled beef liver mixed with green onion and chili, or the chicken and vegetables with Issan-style red curry. Be warned—this is some of the spiciest food you'll ever try. But another of Lotus's surprises is the phenomenal wine list, on which you might find a vintage to cool your palate. [$] *Average main: $25* ✉ *953 E. Sahara Ave., East Side* ☎ *702/735–3033* 🌐 *www.saipinchutima.com* 🕒 *No lunch weekends.*

$$$ FRENCH 🍴 **Pamplemousse.** The name, which is French for "grapefruit," was chosen on a whim by the late singer—and restaurant regular—Bobby

Where to Eat in Greater Las Vegas

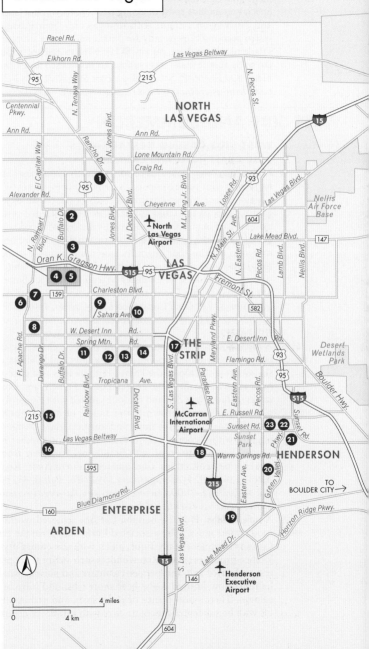

Desert National Wildlife Range

Darin. The dominant color at this old-school restaurant notable for its kitschy pink-glowing sign is burgundy, orchestral music is played over the stereo system, and the food is classic French. There is no printed menu; instead, the waiter recites the daily (and prix fixe) bill of fare. Specialties include roast duckling with cranberry and Chambord sauce and Norwegian salmon with orange-curry beurre blanc. A smaller bistro section is open daily for lunch and serves simpler classics like salade niçoise and coq au vin. ■TIP→ The restaurant is small and popular, so be sure to make reservations far in advance for dinner. $ *Average main: $39* ⊠ *400 E. Sahara Ave., East Side* ☎ *702/733–2066* ⊕ *www.pamplemousserestaurant.com* ⌖ *Reservations essential* ☉ *Closed Mon.*

WEST SIDE AND SUMMERLIN

WEST SIDE CASINO RESTAURANTS
GOLD COAST HOTEL AND CASINO

$

CHINESE

✕ **Ping Pang Pong.** Delicious regional (mostly Cantonese) fare, including marvelous dim sum, compels discerning diners—many who hail from Vegas's large Chinese community—to brave the smoky, low-roller's gaming area of the Gold Coast. This well-regarded restaurant comprises a pair of circular dining rooms decked with red lanterns. Try to get a table in the back of the room to avoid the casino noise, and then tuck into options that might include minced-squab lettuce cups, sautéed lotus root, or julienne fresh abalone with egg white, silver bean sprouts, and chives. The lobster Macau (in a caper-butter sauce) also has plenty of fans. The restaurant is open nightly until 3 am. $ *Average main: $19* ⊠ *Gold Coast Hotel and Casino, 4000 W. Flamingo Rd.* ☎ *702/367–7111* ⊕ *www.goldcoastcasino.com/dine.*

THE PALMS

$$$$

FRENCH

✕ **Alizé.** You may not even notice the priceless china, crystal, and silver in the elegant dining room, given its unbeatable views of the Vegas skyline from the top of the Palms. But you may just become distracted once you sample the artful contemporary French fare. Complex dishes might include New Zealand abalone sautéed with Perigord black truffle, parsnip puree, and brown butter sauce; or a crispy pork belly with Bartlett pear puree, pine nuts, and mustard glaze. Pepper-crusted filet mignon with a cognac cream sauce makes for another reliable main course. Finish your meal with brandy or Armagnac from one of the world's finest collections. Chef and restaurateur André Rochat truly has outdone himself. $ *Average main: $59* ⊠ *The Palms, 4321 W. Flamingo Rd.* ☎ *702/951–7000* ⊕ *www.palms.com/las-vegas-restaurants-dining* ⌖ *Reservations essential* ☉ *No lunch.*

$$$

ASIAN

✕ **Little Buddha.** France's Buddha Bar has achieved world fame for its food and its music. The associated Little Buddha in the swanky Palms Casino continues the mystique, albeit with sometimes iffy service. The kitchen produces Pacific Rim wonders such as Korabuta pork pot stickers; wok-fried salt-and-pepper calamari and shrimp; sizzled Alaskan halibut; slow-braised Kobe beef short ribs; and hibachi char-grilled salmon. There's also plenty of great sushi and sashimi. Finish things off with liquid-center chocolate cake with vanilla ice cream. $ *Average* *main: $39* ✉ *The Palms, 4321 W. Flamingo Rd.* ☎ *702/942–7778* 🌐 *www.palms.com* 🕓 *Closed Mon. and Tues. No lunch.*

$$$$ ITALIAN 🍴 **Nove Italiano.** Head to the Palms' decadent Fantasy Tower to try out this see-and-be-seen Italian restaurant with vaulted ceilings, classical statuary, and ornately upholstered armchairs—there's an intentionally gaudy look about the place, and that's part of its allure among high rollers and poseurs. The modern Italian food, however, is seriously good and surprisingly restrained: a thin-crust pizza topped with buffalo mozzarella and tomato; grilled octopus with lemon and rosemary; and Sicilian crab cakes with peperonata and arugula pesto. The 24-ounce bone-in rib-eye steak topped with a lobster tail is a particularly memorable treat. [$] *Average main: $59* ✉ *The Palms, 4321 W. Flamingo Rd.* ☎ *702/942–6800* 🌐 *www.palms.com* 🕓 *No lunch.*

$$$$ AMERICAN 🍴 **Simon Restaurant & Lounge.** Chef Kerry Simon has created a stylish, whimsical, restaurant that emphasizes fresh, organic ingredients. Servers wearing sneakers bring a menu that's chock-full of traditional fare with creative twists and a long list of sushi specialties. The Crispy, Creamy Rock Shrimp—a favorite appetizer—is lightly fried, tossed in sweet chili aioli, and served on a bed of apple-and-celery slaw. Seekers of comfort food might also find a tasty meat loaf cooked with beer among the entrées. The dessert offerings include a giant bowl of freshly spun cotton candy—a Simon signature. There's delicious breakfast fare, too. The bright and airy restaurant features floor-to-ceiling windows that look out onto the adjacent swimming pool. [$] *Average main: $49* ✉ *Palms Place, 4381 W. Flamingo Rd.* ☎ *702/944–3292* 🌐 *www.palms.com.*

5

WEST SIDE NON-CASINO RESTAURANTS

$ THAI 🍴 **Archi's Thai Kitchen and Thai Bistro.** In a building that once likely held a fast-food joint, Archi's maintains the apparent Vegas tradition of fabulous Thai restaurants grossly lacking in ambience. Serious fans of Thai food happily overlook the low-frills dining room and flock here for spot-on exceptional (and super-cheap) chow. Few surprises here—just expertly prepared curries, tom yum soups, fish cakes, and pad thais. In particular, the shrimp "ginger ginger ginger" has drawn raves; yes, it really is that gingery. [$] *Average main: $19* ✉ *6360 W. Flamingo Rd.* ☎ *702/880–5550* 🌐 *www.archithai.com.*

$ VEGETARIAN 🍴 **Go Raw Cafe.** The name of this all-vegan, all-organic café refers to the fact that nothing is cooked at temperatures higher than the 100°F-plus it takes to make flatbreads and pizza dough. Devotees of living food—as well as vegans and vegetarians—find much to like here. You can make a healthy choice with dishes such as kale salad, soft-tortilla enchiladas, or lasagna made with zucchini, spinach, carrots, marinara sauce, and nut "cheese." [$] *Average main: $12* ✉ *2910 Lake East Dr.* ☎ *702/254–5382* 🌐 *www.gorawcafe.com.*

$$ MEDITERRANEAN 🍴 **Grape Street Cafe, Wine Bar & Grill.** This smart neighborhood restaurant serves food intended to coordinate nicely with the restaurant's interesting, affordable and plentiful (as in 90 selections by the glass) wine list. The menu features salads, sandwiches, pizzas, and specials that might include grilled salmon and crab-stuffed shrimp. Desserts range from austere Stilton and port to positively decadent dark-chocolate

fondue. The dining room at Grape Street is brick-lined, candlelighted, and cozy, and there's a patio for pleasant evenings (if you don't mind the parking-lot view). [$] *Average main: $24* ✉ *7501 W. Lake Mead Blvd.* ☎ *702/228–9463* 🌐 *www.grapestreetcafe.com.*

$ AMERICAN 🍴 **Hash House A Go Go.** Come to this quirky purveyor of so-called "twisted farm food" with a gargantuan appetite and a considerable sense of humor. The spacious restaurant done up with nostalgic roadhouse accoutrements aims to please its patrons by stuffing them with heaps of savory comfort food, prepared with vaguely modern twists. A typical entrée could serve two. At breakfast, you'll find items such as savory pork tenderloin Benedict with homemade barbecue cream. Dinner options might include sage-fried chicken salad, the Kokomo meatloaf sandwich with griddled smoked mozzarella, and duck mac-n-cheese (with pancetta, of course). You may not have room for the fresh-fruit cobbler, but consider taking it home in a box—it's that good. Additional locations are in the Imperial Palace, the Plaza Hotel & Casino, and M Resort. [$] *Average main: $19* ✉ *6800 W. Sahara Ave.* ☎ *702/804–4646* 🌐 *www.hashhouseagogo.com* 🕑 *No dinner Sun.*

$ JAPANESE Fodor's Choice ★ 🍴 **Ichiza.** Ichiza has developed a cult following for its sublimely delicious, authentic Japanese fare. Open daily until 3 am and jam-packed at all hours, this modest space is on the second floor of a shopping center in the city's Little Asia section along Spring Mountain Road. Seating is at the bar, in a few booths, or at a pair of wooden communal tables. Look beyond the traditional menu of sushi and noodle bowls and instead study the hundreds of signs (written in both English and Japanese) pasted on the walls of this boisterous restaurant, each listing a daily special. Red snapper carpaccio, salmon-skin salad, skewered gingko nut, wasabi–green bean tempura, and stir-fried calamari with ginger butter are a few notables you're likely to see many nights—it's best to order with a sense of adventure. [$] *Average main: $19* ✉ *4355 Spring Mountain Rd. #205* ☎ *702/367–3151* 🕑 *No lunch.*

$ INDIAN 🍴 **Mantra Masala.** Indian-food purists insist it's no big deal to drive 15 minutes from the Strip to the back of a bland strip mall for Mantra Masala's exceptionally authentic cuisine. Beside an Indian grocery and gift shop, the darkly lighted space comprises a pair of rooms with richly upholstered booths. Enter the dining room and smell the aroma of lamb chunks simmering in a rich cardamom sauce—a signature dish. On most days, you'll find the usual tandoori and biryani favorites here, plus a few more unusual offerings, such as Goa prawn curry (cooked in a tamarind-coconut sauce) and *barah kabab* (roast rack of lamb marinated in mustard oil, lemon, and a ginger-garlic sauce). [$] *Average main: $19* ✉ *8530 W. Warm Springs Rd.* ☎ *702/598–3663* 🌐 *www.mantramasala.com* 🕑 *Closed Mon.*

$$$ FRENCH 🍴 **Marché Bacchus.** The list of wines at this French bistro-cum-wineshop tucked into a shopping center in a quiet northwest Vegas neighborhood is nearly 1,000 deep, and free tastings are held on Saturday afternoons from 11:30 until 1:30. You can buy a bottle at retail prices in the store and then enjoy it while dining in the lakeside dining room, or out on the patio directly fronting the water. When you're ready to eat, tuck into country French favorites such as classic mussels marinière

and marinated roasted beets with smoked trout and apple salad. Main dishes might include a traditional seafood paella with chorizo and saffron, and a perfectly prepared confit of duck legs with bordelaise sauce and pan-roasted garlic-parsley potatoes. Hear live music on Wednesday, Friday, Saturday, and Sunday nights. [$] *Average main: $39* ✉ *2620 Regatta Dr.* ☎ *702/804–8008* 🌐 *www.marchebacchus.com.*

$ ASIAN 🍴 **Mayflower Cuisinier.** You'll find creative Chinese dishes with Californian, Pan-Asian, and French accents at this attractive off-the-Strip eatery. It may not have the flashy decor of some of the better-known Asian restaurants, but it offers better food than most. Regulars rave about items such as ginger-chicken ravioli, coconut shrimp with sweet chili sauce, spicy Thai shrimp scampi with basil and garlic, and Mongolian grilled lamb chops with cilantro-mint sauce. For dessert, consider a delectable trio of crèmes brûlées flavored with almond, orange, and pineapple-ginger. [$] *Average main: $19* ✉ *4750 W. Sahara Ave.* ☎ *702/870–8432* 🌐 *www.mayflowercuisinier.com* 🕒 *Closed Sun. No lunch Sat.*

5

$ MEXICAN 🍴 **Viva Mercado's.** The explosion of new chain restaurants in suburban neighborhoods makes it easy to forget the charms of the first Las Vegas restaurant to bring a chef's touch to Mexican food. The outstanding food includes bountiful plates of enchiladas and burritos, but more rewarding are the daily specials and fish dishes, such as orange roughy cooked four ways (including with the ultrahot *salsa de arbol*), or the *banderilla de camarones* (shrimp grilled in garlic, lemon, and spicy salsa). [$] *Average main: $19* ✉ *3553 S. Rainbow Rd.* ☎ *702/871–8826* 🌐 *www.vivamercadoslv.com.*

SUMMERLIN

JW MARRIOTT LAS VEGAS RESORT & SPA

$ IRISH 🍴 **J.C. Wooloughan's Irish Pub.** What do you get when you build a pub in Ireland, dismantle it, and ship it across the ocean, to be reconstructed in the desert? An Irish pub in one of the city's most elegant off-Strip resorts that looks like a wee bit o' the Emerald Isle. J.C. Wooloughan's offers Irish beers and beer blends, an extensive list of fine Irish whiskeys, and a hppy hour with great drink specials. The joint also serves up authentic Irish foods: Irish sausage rolls, beef-and-Guinness pie, and all-day Irish breakfast. [$] *Average main: $16* ✉ *JW Marriott Las Vegas Resort & Spa, 221 N. Rampart Blvd.* ☎ *702/869–7725* 🌐 *www.jwlasvegasresort.com.*

$$$ ITALIAN 🍴 **Spiedini Ristorante.** Gustav Mauler, who had long been chef and restaurant developer for the former Mirage Resorts company, struck out on his own with this stylish yet affordable Italian restaurant. The menu presents a contemporary take on traditional favorites. Starters might include spicy Italian sausage and clams with a seafood broth, and sweetwater shrimp wrapped in prosciutto with a lemon–sun-dried tomato sauce. Entrées usually comprise a number of handcrafted pastas, spit-roasted herb chicken with garlic-mashed potatoes, and wild Alaskan halibut with shrimp, capers, grape tomatoes, and a lemon-butter sauce. Desserts are often whimsical and delicious. [$] *Average main: $39* ✉ *JW Marriott Las Vegas Resort & Spa, 221 N. Rampart Blvd.* ☎ *702/869–7790* 🕒 *No lunch.*

RED ROCK CASINO, RESORT & SPA

$ BURGER 🍴 **LBS.** Cleverly decorated with a folk-art-meets-roadhouse assemblage of pressed-license-plate ceilings, hardwood floors, exposed-brick walls, and copper-top tables, this hip yet unfussy joint pays homage to the great American hamburger and all of its permutations, including a slew of turkey and veggie varieties. You can build your own, order a three-pack of sliders, or try one of the many designer selections, such as the Frenchie (topped with blue cheese, grilled wild mushrooms, lettuce, and alfalfa sprouts), or El Caliente (with pepper jack cheese, avocado, chipotle sauce, lettuce, tomato, and jalapeño). Apps include fantastic buttermilk-batter onion rings, and a noteworthy dessert list tempts sweet-tooths with giant cookies, cupcakes, and cookie-crumble malted milk shakes. [$] *Average main: $15* ✉ *Red Rock Casino, Resort & Spa, 11011 W. Charleston Blvd.* ☎ *702/797–7777* 🌐 *www.redrocklasvegas.com/dining.*

$$$$ STEAKHOUSE 🍴 **T-Bones Chophouse.** Locals insist that high-priced Strip steak houses have nothing on this modern and lively eatery. The menu features oversize dry-aged prime steaks, signature bone-in meats, and fresh fish flown in daily. There's also a 7,500-bottle wine loft. But the most happening part of the restaurant is the lounge, a spacious area with floor-to-ceiling windows that overlook the pool. During the "T-Time" Happy Hour (offered Sunday through Thursday), you can choose from 50 items (including beers and wines by the glass) for $5. Some of the more popular offerings include pulled pork sliders and chili-and-cheese tater tots. Value in Vegas has never looked or tasted so good. [$] *Average main: $49* ✉ *Red Rock Hotel, Casino & Spa, 11011 W. Charleston Blvd.* ☎ *702/797–7576* 🌐 *www.redrocklasvegas.com/dining.*

SUMMERLIN NON-CASINO RESTAURANTS

$$$ MEDITERRANEAN 🍴 **Vintner Grill.** Once you get past the bland office-park setting, you'll find that this sumptuously decorated spot near Red Rock Resort has plenty to recommend in the way of contemporary Mediterranean fare. Start with one of the wood-fired flatbreads, or an item such as pan-seared crab cakes with tarragon cream and roasted peppers. From here the menu branches out to pastas and risottos on one side, and a range of meat and seafood grills on the other. A highlight is the spicy Moroccan ahi with baby fennel salad, pecorino, sea asparagus, and preserved lemon aioli. As the restaurant's name suggests, there's an impressive wine list here. On cool evenings, ask for a table on the outdoor patio. [$] *Average main: $32* ✉ *10100 W. Charleston Blvd.* ☎ *702/214–5590* 🌐 *www.vglasvegas.com.*

HENDERSON

GREEN VALLEY RANCH

$$ SEAFOOD 🍴 **Tides Oyster Bar.** For affordable seafood, this futuristic incarnation of a 50s coffee shop does the trick. The space is groovy and inviting, with blue mosaic columns soaring above the dining space, a long counter facing the kitchen, and big-screen TVs showing sporting events. Here you can sit on a blond-wood bar stool and slurp clams and oysters

Continued on page 219

BEST BUFFETS

Despite Vegas's hoity-toity culinary makeover, there's nothing we like more than the city's famous and fabulous buffets that continue to rake in the masses. Why? Because who doesn't love that uniquely American obsession—unlimited gorging for one set price?

Buffets originated in the late 1940s as an attention-grabbing loss leader that would attract hungry gamblers to the casinos (and keep them there). Now the buffet concept has grown into an important tradition at virtually every resort. Bargain-hunters will still find plenty of economical deals, but the top buffets typically charge upwards of $25, or even $40, per person at dinner. Hey, there are lobster tails, Kobe beef, and unlimited Champagne at some of these spreads—you get what you pay for. With that in mind, here's a look at some of the best buffet bangs for the buck, from the chichi Buffet at Bellagio to the value-packed Feast Around the World.

Updated by Matt Villano

TOP PICKS

The Buffet at Bellagio

Step into the regal dining room, tricked out with opulent chandeliers and elegant artwork, and any hesitation that a buffet could be gourmet enough to deserve Bellagio's hefty price tag vanishes. Even the most discerning foodie should find something to like among urbane cuisine like venison chops, apple-smoked sturgeon, and (especially) elaborate pastries.

Some say the Buffet is overrated and overcrowded, but don't be put off by the naysayers—if you skip items that you could easily get at any Vegas buffet (such as pizzas from the wood-fired oven), you'll do well here. The staff does a first-rate job tending to everybody's needs.

If you want to try to avoid the dinner lines, show up right when dinner starts (4 pm nightly). You might be eating earlier than normal, but the trade-off is worth it.

BEST DISHES: Eggs Benedict, crab omelets (with real lump crab meat), Kobe beef, Chilean sea bass, baby squid, crab legs, sushi, smoked Scottish salmon, tandoori game hen, steamed clams, the salad bar.

PRICES: Breakfast $17, champagne brunch $31, lunch $20, dinner $30–$37.

☎ 702/693-7111
🌐 www.bellagio.com

Le Village Buffet/Paris

Let other buffets touch on international foods— Paris Las Vegas owns the world's foremost cuisine, and Francophiles unite jubilantly here to sample Vegas's take on French fare. The verdict? Okay, this isn't going to beat out Joël Robuchon's Left Bank L'Atelier, but in terms of buffets and other similarly priced Strip dining, the food here is mouthwatering.

The cooking stations are themed to the regions of France, such as Burgundy, Normandy, Alsace, and Brittany (head here for the delicious dessert crepes). Raclette (a dish of melted aged cheese) is served at one station; grillade (sausages, grilled seafood, and skewered meat) in another. There's also an impressive spread of cheese (naturally).

Drop by Le Flambé station for bananas Foster to top off your meal. The dining room, fashioned after a quaint French village, is a kick: stone walls and floors lend a charming feel, if not one that's especially conducive to quiet conversation, and the flattering, soft lighting is a rarity among Vegas buffet restaurants.

BEST DISHES: Chicken chasseur (sautéed in a brown sauce), roasted duck, bouillabaisse, veal marengo (in olive oil with tomatoes, onions, olives, garlic, and white wine), salmon-scrambled eggs, raclette, braised lamb, chocolate mousse, made-to-order crêpes, Belgian waffles, French bread pudding.

PRICES: Breakfast $16–19, champagne brunch $31, lunch $22, dinner $31.

☎ 702/946-7000
🌐 www.parislasvegas.com

TOP PICKS

Cravings/Mirage

A chic reinterpretation of the usual Vegas buffet, Cravings was designed in bold colors by noted designer Adam Tihany (who designed Bouchon, Aureole, and Spago, among many others). Aesthetically, it's the anti-buffet—the futuristic back-lighted glass walls, dramatic geometric patterns, and low-slung chairs and tables give it the feel of a mod cafeteria from the next century. The brash lighting can be headache-inducing, but otherwise this is a fun, stylish place to nosh. You can even watch cooking shows on the several flat-screen TVs.

BEST DISHES: Dim sum, peel-and-eat shrimp, red-chile pork tamales, bruschetta, fried chicken, chipotle-mashed potatoes, Asian noodles, wonton duck soup, macaroons, croissant pudding.

PRICES: Breakfast $16, champagne brunch $26, lunch $23, dinner $30.

☎ 702/791–7111
🌐 www.mirage.com

Eleven separate cooking stations freshly prepare all types of eats, including all-American barbecue, wood-fired pizza, Chinese entrées, Southwestern dishes, and even sushi. Many selections are made to order, and the Asian items consistently draw top praise. The mouthwatering dessert section—with hand-scooped Italian ice cream, coffee gelato, and chocolate mousse with raspberry puree—may entice you to skip the main course.

Village Seafood Buffet/Rio

For lovers of all creatures from the water, the notion of an all-you-can-eat seafood buffet sounds almost too amazing to be true. And, well, it is. This nautical-theme dinner buffet at the Rio isn't the seafood nirvana that you'll find at pricey restaurants like Mandalay Bay's RM Seafood or the MGM Grand's SeaBlue. But hey, it's still impressive—and in 2008, the restaurant completed a stunning new makeover, complete with a dramatic new sound-and-light system. In keeping with the around-the-world theme of Rio's standard buffet (Carnival World), the Village Seafood seven seas-themed spread ventures to Mexico (with seafood fajitas), Italy (try the cioppino), China (delicious kung pao scallops), and elsewhere. The relatively steep price still rewards you with plenty of value—just think what you'd pay à la carte for heaping platters of sushi, lobster, raw shellfish, and the like. Fear not if you despise fish and you're just going along to placate a seafood lover—there's plenty of chicken and beef, including delicious barbecue beef ribs.

BEST DISHES: Oysters Rockefeller (above), seafood cannelloni, broiled swordfish, lobster tail, peel-and-eat shrimp, seafood gumbo, snow-crab legs, clams and oysters on the half-shell, chocolate cheesecake.

PRICES: Dinner $40 (no lunch).

☎ 702/777–7777
🌐 www.riolasvegas.com

HONORABLE MENTIONS

Wicked Spoon

The newest addition to the Vegas buffet scene has become a cult favorite for desserts such as gelato and homemade macaroons, and dishes such as "Angry Mac N Cheese," traditional macaroni-and-cheese with a touch of spice. Unlike other buffets, which serve items family-style, here items are presented as individual portions—a strategy that is infinitely more hygienic but likely creates lots of dishes. Another bonus: The music selection here is modern and fun.

BEST DISHES: House made gelato, Angry Mac N Cheese, French Toast, Asian-style pork ribs, Nutella mousse, bone marrow, prime rib.

PRICES: Brunch $22–$29, champagne brunch $37, dinner $35

☎ 702/698–7000 ⊕ www.cosmopolitanlas vegas.com

The Buffet at Wynn Las Vegas

Steve Wynn prides himself on doing everything bigger and better than others in town, so the fact that buffet fans rave about his buffet is no surprise. The place boasts 16 live cooking stations, including those specializing in Asian, Indian, and Thai cuisine (to name a few). Across the board, the real star here is meat—veal short ribs, lamb T-bones, and char-grilled quail are just some of the options. Of course there usually are Alaskan King Crab legs, too. And the dessert table never disappoints.

BEST DISHES: Veal short ribs, char-grilled quail, slow-roasted prime rib, Alaskan King Crab legs.

PRICES: Breakfast $20, weekend brunch $32 or $42 (with champagne), lunch $24, dinner $37 (weeknights) or $40 (weekends).

☎ 702/770–3463 ⊕ www.wynnlasvegas.com

CHAMPAGNE BRUNCH

Virtually every buffet mentioned here offers an elaborate Champagne brunch, usually on Saturday and Sunday mornings. But there are also a few regular restaurants that offer special weekend brunch spreads. Here are the ones you shouldn't miss.

At Mandalay Bay, tap your toes at the wonderful gospel brunch served at the **House of Blues** (☎ 702/632–7607 ⊕ www.hob.com), where you feast on terrific soul food. For sheer over-the-top opulence, don't miss the weekly **Bally's Sterling Brunch** (☎ 702/967–7777 ⊕ www.ballylasvegas.com), a swanky affair set inside the casino's handsome steak restaurant. Menu items include fresh broiled lobster and massive plates of crab claws, as well as American Sturgeon caviar. The best part: the bubbly is real Champagne, as in Perrier Jovet from France.

on the half shell or a dinner-size bowl of gumbo. A particular specialty is the traditional crab roast, prepared in an old-timey steam kettle with tomato, herbs, butter, and brandy. Also consider the all-you-can-eat crab leg dinner for $29.95. $ *Average main: $29* ⊠ *Green Valley Ranch, 2300 Paseo Verde Pkwy.* ☎ *702/617–7075* ⊕ *www.greenvalleyranchresort.com/dining.*

HENDERSON NON-CASINO RESTAURANTS

$ ✕ **Grimaldi's.** A branch of the legendary coal-fired pizza-baker nestled beneath the Brooklyn Bridge, this casual little joint in Henderson (with other outposts in the Palazzo and in Summerlin) doesn't quite conjure up the atmosphere of the original, despite exposed-brick walls and red-checked tablecloths—it's in a shiny upscale shopping center, after all—but it does have a wine list and a martini menu. What counts, of course, is the pizza, and in this regard, Grimaldi's deserves high praise. The oven-hot pies come in three sizes and with staple toppings as spicy sausage, meatballs, and ricotta cheese. Finish off your meal with a cannoli. $ *Average main: $18* ⊠ *9595 S. Eastern Ave.* ☎ *702/657–9400* ⊕ *www.grimaldispizza.com.*

PIZZA

$ ✕ **SuperMex Restaurant & Cantina.** Here's a superlative case of truth in advertising: the California-based SuperMex, a dimly lighted, attractive space with Old Mexico doors and slate floors, has a super-massive menu—32 combination plates, plus countless types of burritos in two sizes, salads, tostadas, appetizers, fajitas, tacos, *taquitos,* and more. You can even get a chile relleno burrito or Mexican sausage with scrambled eggs or an enchilada and a tamale or . . . you get the picture. "Extras are extra," the menu says, and you can tailor them to your tastes. There's even a "lite" menu, for those seeking, say, a whole-wheat quesadilla. It's open 24 hours daily. $ *Average main: $12* ⊠ *3460 E. Sunset Rd.* ☎ *702/436–5200* ⊕ *www.supermexnv.com.*

MEXICAN

$$$ ✕ **Todd's Unique Dining.** What's really unique (for Vegas) about this intimate spot a short drive southeast of the airport is the easygoing pace and unpretentious vibe contrasted with artful, creative contemporary cooking. The dining room is stark (almost homely, actually), perhaps to show off colorful fare such as goat-cheese wontons with berry-basil butter; and a juicy Kobe skirt steak fire-grilled with a spicy black bean–and-chili sauce. Still, some of the dishes feel overworked. This place used to be something of a sleeper, but it's becoming better known, so book a couple of days ahead if you want to dine Thursday through Saturday. $ *Average main: $39* ⊠ *4350 E. Sunset Rd.* ☎ *702/259–8633* ⊕ *www.toddsunique.com* ⊗ *Closed Sun. No lunch.*

ECLECTIC

Shopping

WORD OF MOUTH

"The Forum Shops—it's a mall, never for a second would you doubt you were in a mall (that is NOT the feeling you get at Venetian and Paris) but it's a nice mall, with the second story over the shop fronts made to look like an Italian city—and three large fountains in 'piazzas' throughout. One does an animatronics show every hour with fountains, lights, fire and noise."

—isabel

Updated by
Xazmin Garza

WORLD-CLASS SHOPPING IN VEGAS? YES, among the scads of kitsch and Elvis memorabilia (looking for a piece of the King's pillowcase?), there's also the ne plus ultra from Cartier and Yves Saint Laurent. The square footage in the Forum Shops at Caesars alone is the most valuable retail real estate in the country; bankrolls are dropped there as readily as on the gaming tables. It's the variety that has pushed Las Vegas near the ranks of New York City, London, and Rome: you could send home a vintage slot machine or tote home a classic Hermès handbag. You might start to think those pesky casinos only get in the way of your shopping safaris.

Most Strip hotels offer designer dresses, swimsuits, jewelry, and menswear; almost all have shops offering logo merchandise for the hotel or its latest show. Inside the casinos the gifts are elegant and exquisite. Outside, all the Elvis clocks and gambling-chip toilet seats you never wanted to see are available in the tacky gift shops. Beyond the Strip, Vegas shopping encompasses such extremes as a couture ball gown in a vintage store and, in a Western store, a fine pair of Tony Lamas boots left over from the town's cowboy days. Shoppers looking for more practical items can head for neighborhood malls, supermarkets, shopping centers, and specialty stores. And to avoid the stratospheric prices on the Strip, shoppers not averse to driving a bit can find the same high-ticket items at lower prices at the town's factory outlet malls.

SHOPPING PLANNER

GETTING AROUND

Las Vegas shopping—so demanding, yet so rewarding. With malls encompassing millions of square feet of retail space, you won't have any trouble finding ways to part with your hard-earned cash. But to make the most of your time, you should map out your shopping safari. Distances are deceiving because of the scale of the resort casinos. What looks like a quick walk might take a half hour. Due to crowd-control measures, you'll find yourself squeezing around barriers and leaping over bridges instead of just crossing a street. Grab a cab or ride the monorail ($5 a trip) and save the time for shopping. Buses, which are $2 along the Strip, are a cheaper option, but crowded at all hours.

Got a car? All resorts offer free parking and free valet service (don't worry—they'll still get your money).

SEND THEM PACKING

Who wants to lug packages from store to store? Most stores are happy to send your purchases back to your hotel, or even ship them back home for you.

HOURS OF OPERATION

Although Las Vegas may be up all night, the people who work in the retail establishments need a little rest. Many places are open from 10 am to 11 pm during the week, and stay open an hour later on weekends. And the shopping, like the gambling, goes on every day.

FIND OUT WHAT'S GOING ON
The city's daily newspaper, the *Las Vegas Review-Journal* (⊕ *www. reviewjournal.com*), offers a guide to local malls and printable discount coupons.

MALLS ON THE STRIP

Fodor's Choice ★ **Appian Way at Caesars Palace.** The marble halls of Appian Way are centered around an exact replica of Michelangelo's *David* in Carrara marble. The upscale shops include Cartier and Bernini Couture for Italian men's and women's clothes.

Fodor's Choice ★ **Crystals.** Imagine visiting a huge neighborhood shopping mall, except in the place of stores like Bebe, Express, and GAP, you'll find boutiques like Marni, Mikimoto, and Tom Ford. Now add premiere architecture to the equation and you have the new Crystals at CityCenter shopping venue.

This 500,000-square-foot mall can be accessed from the Strip, a first for luxury retail on Las Vegas Boulevard. Boutiques such as Lanvin and Miu Miu affirm that the Strip gives Rodeo Drive and Fifth Avenue a run for their money. Roberto Cavalli has a two-story boutique that sells everything Cavalli—even the pet line—and features a built-in catwalk. Louis Vuitton has opened one of its largest locations in North America with two levels that extend beyond just leather goods to include men and women's ready-to-wear, shoes, jewelry, textiles, ties, and more.

Food options aren't too shabby either. You'll find Eva Longoria's celebrity hot-spot restaurant, Beso and two Wolfgang Puck eateries: Puck and The Pods. ⊠ *CityCenter, 3720 S. Las Vegas Blvd., Center Strip* ☎ *866/754–2489* ⊕ *www.crystalscitycenter.com.*

Fashion Show. The front of this swanky, fashion-devoted mall is dominated by The Cloud—a giant, oblong disc that looms high above the entrance. Ads and footage of the mall's own fashion events are continuously projected across the expanse of this odd shaped screen. Inside, the mall is sleek, spacious, and airy, a nice change from some of the claustrophobic casino malls. The mall delivers on its name—fashion shows are staged in the Great Hall on an 80-foot-long catwalk that rises from the floor Friday through Sunday, every hour noon–6 pm.

Although you do find many of the same stores that are at the casino malls, there's also a smattering of different fare: Sandwich, the European-based brand that distinguishes itself from the competition with comfort-focused, naturally made clothes; and the yoga-inspired store lululemon. Neiman Marcus, Saks Fifth Avenue, Macy's, Bloomingdale's Home, Nordstrom, and Dillard's serve as the department-store anchors. Fashion Show is next to the Trump Hotel Las Vegas. ⊠ *3200 Las Vegas Blvd. S, North Strip* ☎ *702/369–8382* ⊕ *www.thefashionshow.com.*

Fodor's Choice ★ **The Forum Shops at Caesars Palace.** The Forum Shops resemble an ancient Roman streetscape, with immense columns and arches, two central piazzas with fountains, and a cloud-filled ceiling with a sky that changes from sunrise to sunset over the course of three hours (possibly goading shoppers to step up their pace of acquisition when it appears that

6

DID YOU KNOW?

St. Mark's Square, inside the Grand Canal Shoppes, is full of little gift-shop carts and street performers. Shoppers may experience one or more of the approximately 30 "street" performances that go on each day.

time is running out?). The Festival
Fountain (in the west wing of the
mall) puts on its own show every
hour on the hour daily starting at
10 am: a robotic, pie-eyed Bacchus
hosts a party for friends Apollo,
Venus, and Mars, complete with
lasers, music, and sound effects; at
the end, the god of wine and merri-
ment delivers—what else?—a sales
pitch for the mall. The "Atlantis"
show (in the east wing) is even more
entertaining: Atlas, king of Atlantis,
can't seem to pick between his son,
Gadrius, and his daughter, Alia, to
assume the throne. A struggle for
control of the doomed kingdom
ensues amid flames and smoke.

> ### NONSTOP SHOPPING
>
> Can't wait to hit another mall?
> A pedestrian bridge from the
> Fashion Show mall to the Wynn
> Esplanade gives you access to
> millions of square feet of retail
> bliss. Start at the Fashion Show,
> which houses such heavy hitters
> as Neiman Marcus and Nevada's
> only Nordstrom as well as hip
> boutiques like Betsey Johnson.
> Head across to the Esplanade,
> where you can pick up high-end
> goodies at Alexander McQueen
> or Outfit.

If you can tear yourself away from the animatronic wizardry, you find
designer shops and the old standbys. For fashionistas, there are all the
hard-hitters: Christian Dior, Gucci, Fendi, Pucci, Louis Vuitton, Dolce
& Gabbana, Marc Jacobs, and Balenciaga (whew!). Pick up your diamonds at Harry Winston, DeBeers, or Chopard, or go for a sparkling
handbag at Judith Leiber. If your purse strings are a little tighter, there
are always the ubiquitous Gap or Abercrombie stores. Cosmetics queens
will keep themselves busy at the MAC Pro Store, one of only six in
the country. And, you can't miss the flagship Victoria's Secret with its
provocatively posed mannequins designed to look like the Victoria's
Secret Angels. The mall is open late (until 11 Sunday through Thursday, until midnight Friday and Saturday). ⊠ *Caesars Palace, 3500 Las
Vegas Blvd. S, Center Strip* ☎ *702/893–4800 Forum Shops* ⊕ *www.
forumshops.com.*

Fodor'sChoice **Grand Canal Shoppes.** This is one of the most unforgettable shopping
★ experiences on the Strip. Duck into shops like Dooney & Bourke,
Lior, Sephora, or Paige Premium Denim. Amble under blue-sky ceilings alongside the Grand Canal. All roads, balustraded bridges, and
waterways, lead to St. Mark's Square, an enormous open space full of
gift-shop carts and street performers. If you're loaded down with bags,
hail a gondola! ($16 per person)

Two must-see stores are Il Prato, which sells unique Venetian collectibles, including masks, stationery sets, and pen-and-inkwell sets, and
Ripa de Monti, which carries luminescent Venetian glass. The mall is
open late (until 11 Sunday through Thursday, until midnight Friday
and Saturday). ⊠ *The Venetian, 3355 Las Vegas Blvd. S, North Strip*
☎ *702/414–4500* ⊕ *www.venetian.com.*

Le Boulevard. Petite by Vegas standards, this Parisian-style shopping lane
is chock-full of Gallic delights. Le Journal has that jaunty French beret
you know you're longing for. Keep an eye out for the living statues—
they'll fool you every time. At the Bally's-Paris Promenade, stores such

as Le Paradis provide pieces from Movado, Concord, and Chopard that you can't resist. L'Oasis equips you with everything necessary for that trip to the pool: swimsuits, sunglasses, and sunscreen. ⊠ *Paris Las Vegas, 3655 Las Vegas Blvd. S, Center Strip* ☎ *702/946–7000* ⊕ *www. parislasvegas.com.*

Mandalay Place. This sky-bridge mall spans the gap between Mandalay Bay and the Luxor with lofty stores. You can practice your golf swing with Nike irons and drivers at the first-ever Nike Golf store, or pick up sterling-silver razors at the Art of Shaving, a high-roller "barber spa" and grooming emporium. Beauty lovers will linger at Lush, an all-natural cosmetics boutique with its own "cosmetic deli," and flirty fashion fans will be drawn to Nora Blue, where hot brands like Betsey Johnson and Cassandra Stone can be found. For a relief from eye-popping price tags, head to budget fashion store Maude. ⊠ *Mandalay Bay Resort & Casino, 3950 Las Vegas Blvd. S, South Strip* ☎ *702/632–7777.*

Miracle Mile Shops. If you feel like you're walking in circles here, it's because you are. The shops here line an indoor sidewalk built around the circular Theater of the Performing Arts. You end exactly where you begin. Along the way, you'll find such notable and diverse fashion names as Herve Leger, Betsey Johnson, American Apparel, Urban outfitters, H&M, and Bettie Page. Beauty lovers will enjoy Sephora, the authority in beauty retail stores, which is well worth the walk on the cobblestone flooring. Miracle Mile does an admirable job of balancing fashion designer boutiques with modestly priced shops. Many of the 170 stores are at your local mall, but you still may discover a treasure here. ⊠ *Planet Hollywood Resort & Casino, 3663 Las Vegas Blvd. S, Center Strip* ☎ *702/866–0703, 888/800–8284* ⊕ *www. miraclemileshopslv.com.*

Fodor's Choice ★ **The Shoppes at The Palazzo.** This lavish mall certifies Vegas as one of the world's premier shopping destinations, adding powerhouse names such as Diane von Furstenberg, Michael Kors, Chloé, Bottega Veneta, and Tory Burch to the city's fashion-industry roster. Shoe lovers will swoon over the Christian Louboutin and Jimmy Choo boutiques, and jewelry aficionados will delight in Piaget and Van Cleef & Arpels. The main attraction for many, though, is the mall's anchor, Barneys New York. The reputable department store brings in up-and-coming, cutting-edge designers as well as established, exclusive ones like Balenciaga and Lanvin. ⊠ *Palazzo, 3325 Las Vegas Blvd. S, North Strip* ☎ *702/414–4525* ⊕ *www.palazzolasvegas.com.*

☺ **Showcase Mall.** "Mall" is a bit of a misnomer for this place, where stores are more like highly evolved interactive marketing concepts. First off, there's M&M's World, a rollicking four-story homage to the popular candy. Head up to the fourth level to create your own custom bag of M&M's (all blue! only red! plain and peanut together!). Huge dispensers with every color and every type line one wall. If you're able to pull yourself away from all the chocolate, more sugar awaits at Everything Coca-Cola. Here, you can pony up to the old-time soda fountain and order a Coke float. All sorts of interesting collectibles, like a vintage Coke vending machine, are for sale. Need an outlet for that sugar buzz?

Check out the high-tech Gameworks video arcade (Steven Spielberg had a hand in creating it), visit the Grand Canyon Experience, or suit up for your favorite sport at the Adidas Performance Center, which carries clothes, footwear, and accessories for any sport. Showcase is right next to MGM Grand. ⊠ *3785 Las Vegas Blvd. S, South Strip* ☏ *702/597–3122.*

Ⓒ **Town Square.** Constructed to resemble Main Street America with open-air shopping and dining, this outdoor complex contains more than 150 shops including Juicy Couture, Michael Stars, a 27,000-square-foot H&M, Sephora, Apple, and Patty's Closet. When you tire of shopping (or the kids do anyway), there's also a children's area, an outdoor concert venue, and Rave Motion Pictures, a multiplex cinema. Need to make a quick stop? Town Square offers curbside parking so you don't have to schlep all the way from the parking lot to your shopping destination. ⊠ *6605 Las Vegas Blvd. S, just south of Mandalay Bay, Airport* ☏ *702/269–5000* ⊕ *www.townsquarelasvegas.com.*

★ **Via Bellagio.** Steve Wynn spared no expense to create Bellagio, so be prepared to spare no expense shopping at its exclusive boutiques. Elegant stores such as Prada, Chanel, Giorgio Armani, Gucci, Fred Leighton, and Tiffany & Co line a long passage. When you're ready to cool your heels, dine on the balcony at **Olives,** right in the promenade, to snag the best seat for watching the Fountains of Bellagio (otherwise known as the dancing waters). Children, with few exceptions (such as those of hotel guests), aren't allowed anywhere in the Bellagio casino areas. ⊠ *Bellagio, 3600 Las Vegas Blvd. S, Center Strip* ☏ *702/693–7111* ⊕ *www. bellagio.com/shopping.*

SPECIALTY SHOPS ON THE STRIP

FOOD AND DRINK

Ⓒ **Ethel's Chocolate.** Chocolate lovers will think they've died and gone to chocolate heaven when they walk through the doors of this candy store. A plethora of chocolate assortments, chocolate fondue, cocoa, chocolate-covered fruit, and more awaits you. ⊠ *Fashion Show Mall, 3200 Las Vegas Blvd. S, North Strip* ☏ *702/796–6662* ⊕ *www. ethelschocolate.com.*

La Cave. Take your pick of decadent delights: French imported wines, pâtés, cheeses, and chocolate. ⊠ *Paris Las Vegas, 3655 Las Vegas Blvd. S, Center Strip* ☏ *702/946–4339.*

Ⓒ **M&M's World.** Colorworks, on the second floor, stocks all types and
★ colors of M&M's; the 3-D movie *I Lost My M in Vegas* is shown on the third floor. This popular tourist attraction is usually crowded; it's not easy to maneuver strollers and wheelchairs around the displays. Be sure to catch the 3-D movies even if you're not a kid. ⊠ *Showcase Mall, 3785 Las Vegas Blvd. S, South Strip* ☏ *702/736–7611.*

Shopping on and off the Strip

Bellagio 8▼
Bottega Veneta
Dior
Fendi
Giorgio Armani Boutique
Gucci
Tiffany & Co.
Via Bellagio

Bonanza 16▼

Caesars Palace 9▼
Appian Way
Balenciaga
Bernini
Burberry
Cartier
De Beers
Dior
Ermenegildo Zegna
Forum Shops
Gucci
H&M
Harry Winston
Hugo Boss
John Varvatos
Judith Leiber
Juicy Couture
Louis Vuitton
Marc Jacobs
Nike Town
Tiffany & Co.
Tory Burch
Versace

CityCenter 4▼
Assouline
Bottega Veneta
Cartier
Crystals
Fendi
Hermès
Louis Vuitton
Marni
Paul Smith
Tiffany & Co.
Tom Ford

Cosmopolitan 7▼
All Saints Spitalfields
Beckley
DNA 2050
Stitched

Encore 15▼
Chanel

**Fashion Outlets
Las Vegas** 23▼
Last Call from Neiman Marcus
Williams Sonoma
Marketplace

Fashion Show Mall 14▼
Betsey Johnson
Ethel's Chocolate
Kenneth Cole
Louis Vuitton

Mandalay Bay 1▼
Elton's House of Blues
Mandalay Place

Miracle Mile Shops 5▼
Betsey Johnson
H&M
Herve Leger

Paris Las Vegas 6▼
La Cave
Le Boulevard
Les Memories

**Shoppes at the
Palazzo** 12▼
Bauman Rare Books
Bottega Veneta
Chloé
Diane von Furstenberg
Elton's
Fendi
Tory Burch

Showcase Mall 3▼
Adidas Performance
Center
M&M's World

**Town Square
Las Vegas** 2▼
H&M
Juicy Couture

The Venetian 11▼
Burberry
Ca'd'Oro
Grand Canal Shoppes
Il Prato
Hugo Boss
Kenneth Cole
Ripa di Monti

Wynn Las Vegas 13▼
Cartier
Chanel
Dior
Louis Vuitton
Oscar de la Renta
Outfit

Off-Strip ▼
Buffalo Exchange **19**
The District at Green
Valley Ranch **20**
Houdini's Magic Shop **22**
Las Vegas
Outlet Center **21**
Las Vegas
Premium Outlets **17**
Serge's Showgirl Wigs **18**
Undefeated **24**

GIFTS AND SOUVENIRS

Bonanza "World's Largest Gift Shop". Okay, so it may not, in fact, be the world's largest, but it's the town's largest—and for that matter, the town's best—souvenir store. Although it has most of the usual junk, it also stocks some most unusual junk. Dying for a pair of fuzzy pink dice to hang on your car's rearview mirror? They've got em in spades. Can't go home without your own blinking "Welcome to Fabulous Las Vegas" sign? Or the coveted Elvis aviator sunglasses complete with black sideburns? How about a mechanical card shuffler, dealer's green visor, and authentic clay poker chips for poker nights back home? They're all here. The store is so huge that you won't feel confined, as you might in some of the smaller shops. It's open until midnight, and it's across from the Sahara. ⊠ *2440 Las Vegas Blvd. S, North Strip* ☏ *702/385–7359* ⊕ *www.worldslargestgiftshop.com.*

House of Blues. Buy music, books, hot sauce, and T-shirts at the souvenir shop in the popular bar–restaurant at Mandalay Bay. Browse books about the blues and rest for a bit in the comfortable chairs in the shop's alcove. ⊠ *Mandalay Bay Resort & Casino, 3950 Las Vegas Blvd. S, South Strip* ☏ *702/632–7600.*

Il Prato. Il Prato saves you a shopping foray to Venice, where the original pricey boutique stands. The Vegas outpost offers the same authentic gifts crafted by Italian artisans, such as tooled-leather journals and photo albums, glass-tip quills, wax-seal kits, miniatures, and paintings. And, just as in Venice, there's a huge collection of traditional Carnevale masks here. A back room offers a comprehensive collection of Ferrari collectibles, such as scale models and racing flags. ⊠ *Grand Canal Shoppes at the Venetian, 3377 Las Vegas Blvd. S, North Strip* ☏ *702/733–1201.*

Les Memories. A Francophile's fantasy, this shop stocks Diptyque candles, French-milled soaps, and other French delights. ⊠ *Le Boulevard at Paris Las Vegas, 3655 Las Vegas Blvd. S, Center Strip* ☏ *702/946–4329.*

Ripa di Monti. Exquisite Venetian glass creations—including smaller items like magnets and key chains, as well as the more elaborate vases and figurines—are sold at this store, one of Las Vegas's must-see shops. Buy glass-bead necklaces and earrings or a bowl of glass fruit for your dining-room table. ⊠ *Grand Canal Shoppes at the Venetian, 3377 Las Vegas Blvd. S, North Strip* ☏ *702/733–1004.*

HOME FURNISHINGS

National chains can be found in most Vegas malls, but be sure to hit Las Vegas Outlet Center for reduced prices on brand names such as Waterford Wedgwood, Springmaid, Corning-Revere, Mikasa, and more.

Last Call from Neiman Marcus. Score irresistible discounts on designer clothing as well as housewares and furnishings at this department-store outlet. ⊠ *Fashion Outlets Las Vegas, 32100 Las Vegas Blvd. S, Primm* ☏ *702/874–2100.*

JEWELRY

Most malls and shopping centers on and off the Strip have jewelry stores, including such national chains as Ben Bridge, Gordon's, Lundstrom, Whitehall Co., and Zales. More exclusive jewelers can be found in several of the Strip hotels, most notably Bellagio and the Venetian.

Ca'd'Oro. This store is made up of several exclusive boutiques including the first Damiani boutique in the United States and a Charriol boutique. Oliva and Silvio Hidalgo offer jewel and enamel settings in platinum and 18-karat gold. Lovers of fine watches will find numerous brands, including Ebel, Omega, Tag Heuer, Dubey & Schaldenbrand, and Baume & Mercier. ⊠ *Grand Canal Shoppes at the Venetian, 3377 Las Vegas Blvd. S, North Strip* ☎ *702/696–0080* ⊕ *www.cadorojewelers. com.*

Cartier. There are three outposts of this venerable jeweler in Las Vegas: at the Forum Shops, Wynn Las Vegas, and CityCenter. You'll find a fine collection of jewelry, watches, leather goods, accessories, and fragrances. ⊠ *Forum Shops, 3500 Las Vegas Blvd. S, Center Strip* ☎ *702/418–3904* ⊕ *www.cartier.com* ⊠ *Crystals at CityCenter, 3720 Las Vegas Blvd. S, Center Strip* ☎ *702/487–3160* ⊠ *Wynn Esplanade, 3131 Las Vegas Blvd. S, North Strip* ☎ *702/696–0146.*

De Beers. This jeweler appeals to the diamond connoisseur. Engagement rings, pendants, and high-fashion jewelry are abundant here. ⊠ *Forum Shops at Caesars, 3500 Las Vegas Blvd. S, Center Strip* ☎ *702/650–9559* ⊕ *www.debeers.com.*

Harry Winston. Celebrities continually turn to this exclusive jeweler for red-carpet-worthy diamonds. ⊠ *Crystals at CityCenter, 3720 Las Vegas Blvd. S, Center Strip* ☎ *702/262–0001* ⊕ *www.harrywinston.com.*

Tiffany & Co. Browse through a full selection of Tiffany's timeless merchandise as well as the exclusive jewelry designs of Elsa Peretti, Paloma Picasso, and Jean Schlumberger. ⊠ *Via Bellagio, 3600 Las Vegas Blvd. S, Center Strip* ☎ *702/697–5400* ⊕ *www.tiffany.com* ⊠ *Forum Shops at Caesars, 3500 Las Vegas Blvd. S, Center Strip* ☎ *702/644–3065* ⊠ *Crystals at CityCenter, 3720 Las Vegas Blvd. S, Center Strip* ☎ *702/545–9090.*

6

MEN'S CLOTHING

You can't walk into the shopping areas of the Strip's hotels without encountering high-end men's clothes shops. If the price tags on the Strip are too out-of-reach, the outlet malls have brand names for less, such as Tommy Hilfiger, Eddie Bauer, Ed Hardy, and DKNY.

Bernini. This Rodeo Drive–based men's clothier can dress you to the nines for casual or dressy affairs. ⊠ *Appian Way at Caesars, 3570 Las Vegas Blvd. S, Center Strip* ☎ *702/731–9786.*

Elton's. Exclusive men's designers, both high profile (Hugo Boss, Diesel) and obscure (Great China Wall) come together at this premium men's boutique. ⊠ *The Shoppes at The Palazzo, 3325 Las Vegas Blvd. S,*

Continued on page 241

SPAAAAH

Ah, Vegas. Sin City caters to your every indulgence, and over-the-top luxury day spas are no exception. So go ahead, book that hour-long massage and whatever else your heart desires. Need an excuse for all that pampering? Just remember, you could be spending that money at the tables.

Updated by Matt Villano

The big Strip hotels offer the poshest pampering in luxury spas and the latest in trendy treatments from around the globe. Expect to be smeared with exotic Balinese spices, steambathed in a hammam, swished in a watsu pool, or submerged in a bath enriched with Black Moor mud, all in splashy, stylish spa facilities.

To indulge in these royal treatments, expect to pay anywhere from $20 to $50 to use the fitness facilities, take the waters, and enjoy lavish spa amenities such as lounging areas, whirlpools, steam rooms, saunas, and an array of personal care products in the shower areas. However, most waive the daily facility fee if you purchase treatments, classes, or personal training sessions.

Although most spas are open to the public, many, such as Bellagio, MGM Grand, or Wynn Las Vegas, reserve certain days of the week for the hotel's guests. Some only allow you in if you book a treatment, some don't. Make sure to ask about the spa's policy and usage fees before visiting or while making an appointment.

6

IN FOCUS SPAAAAH

SPA SAVVY

SPA NAME	Body Treatments	Facials	Sun Rescue/ Hydrating	Treatments for Two	Spa Facility Day Pass	Sauna	Steam Room
Aquae Sulis	$75–$215	$75–$245	yes	yes	$35	yes	yes
THE Bathhouse	$85–$265	$80–$170	yes	no	$25	yes	yes
Canyon Ranch Spa Club	$165–$290	$155–$295	yes	yes	$30	yes	yes
Drift at Palms Place	$90–$265	$135–$215	yes	yes	$35	yes	yes
Four Seasons Spa	$90–$200	$165–$245	yes	yes	$30	yes	yes
MGM Grand Spa	$95–$305	$70–$195	yes	yes	$25	yes	yes
Nurture Spa	$70–$200	$75–$155	no	no	$35	yes	yes
Palms Spa	$75–$185	$125–$200	yes	yes	$25	yes	yes
Spa Bellagio	$85–$175	$85–$350	yes	yes	$40	yes	yes
Qua Baths & Spa	$170–$300	$180–$325	yes	yes	$45	yes	yes
Spa at Encore	$100–$425	$95–$310	yes	yes	$40	yes	yes
Spa Mandalay	$85–$265	$85–$225	yes	yes	$25	yes	yes
Spa at Trump	$140–$250	$150–$300	yes	yes	$12	yes	yes
The Spa at Wynn Las Vegas	$100–$280	$170–$300	yes	yes	$30	yes	yes

(Top, right) Spa Bellagio

TOP SPOTS

The Spa, Wynn Las Vegas

■ TIP→ Many spas offer special treatment for bachelorette parties or couples; just ask and a secret party room may open up for you.

The Spa at Wynn Las Vegas

Designed according to Feng Shui principles, and set away from the bells and jangles of the Strip, the Spa exudes an elegant Zen calm while remaining very cozy. There's a fireplace and flat screen TV in the lounge areas, and the hot and cool plunge area is naturally lit, lush with thriving palms and orchids.

Treatments, such as the Sake and Rice Body Treatment, are Asian-inspired. The Good Luck Ritual is based on the Five Elements of Feng Shui, and includes a massage with Thai herbs, an ultra-moisturizing hand therapy, and a wild lime botanical scalp treatment. For the ultimate in combating the drying desert clime, try the Oxygen Rejuvination Facial, which lathers a hydration cream fortified with black currant oil over the face and décolletage.

BODY TREATMENTS. **Massage:** Swedish, aromatherapy, deep tissue, couples massage, pregnancy massage, reflexology. **Exfoliation:** body polish, salt glow, sugar polish, waxing.

BEAUTY TREATMENTS. Anti-aging treatments, hair cutting, facials, manicure, pedicure, waxing, hot-lather shaves for men.

PRICES. **Body Treatments:** $100–$280. **Facials:** $170–$300. **Manicure/Pedicure:** $45–$105. **Waxing:** $30–$75.

Canyon Ranch SpaClub at the Venetian and the Palazzo

Vegas's largest spa—one of the best day spas in the country—is this outpost of Tucson's famed Canyon Ranch connected to the Venetian and the Palazzo. The extensive treatment menu here covers any desire, including Vibrational Therapy and an Ayurvedic herbal rejuvenating treatment. The real treat here is the Aquavana, a European-inspired space that offers a host of water-related experiences. The Wave Room simulates ocean waves; the Finnish Sauna infuses colored light into a dry heat sauna; and the Igloo cools guests off with sparkling fiber optics.

Weekend warriors love the health club, the Strip's largest, with its 40-foot climbing wall and frequent fitness and yoga classes. The nutrition, wellness, and exercise physiology departments also offer free lectures, Lifetime Nutrition Consultation, and acupuncture. An adjoining café serves healthy cuisine and smoothies.

BODY TREATMENTS. **Massage:** Swedish, aromatherapy, stone, couples massage, Ashiatsu, deep tissue, pregnancy massage, ayurvedic rejuvenation, hydromassage, reflexology. **Exfoliation:** body polish, salt glow, sugar polish, Vichy shower, waxing.

BEAUTY TREATMENTS. Anti-aging treatments, facials, manicure, pedicure, hair cutting, waxing, hair extensions, make-up.

PRICES. **Body Treatments:** $165–$290. **Facials:** $155–$295. **Manicure/Pedicure:** $45–$150. **Waxing:** $30–$110.

Canyon Ranch Spa Club

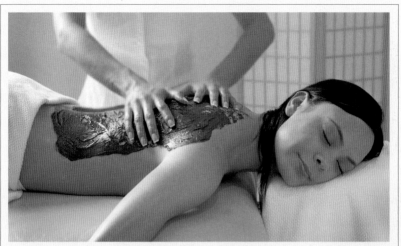

Spa Bellagio

Spa Bellagio

Besides the calming reflecting pools and the Reflexology Pebble Walk, this swank Zen sanctuary has treatments such as Thai yoga massage and Gem Therapy. The 6,000-square-foot fitness center has a gorgeous view of the Mediterranean gardens and the pool. There's even a candlelit meditation room with fountain walls.

If Vegas' over-indulging and the dry climate have gotten to you, try the Thalasso Therapy Session for seaweed and water-based detoxifying and hydrating treatment. Spa Bellagio offers Watsu, an aquatic massage using Zen Shiatsu techniques that takes place in a warm pool while floating.

Spa services are exclusive to Bellagio guests Friday–Sunday.

BODY TREATMENTS. **Massage:** Swedish, aromatherapy, stone, couples massage, Watsu, Ashiatsu, Thai yoga, deep tissue, pregnancy massage, Jamu, Indian head massage, reflexology. **Exfoliation:** body polish, salt glow, sugar polish, coconut scrub Vichy shower, Moor Mud, seaweed, gold, coffee, waxing.

BEAUTY TREATMENTS. Anti-aging treatments, facials, manicure, pedicure, hair cutting, waxing, hot-lather shaves for men.

PRICES. **Body Treatments: $85–$175. Facials: $85–$350. Manicure/Pedicure: $35–$130. Waxing: $25–$100.**

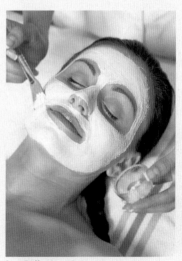

Spa Bellagio

TOP SPOTS

Qua Baths & Spa

Qua Baths & Spa

Caesars Palace's behemoth of a spa bases its philosophy on the calming properties of water. Many of the treatments and special features here draw heavily on this element, beginning with the Roman Baths. Qua's social spa-ing concept of encouraging guests to verbally interact comes naturally when indulging in these three soothing baths.

For guests suffering from heat exhaustion, the Arctic Room offers the perfect solution: snow falling from a glass sky. If traditional treatments bore you, consider visiting the Crystal Body Art Room.

You won't completely experience Qua's water benefits until you've had a Vichy shower treatment that uses seven different showerheads.

Qua also has Men's Zone, a salon for men, and the Tea Lounge where an in-house tea sommelier blends you a cup. Color, a phenomenal hair salon, is right next door.

BODY TREATMENTS. **Massage:** Swedish, stone, deep tissue, Thai, reflexology, Shiatsu, Biofreeze, Hawaiian healing, raindrop therapy, chakra rebalancing, couples, prenatal. **Exfoliation:** Herbal, Microderm, champagne grapeseed, Vichy shower.

BEAUTY TREATMENTS. Facials, waxing.

PRICES. **Body Treatments:** $170–$250. **Facials:** $180–$325. **Waxing:** From $25.

Qua Baths & Spa

HONORABLE MENTIONS

MGM Grand Spa

Though this well-managed spa lacks the stunning architecture of other Strip spas, it makes up for it with accommodating attendants and a serene, Feng Shui–designed atmosphere.

The Ritual Experiences menu offers creative treatments from around the world, including the Turkish Hammam Tradition, the Icelandic Fire and Ice Experience, and a Japanese Yuzu Ritual massage.

Too adventurous? Detox your hangover with the Morning After Arabica, an exfoliating scrub with coffee, Dead Sea salts, and peppermint and rosemary oils.

Spa Mandalay

Spa services are available to nonguests Monday through Thursday only.

BODY TREATMENTS. **Massage:** Swedish, aromatherapy, deep tissue, pregnancy massage, shiatsu, stone, reflexology, ayurvedic treatments. **Exfoliation:** sugar and coffee scrubs. **Wraps/Baths:** herbal wrap, mud wrap, seaweed wrap.

BEAUTY TREATMENTS. Anti-aging treatments, hair cutting, facials, manicure, pedicure, waxing.

PRICES. **Body Treatments:** $95–$305. **Facials:** $70–$335. **Manicure/Pedicure:** $45–$155. **Waxing:** $20–$135

Spa Mandalay

Modeled after a Turkish-style bath, the hot, warm, and cold plunges are surrounded by marble, fountains, and plenty of places to lounge. In what must be a first in Las Vegas, the Spa offers yoga on the beach (of the Mandalay Bay wave pool) mornings at 7 (confirm with the staff).

Try the Ayurvedic Elemental Balancing massage, based on the principals of Ayurveda, a 5,000-year-old healing tradition from India. The spa offers the only Hot Stone Pedicure in town.

BODY TREATMENTS. **Massage:** aromatherapy, Swedish, deep tissue, pregnancy massage, shiatsu, stone, reflexology. **Exfoliation:** herbal, mud, sugar and salt scrubs. **Wraps/Baths:** herbal wrap, aromatherapy wrap. **Other:** hot, warm, cool plunges, sauna, steam room.

BEAUTY TREATMENTS. Anti-aging treatments, hair cutting, facials, manicure, pedicure.

PRICES. **Body Treatments:** $85–$265. **Facials:** $85–$225. **Manicure/Pedicure:** $45–$135. **Wax:** $30–$135.

MGM Grand Spa

Spa at Trump

Customization is the name of the game at this spa. Services are based upon your wishes—Do you want to be calm, balanced, healed, purified, or revitalized?—which then determines everything from your massage oils and candles, to the tea you drink and the music you'll hear during your visit. Services exclusive to this location include the Vegas Recovery Massage and the Royal Facial. The spa's skin care treatments use Kate Somerville products. There's also couples and men specific services.

Last but not least, an attaché service takes care of your every need from shoe shining to clothes steaming.

BODY TREATMENTS. Massage: Swedish, aroma-infused, prenatal, ayurvedic, reflexology, Thai herbal, hot stone. **Exfoliation:** Javanese Lulur, salt scrub, herbal

Spa at Trump

body scrub, yogurt, mud. **Other:** Eucalyptus infused sauna, gemstone massages.

BEAUTY TREATMENTS. Haircut and color, manicure, pedicure, facials, eyelash and brow tinting, waxing, makeup lesson.

PRICES. Body Treatments: $140–$250. **Wraps/Baths:** $40–$275. **Facials:** $150–$300. **Manicure/Pedicure:** $45–$85. **Waxing:** starts at $20.

GLOSSARY

acupuncture. Painless Chinese medicine during which needles are inserted into key spots on the body to restore the flow of *qi* and allow the body to heal itself.

aromatherapy. Treatments using plant-derived essential oils intended to relax the skin's connective tissues and stimulate the flow of lymph fluid.

Ayurveda. An Indian philosophy that uses oils, massage, herbs, and diet and lifestyle modification to restore perfect balance to a body.

body brushing. Dry brushing of the skin to remove dead cells and stimulate circulation.

body polish. Use of scrubs, loofahs, and other exfoliants to remove dead skin cells.

hammam. A Turkish wet spa that bathes you in steam.

hot-stone massage. Massage using smooth stones heated in water and applied to the skin

with pressure or strokes or simply rested on the body.

hydrotherapy. Underwater massage, alternating hot and cold showers, and other water-oriented treatments.

reflexology. Massage of the pressure points on the feet, hands, and ears.

reiki. A Japanese healing method involving universal life energy, the laying on of hands, and mental and spiritual balancing. It's intended to relieve acute emotional and physical conditions. Also called radiance technique.

salt glow. Rubbing the body with coarse salt to remove dead skin.

shiatsu. Japanese massage that uses pressure applied with fingers, hands, elbows, and feet.

shirodhara. Ayurvedic massage in which warm herbalized oil is trickled onto the center of the forehead, then gently rubbed into the hair and scalp.

sports massage. A deep-tissue massage to relieve muscle tension and residual pain from workouts.

Swedish massage. Stroking, kneading, and tapping to relax muscles. It was devised at the University of Stockholm in the 19th century by Per Henrik Ling.

Swiss shower. A multijet bath that alternates hot and cold water, often used after mud wraps and other body treatments.

Temazcal. Maya meditation in a sauna heated with volcanic rocks.

Thai massage. Deep-tissue massage and passive stretching to ease stiff, tense, or short muscles.

thalassotherapy. Water-based treatments that incorporate seawater, seaweed, and algae.

Vichy shower. Treatment in which a person lies on a cushioned, waterproof mat and is showered by overhead water jets.

Watsu. A blend of shiatsu and deep-tissue massage with gentle stretches—all conducted in a warm pool.

North Strip ☎ *702/853–0571* ✉ *Mandalay Place, 3950 Las Vegas Blvd. S, South Strip* ☎ *702/990–0571.*

Ermenegildo Zegna. You'll find the finest in Italian men's suits on this store's racks. Quality craftsmanship, superior fit, and impeccable style dominate here. ✉ *Forum Shops at Caesars, 3500 Las Vegas Blvd. S, Center Strip* ☎ *702/369–5458* ⊕ *www.zegna.com.*

Giorgio Armani Boutique. This elegant store displays the simplicity of the Armani suit as well as signature sportswear, shoes, and accessories. ✉ *Via Bellagio, 3600 Las Vegas Blvd. S, Center Strip* ☎ *702/893–8327.*

Hugo Boss. Both branches (one called Hugo/Hugo Boss and the other called Boss/Hugo Boss, for some mysterious reason) carry styles straight from European and New York runways. ✉ *Forum Shops at Caesars, 3500 Las Vegas Blvd. S* ☎ *702/696–9444* ✉ *Venetian, 3355 Las Vegas Blvd., North Strip* ☎ *702/836–0940.*

John Varvatos. Casual-chic men's clothes and a slew of shoes, belts, and messenger bags make up the offerings here. The Forum Shops location also carries formalwear. ✉ *Forum Shops at Caesars, 3500 Las Vegas Blvd. S, Center Strip* ☎ *702/939–0922* ⊕ *www.johnvarvatos.com.* ✉ *Hard Rock Hotel, 4455 Paradise Rd., Paradise Road* ☎ *702/693–6370.*

Kenneth Cole. The store provides a sleek, realistic approach to men's runway trends. A healthy supply of footwear and accessories is also sold. ✉ *Fashion Show Mall, 3200 Las Vegas Blvd. S, North Strip* ☎ *702/794–2653* ⊕ *www.kennethcole.com* ✉ *Grand Canal Shops at the Venetian, 3377 Las Vegas Blvd. S, North Strip* ☎ *702/836–1916.*

Paul Smith. The designer hails from England and his menswear makes that quite clear. With a strong British tone, the clothes also have a cool quirkiness to them. Some call it geek chic. Most everything in the store is for sale, including the books, art, and furniture. ✉ *CityCenter, 3720 Las Vegas Blvd. S, Center Strip* ☎ *702/796–2640* ⊕ *www.paulsmith.co.uk.*

Stitched. Men who want the best of the latest and greatest fashions will be right at home here. Rag & Bone and George Esquivel are carried here and an on-site tailor can personalize garments. Made-to-measure suits are a specialty. ✉ *The Cosmopolitan, 3708 Las Vegas Blvd. S., Center Strip* ☎ *702/698–7630.*

Tom Ford. The designer made his stamp on the fashion world when he brought Gucci back from the dead. Since then the outstanding craftsmanship of his modern menswear line has dressed Brad Pitt, George Clooney, and Jay-Z on the red carpet. A women's ready-to-wear line was added to the boutique in spring 2011. ✉ *CityCenter, 3720 Las Vegas Blvd. S, Center Strip* ☎ *702/740–2940* ⊕ *www.tomford.com.*

SPECIAL INTEREST

BOOKS

Used-book stores aren't exactly as easy to find in Las Vegas as video-poker machines, but if you venture out into the greater metro area, you inevitably find one. They're stashed among the many strip malls and

Where to Refuel

If you're on a shopping mission, keep your strength up at one of these delicious pit stops.

MALLS ON THE STRIP
Bellagio: Olives

Caesars Palace: Café Lago Buffet

Fashion Show mall: Stripburger, Red Velvet Cafe

The Forum Shops at Caesars: Il Mulino New York, The Palm, or Spago

Mandalay Bay: Burger Bar

Paris Las Vegas: JJ's Boulangerie

Planet Hollywood Resort & Casino: Pink's Hot Dogs

Showcase Mall: La Salsa Cantina

The Venetian: the Coffee Bean & Tea Leaf, or Postrio

OUTLET MALLS
Fashion Outlets Las Vegas: Hot Dog on a Stick or Vegas Burger

Las Vegas Outlet Center: Chao Praya

Las Vegas Premium Outlets: Great Steak and Potato Company

---

neighborhood shopping centers. If you'd rather stick to the Strip, head to the Palazzo for some of the most valuable finds in the literary world.

Assouline. Assouline publishes books that are candy for the eyes. Fashion, photography, architecture—these pages pay tribute to all of it. ⊠ *CityCenter, 3720 Las Vegas Blvd. S, Center Strip* ☎ *702/795–0166* ⊕ *www.assouline.com.*

Bauman Rare Books. Ever wonder what the first edition of James Joyce's *Ulysses* looked like? What about the first issue of *A Farewell to Arms,* inscribed by Hemingway himself? Head here for a look at the classics, life-altering medical works, and special binding services. ⊠ *The Shoppes at The Palazzo, 3327 Las Vegas Blvd. S, #2, North Strip* ☎ *702/948– 1617* ⊕ *www.baumanrarebooks.com.*

Gambler's Book Club. GBC is the world's largest independent bookstore specializing in books about blackjack, craps, poker, roulette, and all the other games of chance. You'll also fine novels about casinos, biographies of crime figures, and anything else that relates to gambling and Las Vegas. ⊠ *5473 S. Eastern Ave., East Las Vegas* ☎ *702/382–7555, 800/522–1777* ⊕ *www.gamblersbookclub.com.*

ONLY IN LAS VEGAS

Fodor'sChoice ★ **Gambler's General Store.** There's a big collection of gambling books, such as *Craps for the Clueless,* as well as poker chips, green-felt layouts, and slot and video-poker machines. Note: the highly collectible vintage slots start at $2,000. The staff will make sure your state allows the type of slot machine you want before you buy. You can buy used casino card decks here but only after they've been resorted and re-packaged by guests of the Nevada state penal system. It's eight blocks south of the Plaza Hotel on Main Street. ⊠ *800 S. Main St., Downtown* ☎ *702/382– 9903* ⊕ *www.gamblersgeneralstore.com.*

☾ **Houdini's Magic Shop.** Magicians are hot tickets in Vegas, and it's no surprise that Houdini's corporate headquarters is in town. There are also seven branches with all the tricks and gags—nearly one for every casino mall. ⊠ *Houdini's Factory Store, 6455 Dean Martin Dr. #L, Airport* ☏ *702/798–4789* ⊕ *www.houdini.com.*

Serge's Showgirl Wigs. If you always wished for the sleek tresses of those showgirls (or female impersonators), head to this Vegas institution. The largest wig store in the world can transform you into a Renaissance angel or Priscilla Presley on her wedding day. After checking out Serge's celebrity wall of fame, head for the wig outlet directly across the parking lot. ⊠ *4515 W. Sahara Ave., West Las Vegas* ☏ *702/732–1015* ⊕ *www. showgirlwigs.com.*

SPORTING GOODS AND CLOTHING

Adidas Performance Center. The coolest Adidas technology is displayed in a minimalist design at this two-story store, one of only a handful of Performance Centers in the United States. There's everything that men and women would need for any sport, all touted on interactive screens and text tickers. The black store is divided into sport preferences: running, basketball, training. Women shouldn't miss British designer Stella McCartney's signature line of fashion-inspired sportswear. You won't know whether to hit the track or the runway in her designs. And if you like old-school style, check out the Adidas Originals collection, which includes the Original Superstar Zoom (based on a 1969 basketball shoe). ⊠ *Showcase Mall, 3791 Las Vegas Blvd. S, South Strip* ☏ *702/262–1373.*

Nike Town. This multilevel Nike theme park features inspirational signs—"The Resolution Starts Now"—and giant swoosh symbols amid the latest cool technology in athletic shoes displayed in glass cases. Flashy and crowded, it's full of "Nike athletes" yelling into two-way radios. On the second floor, the swoosh info desk has the scoop on local sporting events, bike races, and hiking spots. ⊠ *Forum Shops at Caesars, 3500 Las Vegas Blvd. S, Center Strip* ☏ *702/650–8888.*

VINTAGE CLOTHING

AllSaints Spitalfields. The British brand uses vintage themes as its inspiration for graphic tees and dresses perfect for a night on the Strip. Celebrities like Halle Barry have been known to wear the edgy styles here. ⊠ *Cosmopolitan, 3708 Las Vegas Blvd. South, Center Strip* ☏ *702/722–5252.*

WOMEN'S CLOTHING

Vegas shopping can send the most jaded shopper into ecstasy. Prepare to find a great selection of women's wear at area hotel-casino malls and outlet centers. Name a designer, and you should find a signature shop in this town.

Continued on page 246

SIGNATURE VEGAS

By Matt Villano

Even if you travel with designer bath products, sometimes the complimentary, one-of-a-kind soaps, shampoos, conditioners, and lotions that you get in a Las Vegas hotel room are too good to ignore.

Many properties—especially those that have partnered with high-end vendors to create signature brands—sell larger versions of their in-room bath products at spas and on-site gift shops. In most cases, at properties such as Mandalay Bay Hotel & Casino, MGM Grand, and Wynn Las Vegas, these products are only available in Sin City itself. In rare cases (like at Bellagio, for instance), the products are available for purchase online. These sweet-smelling items serve two purposes: they nourish your body, and they smell nice, evoking memories of your trip every time you use them. Here's a closer look at the highlights of Sin City's signature bath products, and a rundown on where you can go to purchase some of the goodies to enjoy at home.

SPOTLIGHT: SYNTHETIC PHEROMONES

In a more subtle approach to keeping customers satisfied, most Vegas resorts circulate fragrances throughout the casino and hotel. These signature scents, dubbed "synthetic pheromones," are concocted to inspire you and stimulate your senses. They range from a piney citrus (at Wynn Las Vegas) to coconut musk (at Mandalay Bay). The catch: few, if any, casino officials like to talk about the scents openly. Behind closed doors, some casino workers describe the science as "olfactory marketing." These folks insist the smells instill a sense of comfort and security that make you feel more at ease, increasing the likelihood of repeat visits. For this reason, you won't find these secret scents for sale in any gift shops.

BATH PRODUCTS

BATHE. Designed exclusively by the English toiletry company Gilchrist & Soames for THEhotel at Mandalay Bay, these vegetable-based soaps, lotions, and hair products smell like lemony sugar and are enhanced with anti-oxidant botanicals. All items are available for sale in THEstore, which is on the first floor of the hotel. Prices start at $14.99.

BAMBU. Rumor has it that Steve Wynn likes things in the shape of eggs, which would explain why the soaps in this tailor-made line of bath products are so elliptical. The products—soaps, shampoo, conditioner, and lotion—smell like fresh, milky lemongrass. The items are for sale at the spas in both

Wynn and Encore, and four different gift shops. Prices start at $12.99.

NURTURE. Concept Amenities makes a line of special products for the Luxor, including green-tea scented conditioner and facial gel, white ginger bar soap, vanilla-cinnamon lotion, and chamomile shampoo. While these specific products aren't available for purchase, guests can buy similar products in The Spa at Luxor. Prices start at $13.99.

BELLAGIO also offers signature bath products, but they're only available at www.bellagioathome.com.

If you like the products at a hotel that we didn't mention, you'll have to hit the maids' carts. Just don't blame us if you get caught.

Balenciaga. Balenciaga is at the top of the style food chain. The Italian fashion house brings an architectural approach to handbags and accessories. ⊠ *Forum Shops at Caesars, 3500 Las Vegas Blvd. S, Center Strip* ☎ *702/732–1660* ⊕ *www.balenciaga.com.*

Beckley. It's an all-in-one experience at this boutique that originated in L.A. You'll find clothes appropriate for a casual walk on the Strip and gear made for a night of club-hopping. A stylist and tailor on-site make your shopping experience that much more convenient. ⊠ *The Cosmopolitan, 3708 Las Vegas Blvd. South, Center Strip* ☎ *702/698–7600.*

Betsey Johnson. This store is for the girly-girl with edge as pouffy party dresses mingle with untamed animal prints. ⊠ *Fashion Show Mall, 3200 Las Vegas Blvd. S, North Strip* ☎ *702/735–3338* ⊕ *www.betseyjohnson. com* ⊠ *Miracle Mile Shops at Planet Hollywood, 3663 Las Vegas Blvd. S, Center Strip* ☎ *702/731–0286.*

Bottega Veneta. Renowned for its modern take on old classics, this Italian fashion house melds elegant style with leather fabrics. The line appeals to the woman with a taste for timelessness. ⊠ *The Shoppes at The Palazzo, 3325 Las Vegas Blvd. S, North Strip* ☎ *702/369–0747* ⊕ *www. bottegaveneta.com* ⊠ *Via Bellagio, 3600 Las Vegas Blvd. S, Center Strip* ☎ *702/369–2944* ⊠ *Crystals at CityCenter, 3720 Las Vegas Blvd., Center Strip* ☎ *702/220–4751.*

Burberry. The luxury British brand features its famous trench coats and rain gear as well as hot fashion accessories. ⊠ *Grand Canal Shoppes at the Venetian, 3377 Las Vegas Blvd. S, North Strip* ☎ *702/735–2600* ⊠ *Forum Shops at Caesars, 3500 Las Vegas Blvd. S, Center Strip* ☎ *702/731–0650.*

Chanel. Las Vegas boasts three branches of this fine French couturier. The boutique at Encore, however, marks the world's first ultraluxe Chanel boutique. ⊠ *Wynn Esplanade, 3131 Las Vegas Blvd. S, North Strip* ☎ *702/765–5055* ⊠ *Encore Esplanade, 3131 Las Vegas Blvd. S, North Strip* ☎ *702/765–5255* ⊠ *Via Bellagio, 3600 Las Vegas Blvd. S, Center Strip* ☎ *702/765–5505.*

Chloé. The French fashion house puts out ultrafeminine takes on current trends. ⊠ *The Shoppes at The Palazzo, 3325 Las Vegas Blvd. S, North Strip* ☎ *702/266–8122* ⊕ *www.chloe.com.*

Diane von Furstenberg. Head here for something figure-flattering, comfortable, and high on the style scale. Diane von Furstenberg, or DVF as she's known to longtime followers, first made her fashion presence known in 1972 with her iconic wrap dress, which is still a staple in her collections to this day. ⊠ *The Shoppes at The Palazzo, 3325 Las Vegas Blvd. S, North Strip* ☎ *702/818–2294* ⊕ *www.dvf.com.*

Dior. Clothes from this storied fashion house appeal to the sophisticated woman who still wants to stand out in a crowd. ⊠ *Forum Shops at Caesars, 3500 Las Vegas Blvd. S, Center Strip* ☎ *702/737–9777* ⊠ *Wynn Esplanade, 3131 Las Vegas Blvd. S, North Strip* ☎ *702/735–1345* ⊠ *Via Bellagio, 3600 Las Vegas Blvd. S, Center Strip* ☎ *702/731–1334.*

DNA2050. Shopping for jeans has never been so easy. DNA2050 specializes in denim, carrying all the old faithfuls as well as brands you've never heard of before. ⊠ *The Cosmopolitan, 3708 Las Vegas Blvd. South, Center Strip* ☎ *702/698–7610.*

Fendi. The Italian designer offers elegant garments, furs, shoes, and handbags that transcend trends. ⊠ *Forum Shops at Caesars, 3500 Las Vegas Blvd. S, Suite C1, Center Strip* ☎ *702/732–9040* ⊕ *www.fendi. com* ⊠ *The Shoppes at The Palazzo, 3327 Las Vegas Blvd. S, North Strip* ☎ *702/369–0587* ⊠ *Via Bellagio, 3600 Las Vegas Blvd. S, Center Strip* ☎ *702/732–7766* ⊠ *Crystals at CityCenter, 3720 Las Vegas Blvd. S, Center Strip* ☎ *702/262–5638.*

Gucci. If you must drop a grand on a pair of loafers, come here. Though the salespeople's noses are definitely turned up, the Gucci reputation prevails. ⊠ *Forum Shops at Caesars, 3500 Las Vegas Blvd. S, Suite C1, Center Strip* ☎ *702/369–7333* ⊠ *Via Bellagio, 3600 Las Vegas Blvd. S, Center Strip* ☎ *702/732–9300.*

H&M. The crème de la crème of fast fashion, this Swedish retailer features affordable apparel and accessories that rival what you'll see on high-profile runways. Diffused lines from acclaimed designers are also prevalent here. The location at the Forum Shops is the biggest H&M in the country. ⊠ *Town Square, 6605 Las Vegas Blvd. S, Airport* ☎ *702/260–1481* ⊕ *www.hm.com* ⊠ *Miracle Mile Shops at Planet Hollywood, 3663 Las Vegas Blvd. S, Center Strip* ☎ *702/369–1195* ⊠ *Forum Shops, 3500 Las Vegas Blvd., Center Strip* ☎ *702/893–4800*

Hermès. The Parisian brand's Birkin bags are so exclusive you could be on a waiting list for several years—yes, years—before securing one. The scarves and clothes carry the same prestige without the waiting game. ⊠ *Encore Esplanade, 3131 Las Vegas Blvd. S, North Strip* ☎ *702/650– 3116* ⊕ *www.hermes.com* ⊠ *Crystals at CityCenter, 3720 S. Las Vegas Blvd., Center Strip* ☎ *702/893–8900.*

Herve Leger. Expect to find the famous bandage dresses that put this brand on the map here. The clothes aren't modest and neither are the price tags. ⊠ *Miracle Mile Shops at Planet Hollywood, 3663 Las Vegas Blvd. S, Center Strip* ☎ *702/732–4529* ⊕ *www.herveleger.com.*

Judith Leiber. These bejeweled handbags qualify as fine jewelry, with prices in the thousands of dollars to match. ⊠ *Forum Shops at Caesars, 3500 Las Vegas Blvd. S, Center Strip* ☎ *702/792–0661* ⊕ *www. judithleiber.com.*

Juicy Couture. To think, it all started with a velour tracksuit. The line has since evolved into a full-fledged lifestyle brand of flirty, irreverent fashion. ⊠ *Forum Shops at Caesars, 3500 Las Vegas Blvd. S, Center Strip* ☎ *702/452–5777* ⊕ *www.juicycouture.com* ⊠ *Town Square, 6605 Las Vegas Blvd. S, Airport* ☎ *702/269–3199.*

Louis Vuitton. Stash your winnings in a designer bag from one of four Vegas branches of this famous French accessories maker. ⊠ *Wynn Esplanade, 3131 Las Vegas Blvd. S, North Strip* ☎ *702/650–9007* ⊠ *Crystals at CityCenter, 3720 Las Vegas Blvd. S, Center Strip* ☎ *702/262–6189* ⊠ *Forum Shops at Caesars, 3500 Las Vegas Blvd. S, Center Strip* ☎ *702/732–1227* ⊠ *Fashion Show Mall, 3200 Las Vegas Blvd. S, North Strip* ☎ *702/731–9860.*

Marc Jacobs. The American designer is known for his innovative silhouettes and creative apparel. Ladylike elegance meets cutting-edge fashion here. ⊠ *Forum Shops at Caesars, 3500 Las Vegas Blvd. S, Center Strip* ☎ *702/369–2007* ⊕ *www.marcjacobs.com.*

Marni. If you like a classic look with a twist, this is the store for you. The brand is known for turning the predictable into something unpredictable. The 2,500-square-feet of space offers men's and women's ready-to-wear, leather goods, shoes, and accessories. ⊠ *CityCenter, 3720 Las Vegas Blvd. S, Center Strip* ☎ *702/726–9360* ⊕ *www. marniinternational.com.*

Oscar de la Renta. Stop here for the finest offerings of this Dominican couturier. ⊠ *Wynn Esplanade, 3131 Las Vegas Blvd. S, North Strip* ☎ *702/770–3487.*

Outfit. If it's graced the pages of *Vogue*, it's hanging on the racks of Outfit. Only the crème de la crème make it into this boutique. Names like Lanvin, Ungaro, Zac Posen, Narciso Rodriguez, and Nina Ricci all call this place home. ⊠ *Wynn Esplanade, 3131 Las Vegas Blvd. S, North Strip* ☎ *702/770–3465.*

Tory Burch. Think ladies who lunch circa 1972. Interesting prints, bib dresses, tunics, and ballet flats are staples here. ⊠ *Forum Shops at Caesars, 3500 Las Vegas Blvd. S., Center Strip* ☎ *702/369–3459* ⊠ *The Shoppes at the Palazzo, 3327 Las Vegas Blvd. S., Center Strip* ☎ *702/369–0541.* ⊠ *The Shoppes at The Palazzo, 3325 Las Vegas Blvd. S, North Strip* ☎ *702/369–0549.*

Versace. This boutique features a body-conscious, seductive line of ready-to-wear clothes that speaks to a confident woman. Remember Jennifer Lopez's provocative green Versace dress at the Grammy's? Enough said. ⊠ *Forum Shops at Caesars, 3500 Las Vegas Blvd. S, Center Strip* ☎ *702/932–5757.*

MALLS OFF THE STRIP

Fodor's Choice ★ **Fashion Outlets Las Vegas.** This outlet mall is definitely worth a shopping safari to nearby Primm, Nevada, about a half hour south down Interstate 15. Here you find many of the same stores as on the Strip but at prices slashed by as much as 75%. And you don't often see these stores represented at an outlet mall: Williams-Sonoma Marketplace, St. John Company Store, and Michael Kors (USA) Inc. Last Call from Neiman Marcus stocks designer labels as well as its private labels. You'll also find a plethora of the usual outlet-mall suspects: Banana Republic Factory Store, Polo Ralph Lauren Factory Store, the Kenneth Cole Outlet, and the Gap Outlet. If you don't want to battle the traffic, take the shuttle service ($15 round-trip) that runs daily from the MGM Grand, Fashion Show, and Miracle Mile shops. ⊠ *32100 Las Vegas Blvd. S, Primm* ☎ *702/874–1400* ⊕ *www.fashionoutletlasvegas.com.*

Las Vegas Outlet Center. Immerse yourself in one of the country's largest discount malls, which is, ironically, just a few miles from the Strip's most exclusive and expensive shopping. Anne Taylor Factory Store, Jones New York, Tommy Kids, and Calvin Klein are among the 130

Town Square Las Vegas is an outdoor shopping mall designed to look like Main Street America. There are more than 150 shops, as well as numerous eateries, and a multiplex cinema to entertain you.

stores selling pretty much everything at discount prices: clothing, jewelry, toys, shoes, beauty products, souvenirs, and more. The mall has two food courts and a full-size carousel. Saks Fifth Avenue Off 5th occupies the majority of space at Las Vegas Outlet Center Annex, a small separate building on the south side. To get here, take Las Vegas Boulevard South 3 miles south from the Tropicana Avenue intersection. ⊠ *7400 Las Vegas Blvd. S, Airport* ☎ *702/896–5599* ⊕ *www. lasvegasoutletcenter.com.*

Fodor's Choice ★ **Las Vegas Premium Outlets.** The upscale mix at this racetrack-shape Downtown outlet mall includes names you can find at your own mall, such as Nine West, Charlotte Russe, and Quiksilver, but with better discounts; and rarely seen outlets of fashion heavyweights, such as Dolce & Gabbana, St. John Company Store, Brooks Brothers Factory Store, Juicy Couture, Michael Kors, Ted Baker, Ed Hardy, and A/X Armani Exchange. Fashion jeweler David Yurman and coveted shoe designer Stuart Weitzman are also here. This is one of the few outdoor malls in town, and there's plenty of shade as well as misting towers to keep you cool in the Vegas desert. The mall runs a $1 shuttle from the California Hotel, the Golden Nugget, and the Downtown Transportation Center, but if you want to drive, two parking garages allow easy access to the mall. ⊠ *875 S. Grand Central Pkwy., Downtown* ☎ *702/474–7500* ⊕ *www.premiumoutlets.com.*

SPECIALTY SHOPS OFF THE STRIP

BOOKS

Psychic Eye Book Shop. Behind the innocuous strip-mall facade are all sorts of esoteric books, lucky talismans, tarot cards, and candles. Get a psychic reading or an astrological chart on where to place your bets. ⊠ *6848 W. Charleston Blvd., East Side* ☎ *702/255–4477* ⊕ *www. pebooks.com* ⊠ *5835 S. Eastern Ave., Henderson* ☎ *702/451–5777.*

FOOD AND DRINK

↻ **Ethel M Chocolates Factory and Cactus Garden.** The *M* stands for Mars, the name of the family (headed by Ethel in the early days) that brings you Snickers, Milky Way, Three Musketeers, and M&M's. Come here for two special reasons: one, to watch the candy making, and two (more important), to taste free samples in the adjoining shop. As for the other, not-quite-as-exciting half of this place's name, yes—there is, indeed, a cactus garden with more than 350 species of succulents and desert plants. It's at its peak during spring flowering. ⊠ *2 Cactus Garden Dr., Henderson* ☎ *702/435–2655* ⊕ *www.ethelm.com.*

HOME FURNISHINGS

Williams-Sonoma Marketplace. Here's the place for the hard-to-buy-for domestic goddess in your life. Gourmet cooking tools and home-decor items—spectacular wreaths, ornate candles—keep visitors occupied for hours. ⊠ *The District at Green Valley Ranch, 2255 Village Walk Dr., Henderson* ☎ *702/897–2346* ⊠ *Rampart Commons, 1001 S. Rampart Blvd., Summerlin* ☎ *702/938–9480* ⊠ *Fashion Outlets, 32100 Las Vegas Blvd. S, Primm* ☎ *702/874–1780.*

MEN'S CLOTHING

Undefeated. This store is the authority in premium sneakers and street wear, which is why you'll see patrons sleeping outside its doors when limited-edition lines debut. ⊠ *4480 Paradise Rd., #400, Paradise Road* ☎ *702/732–0019* ⊕ *www.undftd.com.*

VINTAGE CLOTHING

Buffalo Exchange. This is a must-stop for the terminally hip. The extensive collection of great vintage clothing at reasonable prices makes for satisfying shopping. You also can find great recycled discards and, since we all could use the help, lots of suggestions from the friendly staff. ⊠ *4110 S. Maryland Pkwy., East Side* ☎ *702/791–3960* ⊕ *www. buffaloexchange.com.*

WESTERN WEAR

Shepler's. Since 1946, thousands of cowboys (and cowgirls) have bought their Wranglers and Stetsons here. ⊠ *4700 W. Sahara Ave., West Side* ☎ *702/258–2000* ⊕ *www.sheplers.com* ⊠ *Sam's Town, 5111 Boulder Hwy., Boulder Strip* ☎ *702/454–5266 .*

Shows

WORD OF MOUTH

"Go see Ka or Le Rev. Don't spend anything extra on tix for Le Rev. There's not a bad seat in the house."

—mike61

Updated
by Mike
Weatherford

THE VERY NAME "LAS VEGAS" has been synonymous with a certain style of showbiz ever since Jimmy Durante first headlined at Bugsy Siegel's Flamingo Hotel in 1946. Through the years this entertainment mecca has redefined itself a number of times, but one thing has remained consistent—doing things big.

The star power that made the old "supper club" days glitter with names like Frank Sinatra and Dean Martin is making a latter-day comeback in showcases by veteran concert acts Rod Stewart and Celine Dion. Nationally known performers such as Penn & Teller and Carrot Top have come to roost on the Strip after years of living out of a suitcase. *Jubilee!* hangs in there as a shimmering example of the "feather shows" that made an icon of the showgirl, while technologically advanced shows such as *Blue Man Group* and Cirque du Soleil's *O* have modernized the spectacle. Female impersonators, "dirty" dancers, comedians— all perpetuate the original style of razzle-dazzle entertainment that Las Vegas has popularized for the world.

In the not-so-olden days, shows were intended to draw patrons who would eventually wind up in the casino. Nowadays the accounting's separate and it can cost you around $100 to see Elton John or Donny and Marie Osmond and $253 for Garth Brooks. To hold ticket prices around the $30 line bargain-hunters have learned to look to afternoon shows, such as the comedic magic of Mac King at Harrah's.

On the right weekend you still might run into one of the old names, such as Don Rickles or Tony Bennett. But the new generation of resident headliners ranges from ventriloquist Terry Fator to "mindfreak" Criss Angel to Cee Lo Green, who reinvented himself as "Loberace" for a test run at the Strip in 2012. The Cirque spectaculars continue to dominate, presenting little or no language barrier to the city's large numbers of international tourists.

SHOWS PLANNER

RESERVED-SEAT TICKETING

Most hotels offer reserved-seat show tickets, and nearly all the Las Vegas shows are available through corporate ticketing networks such as Ticketmaster or Vegas.com. If you don't buy in advance, an old-fashioned visit to the show's box office is still your best bet for minimizing add-on charges. It's advisable to purchase tickets to concerts or the hotter shows, such as the Cirque du Soleil productions, ahead of a visit. For smaller shows or spontaneous decisions, "half price" has become the new "full price," thanks to an explosion of discount kiosks along the Strip. Only pay full face value for a headliner name or a show you really want to see. Remember that for the popular titles, casinos control their inventory and make sure their big players are always taken care of. If advance tickets are no longer available, check for last-minute cancelations. Your chances of getting a seat are usually better when you're staying—and gambling—at the hotel.

If you plan on spending a fair amount of time at the tables or slots, call VIP Services or a slot host to find out what their requirements are for getting a comp, paid tickets that have been withheld for last-minute release, or perks such as premium seating or a line pass (it allows you to go straight to the VIP entrance without having to wait in line with the hoi polloi).

CONTACTS AND RESOURCES

Ticketmaster. As most of the venues in town are part of Ticketmaster, you can buy tickets at any Ticketmaster outlet or on the website. ☎ 800/745–3000 ⊕ *www.ticketmaster.com.*

Vegas.com. Vegas.com has become a major sales outlet for full-priced tickets. "Convenience" and "processing" fees are spelled out clearly before you hit the final button to place your order. ⊕ *www.vegas.com.*

Tix4tonight. With 10 locations and counting, Tix4tonight is the place to visit for most ongoing shows (but not the hot concert acts or headliners). There's a service charge for each ticket and the majority of business is for same-day walk-up sales. Strip booths are in Circus-Circus, Slots-A-Fun, the Fashion Show Mall, the Hawaiian Marketplace shopping center, two outlets at the Showcase Mall (look for the giant Coke bottle), Bill's Casino, and the Casino Royale. The Downtown location's inside the Four Queens casino. Another outlet is on Las Vegas Boulevard, way south of the pedestrian part of the Strip, in the popular Town Square shopping center. Originally, prices were half price across the board and only for that day's performance. But the company's now such a dominant source that some producers try to get away with lesser discounts and some make their titles available a day in advance or via phone reservations. ☎ 877/849–4868 ⊕ *www.tix4tonight.com.*

FIND OUT WHAT'S GOING ON

Information on shows, including their reservation and seating policies, prices and suitability for children (or age restrictions), is available by calling or visiting box offices. It's also listed in several local publications or websites.

The **Las Vegas Advisor** (✉ *3687 S. Procyon Ave., West Side* ☎ *800/244–2224* ⊕ *www.lasvegasadvisor.com*) is available as a monthly printed newsletter at its office for $5 per issue or $50 per year. An online membership is $37 and the website has become a font of free news and coupons. It's a bargain-focused consumer's guide to Las Vegas dining, entertainment, gambling promotions, comps, and news.

The stories tend to be of the fawning press-release variety, but two free visitor publications are filled with show listings and discount coupons: *Today in Las Vegas* (⊕ *www.todayinlv.com*) and *What's On, the Las Vegas Guide* (⊕ *www.whats-on.com*) are available at hotels and gift shops.

The *Las Vegas Review-Journal,* the city's morning daily newspaper, publishes a pullout section each Friday called *Neon,* with free distribution separately. It provides entertainment features and reviews, and showroom and lounge listings with complete time and price information. In the tourist corridor, the daily *Review-Journal* is wrapped inside a Daily Visitor's Guide that includes show listings. The newspaper also maintains a website (⊕ *www.lvrj.com*), and entertainment reporters blog about the latest developments. The *Las Vegas Sun,* a competing daily that once had separate distribution, is now a section inside the *Review-Journal* but maintains its own editorial staff and website, ⊕ *www.lasvegassun.com.*

Three alternative weekly newspapers are distributed at retail stores and coffee shops around town and maintain comprehensive websites. They tend to be the best source for coverage of the nightclub scene and music beyond the realm of the casinos: *Las Vegas Weekly* (⊕ *www.lasvegasweekly.com*), *Vegas Seven* (⊕ *www.weeklyseven.com*), and *Las Vegas City Life* (⊕ *www.lasvegascitylife.com*).

WHAT'S NEW?

Cirque du Soleil's Michael Jackson tribute The Immortal is due to land at Mandalay Bay in May 2013 as the company's latest resident Vegas title. Elvis has left the building though; Cirque replaced the underperforming Viva Elvis with Zarkana in late 2012.

Celine Dion, Rod Stewart, and **Elton John** continue to rotate dates in the 4,300-seat Colosseum at Caesars Palace, where they were set to be joined by resurgent country-pop diva **Shania Twain** in late 2012. **Carlos Santana** moved into the House of Blues at Mandalay Bay for about 30 shows a year in 2013, and 2012's two-week stand by **Motley Crue** at the Hard Rock Hotel was a home run that will not only command an encore by the Crue, but will inspire other rockers to copy the model of a limited run.

Blue Man Group was set to move from the Venetian to the Monte Carlo in late 2012, with the campy Broadway hit **Rock of Ages** set to replace it. Blue Man Group displaced the hip-hop dancing **Jabbawockeez**, who planned to move from the Monte Carlo to a new theater on the attractions level of the Luxor in 2013.

Despite the economic downturn and the pinch of competition from nightclubs, restaurants, and shopping, the number of shows in Vegas is increasing. Depending on how you count comedy clubs and short-haul headliners such as Dion, the total number of shows in 2012 was more than 100. It seems the city isn't ready to surrender its self-appointed status of "The Entertainment Capital of the World" just yet.

AFTERNOON SHOWS

Las Vegas has become a wider-reaching and more family-friendly destination. But at the same time, evening show prices can be in the triple digits. These factors are sometimes at odds with one another and help explain a few afternoon shows that hold their ticket prices down or discount heavily with promotional coupons. The following are the most proven and popular.

⟲ **Mac King.** The reigning king of Las Vegas afternoons—12 years and counting at Harrah's Las Vegas—seems more like a Ragtime-era court jester with his plaid suit and folksy "Howdy!" King stands apart from the other magic shows on the Strip with a one-man hour of low-key, self-deprecating humor and the kind of close-up magic that's baffling, but doesn't take the focus away from the running banter. But watch out

Fodor's Choice
★

RAVES AND FAVES

Splashiest opening: It's a curtain war. The beginning of *O* gets things off to an astonishing start when a regal curtain is whooshed away into the backstage recesses as though sucked into a giant vacuum cleaner. Not to be outdone, Celine Dion's new show drops and then whisks away a 2,000-pound white scrim to reveal the orchestra.

Best finale: The climactic scene of *LOVE* just had to be "A Day in the Life." Cirque du Soleil rises to the challenge of the famous orchestral buildup with a symbolic, moving scene featuring an angelic, floating mother figure. (Remember that both John Lennon and Paul McCartney's mothers died young.)

Best band in town: The blue baldies in the Blue Man Group never talk, so it's even more important that their silent antics be backed by a rocking sound track. The seven-piece band keeps the sound percussive and otherworldly.

Most words per minute: Penn & Teller discuss everything from "ocular hygiene" to "petroleum by-products" (meaning Solo cups), conveniently overlooking the fact that most Vegas shows push spectacle over words. What's even more amazing? Only one of them (Penn) talks.

Most deliberately provocative: There was much speculation about whether a man-to-man kiss would stay in Cirque du Soleil's *Zumanity*. It did, although now it's later in the show and placed in a more comedic context.

Best guilty pleasure: *Crazy Horse Paris* has the faux sophistication of the soft-core *Emmanuelle* flicks of the '70s, which makes it even more jolting when off-the-wall specialty acts such as "Micro Jackson" break the spell of the kaleidoscopically lighted dancers.

for that bear! ⊠ *Harrah's Las Vegas, 3475 Las Vegas Blvd. S, Center Strip* ☎ *702/369–5111* ☎ *$33* ⊙ *Tues.–Sat. 1 and 3.*

☺ **Nathan Burton Comedy Magic.** The likable magician whom many came to know on *America's Got Talent* puts a fun spin on familiar illusions— behold! The "Microwave of Death"—and is family-friendly for those with older children. ⊠ *Flamingo Las Vegas, 3555 Las Vegas Blvd. S, Center Strip* ☎ *702/733–3333* ☎ *$37–$47* ⊙ *Tues.–Sun. 4.*

The Price Is Right. Come on down! Audience members get called by familiar hosts such as Todd Newton and Joey Fatone to play favorites such as Plinko and Cliffhangers on a set just like the TV version, for real prizes. Contestants must be 21 and preregister. ⊠ *Bally's Las Vegas, 3535 Las Vegas Blvd. S, Center Strip* ☎ *702/967–4567* ☎ *$56* ⊙ *Wed.– Sun 2:30 pm.*

COMEDY CLUBS

Even when Las Vegas wasn't the hippest place to catch a musical act, it was always up-to-the-minute in the comedy department. From Shecky Greene to Daniel Tosh, virtually every famous comedian has worked a Las Vegas showroom or lounge. Although the franchised comedy-club

Blue Man Group is a show for the whole family.

boom of the 1980s went bust in most cities, the Strip still has dependable comedy clubs with multiple-act formats featuring top names on the circuit. Cover charges are in the $30 range, but two-for-one coupons are easy to come by in freebie magazines and various coupon packages.

Brad Garrett's Comedy Club. Brad Garrett returned to his stand-up roots and after establishing a comedy club at the Tropicana, moved it across the street in 2012 to a retail area of the MGM Grand. This is a new space, not a retrofit, which the comedian fashioned after a 1930s speakeasy. He still hand-picks the comedians and headlines several times per year himself: "It was either this or 'Jews on Ice' at the Stratosphere," he likes to tell audiences. ⊠ *MGM Grand, 3799 Las Vegas Blvd. S, South Strip* ☎ *702/891–7318* ☾ *Sun–Thurs. 8 pm, Fri. and Sat. 8 and 10 pm.*

The Improv. Comedy impresario Budd Friedman oversees the bookings for this 300-seat showroom on the second floor of Harrah's. It has the occasional bigger name such as Jay Mohr and is frequently packaged with room or player's club discounts. ⊠ *Harrah's Las Vegas, 3475 Las Vegas Blvd. S, Center Strip* ☎ *702/369–5223* ☾ *Tues.–Sun. 8:30 and 10:30 pm.*

Louie Anderson. The veteran Vegas comedian plays to tourists and locals alike at Palace Station, slightly off the Strip. His "Louie LOL" forum pulls the "greatest hits" of his childhood and family material back into focus, but touches on present-day concerns as well. The Florida-based Bonkerz chain of comedy clubs produces Anderson's show and lines up substitute headliners when he is on the road. ⊠ *Palace Station, 2411 W. Sahara Ave., West Side* ☎ *702/547–5300* ☾ *Wed. –Sat. 7 pm.*

Celine Dion takes center stage at Caesars Palace for a limited number of must-see special engagements.

Sin City Comedy. Veteran comedian John Padon gave the usual stand-up formula a new twist by mixing (covered) burlesque numbers in between comedians. It's a fun variation that might sway gents who are unfamiliar with the names on any particular lineup. ⊠ *Miracle Mile Shops at Planet Hollywood, 3663 Las Vegas Blvd. S, South Strip* ☎ *702/260–7200* ⊙ *Daily 9 pm.*

EVENING REVUES

Fodor's Choice
★

Blue Man Group. The three bald, blue, and silent characters in utilitarian uniforms have become part of the Las Vegas landscape. At the end of 2012, Blue Man Group was set to move from the Venetian to a remodeled theater at the Monte Carlo. As they did at the Venetian, they promise new, large-scale sequences to go with the classics that stem from the group's humble off-Broadway origins: paint splattering, marshmallow catching, and banging on PVC pipe contraptions to their unique brand of interstellar rock and roll. ⊠ *Monte Carlo, 3770 Las Vegas Blvd. S, Center Strip* ☎ *702/730–7160* ⊕ *www.blueman.com* ⊠ *$65–$148* ⊙ *Daily 7 and 10 pm (with seasonal variations).*

Chippendales: The Show. Score one for the ladies: The Rio builds a theater dedicated to the men of Chippendales, surrounds it with a lounge and gift shop, and gives the historically male-oriented entertainment in this town a jolt. The show has fancier staging than any G-string revue traveling on the nightclub circuit, and the bow-tied hunks keep it respectable enough to let Mom tag along with the bachelorette party. To sustain interest amid competition, the Chips have taken to guest hosts such as Jeff Timmons of the boy band 98 Degrees and Jake Pavelka of "The Bachelor." ⊠ *Rio All-Suite Hotel & Casino, 3700 W. Flamingo Rd., West Side* ☎ *702/777–7776* 💺 *$47–$58* ☼ *Daily 8 pm, also Fri. and Sat. 10:30 pm.*

Crazy Girls. The Riviera staged this low-rent version of the Crazy Horse Cabaret in Paris long before the real Crazy Horse opened at the MGM Grand Hotel. The topless revue got a much-needed sprucing up along with the rest of the Riviera in 2011, helping both to stay competitive as the show celebrates its 25th anniversary in the fall of 2012. ⊠ *Riviera Hotel and Casino, 2901 Las Vegas Blvd. S, North Strip* ☎ *702/794–9433* 💺 *$56–$72* ☼ *Tues.–Sat. 9:30 pm.*

Crazy Horse Paris. The MGM Grand wooed Paris's Crazy Horse Cabaret to Las Vegas by remodeling a lounge into a near spitting image of the French institution, complete with a carefully sized stage that creates a wide-screen movie effect. It remains a mock-sophisticated affair in which *les femmes* are symmetrically matched, naturally endowed women expertly choreographed and "painted in light" for humorous or erotically mimed vignettes. The show was set to take a break in the summer of 2012 as the casino around it was remodeled, and planned to reopen with a format tweak that would make the room more of a nightclub instead of merely hosting the show. ⊠ *MGM Grand Hotel & Casino, 3799 Las Vegas Blvd. S, South Strip* ☎ *702/891–7777* 💺 *$50–$60* ☼ *Wed.–Mon. 8 and 10:30 pm.*

Criss Angel—Believe. When no one seemed to appreciate the odd-couple pairing of Cirque du Soleil and the star of television's *Mindfreak,* Cirque backed off and left Angel on his own to rework the show in 2010. He stripped down the production, eliminated most of the artsy theatrics, and transformed it into a more predictable magic showcase—one that's rockin' loud and full of pyrotechnics as Angel bustles through one illusion after another like a young(er) David Copperfield. Consider the changes a good thing if you're a fan of his, maybe less so if it was Cirque's name and contribution that intrigued you. ⊠ *Luxor Las Vegas, 3900 Las Vegas Blvd. S, South Strip* ☎ *702/262–4400* 💺 *$74–$185* ☼ *Tues.–Sat. 7 and 9:30 pm.*

Defending the Caveman. Rob Becker's anthropological take on the battle of the sexes is a popular touring one-man show that brought something new to Las Vegas: theatrical long-form comedy, in the form of a likable schlub. Kevin Burke delivers an extended monologue (with lighting and sound cues, plus a funny opening video with his real-life wife) that preaches greater understanding on a set that looks like it's right out of *The Flintstones.* ■ TIP➔ Two of the weekly performances are in the afternoon (4 pm Sunday and Monday). ⊠ *Harrah's Las Vegas, 3475 Las Vegas Blvd. S, Center Strip* ☎ *702/369–5111* 💺 *$46–$74* ☼ *Daily 7 pm; also Sun. and Mon. 4 pm.*

Fantasy. It's not uncommon to see couples in the audience here. Fantasy is a topless show that would rather be a pop variety show, and it acts upon that particular fantasy with power-pop belting by fireball host Lorena Peril and impressions and clowning from Sean Cooper. ⊠ *Luxor*

7

Las Vegas, 3900 Las Vegas Blvd. S, South Strip ☎ *702/262–4400* ✉ *$46–$68* ☉ *Nightly 10:30 pm.*

Jersey Boys. Las Vegas proved to be a fine location for a permanent company of the runaway hit biography of Frankie Valli and the Four Seasons, which moved to Paris Las Vegas in early 2012 after three years at the Palazzo. The show has become a phenomenon, thanks to familiar music combined with the the little-known story of the group's rough-and-tumble beginnings, a surprising saga that contrasts dynamically with the familiar songs. It's all told at a cinematic clip with an edge of grit. One of the actors says the creators always reminded the cast, "You're in a Scorsese film. You're not in 'Guys & Dolls.'" The Vegas version is slightly trimmed but still runs in two acts. ✉ *Paris Las Vegas, 3325 Las Vegas Blvd. S, Center Strip* ☎ *877/874–7469* ✉ *$100–$227* ☉ *Wed.–Fri. and Sun. 7 pm, Tues. and Sat. 6:30 and 9:30 pm.*

Jubilee!. This is the last place to experience the over-the-top vision of Vegas showman Donn Arden, who produced shows on the Strip from 1952 to 1994. A cast of 80 performs a spectacle that marked its 30th birthday in 2011. It's the last bastion of showgirls parading around in feathers and headdresses amid gargantuan sets and props, such as the sinking of the *Titanic*. If you embrace how silly and dated it all is you will enjoy it that much more. ■ **TIP→** The early show on Saturday is "covered" (i.e., a bit more chaste) if you want to take the whole family. ✉ *Bally's Las Vegas, 3645 Las Vegas Blvd. S, Center Strip* ☎ *702/967–4567* ✉ *$57–$117* ☉ *Sat.–Thurs. 7:30 and 10:30 pm.*

KÀ. *KÀ* is Cirque du Soleil's bold interpretation of live martial-arts period fantasies like *Crouching Tiger, Hidden Dragon* in the adventures of two separated twins. The spectacle includes huge puppets and a battle on a vertical wall. A fixed stage is replaced by an 80,000-pound deck that's maneuvered by a giant gantry arm into all sorts of positions, including vertical. Though no Cirque since rivals it for sheer spectacle, the operatic tone remains divisive; those not sitting close enough to see faces can be confused by the story, which is told without dialogue. If nothing else, it's an amazing monument to the sky's-the-limit mentality that fueled Vegas in the go-go 2000s. ✉ *MGM Grand Hotel & Casino, 3805 Las Vegas Blvd. S, South Strip* ☎ *702/891–7777* ✉ *$85–$174* ☉ *Tues.–Sat. 7 and 9:30 pm.*

Legends in Concert. After 26 years at the Imperial Palace, the durable *Legends* moved next door to Harrah's Las Vegas with a much needed punch-up of production values. It's still the same basic formula of "mini-concerts" by a rotating lineup of celebrity impersonators, a vast range that includes Madonna, Toby Keith, Bobby Darin, and Lady Gaga. The Elvis Presley finale was the only constant, at least until the death of Michael Jackson brought a second tribute that's in the show as often as possible (there still aren't as many Jackson impersonators as there are Elvis). There's no lip-syncing and always a band. ✉ *Harrah's Las Vegas, 3475 Las Vegas Blvd. S, Center Strip* ☎ *702/369–5111* ✉ *$55–$65* ☉ *Sun.–Fri. 7 and 9:30 pm.*

Le Rêve. Perhaps befitting the surreal dream implied in the title, it has been a long, strange voyage for this aquatic spectacle created by orignial

O and *Mystere* director Franco Dragone. Le Rêve was heavily revised after it was deemed too reminiscent of *O*, and the theater-in-the-round now has a deluxe seating area with champagne service. Darker elements were toned down and the sex appeal turned up in the tale of a female dreamer adrift in a surreal journey to find love. Max Chmerkovskiy from *Dancing with the Stars* added a ballroom element to the water-based stunts and aerial acrobatics. You're likely to remember the sensual image of the dreamer in her dripping-wet dress as much as the 80-foot dives from an upper bell tower. ✉ *Wynn Las Vegas, 3131 Las Vegas Blvd. S, North Strip* ☎ *702/770–9966* 🎟 *$109–$214* ⏰ *Fri.–Tues. 7 and 9:30 pm.*

LOVE. Meet the Beatles again, well sort of, in a certified home run for Cirque du Soleil. Before he died, George Harrison convinced the surviving Beatles (and Yoko Ono) to license the group's music to Cirque for its fifth Las Vegas production. Even if you keep your eyes closed, the remixed music by producer George Martin and his son Giles is revelatory on the state-of-the-art sound system, often like hearing the songs for the first time. Coming up with visuals to match was more of a challenge. Cirque created a theatrical and fanciful version of Liverpool, telling the story of Beatlemania and the postwar generation without literally depicting the Fab Four. It's a lot to absorb, and one's attention can be split between the aerial stunt work and the action on the ground. But that just gives Beatles fans a reason to see it twice. ✉ *Mirage Las Vegas, 3400 Las Vegas Blvd. S, Center Strip* ☎ *702/792–7777* 🎟 *$85–$174* ⏰ *Thurs.–Mon. 7 and 9:30 pm.*

Michael Jackson "The Immortal". After two years on the road, Cirque du Soleil's salute to Michael Jackson will settle on the Strip in a remodeled Mandalay Bay theater in May 2013. The touring version was designed to play big in sports arenas, but Cirque officials say they want the permanent installation to be more theatrical and to use cutting-edge technology that would not be possible to pack along on tour. The road show inevitably played like a concert missing its star, but its creators included longtime collaborators of Jackson who worked hard to convey the themes of his childlike optimism and aesthetic. For better or worse, it was appropriately eccentric and naive, avoiding the easy road of simply using his music as a sound track for the usual Cirque shenanigans. ✉ *Mandalay Bay Resort & Casino, 3950 Las Vegas Blvd. S, South Strip* ☎ *702/531–2166.*

Mystère. Since 1993 Cirque du Soleil's new-age circus has been the town's most consistent family show. *Mystère* most purely preserves the original Cirque concept, and has held up to the increased spectacle of its sister shows by being the funniest of the bunch, and by keeping the spectators close to the action and the human acrobatics in the spotlight. Perhaps more than the other Cirque productions, you're intimately involved with this surreal wonderland and the comic characters who interact with the audience. In early 2012, the show swapped out the climactic trapeze number for an aerialist display from a closed show in Japan, providing new incentive to re-explore *Mystère*. ✉ *Treasure Island Las Vegas, 3300 Las Vegas Blvd. S, North Strip* ☎ *800/392–1999* 🎟 *$85–$129* ⏰ *Sat.–Wed. 7 and 9:30 pm.*

Continued on page 264

ANATOMY OF A SHOWGIRL

By Matt Villano

Move over, Old Blue Eyes. Sit down, Wayne Newton. You may be legends, but no one embodies the spirit of Sin City better than showgirls and their sequins, fishnets, and feathers.

For generations, these sexy, confident ladies have been the subject of boyhood (and manhood) fantasies. Whether entirely topless or merely scantily clad, showgirls have a timeless pinup-girl allure. What could be more Vegas?

Perhaps the best place to find the quintessential showgirl is Donn Arden's *Jubilee!*, a show that has played nonstop at Bally's Las Vegas for almost 25 years. It employs nearly 100 showgirls and still incorporates some of the costumes that Bob Mackey (creator of Cher's current Vegas show costumes) designed for the show's 1984 debut. For a rundown of showgirl accessories and attire, see opposite page.

DID YOU KNOW?

Over the course of a 90-minute *Jubilee!* show, the girls make between 7 and 11 costume changes. To reach the right parts of the three-level stage, they also run an average of 400 steps per night.

Top & Above, Don Arden's *Jubilee!*, Bally's Las Vegas

7

HEADDRESSES
Made of goose and rhea feathers, Swarovski crystal, and a whole lot of fabric, some of these headdresses can soar 5 feet and weigh up to 35 pounds.

WINGS
During the *Jubilee!* show, girls appear on stage with angel-like wings that are attached to tiny backpacks—the combination weighs 30 to 40 pounds.

FEATHER BOAS
Made from dyed ostrich feathers, these boas stretch up to 4 feet in length and can weigh as much as 5 or 6 pounds.

SEQUIN DRESSES
According to *Jubilee!*, the average costume contains 100,000 sequins in silver, gold, and a kaleidoscope of other colors. Each dress weighs 7–8 pounds.

G-STRINGS
This is a showgirl must. *Jubilee!* G-strings are made with a nude-colored fabric so they appear invisible to audience members.

FISHNETS
Jubilee! employs sewing technicians exclusively to keep fishnets looking good. In an average week, showgirls go through as many as six pairs.

HEELS
What's a showgirl without towering heels? Most dancers stomp around in three- or four-inchers; shorter gals opt for heels that are even higher.

JEWELRY
These pieces might contain rhinestones rather than diamonds but they're still substantial. Some of the jewelry can weigh up to 20 pounds.

Discount Tickets Vegas Style

It seemed like a welcome idea at the time. Visitors had long wondered when Las Vegas would get those kiosks for discount show tickets that people are used to looking for in New York's Broadway theater district.

When the first such outlet finally arrived on the Strip, producers were assured that they would remain in control of their own ticket inventory. Sell all the full-priced seats you can, the argument went, but why not fill any remaining seats at half price once it appeared full-price sales had peaked for the day?

And so it went. For a time. What the producers learned they couldn't control was the number of discount outlets. But, isn't that a win-win for the consumer, finding 10 or more of these booths all along the Strip now? Sort of. What happens now is that producers mark 'em up to mark 'em down. A middle-tier show such as *Fantasy* charges $46 to $68 in order to get half that. *The Amazing Johnathan* has gone from $54 a few years ago to $69. Now, any budget-minded person is almost forced to seek out the discount outlets for all but a handful of shows that still sell out at full face-value: Cirque du Soleil's *O* and *LOVE,* headliners such as Celine Dion with a limited number of performance dates, or touring concert acts.

And discount vendors are bending what once used to be simple, across-the-board pricing—all seats half price, plus a service charge—to experiment with discounts of less than 50% and some shows available a day in advance or by telephone. "Half-price outlets are like crack," noted one veteran of the ticket wars. "You start with a few and get that easy sale, so you start doing more and more."

The same-day outlets still make it deliberately inconvenient with no Internet sales, prodding those who have their hearts set on a title to buy ahead. But other discounts are out there as well, from coupon ads to room-and-show promotions bundled by the hotels. All of these, one producer explained, factor in to get prices from one number—the face value of a full-price ticket—to the real number a producer uses after averaging all the various discounts.

One magician says another who was new to town told him, "I figure if I can get just 100 full-priced sales a day, I'll be fine."

"Do you know how rare that is?" The veteran told him. "You will be lucky to get 30 on a good day."

—Mike Weatherford

Fodor's Choice ★ **O.** More than $70 million was spent on Cirque du Soleil's theater at Bellagio, and its liquid stage is a centerpiece of the show. It was money well spent: *O* is in its 14th year and remains one of the best-attended shows on the Strip. The title is taken from the French word for water (*eau*), and water is everywhere—1.5 million gallons of it, 12 million pounds of it, contained by a "stage" that, thanks to hydraulic lifts, can change shape and turn into dry land in no time. The intense and nonstop action by the show's acrobats, aerial gymnasts, trapeze artists, synchronized swimmers, divers, and contortionists takes place above, within, and even on the surface of the water, making for a stylish spectacle that manages to have a vague theme about the wellspring of theater and imagination. To grasp some of the deeper themes, which can be a bit elusive, and catch all that's going on, many people become repeat visitors. ⊠ *Bellagio Las Vegas, 3600 Las Vegas Blvd. S, Center Strip* ☎ *702/693–7722* ✉ *$117–$179* ⊗ *Wed.–Sun. 7:30 and 10 pm.*

Peepshow. Reality TV succeeded where Broadway director-choreographer Jerry Mitchell fell short. Mitchell conceived this one as a big-budget attempt to reinvent burlesque and striptease with a Broadway aesthetic. When audiences didn't respond in large enough numbers to his ribald riffs on classic fairy tales (What? Red Riding Hood isn't a turn-on?) it downsized and became a vehicle for former Playmate and "Girl Next Door" Holly Madison. So far the gambit has worked. The reality TV series *Holly's World* not only sustained Madison's curiosity value, but made reality-TV stars of her BFFs: male singer Josh Strickland and personal assistant Angel Porrino. ⊠ *Planet Hollywood Resort & Casino, 3667 Las Vegas Blvd. S, Center Strip* ☎ *702/785–5000* ✉ *$71–$137* ⊗ *Fri. and Mon. 9 pm, Sat. and Thurs. 8 and 10:30 pm.*

Rock of Ages. The unlikely Broadway hit, a salute to '80s-era hair metal and power ballads, actually played on the Strip very briefly in 2006 before it went on to the Great White(snake) Way. Now it's back, buoyed by the movie version starring Tom Cruise as an over-the-top rocker. The jukebox musical makes show tunes out of fist-pumpers such as "Sister Christian" and "Don't Stop Believin'," as it tells a story as old as rock and roll itself: The kids try to save their beloved club from greedy developers. ⊠ *The Venetian, 3355 Las Vegas Blvd., North Strip* ☎ *702/414–7469.*

☾ **Tournament of Kings.** One of the last vestiges of Las Vegas's "family" phase is 20-plus years of this Arthurian stunt show in a dirt-floor arena, with the audience eating a basic dinner (warning: no utensils) and cheering on fast horses, jousting, and swordplay (those familiar with Medieval Times around the country will recognize it in all but name). It's still a great family gathering—especially for preadolescents, who get to make a lot of noise—and the realistic stunts speak to the commitment of the cast. However, corporate indecision about the show's future has kept upgrades in limbo when it could use an overall sprucing up. ⊠ *Excalibur, 3850 Las Vegas Blvd. S, South Strip* ☎ *702/597–7600* ✉ *$68* ⊗ *Thurs.–Sun. 6 and 8:30 pm, Mon. and Wed. 6 pm.*

X Burlesque. There's no old-time burlesque here. Instead, an edgy modern-rock attitude permeates this dance-intensive topless revue. A comedian doing a 10-minute set is the only spoken contact with the audience. It's much closer to a strip-club vibe than the more theatrical *Fantasy* or *Peepshow*, which should serve as a recommendation to some and a warning to others. But even the more intense gyrations are leveled with a knowing humor. ⊠ *Flamingo Las Vegas, 3555 Las Vegas Blvd. S, Center Strip* ☎ *702/733–3333* ✉ *$49–$62* ⊗ *Daily 10 pm.*

Zumanity. For its third Las Vegas production, Cirque du Soleil deliberately turned away from the family market to indulge in an erotic, near-naked exploration of sexuality. The end product also followed the lead of Baz Luhrmann's movie *Moulin Rouge* by fusing Cirque

SAVE OR SPLURGE

Whether you're rollin' high or down on your luck, Vegas has a show for you. Check out the following steals and splurges:

SAVE

Mac King. The comedy magic of Mac King is worth every penny of the full $33 ticket price, and full-price tickets send you to the front of the line. But if you look for coupon-dispensing showgirls within the casino or check a promotions booth at the Carnaval Court lounge, you can often get in for the price of a $9.95 drink; especially when schools are in session.

Fremont Street Experience. Thought the Downtown Fremont Street Experience was limited to video shows on the overhead canopy covering Glitter Gulch? Not so. The street itself has become a midway, from sidewalk artists to the overhead zip line. Every weekend live performers—heavy on costumed tribute bands with names such as Fan Halen or Led Zepagain—play free gigs on two stages; select weekends even bring in acts with name recognition (breakout country stars Lady Antebellum and Eric Church have played the weekend of the Academy of Country Music Awards). Stages are on 1st and 3rd streets. 🕾 702/678–5777.

Defending the Caveman. Sunday and Monday matinees of this worthwhile one-man comedy are at least $5 cheaper than evening performances, and that's if you pay full price. The show's usually discounted in visitor publications as well. If all else fails, try the half-price ticket outlets.

SPLURGE

Le Rêve. Wynn Las Vegas experimented with an "upsell" ticket for its water show in-the-round, adding a first-class section of seating that's been so successful, the producers say they wish there was room for more. The top $214 ticket includes champagne, chocolate-covered strawberries, and video monitors offering backstage and underwater views of the action.

LOVE. A Beatles fan—and there are said to be a few still out there—will be in orbit over the sound track alone, reengineered to pump from 6,500 speakers. If that's not worth $165, the visuals carry some punch of their own.

O. Cirque's big water show has been around since 1998, but you won't ever see it go on tour. Pony up the $165 and save on your water bill when you get home.

Garth Brooks. The fan-friendly superstar didn't want this to be a "splurge," and argued with Steve Wynn over ticket prices. Wynn won. But fans can justify the $253 because it's the only guaranteed place to see the country icon for a few years (until his daughters are all in college, he says). And the solo-acoustic showcase is such a personal, direct communication, it won't be duplicated even when he starts barnstorming arenas with his band again.

acrobatics with European cabaret and English music-hall tradition. Over the years, *Zumanity* hit a stronger balance of comedy, omni-sexual titillation, and the familiar Cirque brand of acrobatics. It's tamer now, but still the most divisive of the local Cirques, and (still somewhat proudly) not meant for everyone. ⊠ *New York–New York, 3790 Las Vegas Blvd. S, South Strip* ☎ *702/740–6815* 🎟 *$85–$146* 🕐 *Fri.–Tues. 7:30 and 10 pm.*

RESIDENT HEADLINERS

The turn of the 21st century took Las Vegas back to one of the traditions from its past. The success of the late impressionist Danny Gans—not to mention the hassles of modern air travel—opened the doors to a wave of resident headliners, those who live in Las Vegas and perform on a year-round schedule comparable to the revues. Donny and Marie Osmond, George Wallace, and Carrot Top all bet that audiences were ready to embrace the down-front performing tradition (not letting anything get between the performer and the audience) that put Las Vegas on the map.

Now Las Vegas is going full circle by returning to its 60s and 70s-era concept of stars who don't live here, but come in several times a year for extended stretches. Rod Stewart and Elton John assembled custom showcases, and Celine Dion returned with her second Las Vegas residency in March 2011. Plenty of other stars seem willing to get in line, with Cee Lo Green, Shania Twain, and Carlos Santana the latest to test the waters. With nonstar production shows having hit a creative wall outside of Cirque, count on this star-plus-spectacle formula to continue for some time.

The Amazing Johnathan. The crackpot comedian and almost-magician is profane and twisted even for the Strip, and that's saying something. The bellicose and belligerent Johnathan has now made a long career of drawing (fake) blood and torturing both his dingbat stage assistant and a hapless audience volunteer who never fails to spend an inordinate amount of time onstage. ⊠ *Harmon Theater at Planet Hollywood, 3667 Las Vegas Blvd. S, Center Strip* ☎ *702/836–0836* 🎟 *$69–$80* 🕐 *Tues.–Sat. 9 pm.*

Carrot Top. After years on the college circuit, the prop comic moved his trunks full of tricks into the Luxor, where a lot of people realize he's funnier than they thought he would be. The Florida native known offstage as Scott Thompson still is most unique when wielding his visual gags, but he sells them with an unrelenting manic energy and a whole running commentary on the act itself, perhaps a sly nod to his eternal lack of respect. ⊠ *Luxor Las Vegas, 3900 Las Vegas Blvd. S, South Strip* ☎ *702/262–4400* ✉ *$58–$69* ⊙ *Wed.–Mon. 8:30 pm.*

Celine Dion. Celine Dion became a divisive pop star in the 90s, and so may be singing to the converted at this point. Too bad, because those willing to approach with an open mind will be treated to a universally entertaining showcase by an immensely talented performer. Dion goes beyond her expected hits and steers her powerhouse voice into challenging new directions. The new show puts the focus squarely on the music, trading the large ensemble of dancers from the five-year run of "A New Day" for an onstage orchestra and a few visual enhancements. The song list provides fun surprises, from a medley of James Bond movie themes to Ella Fitgerald and Michael Jackson tributes. ■ TIP➔ Those planning a trip around Celine should know the 150 or so annual performances of "A New Day" have been cut back to a modest 70-plus shows a year. Check the schedule on her website (www.celinedion.com) or Caesars'. ⊠ *Caesars Palace, 3570 Las Vegas Blvd. S, Center Strip* ☎ *702/731–7110* ✉ *$61–$275* ⊙ *7:30 pm selected dates (no shows Mon. and Thurs.).*

Donny and Marie Osmond. The Mormon siblings who grew up in front of America still look and sound great, and their variety training on the Strip back in the 1970s allows them to work this old-school showroom setting with ease. The two are quick to split into lengthy solo sets that let Marie sing opera and rock out to Aerosmith, while Donny gives the old Osmonds pop ditty "Yo-Yo" a Justin Beiber treatment. The time apart just makes their time together more valuable. The production numbers with a campy squad of badly costumed dancers will rekindle memories of their toothier, bad-hair days on variety TV. ⊠ *Flamingo Las Vegas, 3555 Las Vegas Blvd. S, Center Strip* ☎ *702/733–3333* ✉ *$104–$137* ⊙ *Tues.–Sat. 7:30 pm.*

Garth Brooks. Casino developer Steve Wynn lured Brooks, one of the biggest-selling acts in music history, out of early retirement to play on the Strip one weekend each month, commuting from Oklahoma by private jet. Wynn at least recoups on production costs for this stripped-down, solo (not counting the usual guest appearance by Garth's wife, Trisha Yearwood) acoustic showcase where Brooks strolls a bare stage with his guitar. The sets have evolved into a tighter musical biography of Brooks and his generation, one which balance his own hits with covers of singers that inspired him, from Merle Haggard to Billy Joel. It's charming, funny, and memorable. Though casual fans might find the ticket price prohibitive, it will remind the less devout why everyone went crazy over this guy in the first place. ■ TIP➔ Brooks is known to play longer on Fridays, when there is only one show, than he does on two-show Saturdays. ⊠ *Wynn Las Vegas, 3131 Las Vegas Blvd., Center Strip* ☎ *702/770–7469* ⊕ *boxoffice.wynnlasvegas.com* ✉ *$253* ⊙ *Fri. 8 pm, Sat. 8 and 10:30 pm.*

Gordie Brown. The Canadian impressionist has been a Las Vegas presence for years, with a needed jolt of exposure as the opening act for Celine Dion's U.S. arena tour in 2009. Women will warm up to a guy good-looking enough to be a retro crooner, while men will recognize the kid from their middle school who memorized *MAD* magazine. Brown's terrain is the song parody, delivered with a manic silliness that sometimes goes by so fast you're not sure if it even makes sense. But you won't take the effort for granted. ⊠ *Golden Nugget, 129 E. Fremont St., Downtown* ☎ *866/946–5336* ☎ *$37–$75* ⊘ *Tues.–Sat. 7:30 pm.*

Fodor's Choice
★

Penn & Teller. Eccentric comic magicians Penn & Teller once seemed an unlikely fit for Las Vegas, but they're more popular now than when they came to town more than a decade ago. The two have spread into mainstream culture beyond the Strip, thanks to Penn (the big loud one to Teller's short mime) becoming a cable news pundit and *Celebrity Apprentice* contestant. Their off-kilter humor now seems less jarring as they age gracefully at the Rio. Their magic in a gorgeous 1,500-seat theater is topical and genuinely baffling, the only show in town to push the form into new creative directions. And their comedy is satiric, provocative, and thoughtful. ⊠ *Rio All-Suite Hotel & Casino, 3700 W. Flamingo Rd., West Side* ☎ *702/777–7776* ☎ *$86–$97* ⊘ *Sat.–Wed. 9 pm.*

Rod Stewart. Wearing the second half of his 60s as comfortably as a mop of sandy hair, Rod Stewart breezes through a gentle-rocking showcase of his hits. You can almost see him winking from the back row as he still agitates the ladies with a bit of the soft shoe on "Tonight's the Night." And yet, in some of his 2011 shows, Stewart also buckled down in a few places to remind audiences of the more credible moments of his past, offering more serious tunes such as "The Killing of Georgie." ■TIP➔ Fans will want to plan in advance a Las Vegas visit around Stewart's blocks of shows at the Colosseum; he's only there a couple of stretches per year. ⊠ *Caesars Palace, 3570 Las Vegas Blvd S, Center Strip* ☎ *702/731–1333* ⊕ *www.caesarspalace.com* ☎ *$49–$250* ⊘ *Select dates 7:30 pm.*

Terry Fator. Las Vegas has long been a haven for impressionists, only this one lets his puppets do the talking. Fator is the likable second-season winner of *America's Got Talent* who does singing impressions as well as ventriloquism. During his run at the Mirage he's added new puppets to the act, including Vicki the Cougar (on the prowl for younger men) and a beetle who sings the Beatles. In just a few years, Fator has become one of the more accomplished and consistent headliners on the Strip. ■TIP➔ Fator's Christmas show, during the holiday stretch when many titles go on vacation, is even more charming. It tones down some of the humor that makes the year-round version less suitable for children than you'd think a puppet show would be. ⊠ *Mirage, 3400 Las Vegas Blvd. S, Center Strip* ☎ *702/792–7777* ☎ *$75–$174* ⊘ *Tues.–Sat. 7:30 pm.*

Vinnie Favorito. Don Rickles has an heir apparent in this insult comic who devotes all but the first five minutes of his set to working the crowd, singling out victims for all sorts of racial profiling and raunchy interrogation. The politically correct should stay far away or try to hide in the back of the room, but it usually doesn't help. He will find you. And most people end up not minding so much, or forgetting they should know better. ⊠ *Flamingo Las Vegas, 3555 Las Vegas Blvd. S, Center Strip* ☎ *702/733–3333* ☎ *$60–$72* ⊘ *Nightly 8 pm.*

7

O, at the Bellagio, is one of Las Vegas's seven Cirque du Soleil shows.

FINE ARTS

Although it's known more for theatrical spectacles than serious theater, Las Vegas does have a lively cultural scene. The arrival of a new performing arts center Downtown in 2012 could be a game-changer for the city's ballet and philharmonic, which already offer full seasons of productions each year. And while some musicals such as "Jersey Boys" dig in for long runs on the Strip, The Smith Center for the Performing Arts also filled the previously missing niche of touring Broadway musicals that drop in for a week or so.

BALLET

Nevada Ballet Theatre. The city's longest-running fine-arts organization (this being Las Vegas, it only dates from 1973) stages three or four productions each year, anchored by an annual December presentation of *The Nutcracker*. In May 2012, the company moved its productions from the UNLV campus to the new Smith Center for the Performing Arts Downtown. ⊠ *1651 Inner Circle Dr., Summerlin* ☎ *702/243–2623, 702/982–7805 for tickets* ⊕ *www.nevadaballet.com.*

CLASSICAL MUSIC

Las Vegas Philharmonic. Formed in 1998, the Philharmonic performs both a "Masterworks" and "Pops" series, the latter often using guest vocalists from shows on the Strip. In the spring of 2012, the orchestra moved its concerts into the new Smith Center to join the ballet Downtown. ⊠ *361 Symphony Park A, Downtown* ☎ *702/258–5438 for schedule information, 702/982–7805 for tickets* ⊕ *www.lvphil.com.*

THEATER

Away from the Strip, a booming community theater scene caters to the area's many new residents, retirees in particular, who are looking for a low-cost alternative to the pricey shows. With the exception of Las Vegas Little Theatre, most don't have their own performance spaces and instead rent municipal auditoriums or the offbeat Onyx Theatre for their productions.

Las Vegas Little Theatre. Las Vegas's oldest community theater has branched out beyond the Neil Simon basic. Its main-stage season is augmented by a "Black Box" season of smaller, more adventurous works and it hosts the Vegas Fringe Festival of new works in June. The productions are staged in a cozy, comfortable theater in a strip mall. ⊠ *3920 Schiff Dr., West Side* ☎ *702/362–7996* ⊕ *www.lvlt.org.*

Onyx Theatre. Some wild and challenging theater has emerged in the back of a fetish store in a run-down shopping center. The small venue has presented everything from Shakespeare to *Naked Boys Singing* and a musical adaptation of *The Evil Dead.* Artistic frictions and turnover left the theater's future direction in question in 2012, but it seemed it wouldn't easily abandon its mission to provide an alternative to the safer offerings of the Strip and community theater. ⊠ *953 E. Sahara #16b, East Side* ☎ *702/732–7225* ⊕ *www.onyxtheatre.com.*

University of Nevada–Las Vegas Theater Department. UNLV's Nevada Conservatory Theatre brings in outside professionals and holds community-wide auditions for a full season of five productions each academic year, one of them a musical. Most performances are held in the Judy Bayley Theatre on campus. ⊠ *4505 S. Maryland Pkwy., University District* ☎ *702/985–2787 for tickets, 702/895–3663 for information.*

7

Nightlife

WORD OF MOUTH

" . . . At XS, the hot nightclub . . . we flaunted our fancy selves. While there is a dedicated dance floor, the action can also be found outside (this is the Encore pool during the day). Away from the crush of sweaty people, we had fun sipping cocktails."

—goddessintl

Updated by
Matt Villano

LAS VEGAS IS THE NIGHTLIFE capital of the United States. Eight of the top 10 venues on *Nightclub & Bar* magazine's "Top 100" list for 2012 are in Sin City, with each bringing in a minimum of $35 million in revenue. Still fueled by the "What happens in Vegas, stays in Vegas" advertisements (read: "All your sins here get expunged completely as soon as you pay your bookie, loan shark, and/or credit card bill"), nightlife impresarios on the Strip keep dipping into their vast pockets in order to create over-the-top experiences where party-mad Visigoths—plus, well, you and me—can live out some wild fantasies. The number of high-profile nightclubs, trendy lounges, and sizzling strip bars continues to grow, each attempting to trump the other in order to attract not just high rollers, but A-list celebrities and the publicity that surrounds them. Many of the newest clubs even have gambling. Though, we ask: Why bother when you can lounge beside the pool by day and bellow at the moon by night while dancing half clad at a club until noon the following day (when it's back into the pool you go)?

In the late 1990s, once the Vegas mandarins decided that the "family experience" just wasn't happening, Sin City nightlife got truly sinful again, drawing raves from clubbers worldwide. A wave of large dance clubs, such as the Luxor's (now-defunct) Ra, opened their doors, followed by a trendy batch of cozier ultralounges—lounges with dance floors—like the MGM Grand's Tabú.

The game of one-upmanship has continued—recent additions that have kept the city hopping include Surrender at Encore, Marquee at The Cosmopolitan, and Chateau Nightclub & Gardens at Paris Las Vegas. What's more, bawdy 50s-era burlesque lounges are continuing their comeback with a gaggle of clubs now dedicated to the art of striptease.

Few cities on Earth match Vegas in its dedication to upping the nightlife ante. So with all these choices, no one—not even the Visigoths—has an excuse for not having fun, however you define the "f" word.

AFTER DARK PLANNER

FIND OUT WHAT'S GOING ON

With the number of nightlife options in Las Vegas, it's not hard to be overwhelmed. *These local publications can steer you in the right direction and help you plan your ultimate Vegas night out.* Remember that party schedules—as well as the popularity of any one spot—can change overnight, *so the best way of keeping current is to consult these publications.*

Anthony Curtis' *Las Vegas Advisor* (☎ 702/252–0655 ⊕ *www.lasvegasadvisor.com*) is a monthly newsletter that's invaluable for its information on Las Vegas dining, entertainment, gambling promotions, comps, and news. If you're here for a short visit, pick up free copies of *Vegas, Today in Las Vegas,* and *What's On in Las Vegas* at hotels and gift shops.

The *Las Vegas Review-Journal,* the city's daily newspaper, publishes a tabloid pullout section each Friday. It provides entertainment features and reviews, and showroom and lounge listings with complete time and

LAS VEGAS NIGHTLIFE BEST BETS

BEST LOCAL LOUNGE
Peppermill's Fireside Lounge, with its lethal Scorpion cocktail.

BEST OUTDOOR PATIO
With cabanas, private tables, a DJ, and a dance floor, **Encore Beach Club** is the perfect way to spend a night under the stars.

BEST ANTIDOTE TO THE STRIP
For an alternative scene, the no-frills **Double Down Saloon** rules, although charming lounges like the

Griffin, the **Downtown Cocktail Room**, and the **Artisan Lounge** are giving it a run for its money.

BEST LEGAL HIGH
The "hookahs" at **Paymon's Mediterranean Café and Lounge**.

BEST ALL-AROUND "HANG"
The Chandelier at The Cosmopolitan, where mixologists serve up dozens of handcrafted cocktails in a three-story bar—all inside the world's largest chandelier.

price information. The *Review-Journal* maintains a website (⊕ *www. lvrj.com*) where show listings are updated each week. The *Las Vegas Sun,* once a competing daily, is now a section inside the *Review-Journal* but maintains its own editorial staff and website, ⊕ *www.lasvegassun. com.*

Two excellent alternative weekly newspapers are distributed at retail stores and coffee shops around town and maintain comprehensive websites. *Las Vegas Weekly* (⊕ *www.lasvegasweekly.com*) and *Las Vegas City Life* (⊕ *www.lasvegascitylife.com*) offer some timely and incisive reflections on the nightclub scene and music outside the realm of the casinos. Vegas Seven (⊕ *www.weeklyseven.com*) also has reliable listings. And nothing imparts the flavor of "Viceville" (our proposed alternate nickname for "Sin City") better than ShulmanSays.com (⊕ *www. shulmansays.com*), a website published by Michael Shulman, the former gossip columnist for *Vegas Magazine* (⊕ *www.vegasmagazine.com*).

HOW TO GET IN

Nobody comes to Las Vegas to wait in line. So how exactly do you get past those velvet ropes? Short of personally knowing the no-nonsense bouncers and serious-looking women holding clipboards that guard the doors, here are a few pointers.

First, know that even though this is a 24-hour town, lines start forming around 10 (or earlier). If you're not on a list, get there after dinner and dress the part—which is to say, don't expect to go straight from the pool to the club. Vegas bars and clubs have pretty strict dress codes, so leave those T-shirts, baseball caps, and ripped jeans in your hotel room (unless you're headed to the Griffin Lounge or some other hipster haven). Arguing that your sneakers were made by Alexander McQueen probably won't help, either. At most of the trendier spots, at least for women, skin is in—this *is* Sin City, after all. And needless to say, the universal rule of big-city nightlife also applies in Vegas: groups of guys almost always have a harder time getting in without a few women in the mix. If your group is gender impaired, consider politely asking some unaccompanied women to temporarily join you, perhaps in exchange for some drinks once you're all inside. Too shy, you say? If there was ever a place to check your shyness at the airport, it's this town.

Most spots have two lines: a VIP line (for those on the guest list or who have a table with bottle service reserved) and a regular line. You can either ask your hotel concierge for help contacting a club to get on a guest list, or contact the club directly. Some websites such as ⊕ *www. vegas.com* sell passes they guarantee will get you past the crush, but save your money for the door—better to slip the bouncer $20 per person than hope they'll acknowledge the Internet ticket you've bought for the same amount. If you have a few people in your group, it might be worth it to splurge on a table reservation: without one, a group of five could easily spend $20 each getting in good with the bouncers, plus $20 each for the cover charge, and then there's always the expensive drinks.

A further note on going deluxe: if you're getting a table with bottle service, note that your VIP host will expect something from you, as will the busboy who actually lugs over your booze. (The waitress or waiter usually gets an automatic 20%–30% tip on your bill.) On holiday weekends and New Year's Eve, expect to multiply what you plan to give them by at least two.

ON THE STRIP

BARS AND LOUNGES

"ULTRALOUNGES" AND THEN SOME

The lounges of the Las Vegas casino-hotels were once places where such headliners as Frank, Dean, and the gang would go after their shows, taking a seat in the audience to laugh at the comedy antics of Shecky Greene or Don Rickles. For a while lounges were mostly reduced to small bars within the casino where bands played Top 40 hits in front of people pie-eyed from the slots. The turn of the 21st century, however, brought an explosion of hybrid nightspots—the so-called "ultralounges"—that aimed for the middle ground between dance club and conventional lounge. Some of the best of them—MGM Grand's Tabú, Bellagio's Hyde Lounge, and the Mandarin Oriental's Mandarin Bar—are worth a separate trip, given how much of a pleasure-jolt they offer.

Fodor's Choice ★ **The Beatles Revolution Lounge.** Designed for synergy with Cirque du Soleil's Beatles-theme *Love* next door, the "Rev" wows tourists and locals alike with its private alcoves, hippie-outfitted servers, beanbag chairs, and eye-popping, ever-shifting psychedelic fractal wall projections (which patrons can control at their tables). The low lighting and high volume deemphasize the "lounge" aspect here, but late at night, when the inevitable Fab Four tunes give way to pumping dance music, it's rightly all about the "ultra," as in "ultrafun." The lounge has different DJs every night it's open. On weekends, it's also one of the most crowded spots on the Mirage casino floor. ⊠ *The Mirage, 3400 Las*

Out at 4 am

Vegas is a 24-hour town, and when the party starts to wind down in some places, the doors to others are just opening. The following are our picks for after-hours hot spots. Remember, even after 4 am, expect lines—sometimes very long ones—to get in. And bring your sunglasses to protect those bleary eyes from the morning rays when you finally stumble out.

The sin-sational **Drai's** has long been the after-hours king. In three elegant rooms, DJs spin house and hip-hop until well after the sun rises.

Another late-night option is even smaller and more intimate: **Savile**

Row. There's no set menu here; instead, mixologists come by and ask you what sorts of drinks you like, then they concoct cocktails based upon your preferences.

For those seeking a different kind of decadence, go to Sin City's best strip joint, the gloomy yet glorious **Spearmint Rhino**.

Finally, if you're looking for a chill atmosphere rather than a club or strip joint, check out The Cosmopolitan's **Chandelier** for three levels of cocktail splendor, or hang and gamble at the Aria's lounge/high-limit room, **The Deuce Lounge**.

Vegas Blvd. S, Center Strip ☎ *702/693–8300* ⊕ *www.mirage.com/nightlife* ⊘ *Closed Mon.–Wed.*

Cathouse. A plush 19th-century French bordello inside a giant black pyramid? Only in Vegas. The decor of this funky gem of an ultralounge is red-velvet-y, chandelier-y, and lavish, and so are the physical charms and wardrobes of the staff. (They've got the most revealing cocktail uniforms this side of a strip club.) There are two decadent rooms to choose from, and bottle service available in each. ✉ *Luxor, 3900 Las Vegas Blvd. S, South Strip* ☎ *702/403–7174* ⊕ *www.luxor.com/nightlife.*

The Chandelier. True to its name, this uber-swanky lounge sits in a chandelier with 2 million crystal beads, making it the largest chandelier in the town (and, perhaps, the world). The bar is separated into three separate levels, and mixologist Meriena Mercer has assigned different themes to each one. The ground floor—dubbed "Bottom of the Chandelier," for those of you scoring at home—is dedicated to intricate specialty drinks; the kinds of cocktails you'll only find here. The second floor pays homage to molecular gastronomy in cocktail form; spiked sorbets and dehydrated fruits are common in drinks here. Finally, at the top of the Chandelier, everything's coming up floral, with rose and lavender syrups and violet sugar. If you're particularly adventuresome (and you can get a seat on the first floor), try the Verbena cocktail with a "buzz button." This desiccated flower from Africa numbs your mouth to make flavors more potent; it also prompts you to down your cocktail in mere seconds. ✉ *The Cosmopolitan, 3708 Las Vegas Blvd. S, South Strip* ☎ *702/698–7000* ⊕ *www.cosmopolitanlasvegas.com.*

The Deuce Lounge. James Bond—he of the martinis shaken, not stirred—would have frequented this swanky and sophisticated lounge. Part restaurant-bar, part high-roller pit, The Deuce Lounge is a great spot for

8

"Turn off your mind, relax…." Beanbag chairs and modern psychedelic touches such as fractal wall imagery are what make the Beatles Revolution Lounge the future of retro.

revelers who like to mix business (that is, high-stakes gambling) and pleasure (that is, boozing) all night long. Bartenders serve up custom cocktails, with pretty much whatever liquors you prefer. There's also appetizer service until 10 pm every night. Before 8 pm, The Deuce is a great spot to take in a ballgame, especially since Aria's sports book is so small (yet close enough to run in those last-minute wagers). ✉ *Aria, 3730 Las Vegas Blvd. S, Center Strip* ☎ *702/693–8300* ⊕ *www. arialasvegas.com/nightlife.*

Fodor's Choice
★
Drai's. All hail Victor Drai, classiest of Vegas nightlife sultans. Once the tables of his tony restaurant are cleared away, the wild scene inside this after-hours titan is closer to a dance club or a rave than to a lounge, even though its three modestly sized rooms are as gorgeous as any lounge in town. The vibe of decadence can reach an extraordinary pitch, but this, of course, is exactly how an after-hours club *should* be, right? Besides, you'll be hard-pressed to find a more beautiful insider crowd anywhere in city limits. ✉ *Bill's Gamblin' Hall & Saloon, 3595 Las Vegas Blvd. S, Center Strip* ☎ *702/737–0555* ⊕ *drais.net/flash.*

eyecandy. High technology hits the Strip at this vast "interactive" ultralounge in the center of Mandalay's casino floor. For "future shock" freaks, there are video feeds of various bar locales, tented "touch tables" onto which you can draw messages and words and images that other tables can receive and respond to, and "sound stations" that let you send music of your choice to the deejay. More important than the technology here, though, is the cocktail menu; crafted by master mixologist Tony Abou-Ganim, drinks are so scrumptious they could call the place "mouthcandy," too. ✉ *Mandalay Bay, 3950 Las Vegas Blvd. S, South*

Strip ☎ *702/632–7777* ⊕ *www. mandalaybay.com/nightlife.*

Fodor's Choice ★ **Foundation Room.** This lounge takes aesthetic appeal to an unprecedented level. Ancient statues, tapestry-covered walls, pirated Mississippi road signs; the place has it all. Though it used to be open to members only, this secluded subsidiary of the House of Blues is now open to everyone seven nights a week—provided nonmembers are willing to wait on line. (If you're interested in becoming a member see phone number below.) The venue itself is a series of different rooms, each with its own set of design themes and type of music (disco, house, etc.). A main attraction is the view of the Strip; because the club is on the 43rd floor, it provides panoramic vistas of the entire town. ⊠ *Mandalay Bay, 3590 Las Vegas Blvd. S, South Strip* ☎ *702/632–7631, 702/632–7614 for information about membership* ⊕ *www.houseofblues.com/venues.*

Hyde Lounge. Before he rebuilds the Sahara, SBE founder and CEO Sam Nazarian has established a foothold in the local nightlife scene with this posh ultralounge, famous for its front-and-center view overlooking the Bellagio Fountains. Inside, the theme is library chic—there are actual books on the walls. Outside, a small patio harbors what some deem the most romantic table in Vegas—a two-top that looks out on the water show. The real star at this swanky lounge, however, is the cocktail program, complete with roving Bellini carts. On most nights, food (small plates only) also is available from Circo next door. ⊠ *Bellagio, 3600 Las Vegas Blvd. S, Center Strip* ☎ *702/693–8700* ⊕ *www. bellagio.com/nightlife.*

Koi Lounge. Circles are a big theme at this lounge that fronts Koi restaurant. More than 20 Tibetan hand-carved prayer wheels are positioned around the room, interspersed with circular banquettes that are great for big groups and lousy for small ones. Be sure to visit during happy hour, when mixologists oblige by offering half price on signature drinks and select appetizers. Unlike other lounges around town, this joint's happy hour runs seven days a week (with limited hours on weekends). ⊠ *Planet Hollywood Resort & Casino, 3667 Las Vegas Blvd. S, Center Strip* ☎ *702/454–4555* ⊕ *www.planethollywoodresort.com.*

Level 107 Lounge. The Stratosphere might be downscale compared to other Vegas hotels, but there ain't nothing "down" about the high-in-the-sky experience to be had here. From this sleek, attractive room, the view of Sin City is truly amazing (if slightly remote). For an even bigger thrill, head upstairs and outside (to level 108, of course) to Air Bar. The signature drink: something called Jet Fuel. Consider yourself warned.

8

✉ *Stratosphere, 2000 Las Vegas Blvd. S, North Strip* ☎ *702/380–7777* ⊕ *www.stratospherehotel.com.*

Lily Bar & Lounge. This colorful (hence the name) ultralounge is quite literally at the center of the action in Bellagio; it's smack-dab in the middle of the casino floor, which you can view through windows on two sides. Community-style ottomans lend themselves to conversation. At the bar, expert mixologists pour cocktails made with seasonally fresh ingredients. DJs spin most nights until the venue closes around 4. ✉ *Bellagio, 3600 Las Vegas Blvd. S, Center Strip* ☎ *702/693–8300* ⊕ *www.bellagio.com/nightlife.*

Mandarin Bar. Few views of the Strip are as breathtaking as the one you'll get from this über-chic lounge on the 23rd floor of the Mandarin Oriental at CityCenter. The room has two walls of floor-to-ceiling windows, meaning just about every one of the plush banquettes is a winning seat. Mixologists concoct cocktails based on individual preferences, though Dom Perignon is always on hand. There's also a small menu of bite-size (literally, they come on spoons) appetizers. Doormen are particular about the business-casual dress code so make sure you're dressed appropriately. ✉ *Mandarin Oriental, 3752 Las Vegas Blvd. S, Center Strip* ☎ *888/881–9367* ⊕ *www.mandarinoriental.com/lasvegas.*

Minus 5 Ice Bar. Did you ever think you'd be wearing a winter parka in the Las Vegas desert? If not, then you've underestimated just how gimmicky these 21st-century bars can be. So don that parka, pay attention to your orientation speech, buy those drink tickets, and step into Minus 5's bar area, where the temperature is always minus five below zero. This frosty clime ensures that you'll have a "cool" time here, but it also keeps the walls, bar, cocktail glasses, ashtrays, chairs, couches, and decorative sculpture in their frozen-solid state. Expensive fun for the sheer weirdness of it? Definitely! The drinks are tasty, too. (And they're available at the Mandalay Place location, or a second spot in the Monte Carlo.) ✉ *Mandalay Bay, 3950 Las Vegas Blvd. S, South Strip* ☎ *702/740–5800* ⊕ *www.minus5experience.com* ✉ *Monte Carlo, 3770 Las Vegas Blvd. S, South Strip* ☎ *702/643–7800..*

Mix Lounge. Floor-to-ceiling windows, an appealing curved bar, an equally appealing staff—what could top all that? An outdoor, 64th-floor deck that offers stunning views of the Strip, that's what. At this spot atop THEhotel at Mandalay, even the glass-walled restrooms give you a window onto the city. Black leather accented by red lighting creates a hipper-than-thou vibe. ✉ *Mandalay Bay, 3590 Las Vegas Blvd. S, South Strip* ☎ *702/632–9500* ⊕ *www.mandalaybay.com/nightlife.*

Fodor'sChoice
★

Parasol Up. Not to be confused with sister lounge "Parasol Down," this exquisite-looking—and exquisitely tranquil—setting near the entrance of Wynn Las Vegas ensures you can indulge in that most endangered of all pleasures: a good conversation. Tufted leather chairs and an extensive menu of house martinis certainly contribute to the vibe. Best of all, the menu features a handful of snacks, and the place stays open all night. ✉ *Wynn Las Vegas, 3131 Las Vegas Blvd. S, North Strip* ☎ *702/770 7000* ⊕ *www.wynnlasvegas.com.*

★ **Tabú Ultra Lounge.** Here you'll find the high-tech touches of a big dance club, with square tables that double as "canvases" for projected images and "murals" of light that change depending on the perspective of the viewer. At the same time, peach-color banquettes and mirrored columns lend the space the coziness of a lounge. The fine deejays spin everything from hip-hop to rock, techno to country. Perhaps the only problem: The club is closed Tuesday, Wednesday, and Thursday every week. ⊠ *MGM Grand, 3799 Las Vegas Blvd. S, South Strip* ☎ *702/891–7183* ⊕ *www. mgmgrand.com/nightlife* ⊗ *Closed Tues.–Thurs.*

Talon Club. This swanky little pocket bar is open to everyone, but its spot in the high-limit gaming area on the second floor of the casino (no, you don't have to play) makes it a well-kept secret for drinkers who want some privacy. Mixologists don't usually offer a cocktail menu; instead they simply ask you what you like and craft drinks from there. Perhaps the only downside is the price; martinis start at $16 apiece and go up from there (depending on the liquor). ⊠ *The Cosmopolitan, 3708 Las Vegas Blvd. S, Center Strip* ☎ *702/698–7000.*

DANCE CLUBS AND NIGHTCLUBS

Vegas dance clubs come in three basic flavors—up-to-the-moment trendy (e.g., Marquee, 1 OAK and XS), established classic (Tao, LAX, Tryst, and Bank), and fun for the great unwashed masses (Rain, PURE, and Moon). The usual Catch-22 of nightlife applies: the more "in" the place, the harder it is to get in, and the more oppressively crowded and noisy it will be once you do. Cover charges have crept into the $20 to $30 or $40 range—and don't be surprised to find that, even in these enlightened times, men pay higher cover charges than women. Although the level of capital investment gives these clubs a longevity their New York counterparts don't enjoy, dance clubs are still by nature a fickle, fleeting enterprise, so check with more frequently updated sources (such as the Fodor's website as well as local periodicals) to ensure they are still hot.

1 OAK. The "OAK" in this nightclub's name is an acronym for "Of A Kind," and, indeed, it is bigger, darker, and louder than just about any other dance club in Vegas. And on a good night, sexy revelers are packed in and pumping like you wouldn't believe. The space, which replaced Jet in early 2012, is two separate rooms, each with its own bar and DJ (music styles change weekly). An animal theme is prevalent throughout, with zebra stripes, jaguar spots, and other patterns visible from just about every angle. The influence is subtle, but don't be surprised if your inner beast bursts out. ⊠ *Mirage Las Vegas, 3400 Las Vegas Blvd. S, Center Strip* ☎ *702/693–8300* ⊕ *www.mirage.com/ nightlife.*

Bank. "Status is everything!" goes the motto at this white-hot, megadance club, which has replaced an old favorite known as Light. One of the biggest celeb-hangs in town, Bank sets itself apart with etched-glass walls, avant-garde chandeliers, and an entrance foyer lined floor to ceiling with illuminated Cristal bottles. The staff is every bit as classy and hot-looking as at other Vegas nightspots. Weekends generally draw

8

the biggest crowds, but other nights boast special parties, promo events, and live performances (by, say, Gavin Rossdale, among others). In fact, the only thing really wrong about Bank is its motto, because status isn't *everything*. Or is it? ⊠ *Bellagio, 3600 Las Vegas Blvd. S, Center Strip* ☎ *702/693–8300* ⊕ *www.bellagio.com/nightlife* ☉ *Thurs.–Sun.*

Chateau Nightclub and Gardens. A marble staircase leads revelers straight from the Strip up to this French-inspired nightclub. The entrance is not only marvelously elegant, but also it's the first one on the Strip that you don't have access from inside the resort. The space itself offers three distinct experiences: a main dance room, a bar, or the open-air terrace, which is flanked by exquisite gardens (hence the name). In the main room, house deejays spin from a booth atop a 10-foot-high fireplace, and go-go dancers in French maid costumes abound. If you're looking for something different, don't miss the chandeliers made of globes near the bar; with LED screens in every nightclub these days, the handmade fixtures are wonderfully unique. ⊠ *Paris Resort, 3655 Las Vegas Blvd. S, South Strip* ☎ *702/776–7770* ⊕ *www.chateaunightclublv.com* ☉ *Tues., Fri. and Sat.*

Haze. Dioramas with living, breathing humans catch your attention the moment you walk into this oversexed nightclub inside Aria, and you know this place is different. Inside, suede walls and plush surfaces give way to a 20-foot wall of lights and a bunch of interactive projection screens. There are laser light shows, and a state-of-the-art sound system that is, essentially, surround-sound on steroids. Did we mention that drinks and deejays here are top-notch, too? Perhaps the only downside to Haze is the line; because of its location on the ground floor of the resort, queuing can get messy, especially when folks are drunk. ⊠ *Aria, 3730 Las Vegas Blvd. S, Center Strip* ☎ *702/693–8300* ⊕ *www. arialasvegas.com/nightlife* ☉ *Thurs.–Sat.*

Krâve. Live entertainers, acrobats, and go-go dancers put a mixed crowd in motion at this club, which is popular among young gay males. The club hosts events every night of the week, most of which revolve around well-endowed men dancing suggestively in tiny, tiny thongs. Seasonal events are popular—Valentine's Day in particular tends to draw a colorful crowd. The club also has embraced social networking and sends out drink specials, free bottle service, and other promotions to followers of its Twitter handle, @KraveLasVegas. ⊠ *Miracle Mile Shops at Planet Hollywood, 3663 Las Vegas Blvd. S, Center Strip* ☎ *702/836–0830* ⊕ *www.kravelasvegas.com.*

Lavo. From the people who brought us the titanic Tao comes this restaurant-lounge-dance club with a vaguely—though attractive—Middle Eastern vibe. Although Lavo's advertising tagline reads, "Hookahs Not Included," it's actually all about the water pipes here (the theme is a bathhouse, you see), at least until you finish dinner and ascend past cisterns and ceramics to the top floor's dome-roofed dance floor, complete with go-go dancers, chandeliers, boa-clad servers, eccentrically shaped bars, and a bendy-trendy crowd. ⊠ *The Palazzo, 3325 Las Vegas Blvd. S, North Strip* ☎ *702/791–1818* ⊕ *www.palazzo.com/Las-Vegas-Nightlife* ☉ *Closed Mon. and Thurs.*

The Cosmopolitan's Marquee nightclub promises epic dance parties with a huge floor surrounded by four-story projection screens.

LAX. At one point in recent Vegas history (circa 2007/08), this tremendous club was the hottest ticket in town. And while no single club in Vegas reigns supreme for too long, LAX still shines: crazy flashing lights, deafening music, and shaking sweaty bodies. Preferred spots to dance here are the anarchically crowded stage or the less frenetic wraparound balcony, which offers a delightful bird's-eye view of all the heaving, writhing behavior down below. Our favorite spot of all, though, doesn't really involve dancing: it's **Savile Row**, the elegant, tiny, and eminently chill private lounge-within-a-club downstairs. By private we mean private service—the bartender will ask you what your tastes are before bringing you an appropriate signature cocktail. It's the ultimate in VIP treatment. And when you're ready to face the masses again, LAX is just a few steps away. ✉ *Luxor Las Vegas, 3900 Las Vegas Blvd. S, South Strip* ☎ *702/262–4529, 702/222–1500 Savile Row* ⊕ *www.luxor. com/nightlife* ⊗ *Wed.–Sat.*

Marquee. This cavernous joint, run by the same company that operates Tao and Lavo elsewhere in town, boasts three different rooms spread across two levels, as well as 50-foot ceilings. In the main area, stadium-style seating surrounds the dance floor, while four-story LED screens and projection walls display light and image shows customized for every performer. For a more intimate experience, check out the "Boom Box," a smaller room (usually featuring something other than house music) with windows overlooking the Strip. On the top level, the Library provides a respite from the thumping downstairs with dark wood, books (actual books!), and billiard tables. In spring and summer, the hotspot opens Marquee Dayclub, which features two pools, several bars, a gaming area, and deejays all day long. Resident spin-masters for 2012 included Kaskade and DJ Chuckie, two huge names on the scene. ⊠ *The Cosmopolitan, 3708 Las Vegas Blvd. S, South Strip* ☎ *702/698–7000* ⊕ *www.marqueelasvegas.com* ☾ *Mon. and Thurs.–Sat.*

Fodor's Choice ★ **PURE.** Although a few Vegas dance clubs are more provocative—and thereby more tabloid-friendly— PURE still takes the cake for best all-around shake appeal. In addition to multiple rooms and its sexy Pussy-cat Dolls Lounge, the club has a secret weapon—an outdoor terrace, complete with waterfalls, private cabanas, dance floor, and an up-close view the center Strip. No wonder celebrities and celebrity deejays love coming here for big events. ⊠ *Caesars Palace, 3570 Las Vegas Blvd. S, Center Strip* ☎ *702/731–7873* ⊕ *angelmg.com/venues/pure* ☾ *Tues. and Thurs.–Sun.*

Rok. For some Vegas partiers, a 20-foot high, 360-degree screen that blasts lasers, live feeds, animation, and music videos into their eyeballs while crazy-loud music blares is an exciting prospect. For others, nausea (physical and/or cultural) will ensue. Either way, there's no denying the visceral appeal of this lounge/bar/nightclub, especially when the deejays play particularly cool mashups. ⊠ *New York–New York, 3790 Las Vegas Blvd. S, South Strip* ☎ *702/740–6745* ⊕ *www.rokvegaslv. com* ☾ *Wed.–Sun.*

Fodor's Choice ★ **Surrender.** Steve Wynn and nightclub impresario Sean Cristie came together in 2010 to concoct this one-of-a-kind, indoor/outdoor lounge that's unlike anything else on the Strip. The experience begins indoors, in a giant living room designed by Roger Thomas, the same aesthetic genius behind Encore itself. At the back, the space transitions into the Encore Beach Club, an intimate, open-air dayclub that is transformed into a nightclub after dark. Some of the private cabanas out here feature balconies that overlook Las Vegas Boulevard. There's also an open-air gaming pit. Perhaps the highlight of the entire facility is the 120-foot-long silver snake over the bar inside; this artwork, much like Surrender itself, glistens all night long. ⊠ *Encore, 3121 Las Vegas Blvd, S, Center Strip* ☎ *702/770* ⊕ *www.surrendernightclub.com* ☾ *Wed., Fri., and Sat.*

Fodor's Choice ★ **Tao.** Nowhere else in Vegas furnishes you with the four D's—dining, drinking, dancing, and drooling—in quite as alluring a mix as this multilevel (and multimillion-dollar) playground. The ground floor and mezzanine levels are exquisite enough (you almost tumble into rosewater baths before you're in the door), but once you get off the elevator at the top floor, where an army of dramatically lighted stone deities greets you, the party truly begins. Chinese antiques, crimson chandeliers, and a so-called Opium Room set the mood. It's still one of the best dance clubs in Vegas, with one of the most popular theme parties with its Thursday locals' "Worship" night. ⊠ *The Venetian, 3355 Las Vegas Blvd. S, North Strip* ☎ *702/388–8588* ⊕ *www.taolasvegas.com/ tao.html* ☾ *Thurs.–Sat.*

Fodor's Choice ★ **Tryst.** No other club in Vegas has its own 90-foot waterfall, a distinction that sets Tryst apart from competitors right off the bat. Other touches worth digging: the eerie red lighting, the open-air dance floor, the gorgeous stairway at the entrance, and the discreetly curtained VIP

CLOSE UP

Specialty Bars

CIGAR BARS

Casa Fuentes. Casa Fuentes reproduces the decor and atmosphere of El Floridita, Ernest Hemingway's favorite Havana watering hole. A sophisticated lounge was added in 2010. ⌧ *Caesar's Palace Forum Shops, 3570 Las Vegas Boulevard S, Center Strip* ☎ *702/731–5051.*

Napoleon's Dueling Piano Bar. This baroque Paris piano bar can get loud, but it's all good fun. ⌧ *Paris, 3655 Las Vegas Blvd. S, Center Strip* ☎ *702/946–7000.*

IRISH BARS

Brendan's Irish Pub ⌧ *Orleans Hotel & Casino, 4500 Tropicana Ave., West Side* ☎ *702/365–7111* ⊕ *www. orleanscasino.com/entertain.*

Nine Fine Irishmen. Don't be surprised to see patrons break into impromptu bouts of step-dancing at this authentic Irish Pub inside New York–New York. It's so authentic that the place was built in Ireland, shipped over, and reassembled in Vegas. Today, barkeeps pour all sorts of Irish whiskeys, and cooks crank out Irish food and traditional Irish breakfast all day long. ⌧ *New York–New York, 3790 Las Vegas Blvd. S, South Strip* ☎ *702/740–6969* ⊕ *www.ninefineirishmen.com.*

Quinn's Irish Pub. At the Green Valley Resort, this rollicking establishment mixes straight-from-Ireland whiskeys and beers, authentic Irish fare, and live Irish music (on most nights). The place offers great drink specials, too. ⌧ *Green Valley Ranch Resort & Spa, 2300 Paseo Verde Pkwy., Henderson* ☎ *702/617–7777* ⊕ *www.greenvalleyranchresort.com/ entertainment.*

Rí Rá Irish Pub ⌧ *Mandalay Bay, 3950 Las Vegas Blvd. S, South Strip* ☎ *702/632–7771* ⊕ *www. mandalaybay.com.*

SPORTS BAR

Lagasse's Stadium. Jumbo video screens on the walls, 100 high-def TVs, and delicious down-home cooking are all found at Lagasse's Stadium. Add in mobile sports betting devices from the Palazzo's sports book (located next door) and there's no better place to enjoy a game. ⌧ *Palazzo, 3325 Las Vegas Blvd. S, North Strip* ☎ *702/607–2665* ⊕ *www.palazzo. com/Las-Vegas-Nightlife.*

A TEQUILA SUNRISE

Tequila Bar & Grille. Latin music, Mexican meals, and more than 50 brands of tequila—all these are found at Tequila Bar & Grille. The $2 menu (tacos, margaritas, shots, and draft beers) offers great value. ⌧ *Bally's, 3645 Las Vegas Blvd. S, Center Strip* ☎ *702/739–4111* ⊕ *www. ballyslasvegas.com.*

WINE BAR

Grape Vegas. Grape Vegas, in the Town Square Mall, provides more than 200 different wine selections to in a pleasing, relaxing space, as well as tapas aplenty and friendly bartenders. ⌧ *Town Square Mall, 6599 Las Vegas Blvd. S, #150, Airport* ☎ *702/220–4727.*

8

section. Indeed, this club has firmly established itself as one of the best in the business. We're not the only ones who think so, either: *Nightclub & Bar* regularly names this one of the top nightclubs in town. Our only gripe: The queue, which stretches past Wynn hotel registration and sometimes back into the casino, but good things come to those who wait. ⊠ *Wynn Las Vegas, 3131 Las Vegas Blvd. S, North Strip* ☏ *702/770–3375* ⊕ *www.trystlasvegas.com* ☉ *Thurs.–Sat.*

Fodor's Choice
★
XS. As its name suggests, everything about XS is superlative. At the time it opened, it was the biggest club in Vegas (it has since been supplanted by Marquee at The Cosmopolitan). It backs up onto a pool that converts into one of the most spacious open-air dance floors in town. The club also features Wynn's signature attention to detail with touches such as red and leopard-print decor, a chandelier that turns into a psychedelic disco ball, light fixtures that turn into stripper poles, and walls imprinted with golden body casts (the waitresses modeled for them). At the pool are 31 cabanas, another bar, and outdoor gaming, where the sexiest croupiers in town ply their trade. "Excess" is a pretty good word for all of this, indeed. ⊠ *Encore, 3131 Las Vegas Blvd. S, North Strip* ☏ *702/770–0097* ⊕ *xslasvegas.com/flash2* ☉ *Fri.–Mon.*

LOCAL HANGOUTS

Outside the realm of the big casinos, the Las Vegas bar scene is dominated by so-called video-poker taverns, named for the 15 video-poker machines they are legally allowed to have. Most other Vegas bars are generic, but there are exceptions—in some cases, glorious exceptions. ■TIP➔ Combine a visit to some of the superb *below-listed* Downtown bars with a stroll around the area. Despite the touristy "Fremont Street Experience," Downtown is the gritty original part of town, and though it can be dangerous at night (read: people-with-guns-dangerous), it is essential to see if you want to claim you truly know Vegas.

Blue Martini Lounge. It's in a shopping mall eight minutes from the Strip (by taxi), but we won't hold that against the Blue Martini, because it's still pretty cool. The cream of local bands plays here nightly, an attractive blue interior curves from room to room, and the cocktail menu is impressive (the signature martinis are served in the shaker). Also, there's a legendary happy hour from 4 to 8. Best of all, hordes of the kind of people you'll want to meet (that is, sexy nontourists of both genders) keep pouring in. ⊠ *Town Square Mall, 6593 Las Vegas Blvd. S, Airport* ☏ *702/949–2583* ⊕ *www.bluemartinilounge.com.*

Fodor's Choice
★
Peppermill's Fireside Lounge. Many visitors to Viceville leave disappointed, finding the wrecking ball has left behind little but massive movie-set-like resort-casinos to dominate the landscape. But benign neglect has preserved this kitschy and shagadelic lounge, one of the town's truly essential nightspots. Near the site of the old Stardust Hotel, this evergreen ironic-romantic getaway serves food, but what you're really here for is the prismatic fire pit, the crazy waitress outfits, and the lethal Scorpion cocktail. ⊠ *2985 Las Vegas Blvd. S, North Strip* ☏ *702/735–4177* ⊕ *www.peppermilllasvegas.com.*

Continued on page 291

BRIDAL PARTIES GONE WILD

New York may be the city that never sleeps, but Las Vegas makes the Big Apple look positively somnolent. Activities aren't merely available to you at all hours of the day and night; they practically follow you around, demanding you to take part in Vegas's fun and games.

The best man and maid-of-honor know that Vegas is the only place in the world to sate the needs of the partiers for one brief, hot-burning, 48-hour flame of a weekend.

So take a peek at a sample bachelorette party. Go to the places they go, do what they do, giggle like they do. Then check out the bachelor party. Watch the boys be boys. Hey, just because they grew up doesn't mean they grew out of it.

STAY WHERE YOU PLAY

Don't skimp on the hotel. Things aren't as close as they appear, and cabs can be a hassle. The best plan is to stay where you play. If your party has a certain scene in mind, whether it's a casino, bar, club, or pool, minimize travel and maximize fun.

Updated by Matt Villano

FRIDAY

The hunks from *Thunder from Down Under*

GIRLS

Eight girls fly in and head to the Strip. There are hugs all around and mischief in the air as they gather in the lobby.

Timeline

CHECK-IN & COCKTAILS: First stop—the lavish rooms at the **Cosmopolitan** for freshening up before gathering downstairs at **The Chandelier**. The girls sip funky martinis and catch up before presenting the bride-to-be with her veil, not to be removed until beyond Nevada state lines.

DINNER: For Mediterranean tapas-style dishes, the girls head for **Lavo** (Palazzo), home of popcorn-battered chicken and other mouth-watering dishes.

MALE REVUE: The shoulder devil wins the first major scuffle of the trip as the group heads to *Thunder from Down Under*, (Excalibur) where, as the men of the Aussie all-male revue gyrate, the bride-to-be has just enough to drink to do things she won't tell her fiancé about.

LATE-NIGHT: The girls get down on the dance floor at **10ak** (The Mirage). The music fades from techno to 80s to bhangra as ladies sip drinks from a bottle of Ciroc vodka as they watch the sexy crowd bump and grind.

BOYS

For Bachelor Parties, the first night includes some action on and off the strip.

Timeline

CHECK-IN & COCKTAILS: Our boys are kicking it at the **Hard Rock Hotel**. The **Center Bar** in the middle of the casino provides the perfect meet-up location for the bachelor, the best man, and the groomsmen (one of whom is already down two large at the Blackjack tables).

DINNER: The guys head over to the **Prime Steakhouse** (Bellagio) for some hefty ribeyes and a hearty cabernet.

CLUBBING: After a gut-busting dinner, it's off to the **Playboy Club** (Palms), the ultimate guys' nightclub on the 52nd floor of the resort's appropriately named **Fantasy Tower**. With the number of bunnies wandering around, it's surprising that Hugh Hefner himself isn't lurking in the corner.

EVEN LATER: After a night of canoodling with Playboy bunnies, the boys blow off steam at a $25 craps table at **Mandalay Bay**. John Patrick, the turtleneck-wearing craps legend, would be proud.

SATURDAY

GIRLS
The Maid-of-Honor brings out the bottle of ibuprofen she bought for this trip.

Timeline
SHOPPING: After everyone's recovered from the night before, they're off to the **Miracle Mile Shops** (Planet Hollywood) for therapeutic shopping.

LUNCH: The girls settle on patio-seating at **Spago** (Caesars Palace) for unrivaled people-watching and Wolfgang Puck creations.

SPA: The group hits **Qua Baths & Spa** (Caesars Palace) for a deep-freeze in the arctic ice room, then indulges in seaweed wraps and hot-stone massages.

DINNER: The girls clean up and head back to Planet Hollywood for a sushi dinner at **Koi**.

CLUBBING: It's time for **Vanity** (Hard Rock): pounding music, a posh VIP section, and the sounds of some of the city's most talented DJs provide the perfect backdrop for some of the best celebrity-sighting in town.

LATER: All danced out, the girls move on to **Hyde Lounge** (Bellagio), where mixologists craft them cocktails based on their individual preferences. In the taxi back to the hotel, the glimmers of dawn are just beginning to appear over the mountains to the east.

BOYS
The sun tortures their eyes, but the ride west towards the Spring Mountains is oh so worth it . . .

Timeline
BREAKFAST: The best cure for hangovers is a greasy breakfast, and the boys make a bee-line for the **Grand Café** (Red Rock), where overstuffed omelets are complimented perfectly with gin greyhounds. After chowing down, the fellas digest around a $1/$2 no-limit poker table in the poker room.

GOLF: The boys tee off at **TPC Las Vegas**, a championship-level course designed by Raymond Floyd.

DINNER: After a day on the links and showers in the room, the evening kicks off back at the Hard Rock with a feast at **Ago**, where the Tuscan-style Italian food transports everyone to Italy for a few hours.

CLUBS: The starting point is **Pure** (Caesars Palace), one of the hottest clubs in Vegas (and a Fodor's Choice): its mix of hip-hop, house, and rock is split into 3 sub-clubs within the 36,000 square-foot space.

STRIP CLUB: This is a bachelor party, so a strip-club visit is de rigeur. **Spearmint Rhino's** clubby setting gives it a classy feel (well, as classy as classy gets at a strip club).

AFTER-HOURS CLUB: The boys hit **Deja Vu presents Vince Neil's Girls, Girls, Girls**, a club/strip club where the music is almost as hot as the performers.

SUNDAY

GIRLS

Last on the weekend's agenda is a Vinyasa yoga class at **Sherry Goldstein's Yoga Sanctuary** (☎ 702/240–7666 ⊕ www.lasvegasyoga.com) in West Las Vegas. Then it's back to the pool for an hour or two before the girls start making their way to the airport. For the bachelorette, it's a weekend she'll never forget—although she may want to when the maid of honor pulls out the pictures at the wedding reception.

BOYS

Manly-man hugs abound as the guys begin to make their way to the airport. For those with late flights, there's time to ride the go-karts and compete in pop-a-shot at the **Las Vegas Mini Gran Prix** (☎ 702/259–7000 ⊕ www.lvmgp.com). The bachelor's going to need to work up some cover stories on what to tell the fiancée about what happened. Of course, she's probably working on her own.

The Game Plan

No matter what the nature of your bachelor or bachelorette party is, here are some tips:

YOU CAN'T EXPECT EVERYONE TO STICK TOGETHER all the time. Build anchor events into the trip that everyone will be expected to attend, like a fancy dinner or club outing for a Saturday night so that those who have to arrive late or leave early can attend.

WANT TO GET INTO THE CLUBS? So do a trillion other people. Above all else, dress the part. Clubs want well-put-together patrons who look like they belong with the beautiful people.

DISNEYLAND FIGURED IT OUT A FEW YEARS AGO: position in line is a product that can be sold just like anything else, so higher-budget parties can buy Front-of-the-Line passes that give you license to cut. Sounds good, right? The thing is, it doesn't actually work. Front-of-Line passes just move you to the front of one line but to the back of another. Don't waste your money. Instead, to secure a reservation, call ahead and book a table with bottle service.

PLAN AHEAD. That means dinner and show reservations, golf and other outdoor excursions, and especially night-time activities. The further ahead you plan, the more likely you are to get seats for the shows and meals you want, and the more likely you are to gain entrance to the hottest clubs. Even though Vegas has a lot of places to play, start building an itinerary at least a month before your trip.

Club Surrender

LIVE MUSIC

Small, medium, or large? From bohemian indie-band showcases (the Art Bar, the Beauty Bar) and kooky kitschy lounges (the Bunkhouse, the Rocks Lounge) to big concert halls (the House of Blues, the Joint, and the Pearl)—and *then* on to truly *gargantuan* venues like the new Smith Center for the Performing Arts and the MGM Grand Arena—Vegas is a world capital of live music. The trick, as always with local nightlife, is to check current news listings for performers, showtimes, and locations. (Why locations? Because even certain hot spots not ordinarily given over to live music—the Bank dance club, for example—will host concerts when you least expect it.) And, of course, the Vegas lounge act has come a long way. Nearly every big Strip resort features a high-energy dance band that ably performs hits from the 60s to today's hottest tunes.

Book & Stage. Book & Stage started as Cosmopolitan's sports book, but now the area provides a comfortable and intimate spot (with great acoustics) to see free live music (the book has moved upstairs). What's more, the modest stage has attracted some of the biggest up-and-coming bands in Vegas, from Tennis and The Knocks to Chairlift and 100 Monkeys. Shows generally occur nightly at 10 pm and midnight. Because the cushiest seats are first-come-first-served, get there early if you really want to sit. ⊠ *The Cosmopolitan, 3708 Las Vegas Blvd. S, South Strip* ☎ *702/698–7000* ⊕ *www.cosmopolitanlasvegas.com.*

House of Blues. This nightclub–concert hall hybrid at Mandalay Bay was the seventh entry in this chain of successful, intimate music clubs. As if the electric roster of performers taking the stage almost nightly wasn't enough (past acts include Al Green, Bo Diddley, Bob Weir, Sarah Silverman, the Dropkick Murphys, and Seal), the decor is lusciously imaginative. (Our favorite decoration isn't inside, though—it's the Voodoo Mama statue greeting you outside.) The Gospel Brunch on Sunday has great live music and a delicious brunch and is worth a visit. ⊠ *Mandalay Bay, 3950 Las Vegas Blvd. S, South Strip* ☎ *702/632–7600* ⊕ *www.houseofblues.com.*

OFF THE STRIP AND DOWNTOWN

BARS AND LOUNGES

Fodor'sChoice **The Artisan Lounge.** This not-yet-well-known favorite of ours is in the
★ slightly out-of-the-way Artisan Hotel and is sort of an upscale version of the Peppermill (⇨ *review).* The vibe is relatively chill even on weekends, so it can serve as a tonic to the usual Vegas lunacy. The interior is filled with gilt-framed paintings (and sometimes frames without the paintings), which are even on the ceiling. Ordinarily, a crazy ceiling stunt like this one would seem silly, but the muted romantic ambience here (candlelight, soft music, dark wood, comfy leather couches) makes it work. On Friday and Saturday nights, during an event dubbed "Artisan Afterhours," deejays spin electro, house, and techno from 10

pm until dawn. ⊠ *The Artisan Hotel, 1501 W. Sahara Ave., West Side* ☎ *800/554–4092* ⊕ *www.theartisanhotel.com/lounge.html.*

Ghostbar. Perched atop the Palms, this apex of ultralounges has rock music, glamorous patrons, glowing lights, and a glassed-in view of the city. Step outside and you'll find that the outdoor "Ghostdeck" is cantilevered over the side of the building, with a Plexiglas platform that allows revelers to look down 450 feet below. Because of the laughably complicated process to get in the door, some might find this spot frustrating (although, with the right blend of patience and good humor, getting inside can be highly entertaining). Still, for the views of the Strip skyline alone, it's worth the effort. ⊠ *The Palms, 4321 W. Flamingo Rd., West Side* ☎ *702/942–6832* ⊕ *www.palms.com.*

Lucky Bar. This circular bar's casual, lively atmosphere, comfy couch-like seats, sexy staff, and giant chandeliers make it one of the best in town, and worth the trip to the impressive Red Rock complex. What's more, the bar is steps away from Rocks Lounge, another hip spot that features up-and-coming deejays who spin a blend of top 40, flashbacks, rock, and oldskool on Friday and Saturday nights. ⊠ *Red Rock Casino, Resort & Spa, 11011 W. Charleston Blvd., Summerlin* ☎ *702/797–7777* ⊕ *www.redrocklasvegas.com/entertainment.*

Paymon's Mediterranean Cafe and Hookah Lounge. The hookah is an elaborate Middle Eastern water pipe that is used to smoke exotic tobaccos (and yes, we just mean *tobacco*). It also happens to be a trend popular at Vegas lounges and clubs these days. Thanks to a helpful "Hookah Man" and some available samples, no prior experience with water pipes is required. But the hookah is only one part of the appeal here: designed by local entrepreneur Paymon Raouf for the ultimate chill-out experience, this red velvet–laden, exquisitely carpeted, incense-filled environment redefines Vegas plush, and its young, somewhat bohemian crowd and those sexy paintings on the wall don't hurt the romance, either. ⊠ *4717 S. Maryland Pkwy., University District* ☎ *702/731–6030* ⊕ *www.paymons.com* ⊠ *8380 W. Sahara Ave., Northwest Las Vegas* ☎ *702/731–6030.*

The Playboy Club. "The Bunny is back!" The 1960s nightlife legend, now rocks the 52nd floor of the Palms' new Fantasy Tower. A few of the old fixings are absent: the vintage *Playboy* photos projected on multiple LCD screens include no nudity, for example. (This isn't a topless joint, mind you—it's as upscale as ultralounges get.) Still, all the servers and croupiers (yes, there is gambling, Thursday through Saturday) wear the classic Bunny outfits, and the plush dark bachelor-pad-on-a-grand-scale feel here, complete with fireplace and a multitude of couches, proves that everything old can be new again. When you're ready to dance, take the escalator up to Moon. It's connected to the Playboy and is included in your cover charge. ⊠ *The Palms, 4321 W. Flamingo Rd., West Side* ☎ *702/942–7777* ⊕ *www.palms.com.*

VooDoo Rooftop Nightclub. Take in great views of the city at this indoor/outdoor, bi-level club 51 floors atop the Rio. Deejays, great dance bands, and well-trained flair bartenders, serving concoctions such as the rum-packed Witch Doctor, keep things lively. Faux-primitive voodoo paintings on the walls of the dance rooms maintain a tenuous thematic connection. Except for the Thursday-night Industry party, the crowd tends to be slightly older and less, shall we say, sophisticated than at similar clubs. The party starts at 5 pm daily. ⊠ *Rio All-Suite Hotel & Casino, 3700 W. Flamingo Rd., West Side* ☎ *702/777–6875* ⊕ *www. riolasvegas.com.*

DANCE CLUBS AND NIGHTCLUBS

Fodor's Choice
★ **Moon.** Packing in more futuristic technology than a space station, this vast megalopolis of cool occupies the top floor of the Palms' Fantasy Tower. The club has a retractable roof, multiple dance floors, two ample outdoor balconies, banquettes seating 20, stripper poles galore, and some of the best views in town (including a few without glass—it's just you and the vista). And what would a hot new scene be without its celebrity enthusiasts? Justin Timberlake and Lindsay Lohan are among those who've landed at Moon, even seizing control of the turntables on occasion. Oh, and if you'd like to take a breather from the space suits (and look at Bunny outfits instead), simply take the escalator to the Playboy Club. (It's included in your ticket price.) ⊠ *The Palms, 4321 W. Flamingo Rd., West Side* ☎ *702/942–6832* ⊕ *www.palms.com* ☉ *Tues. and Thurs.–Sat.*

Stoney's Rockin' Country. What do you get when you fill a country-themed Texas saloon with slick dance-music-crazed nightclubbers? Madness— 2,000-capacity 10-gallon-hat madness. Despite the Texas-shape neon sign, Stoney's (named after its owner) has all the glam hot-spot fixings: the largest dance floor in Nevada, private tables, a VIP lounge, bottle service, and music that can segue from Merle Haggard to Jay Z. With $10 all-you-can-drink draft beer specials on Thursday and free dance lessons on Friday and Saturday, you can't beat the prices either. ⊠ *9151 Las Vegas Blvd. S, Outskirts* ☎ *702/435–2855* ⊕ *www. stoneysrockincountry.com.*

Vanity. With an interior adorned with antique mirrors and a cyclone chandelier composed of more than 20,000 crystals, the result is something rare in Vegas nightclubs: decent lighting. When it opened in late 2009, Vanity was the hottest ticket in town; though the venue has waned a bit on the buzz-o-meter, Friday and Saturday nights still jam (and often attracts a good number of celebrities). After working up a sweat on the sunken dance floor, grab a drink and a breather on the outdoor terrace, which overlooks the Hard Rock Beach Club. Ladies, be sure to check out the women's lounge; female sources say it's plush. ⊠ *Hard Rock Hotel & Casino, 4455 Paradise Rd., Paradise Road* ☎ *702/693–5555* ⊕ *www.hardrockhotel.com/party* ☉ *Fri.–Sun.*

DIVE BARS AND LOCAL HANGOUTS

Beauty Bar. This charming little Downtown joint, spun off from a popular Manhattan watering hole, is laid out like an old-fashioned hair salon, complete with hair-dryer chairs acquired from a defunct New Jersey salon. It's a kitschy spot to listen to local bands (primarily

8

rockers), get entranced by the curve of the pink walls, sip away at creative cocktails with names like Shampoo and Conditioner, and ogle the hipster crowd. On warm nights, a spacious patio with a bar and stage for live music is opened out back. ⊠ *517 Fremont St., #A, Downtown* ☎ *702/598–1965* ⊕ *www.thebeautybar.com/las_vegas.*

Double Down Saloon. The grand poobah of Vegas dive bars, the Double D is a short walk from the Hard Rock Hotel and a long, long way from Paradise—although a sign above the door has proclaimed it to be "The Happiest Place on Earth." Delicious decadence prevails here; no wonder it's a fave of filmmaker Tim Burton. For the boho crowd, this deliberately downscale bar has everything from great local bands to a satisfying jukebox with truly eclectic selections. Our advice: go late, wear black, and try the (fabled) Ass Juice cocktail. Also, don't miss the clever, mostly obscene graffiti; it'll have you guffawing in minutes. ⊠ *4640 Paradise Rd., Paradise Road* ☎ *702/791–5775* ⊕ *www.doubledownsaloon.com.*

Downtown Cocktail Room. Hiding from your creditors? Seeking a good spot for a séance or a Spin-the-Bottle party? If so, then consider stepping—carefully—into the gorgeous gloom of this hipster hangout, which is just around the corner from the Griffin and the Beauty Bar. The modest-size, minimalist lounge glows from candle-filled tables and thumps with simmering house music, making the vibe mysterious and romantic. Weeknight happy hour, from 4 to 8 pm, is popular among locals (and even offers discounted bottle service). ⊠ *111 Las Vegas Blvd., Downtown* ☎ *702/880–3696* ⊕ *thedowntownlv.com.*

Frankie's Tiki Room. You want Polynesian tiki-bar culture, Vegas-style? You want grass huts, carved wooden furniture, and cocktails such as the Green Gasser, the Thurston Howl, the Lava Letch, and the Bearded Clam? You'll get it all here, and more. On Friday, if you wear an Aloha shirt, your first drink is free. Better still: If you love your mug (and trust us, you will), there's a gift shop where you can buy one to bring the spirit of aloha home with you. ⊠ *1712 W. Charleston Blvd., West Side* ☎ *702/385–3110* ⊕ *www.frankiestikiroom.com.*

Freakin' Frog. Prepare to get carded at this college bar with "1,000 beers in the cooler and 600 whiskeys in the attic." Although booze takes top billing, the two-story joint has a decent-size stage, and attracts all sorts of live music acts from around the country. ⊠ *4700 S. Maryland Pkwy., University District* ☎ *702/597–9702* ⊕ *www.freakinfrog.com.*

The Griffin Lounge. As good as Vegas Bohemia gets, this Downtown bar, close to the Beauty Bar and the Downtown Cocktail Room, is an instant winner. Some wags have likened it to a Peppermill for the younger, looser set, but this description fails to account for the beauty of its hipster crowd as well as its decor, from the kitschy neon sign outside to the fire grills, the barrel-vaulted brick ceiling, the semicircular banquettes, and the griffin insignias on the bathroom walls. Our favorite feature, though, is the back room, which resembles a study owned by King Henry VIII—in the 1950s. ⊠ *511 Fremont St., Downtown* ☎ *702/382–0577.*

GAY AND LESBIAN NIGHTLIFE

Las Vegas was never really known for gay tourism, but things have changed rapidly in the past few years. Now a number of bars and nightclubs cater to different segments of the community, and the gay-friendly **Blue Moon Resort** (⊕ *www.bluemoonlv.com*) has 45 rooms near Sahara Avenue and Interstate 15.

Most gay and lesbian nightlife is concentrated into two areas of town. The most prominent is the so-called "Fruit Loop"—which wins our award for best nickname for a North American gay neighborhood—which you enter near the intersection of Naples Drive and Paradise Road, just north of the airport and close to the Hard Rock. The other is the area in and around Commercial Center, one of the city's oldest shopping centers, on East Sahara Avenue, just west of Maryland Parkway. If there are cover charges at all, expect them to be around $10 for dance clubs on weekends.

Unfortunately, there are no all-out lesbian bars in Vegas, although many of the gay bars (most prominently Freezone and Krâve) host special nights for their Sapphic sisters. These parties, like so much in Sin City, change frequently, so it's best to consult a copy of *Q Vegas*, the city's gay monthly, or visit its website ⊕ *www.qvegas.com*.

Backdoor Lounge. For those of you who believe that Latinos are the sexiest men in this galaxy (if not the surrounding galaxies, as well), step—or dive—into this 24-hour establishment that caters to your taste with weekend drag shows and $2 drinks. ⊠ *1415 E. Charleston Blvd., East Side* ☎ *702/385–2018.*

Badlands Saloon. Consider the "Badlands" a 24-hour haven for local gay cowboys. It's decorated with a mock-log-cabin facade and offers cubbyholes in which regulars can store their beer steins. There's also a jukebox crammed to the coin slot with country-and-western hits. Plus, the Nevada Gay Rodeo Association hosts its fundraisers here. Perhaps the only downside is the smoke; in true Old West fashion, the Badlands is one of the few places where smoking is permitted. ⊠ *953 E. Sahara Ave.(inside Commercial Center), East Side* ☎ *702/792–9262.*

Flex. A small, neighborhood-oriented club for men, this 24-hour hotspot sometimes has floor shows, banana-eating contests, and entertainment (think male strippers, folks, sometimes in drag). Of course we like the strong and inexpensive drinks. ⊠ *4371 W. Charleston Ave., West Side* ☎ *702/385–3539* ⊕ *flexlasvegas.com.*

Fodor's Choice ★ **Freezone.** An egalitarian mix of (straight and gay) men and women congregates at this 24-hour bar with a dance floor, pool tables, karaoke, and video-poker machines. Each night brings a different theme: Ladies' Night is Tuesday (lesbians, unite!), male go-gos "come out" on Thursday, and the Queens of Las Vegas drag show is held Friday and Saturday. ⊠ *610 E. Naples Dr., University District* ☎ *702/794–2300* ⊕ *www.freezonelv.com.*

Gipsy. The oldest, largest, and most famous alternative dance club in Las Vegas is within walking distance of the Hard Rock. Predominantly a male club, it has always welcomed the open-minded regardless of sexual

8

preference. Competition from newer mainstream nightclubs has taken a little of the edge off its crossover appeal, but the "Gip" manages to stay busy, and then some—its modest size often leads to brutal overcrowding. There are nightly drink specials, and deejays spin hip-hop on Friday and Saturday. We also love the "cabaret" show on the last Sunday of every month. ✉ *4605 Paradise Rd., Paradise Road* ☎ *702/731–1919* ◷ *Thurs.–Sun.*

Piranha Boutique Nightclub. As the sister establishment to the ever-popular Gipsy (across the street), this gorgeous spot packs in revelers every night of the week. While the dance floor at Piranha is legendary, the best spot in the house is the spacious, fireplace-ringed open-air patio out back. The club also runs promotions whereby patrons can receive free drinks by checking in on Facebook. ✉ *4633 Paradise Rd., Paradise Road* ☎ *702/491–0100* ⊕ *www.piranhavegas.com.*

LIVE MUSIC

COUNTRY AND WESTERN

Dylan's Dance Hall & Saloon. This Boulder Highway honky-tonk is the spiritual heart of Las Vegas country-and-western music. It's open Thursday through Saturday from 7 pm., and offers two-for-one drink specials every night. ✉ *4660 Boulder Hwy., Boulder Strip* ☎ *702/451–4006* ⊕ *dylanslv.com* ◷ *Thurs.–Sat.*

JAZZ AND CLASSICAL

Fodor's Choice ★ **The Smith Center for the Performing Arts.** Las Vegas got its very own ($150-million) world-class performing arts center in early 2012, and what a spot it is. The multi-building complex (complete with a bell tower) was designed to invoke 1930s-era art deco construction; the same motif you'll find at the Hoover Dam. Here, this elegance graces the main concert hall, which hosts everything from rock bands to traveling orchestras. The cabaret across the breezeway hosts live jazz every weekend. In the summer, the "Smith" also hosts open-air concerts on the lawn. ✉ *361 Symphony Park Ave., Downtown* ☎ *702/749–2000* ⊕ *www.thesmithcenter.com.*

ROCK

Bunkhouse. Offering raucous rock in a raucous Downtown saloon, this is where the most clued-in locals go to shake, rattle, headbang, and roll. ✉ *124 S. 11th St., at Fremont Experience, Downtown* ☎ *702/384–4536.*

The Joint. Arenas acts such as the Rolling Stones, the Eagles, and Sting, as well as smaller acts more often matched to an intimate club, play at the Joint. From Tim McGraw to Bon Iver, the Joint hosts some of the best touring acts in the nation. ✉ *Hard Rock Hotel & Casino, 4455 Paradise Rd., Paradise Road* ☎ *702/693–5583* ⊕ *thejointlasvegas.com.*

Fodor's Choice ★ **The Pearl.** Look out, Hard Rock. Not only does the Palms Casino Resort have its own recording studio and tie-in deal with iTunes, it's got this gorgeous, state-of-the-art concert venue, which boasts a stream of big-name rock, country, and hip-hop acts year-round. ✉ *The Palms, 4321 W. Flamingo Rd., West Side* ☎ *702/942–7777* ⊕ *www.palms.com/las-vegas-pearl-theater.*

The Railhead. This comfortable venue started as an open casino and lounge that occasionally hosted ticketed concerts. It has since become an enclosed club, nearly perfect for a diverse range of local and mid-level concerts that range from rock to country and just about everything in between. ⊠ *Boulder Station Hotel & Casino, 4111 Boulder Hwy., Boulder Strip* ☎ *702/432–7777* ⊕ *www.boulderstation.com/entertainment.*

STRIP CLUBS

It's not called Sin City for nothing. "Exotic dancing" clubs are a major industry here, but they do have some quirks. Zoning laws restrict most clubs to industrial areas not far off the Strip. Fully nude clubs are available in Vegas but such venues cannot carry liquor licenses. (The Palomino Club, in North Las Vegas, is the one exception.) Joints with liquor licenses have the sharper designs, the bigger spaces, the more savory customers, and the more glamorous gals. Some, depending on how loosely you define the term, can be pretty classy.

Wherever you go, be prepared to shell out some serious cash. Most places have instituted cover charges of $20 or more, but that's just the beginning. The real money's made on the table dances continuously solicited inside, with most going for $20 per song (and four VIP dances often for a C-note).

Cheetah's. This gentleman's club is no stranger to headlines. It has been featured in that pinnacle of late-20th-century cinematic excellence, *Showgirls,* and also was a favorite hangout of famous Vegas casino scion and murder victim Ted Binion. The place ain't the Rhino, but it does have plenty of hotter-than-average dancers, plus a free shuttle from the Strip, cheap lap dances (2 for $20) during daylight hours and free pizza and wings every day between noon and 5. The bad news for a gentlemen's club, where zing is the thing, is that the joint is looking a bit tired. ⊠ *2112 Western Ave., West Side* ☎ *702/384–0074* ⊕ *www. cheetahslv.net.*

Crazy Horse III. Rising from the ashes of two previous strip clubs (Sin and the Penthouse Club) on the same site is this mammoth tribute to flesh and hedonism. Unlike many other strip clubs in town, this one offers a number of promotions throughout the week, including free food, free limo rides, and free drinks. Private cabanas off the main room require a one-drink minimum, one of the best "deals" in town. ⊠ *3525 W. Russell Rd., West Side* ☎ *702/673–1700* ⊕ *www.ch3lv.com.*

Deja Vu Presents Vince Neil's Girls Girls Girls. This place isn't just a topless bar—it's also an ultralounge and a super-popular after-hours dance club, where you don't have to be a stripper or stripperphile to get your groove on. The joint was rebranded (from something called an "erotic ultralounge") in March 2012 with Mötley Crüe singer Vince Neil and a live music component was added to the mix. Could such three-in-one spots be the next wave of Vegas nightlife? Come see for yourself. ⊠ *4740 S. Arville St., West Side* ☎ *702/227–5200* ⊕ *www.dejavu.com.*

OG. Yes, it's the granddaddy of Vegas strip clubs, and the first to install several smaller stages to take the place of the single stage found in older

8

clubs. The cover charge is $30, but the fee is waived if you get there on your own before 6 pm (our advice: cab it to the Stratosphere, and walk the two blocks to the OG). Inside, a separate room has male revues for the ladies. ✉ *1531 Las Vegas Blvd. S, North Strip* ☎ *702/385–9361* ⊕ *www.ogvegas.com.*

Palomino Club. This is one of the oldest strip clubs in the area (the Rat Pack used to hang out here), as well as the most notorious; two separate owners have been accused of murders, and it was also owned briefly by a noted heart surgeon. Because the "Pal" was grandfathered into the North Las Vegas zoning codes, it's allowed to have both a full bar *and* full nudity. There's also a burlesque stage and an all-male revue. ✉ *1848 Las Vegas Blvd. N, North Side* ☎ *877/399–2023* ⊕ *www.palominolv.com.*

Sapphire. The owners claim to have spent $26 million for the bragging rights of proclaiming their club the "largest adult entertainment complex in the world," which means that what it loses in intimacy it makes up for in excess. Formerly a gym, this place provides 40,000 square feet of topless dancing, complete with 13 second-floor "skyboxes" and a phalanx of dancers who rank among Vegas's most proficient. For their big entrances, dancers descend a ramp to a clear, elevated main stage that towers over the floor. ✉ *3025 S. Industrial Rd., West Side* ☎ *702/796–6000* ⊕ *www.sapphirelasvegas.com.*

Fodor's Choice
★

Spearmint Rhino. At the "Rhino," as everyone calls it, you can expect a veritable onslaught of gorgeous half-clad women: possibly the best-looking dancers west of the Mississippi. The national chain got a late start in Vegas, but it grew fast, expanding its original space to 18,000 square feet. It's also the rare topless club that offers lunch, including pizza, burgers, and steak sandwiches, not to mention an adjoining shop for lingerie, sex toys, and various other implements of physical naughtiness. Of course it's always crowded, but tipping the staff lavishly will get you a table, not to mention anything else that's not too illegal, immoral, or fattening. (Further tipping might even snag you some of that immoral and fattening stuff.) Our only gripe: The lighting here is usually so low that you can't get a good enough gander at all the wonders worth gandering at. Still, that's a small price to pay for American beauty in all its glistening grandeur. ✉ *3340 S. Highland Dr., West Side* ☎ *702/796–3600* ⊕ *www.spearmintrhinolv.com.*

Side Trips from Las Vegas

WORD OF MOUTH

"If you want to do something outdoors during the summer, a good choice is the Mt. Charleston area. At elevations from around 7,000 to 12,000 feet, it's very different from the desert floor—and much cooler."

–logott

SIDE TRIPS FROM LAS VEGAS

TOP REASONS TO GO

★ **Experiencing geologic history:** The breathtaking 277-mile Grand Canyon was created by the Colorado River over the course of 6 million years, yet it never gets old.

★ **Enjoying the outdoors:** With expansive views and acres upon acres of open space, Mt. Charleston and the Lake Mead National Recreation Area are great places to reconnect with nature.

★ **Celebrating engineering:** It's hard to find a monument to man's ingenuity more impressive than the 1,244-foot concrete span of Hoover Dam.

1 Mt. Charleston Area. The highest point in the Spring Mountain range is a favorite spot for Las Vegans to ski and hike. Take Route 157 to its end and enjoy the view (or a cocktail) at the Mt. Charleston Lodge.

2 Lake Mead Area. Lake Mead, the largest reservoir in the United States, and Hoover Dam are about 34 miles from Las Vegas. Nearby, Valley of Fire is a seemingly infinite landscape of sandstone outcroppings, petrified logs, and miles of hiking trails.

3 Grand Canyon. About four hours' drive from Las Vegas—less if you head to the West Rim—much of the Canyon is a National Park. The South Rim is where all the action is, although the North Rim is more for the adventurer. The Skywalk, a relatively new attraction in the West Rim, provides jaw-dropping views straight down.

4 Death Valley. This is a vast, lonely, beautiful place with breathtaking vistas, blasting 120-degree heat, and mysterious moving rocks. The desert landscape is surrounded by majestic mountains, dry lake beds, spring wildflowers, and Wild West ghost towns.

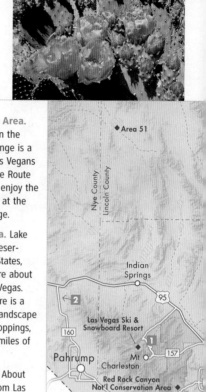

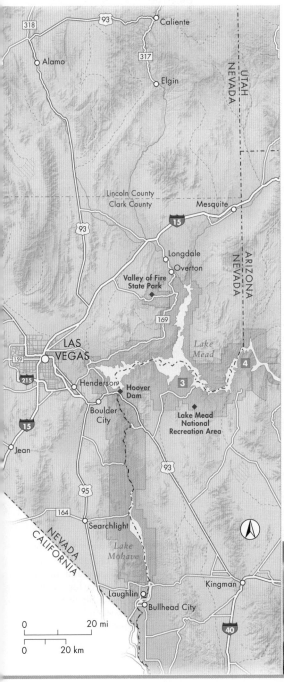

NEVADA

GETTING ORIENTED

In many ways, the expanse of Nevada to the west, south, and east of Las Vegas is a living museum. The breathtaking Grand Canyon offers a glimpse at 6 million years of erosion, while the Hoover Dam is an exhibit on modern engineering. Beyond these attractions, untrammeled places like Lake Mead National Recreation Area and Mt. Charleston provide a perfect counterpoint to the hubbub of Sin City.

9

Updated
by Mike
Weatherford

Nevada takes its name from a Spanish word meaning "snow-covered." So why, you might ask, is the southeastern corner of the state covered in scorching sands and desert landscapes that blend seamlessly with neighboring Arizona? Probably because prior to Nevada's becoming a state, most of the land in what's now Clark County belonged to Arizona's "lost county of Pah-Ute."

At that time Las Vegas was a tiny settlement situated at the crossroads of the Old Spanish Trail and the Mormon Road. The Mormon town of Callville, now drowned beneath the waters of Lake Mead, was the Pah-Ute county seat. A smattering of agricultural communities sat on the banks of the Colorado River, and steamboats plied the river's muddy waters. A lot has changed in the last 150 years.

Today the vast majority of the state's population resides in Clark County and the nearby lakes, state parks, and geological wonders entertain even the most jaded city dwellers. Those pressed for time can take a short drive from Vegas to go skiing at Mt. Charleston, hiking in the Humboldt–Toiyabe National Forest, or rock climbing in Red Rock Canyon. Those with a little more time can explore the wonderland of nearby waterways, stunning rock formations, and laid-back ranching communities. Water enthusiasts head to Lakes Mead, Mohave, and Havasu. Nature lovers find prime wildlife watching along the Colorado River. And those looking for the grandest spectacle in the region can take the longer drive to the Grand Canyon.

SIDE TRIPS PLANNER

WHEN TO GO

There's no bad time to visit the Grand Canyon, though summer and spring break are the busiest times. Visiting during these peak seasons, as well as holidays, requires patience and a tolerance for crowds. Weather changes on a whim in this exposed high-desert region. The more remote North Rim is off-limits during winter. There are no services, and Highway 67 south of Jacob Lake is closed.

The communities in southeastern Nevada and northwestern Arizona don't have distinct high and low seasons. The arid climate and clear winter skies attract retirees escaping harsh northern climes, and the hot, sunny summer months attract sports enthusiasts looking for water—despite 120°F temperatures. Things simmer down a bit during the spring and fall months. Overall, expect crowded weekends during the summer months and sold-out rooms during sporting events.

GETTING HERE AND AROUND

Grand Canyon National Park's South Rim is 278 miles southeast of Las Vegas. Take Highway 93 south to Interstate 40. At Highway 64 drive 60 miles north to the park's southern entrance. In summer, roads are congested, so park your car and take the free shuttle. Traffic's lighter and parking easier October through April.

The North Rim is 275 miles northeast of Vegas. Drive 128 miles north on Interstate 15 to Route 9 and then travel east 10 miles to Route 59/Route 389. Continue east 65 miles to the junction of U.S. 89A and then 30 miles east to Route 67, which dead-ends at the North Rim entrance.

Grand Canyon West is 121 miles southeast of Las Vegas. Travel 72 miles south on Highway 93 to Pierce Ferry Road and travel north 28 miles to Diamond Bar Road. Drive 21 miles on Diamond Bar Road to the entrance at Grand Canyon West Airport, where a shuttle takes visitors to the West Rim.

MAKING THE MOST OF YOUR TIME

Plan ahead if you're going to explore Grand Canyon National Park. Reservations for everything fill up during the busy summer months; mule rides and lodging may be reserved up to 13 months in advance. Perhaps the easiest way to visit the West Rim from Vegas is with a tour (⊕ *www.destinationgrandcanyon.com*). **Bighorn Wild West Tours** (☎ *702/385–4676 or 888/385–4676*) will pick you up in a Hummer at your Vegas hotel for an all-day trip that includes the shuttle-bus package and lunch for $229.

Day-trippers heading to the Lake Mead National Recreation Area can stop at the Alan Bible Visitors Center near Boulder Beach (at this writing the center was being renovated but is expected to reopen by the fall of 2012). For a multiday trip, bunk down in Kingman and explore the ghost town of Oatman or head to the laid-back casino resorts in Laughlin and fill up your itinerary with Colorado River water sports.

WHAT TO DO AND WHERE TO DO IT

Looking to hook the big one? Head to Lake Mead for excellent year-round fishing. To explore ghost towns and the Old West, check out Oatman, Arizona, or the eastern reaches of Nevada en route to Death Valley. Nature buffs will find excellent birding and wildlife-watching at nature preserves along the Colorado River, but the grandest natural spectacle's just a short jaunt away at the Grand Canyon. The South and North rims offer outdoor adventure, multiple viewpoints, and rustic lodging for multiday excursions. Grand Canyon West, easily accessible from Las Vegas by a quick flight or a relaxed bus tour, adds a Native American perspective to the world's grandest gorge with three developed viewpoints, horseback and Hummer rides to the rim, and the Skywalk—a glass U-shape bridge 4,000 feet above the Colorado River. Another geological marvel that's a short drive from Las Vegas is the dramatic red sandstone formations and stark views of the Mohave Desert at Valley of Fire State Park.

SAFETY TIPS

Services can be few and far between in the more remote regions of southwestern Nevada and northeastern Arizona. Play it safe by packing an emergency car kit with basic automotive repairs, plenty of water, and overnight supplies. To avoid being stranded, let someone know where you're going and which route you plan to take. It's also a good idea to check road conditions (*Nevada:* ☎ 877/687–6237 ⊕ *www. nevadadot.com; Arizona* ☎ 888/411–7623 ⊕ *www.azdot.gov; Utah:* ☎ 866/511–8824 ⊕ *www.sr.ex.state.ut.us; Grand Canyon National Park:* ☎ 928/638–7888) before you set out.

ABOUT THE RESTAURANTS

Dining's generally relaxed and casual in southeastern Nevada. For the most part you'll find home-cooked American favorites and "South of the Border" specialties. For the best in fine dining, head to the Laughlin casinos for a sophisticated medley of gourmet restaurants serving everything from seafood to steaks.

Dining options in Grand Canyon National Park are limited. However, inside the park, you'll find everything from cafeteria food to casual café fare to elegant evening specials. On the Hualapai and Havasupai reservations in Havasu Canyon and at Grand Canyon West, options are limited to tribe-run restaurants.

Prices: *Prices in the restaurant reviews are the average cost of a main course at dinner or, if dinner is not served, at lunch; taxes and service charges are generally included.*

ABOUT THE HOTELS

Of the 922 rooms, cabins, and suites in Grand Canyon National Park, only 203—all at the Grand Canyon Lodge—are located at the North Rim. Outside of El Tovar Hotel, the canyon's architectural crown jewel, frills are hard to find. Rooms are basic but comfortable, and most guests would agree that the best in-room amenity is a view of the canyon. Reservations are a must, especially during the busy summer season.

Lodging options are even more limited on the West Rim. The Hualapai Lodge in Peach Springs and the Hualapai Ranch at Grand Canyon West are run by the Hualapai tribe. The Havasupai Lodge in Supai offers the only rooms in Havasu Canyon. Motel chains and laid-back casinos make up the most abundant and affordable options in Laughlin, Kingman, and just outside Boulder City.

Prices: *Prices in the hotel reviews are the lowest cost of a standard double room in high season, excluding taxes, service charges, and meal plans.*

MT. CHARLESTON

45 miles northwest of Las Vegas.

GETTING HERE AND AROUND

Take U.S. 95 from Las Vegas. At the intersection of 95 and Route 157, turn left to Kyle Canyon, home of the township for year-round residents and the two lodges/restaurants. If you are in a hurry to ski, pass this

For a break from the slots during the winter, head to Las Vegas Ski and Snowboard Resort, just 47 miles northwest of Downtown.

turn and stay on the highway to the next left, Route 156, which takes you to Lee Canyon and the ski resort. But don't stress over the decision. If you take the Kyle road first, there's a scenic 25-minute drive midway up, connecting drive Kyle to Lee.

■TIP→ Speed limits on the drive approaching and climbing Mt. Charleston vary and change quickly; it can be an easy ticket on weekends, when police are out in force. The descending drive especially can lead to speed violations—it's easy to exceed 55 mph without even realizing it—leading you right into the waiting arms of the law.

ESSENTIALS

Campground Info U.S. Forest Service ☎ 702/515–5400, 877/444–6777 *reservations* ⊕ *www.recreation.gov.*

Weather Reports Las Vegas Ski and Snowboard Resort ☎ *702/593–9500.*

EXPLORING

Mt. Charleston. In winter Las Vegans crowd the upper elevations of the Spring Mountains to throw snowballs, sled, cross-country ski, and even slide downhill at a little ski area. In summer they return to wander the high trails and escape the valley's 110°F heat (temperatures here can be 20°F–30°F cooler than in the city), and maybe even make the difficult hike to Mt. Charleston, the range's high point. Easier trails lead to seasonal waterfalls or rare, dripping springs where dainty columbine and stunted aspens spill down ravines and hummingbirds zoom. Or they might lead onto high, dry ridges where ancient bristlecone trees have become twisted and burnished with age. ⊠ *Outskirts, Las Vegas.*

Fodor's Choice
★

WHERE TO STAY

For expanded reviews, facilities, and current deals, visit Fodors.com.

$ 🏨 **Mount Charleston Lodge and Cabins.** At the end of Route 157 at 7,717
HOTEL   feet above sea level you find this lodge on the perch of Kyle Canyon, with a well-known restaurant and adjacent cabins (run by a separate operator than the restaurant). **Pros:** the seclusion and spectacular views; trails within walking distance. **Cons:** no cable TV (just DVD players), no phones, no Wi-Fi (Some might call these "pros"—a true escape); outdoor walk across parking lot to the lodge can be chilly. **TripAdvisor:** "cute cabins with an amazing view," "great romantic getaway," "very scenic." [$] *Rooms from: $110 ⌂ 5355 Kyle Canyon Rd., Las Vegas* 🕾 *702/872–5408, 800/955–1314 ⊕ www.mtcharlestonlodge.com ⤳ 24 rooms* ⏐⭘⏐ *No meals.*

$ 🏨 **The Resort on Mt. Charleston.** This is the more upscale of the two lodg-
HOTEL   ing choices in Kyle Canyon, though the views aren't as good. **Pros:** full hotel experience with a spa, open Wednesday through Sunday. **Cons:** not as high up the mountain as the other lodge, so the views aren't as spectacular and the summer temperatures not quite as cool; not much to do in immediate vicinity without getting back in a car. **TripAdvisor:** "beautiful," "nice setting," "outstanding service." [$] *Rooms from: $70 ⌂ 2755 Kyle Canyon Rd., Las Vegas* 🕾 *702/872–5500, 888/559–1888 ⊕ www.mtcharlestonresort.com ⤳ 61 rooms* ⏐⭘⏐ *No meals.*

SPORTS AND THE OUTDOORS

HIKING

🕙   **Mt. Charleston.** In summer, hikers escape the heat by traveling 45 min-
Fodor's Choice   utes up to the Spring Mountains National Recreation Area, known
★   informally as Mt. Charleston, where the U.S. Forest Service maintains more than 50 miles of marked hiking trails for all abilities. Trails vary from the 0.7-mile (one-way) Robber's Roost loop trail to the 6.2-mile Bristlecone Loop trail to the extremely strenuous 10.3-mile (one-way) North Loop Trail, which reaches the Mt. Charleston summit at 11,918 feet; the elevation gain is 4,278 feet. There are also plenty of intermediate trails, along with marathon two-, three-, four-, and five-peak routes only for hikers who are highly advanced (and in peak physical condition). Most trails in the area are open for horseback riding, and the Sawmill and Bristlecone trails are open for mountain-bike use. The Mt. Charleston Wilderness is part of the Humboldt–Toiyabe National Forest; for information, contact the U.S. Forest Service (🕾 702/515–5400 ⊕ www.fs.fed.us). ⌂ Outskirts, Las Vegas.

SKIING AND SNOWBOARDING

🕙   **Las Vegas Ski and Snowboard Resort.** Southern Nevada's skiing headquarters is a mere 47 miles northwest of Downtown Las Vegas. Depending on traffic and weather conditions, it can take less than two hours to go from a 70°F February afternoon on the Strip to the top of a chairlift at an elevation of 9,370 feet. "Ski Lee," as it's affectionately known (for its site in Lee Canyon), is equipped with four chairlifts—two double, a surface or magic carpet, and one triple—a ski school, a half pipe

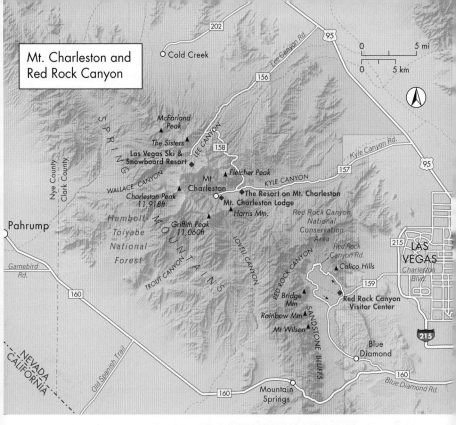

Mt. Charleston and
Red Rock Canyon

and terrain park, a ski shop, rental equipment, and a day lodge with a café and lounge. Clothing rentals are available. There are 40 acres of groomed slopes: 20% of the trails are for beginners, 60% are intermediate, and 20% are advanced runs. The longest run is 3,000 feet, and there's a vertical drop of nearly 1,000 feet. You know you're at the closest ski resort to Las Vegas when you see the slope names: Blackjack, High Roller, Keno, the Strip, Bimbo 1 and 2, and Slot Alley. The lifts are open from about Thanksgiving to Easter for skiing. Lift tickets are normally $50; more on weekends but less if you wait until noon. Shuttle service is available. A telephone call will get you snow conditions (☎ 702/593–9500); driving conditions can be had through the local road report (☎ 511 in NV, 877/687–6237 outside NV ⊕ www.nevadadot.com/traveler). ✉ 6725 Lee Canyon Rd., Mt. Charleston .Take U.S. 95 north to the Lee Canyon exit (Hwy. 156), and head up the mountain ☎ 702/385–2754 ⊕ www.skilasvegas.com.

LAKE MEAD AREA

Southeast of Las Vegas sits Boulder City—prim, languid, and full of historic neighborhoods, small businesses, parks, greenbelts—and not a single casino. Over the hill from town, enormous Hoover Dam blocks the Colorado River as it enters Black Canyon. Backed up behind the dam is incongruous, deep-blue Lake Mead, the focal point of water-based recreation for southern Nevada and northwestern Arizona and the major water supplier to seven Southwestern states. The lake is ringed by miles of rugged desert country. The breathtaking wonderland known as Valley of Fire, with its red sandstone outcroppings, petrified logs, petroglyphs, and hiking trails, is along the northern reach of the lake. And all of this is an hour or less from Vegas.

BOULDER CITY

25 miles southeast of Las Vegas.

In the early 1930s Boulder City was built by the federal government to house 5,000 construction workers on the Hoover Dam project. A strict moral code was enforced to ensure timely completion of the dam, and to this day the model city is the only community in Nevada in which gambling is illegal. (Note that the two casinos at either end of Boulder City are just outside the city limits.) After the dam was completed, the town shrank but was kept alive by the management and maintenance crews of the dam and Lake Mead. Today it's a vibrant little Southwestern town.

GETTING HERE AND AROUND
It takes about 30 minutes via U.S. 93 to get from the Las Vegas tourist corridor to Boulder City.

ESSENTIALS
Visitor Info Boulder City Chamber of Commerce ⊠ *465 Nevada Way* ☎ *702/293–2034* ⊕ *www.bouldercitychamber.com* ☉ *Weekdays 9–5.*

EXPLORING
Boulder Dam Brewing Company. Across the street from the Boulder Dam Hotel, the Boulder Dam Brewing Company is a family-run brewery decorated with historic Hoover Dam photos. A patio garden offers live music on fair-weather weekends. ⊠ *453 Nevada Hwy.* ☎ *702/243–2739* ⊕ *www.boulderdambrewing.com.*

Boulder Dam Hotel. Be sure to stop at the Dutch Colonial– style Boulder Dam Hotel, built in 1933. On the National Register of Historic Places, the 20-room bed-and-breakfast once was a favorite getaway for notables, including the man who became Pope Pius XII and actors Will Rogers, Bette Davis, and Shirley Temple. ⊠ *1305 Arizona St.* ☎ *702/294–5005* ⊕ *www.boulderdamhotel.com.*

Boulder City/Hoover Dam Museum. The Boulder City/Hoover Dam Museum in the rear of the hotel gives you a quick, compact history of the city and dam-building process. If you're going to the dam and paying for the tour and exhibits there, you probably don't need this one as well; but if you don't plan to pop for the dam tour, this one covers the basics. ☎ *702/294–1988* ⊕ *www.bcmha.org* ⊠ *$2* ☉ *Mon.–Sat. 10–5*

NEED A BREAK?

Grandma Daisy's Candy & Ice Cream Parlor. Grandma Daisy's Candy & Ice Cream Parlor makes its own fudge, cloisters, and peanut brittle. ⊠ *530 Nevada Hwy.* ☎ *702/294–6639.*

Lake Mead National Recreation Area

WHERE TO EAT

The old downtown area of Boulder City has become a fun zone for drinks, dining, and antiques shopping. The center of the action is the 500 block of Nevada Highway (aka Nevada Way).

$ DINER 🍴 **The Coffee Cup.** The Coffee Cup is a breakfast-and-lunch diner that's been featured on the Food Network's Diners, Drive-Ins, and Dives. Tourists line up outside on weekends for the quintessential small-town diner experience, complete with newspaper-strewn counter seating and the owners' family photos and memorabilia on the walls. It delivers on the food front, too, with giant portions of vacation-breakfast favorites such as huevos rancheros, chili verde omelets, and skillet scrambles. [$] *Average main: $12* ✉ *512 Nevada Hwy.* ☎ *702/294–0517* 🌐 *www.worldfamouscoffeecup.com* 🕒 *No dinner.*

$$ CAFÉ 🍴 **Milo's Cellar.** At the wine bar Milo's Cellars, the outside sidewalk tables are more popular than its indoor seating, which does evoke a well-stocked wine cellar if you happen to visit in one of the few months when it's too cold to sit outside. But the real appeal for most of the year is to sit outdoors under the ceiling fans — keeping an eye on the quaint main street that Milo's is largely responsible for reviving — while enjoying wine by the glass and the simple but well-considered light menu of salads and sandwiches. If it's too early for the grape, one corner of the place is a coffee and bakery nook. [$] *Average main: $14* ✉ *538 Nevada Hwy.* ☎ *702/293–9540* 🌐 *www.miloswinebar.com.*

HOOVER DAM

8 miles northeast from Boulder City.

GETTING HERE AND AROUND

Hoover Dam is about a 45-minute drive from Las Vegas via U.S. 93; it's about 15 minutes from Boulder City.

EXPLORING

👶 Fodor's Choice ★ **Hoover Dam.** In 1928 Congress authorized $175 million for construction of a dam on the Colorado River to control destructive floods, provide a steady water supply to seven Colorado River Basin states, and generate electricity. Considered one of the seven wonders of the industrial world, the art deco Hoover Dam is 726 feet high (the equivalent of a 70-story building) and 660 feet thick (more than the length of two football fields) at the base. Construction required 4.4 million cubic yards of concrete—enough to build a two-lane highway from San Francisco to New York. Originally referred to as Boulder Dam, the structure was later officially named Hoover Dam in recognition of President Herbert Hoover's role in the project. Look for artist Oskar Hansen's plaza sculptures, which include the 30-foot-tall *Winged Figures of the Republic* (the statues and terazzo floor patterns were copied at the new Smith Center for the Performing Arts in Downtown Las Vegas).

The tour itself is a tradition that dates back to 1937, and you can still see the old box office on top of the dam. But now the ticketed tours originate in the modern visitor center, with two choices of tour. The cheaper, most popular one is the **Powerplant Tour**, which starts every 15 minutes or so. It's a half-hour, guided tour that includes a short film and then a 537-foot elevator ride to two points of interest: a less-than-overwhelming view of a diversion tunnel, and the more impressive eight-story room housing still-functional power generators. Self-paced exhibits follow the guided portion, with good interactive museum exhibits and a great indoor/outdoor patio view of the dam from the river side. The more extensive **Hoover Dam Tour** includes everything on the Powerplant Tour but limits the group size to 20 and spends more time inside the dam, including a peek through the air vents. Tours run from 9 to 5 in the winter and 9 to 6 in the summer. Visitors for both tours submit to security screening comparable to an airport. January and February are the slowest months, and mornings generally are less busy. The top of the dam is open to pedestrians and vehicles, but you have to remain in your vehicle after sundown. The new bypass bridge is the way to and from Arizona. Those willing to pass a security checkpoint (with inspections at the discretion of officers) can still drive over the dam for sightseeing, but cannot continue into Arizona; you have to turn around and come back after the road dead-ends at a scenic lookout (with a snack bar and store) on the Arizona side. ■TIP→ The dam's High Scaler Café is fine for a cold drink or an ice-cream cone, and the outdoor café tables even have misters. But you can skip the $9 burger by having lunch in Boulder City instead. ⊠ *U.S. 93, east of Boulder City* ☎ *702/494–2517, 866/730–9097* ⊕ *www.usbr.gov/lc/ hooverdam* 🖃 *Powerplant Tour $11, expanded Hoover Dam Tour $30, visitor center only $8; garage parking $7 (free parking on Arizona-side surface lots)* ⊘ *Daily 9–5* ☞ *Security, road, and Hoover Dam crossing information: 888/248–1259.*

The Mike O'Callaghan–Pat Tillman bridge. The Hoover Dam now has sightseer competition from the spectacular bridge that was built to bypass it. The Mike O'Callaghan–Pat Tillman bridge (named for the popular Nevada governor and the Arizona football star who was killed in Afghanistan) is the Western Hemisphere's longest single-span concrete arch bridge. It runs 1,905 feet long and towers nearly 900 feet above the river, and 280 feet above Hoover Dam. You don't see much by driving over it—scarcely anything from a sedan—but walking it is quite a thrill. A pedestrian walkway is well separated from the driving lanes, the access path to the bridge has informational signage, and ramps offer an alternative to the steps. There are restrooms in the parking lot (labeled "Memorial Bridge Plaza"), where it can be hard to find a parking space on weekends. (If you can't get a spot, drive a few yards past the parking lot entrance and turn left into the lot for a trailhead on the other side of the road). Bring water and sunscreen for the walk and be prepared for broiling summer temperatures; there is no shade. ■TIP→ Remember to take "Exit 2" if you want to go to the dam instead of the bypass bridge, or you will have to drive across it and turn back to visit the dam. ⊠ *U.S. 93.*

SPORTS AND THE OUTDOORS
RAFTING
Black Canyon, just below Hoover Dam, is the place for river running near Las Vegas. You can launch a raft here on the Colorado River year-round. On the Arizona side, the 11-mile run to Willow Beach, with its vertical canyon walls, bighorn sheep on the slopes, and feeder streams

and waterfalls coming off the bluffs, is reminiscent of rafting the Grand Canyon. The water flows at roughly 5 mph, but some rapids, eddies, and whirlpools can cause difficulties, as can headwinds, especially for inexperienced rafters.

If you want to go paddling in Black Canyon on your own, you need to make mandatory arrangements with one of the registered outfitters. They provide permits ($12) and the National Park Service entrance fee ($5) as well as launch and retrieval services. You can get a list of outfitters at ☎ 702/494–2204, or go to the paddle-craft and rafting-tours section on the Bureau of Land Management's website (⊕ www.usbr. gov/lc/hooverdam).

Black Canyon/Willow Beach River Adventures. If you're interested in seeing the canyon on large motor-assisted rafts, Black Canyon/Willow Beach River Adventures is a group excursion launching most mornings from the Hacienda Casino and Hotel. You only get wet if you want to, and a picnic lunch on the riverbank is included. The trip is $88 for adults, or $33 for a half-hour "post card" tour. ✉ *Depart from Hacienda Casino and Hotel, U.S. 93, Boulder City* ☎ *800/455–3490* ⊕ *www. blackcanyonadventures.com.*

Boulder City River Riders. For a more hands-on approach, try a guided kayak trip through Black Canyon with Boulder City Outfitters. Rates, which include permits, are $210 per person with a two-person minimum for an eight-hour trip. They'll pick you up at the Hacienda Hotel and Casino, or from your hotel on the Strip. ☎ *702/293–1190* ⊕ *www. bouldercityriverriders.com.*

LAKE MEAD

About 4 miles from Hoover Dam.

GETTING HERE AND AROUND

From Hoover Dam, travel west on U.S. 93 to intersection with Lakeshore Drive to reach Alan Bible Visitors Center, which at this writing is being remodeled with a new welcome film for 2013. Public information is available in the lobby of headquarters in downtown Boulder City, 601 Nevada Way. A temporary visitor center there is open daily 8 to 4:30. Call ☎ 702/293–8990 for more information.

EXPLORING

Lake Mead. Lake Mead, which is actually the Colorado River backed up behind Hoover Dam, is the nation's largest man-made reservoir: it covers 225 square miles, is 110 miles long, and has an irregular shoreline that extends for 550 miles. You can get information about the lake's history, ecology, recreational opportunities, and the accommodations available along its shore at the Alan Bible Visitors Center. People come to Lake Mead primarily for boating, but a few areas of shoreline are cultivated for swimming: **Boulder Beach** is the closest to Las Vegas, only a mile or so from the visitor center.

Angling and house boating are favorite pastimes; marinas strung along the Nevada shore rent houseboats, personal watercraft, and ski boats. At least 1 million fish are harvested from the lake every year including

the popular striped and largemouth bass. It's stocked with rainbow trout on a weekly basis from late October through March. You can fish here 24 hours a day, year-round (except for posted closings). You must have a fishing license from either Nevada or Arizona (details are on the National Park Service website), and if you plan to catch and keep trout, a separate trout stamp is required. Willow Beach is a favorite for anglers looking to catch rainbow trout; Cathedral Cove and Katherine are good for bass fishing. Divers can explore the murk beneath, including the remains of a B-29 Superfortress, which crashed into the Overton Arm of the lake in 1948. Other activities abound, including waterskiing, sailboarding, canoeing, kayaking, and snorkeling. ⊠ *601 Nevada Way, Boulder City* ☎ *702/293–8990* ⊕ *www.nps.gov/lame* ⊠ *$10 per vehicle, good for 7 days; lake-use fees $16 1st vessel, good for 7 days. Annual pass is $30 per vehicle or per vessel.*

SPORTS AND THE OUTDOORS

BOATING

Ⓒ **Echo Bay Resort and Marina.** Echo Bay Resort and Marina, on the Overton Arm of the north side of the lake, has boat rentals, RV facilities, a gift shop, and snack bar. It used to have a restaurant and hotel rooms but those are closed indefinitely. However, it has "flotels"—houseboat rentals that stay moored at the marina but do not go out on the lake. ⊠ *600 Echo Bay Rd, Overton* ☎ *702/394–4000* ⊕ *www.echobaylakemead. com.*

Lake Mead Marina. Lake Mead Marina, at Hemenway Harbor near Hoover Dam, has a general store, rentals, and a floating restaurant. It's the closest marina to the public beach, Boulder Beach. If you haven't been to Lake Mead in a few years, the marina was moved in 2008 due to dropping water levels but has stayed put since. Boat rentals and personal watercraft are available through the **Las Vegas Boat Harbor** (☎ *702/293–1191 or 877/765–3745*). ⊠ *490 Horsepower Cove Rd., Boulder City* ☎ *702/293–3484* ⊕ *www.boatinglakemead.com.*

CRUISES

Lake Mead Cruises. At Lake Mead Cruises you can board the 300-passenger *Desert Princess,* an authentic Mississippi-style paddle wheeler that plies a portion of the lake; brunch and dinner cruises are available seasonally. Ninety-minute sightseeing cruises occur year-round. ⊠ *Hemenway Boat Harbor near Boulder Beach* ☎ *702/293–6180* ⊕ *www. lakemeadcruises.com* ⊠ *Prices start at $25. Advance tickets available online.*

SCUBA DIVING AND SNORKELING

The creation of Lake Mead flooded a huge expanse of land, and, as a result, sights of the deep abound for scuba divers. Wishing Well Cove has steep canyon drop-offs, caves, and clear water. Castle Cliffs and Virgin Basin both have expansive views of white gypsum reefs and submerged sandstone formations. In summer Lake Mead is like a bathtub, reaching 85°F on the surface and staying at about 80°F down to 50 feet below the surface. Divers can actually wear bathing suits rather than wet suits to do some of the shallower dives. But visibility—which averages 30 feet to 35 feet overall—is much better in the winter months before the late-spring surface-algae bloom obscures some of the deeper attractions from snorkelers. Be aware that Lake Mead's level has dropped because of low snowfall in the Rockies. This has had some effect on diving conditions; St. Thomas, for example, is now only partially submerged.

Outfitters American Cactus Divers ✉ *3985 E. Sunset Rd., Suite B, Las Vegas* ☎ *702/433–3483* ⊕ *www.americancactusdivers.com.*

Desert Divers Supply ✉ *5720 E. Charleston Blvd., West Side, Las Vegas* ☎ *702/438–1000* ⊕ *www.nsra.info/desertdivers/divers.php.*

VALLEY OF FIRE

50 miles northeast of Las Vegas.

GETTING HERE AND AROUND

From Las Vegas, take Interstate 15 north about 35 miles to Exit 75–Route 169 and continue 15 miles. If you're coming from Lake Mead, look for the sign announcing the Valley of Fire a mile past Overton Beach. Turn left at the sign and go about 3 miles to reach the Valley of Fire Visitors Center. ■**TIP**→ At this juncture it may also be possible to see some of the remnants of St. Thomas, as drought conditions have lowered lake levels dramatically.

EXPLORING

ⓒ **Valley of Fire State Park.** The 56,000-acre Valley of Fire State Park was

Fodor'sChoice dedicated in 1935 as Nevada's first state park. Valley of Fire takes its
★ name from its distinctive coloration, which ranges from lavender to tangerine to bright red, giving the vistas along the park road an otherworldly appearance. The jumbled rock formations are remnants of hardened sand dunes more than 150 million years old. You find petrified logs and the park's most photographed feature—Elephant Rock—just steps off the main road. Mysterious petroglyphs (carvings etched into the rocks) and pictographs (pictures drawn or painted on the rock's surface) are believed to be the work of the Basketmaker and ancestral Puebloan people who lived along the nearby Muddy River between 300 BC and AD 1150. The easy, essential trail is Mouse's Tank, named for an outlaw who hid out here and managed to find water; so will you in cooler months (but not for drinking). It's a short walk, shaded by steep canyon walls. Sci-fi fans also might recognize Fire Canyon as the alien planet in Starship Troopers and several other movies.

The **Valley of Fire Visitors Center** was remodeled in 2011 and has displays on the park's history, ecology, archaeology, and recreation, as well as slide shows and films, an art gallery, and information about the two campgrounds (73 campsites, 20 of them with power and water for RVs) within the park. Campsites at Atlatl Rock and Arch Rock Campgrounds are available on a first-come, first-served basis. The park is open year-round; the best times to visit, especially during the heat of summer, are sunrise and sunset, when the light is truly spectacular. ✉ *Overton* ✢ *From Las Vegas, take 15N to Exit 75. Turn right on Valley of Fire Hwy. Entrance to park is about 14 miles* ☎ *702/397–2088* ⊕ *www. parks.nv.gov* ✎ *$10 per vehicle ($2 discount for Nevada residents) or*

9

$20 per night for a campsite and $30 for full hookups ⊙ Visitors Center daily 8:30–4:30; park sunrise–sunset.

OFF THE
BEATEN
PATH

Lost City Museum. The Moapa Valley has one of the finest collections of ancestral Puebloan artifacts in the American Southwest. Lost City, officially known as Pueblo Grande de Nevada, was a major outpost of the ancient culture. The museum's artifacts include baskets, weapons, a restored Basketmaker pit house, and black-and-white photographs of the 1924 excavation of Lost City. To get to the Lost City Museum from Valley of Fire, turn around on the park road and head back to the T intersection at the eastern entrance to the Valley of Fire. Turn left and drive roughly 8 miles into Overton. Turn left at the sign for the museum. Kids get in free. ⊠ *721 S. Moapa Valley Blvd., Overton* ☎ *702/397–2193* ✉ *$5 ⊙ Thurs.–Sun. 8:30–4:30.*

GRAND CANYON

If you take only one side trip from Las Vegas, make it to the Grand Canyon. The Colorado River has carved through colorful and often contorted layers of rock, in some places more than 1 mile down, to expose a geologic profile spanning a time between 1.7 billion and 2.5 billion years ago—one-third of the planet's life. There's nothing like standing on the rim and looking down and across at layers of distance, color, and shifting light. Add the music of a canyon wren's merry, descending call echoing off the cliffs and spring water tinkling from the rocks along a trail, and you may sink into a reverie as deep and beautiful as the canyon.

GETTING HERE AND AROUND

There are two main access points to the canyon: the **South Rim** and the **North Rim,** both within the national park, but the hordes of visitors converge mostly on the South Rim in summer, for good reason. Grand Canyon Village is here, with most of the lodging and camping, restaurants and stores, and museums in the park, along with the airport, railroad depot, rim roads, scenic overlooks, and trailheads into the canyon. The South Rim can be accessed either from the main entrance near Tusayan or by the East entrance near the Desert View Watchtower. The North Rim, by contrast, stands 1,000 feet higher than the South Rim and has a more alpine climate, with twice as much annual precipitation. Here, in the deep forests of the Kaibab Plateau, the crowds are thinner, the facilities fewer, and the views even more spectacular.

If you don't have the time for the 5-hour drive to the North or South Rim, the **West Rim**—about 2½ hours from Las Vegas—is a more manageable excursion. A self-drive is possible, although it's a 14-mile road that is only partially paved so RVs and motorcycles, in particular, may find it a rough ride leading up to Grand Canyon West. As an alternative to driving, look into a helicopter, Hummer, or coach tour. Many tours will transport you to and from your Vegas hotel; park fees and lunch are usually part of the package. You can also take the shuttle from the Park and Ride Center in Meadview. At the West Rim, which is not part of the Grand Canyon National Park and is run by the Hualapai tribe, you can view the canyon from the controversial Skywalk.

SAFETY AND PRECAUTIONS

To report a security problem, contact the Park Police stationed at all visitor centers. There are no pharmacies at the North or South Rim. Prescriptions can be delivered daily to the South Rim Clinic from Flagstaff. A health center is staffed by physicians from 8 am to 6 pm, seven days a week (reduced hours in winter). Emergency medical services are available 24 hours a day.

Contacts Emergency services ☎ *911, 9–911 in park lodgings.* **North Country Grand Canyon Clinic** ✉ *Grand Canyon Village, Arizona* ☎ *928/638–2551.* **Park Police** ☎ *928/638–7805.*

ADMISSION FEES AND PERMITS

A fee of $25 per vehicle or $12 per person for pedestrians and cyclists is good for one week's access at both rims.

Hikers descending into the canyon for an overnight stay need a backcountry permit ($10, plus $5 per person per night), which can be obtained in person, by mail, or faxed by request. Permits are limited, so make your reservation as far in advance as possible (they're taken up to four months ahead of arrival). Day hikes into the canyon or anywhere else in the national park do not require a permit; overnight stays at Phantom Ranch require reservations but no permits. Overnight camping in the national park is restricted to designated campgrounds.

Contacts Backcountry Information Center ☎ *928/638–7875* ⊕ *www.nps. gov/grca.*

TOURS

Air Tours. Ground tours to the Grand Canyon can be had from the Grand Canyon Tour Company, but if you're short on time (and can check your fear of heights at the bell desk), consider winging your way there in a small plane or helicopter. A host of air-tour companies will give you the bird's-eye view of the Strip, Hoover Dam, and Lake Mead on the way to the Grand Canyon rim and even down to the Colorado River bed itself on tours as brief as two hours and as inexpensive as $200 per person. Helicopter tours are usually more expensive than those in a small fixed-wing plane. All possible permutations of flight plans and amenities are available, from lunch, to river rafting, to overnight accommodations. Most tours include pick-up and drop-off service from your hotel (sorry, Hotshot, you get picked up in a van or limo, not by a chopper). Weekday tours actually fill up faster than weekends; it can't hurt to book a few days in advance. The scenery is spectacular, but the ride can be bumpy and cold, even in summertime.

Air Tour Contacts Grand Canyon Express ☎ *702/501–8470, 800/940–2550* ⊕ *www.airvegas.com.* **Grand Canyon Tour Company** ☎ *702/655–6060, 800/222–6966* ⊕ *www.grandcanyontourcompany.com.* **HeliUSA** ☎ *702/736–8787, 800/359–8727* ⊕ *www.heliusa.com.* **Maverick Helicopter Tours** ☎ *702/261–0007, 888/261–4414* ⊕ *www.maverickhelicopter.com.* **Papillon** ☎ *702/736–7243, 888/635–7272* ⊕ *www.papillon.com.* **Scenic Airlines**

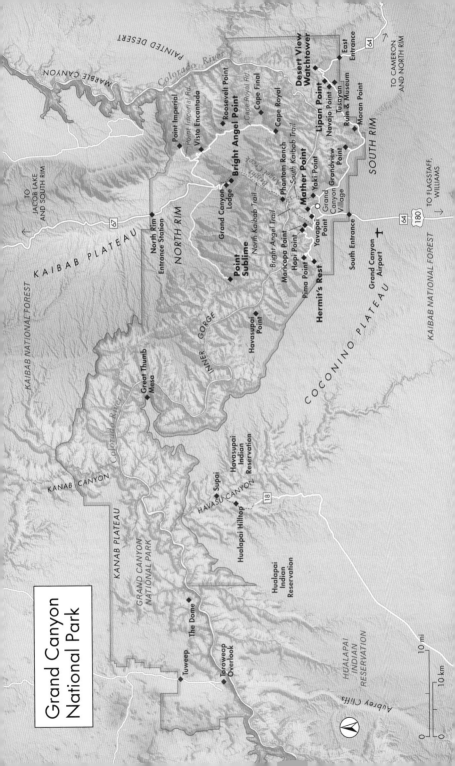

Grand Canyon National Park

PAINTED DESERT

MARBLE CANYON

Colorado River

TO CAMERON AND NORTH RIM

64

East Entrance

Desert View Watchtower

Point Imperial

Point Imperial Rd.

Vista Encantada

Roosevelt Point

Cape Final

Cape Royal Rd.

Cape Royal

Lipan Point

Navajo Point

Tusayan Ruin & Museum

Moran Point

TO JACOB LAKE AND SOUTH RIM

Bright Angel Point

Phantom Ranch

South Kaibab Trail

Yaki Point

SOUTH RIM

NORTH RIM

Grand Canyon Lodge

North Rim Entrance Station

Mather Point

Grandview Point

67

KAIBAB PLATEAU

North Kaibab Trail

Bright Angel Trail

Grand Canyon Village

TO FLAGSTAFF, WILLIAMS

Yavapai Point

64

180

Point Sublime

Maricopa Point

Hopi Point

Yavapai Point

South Entrance

KAIBAB NATIONAL FOREST

Pima Point

Hermit's Rest

Grand Canyon Airport

INNER GORGE

Havasupai Point

COCONINO PLATEAU

KAIBAB NATIONAL FOREST

Colorado River

Great Thumb Mesa

KANAB CANYON

Supai

Havasupai Indian Reservation

HAVASU CANYON

18

KANAB PLATEAU

Hualapai Hilltop

Hualapai Indian Reservation

GRAND CANYON NATIONAL PARK

The Dome

HUALAPAI INDIAN RESERVATION

Tuweep

Toroweap Overlook

Aubrey Cliffs

0

10 mi

0

10 km

0

WHEN TO GO TO THE GRAND CANYON

Time of Year	Advantages	Disadvantages
Mar.–May	Cool temperatures and more elbow room than in summer.	Weather is unpredictable. Be prepared for chilly climate changes.
June–Sept.	Highs in the low to mid-80s but mostly pleasant.	High humidity from frequent afternoon thunderstorms.
Oct.–Feb.	You'll experience the South Rim in a different light, literally and figuratively.	Winter conditions can be extreme. The road to the North Rim is closed from mid-October (or the first heavy winter snow) until mid-May.

WHERE TO GO: SOUTH RIM VS. NORTH RIM

Grand Canyon National Park is located in the northeastern corner of Arizona. The Grand Canyon and the Colorado River physically separate the park's two distinct halves into the North Rim and the South Rim. The average distance from the North Rim to the South Rim is 10 miles, but to travel from rim to rim by car requires a journey of 200 miles. The action's in the South Rim: Grand Canyon Village has year-round lodging, dining, shopping, museums, and shuttle stops. Higher in elevation by 1,000 feet, the North Rim offers more solitude and higher, grander views, but it's only open part of the year.

	SOUTH RIM	NORTH RIM
Distance from Vegas	278 mi.	275 mi.
Distance from Phoenix	231 mi.	351 mi.
The experience	Fast action and a hurried pace, with plenty to see and do.	A leisurely look at the remote rim of this famous national park.
Why?	More amenities than the North Rim.	Geared for outdoor activities
Elevation	7,000 feet	8,000 feet
Timing	It's best to spend at least one night here. One day is good to see the main sites; two days are best for a leisurely exploration.	With the added driving distance, most people spend two days exploring this far-away corner.
Rim drives	Self-guided Desert View Drive and Hermit Road, accessible by shuttle only from March through November.	Self-guided driving tours to developed overlooks on Cape Royal Road and Point Imperial Road.
Trails	9-mile rim hike from Mather Point to Hermits Rest. 8 trails including the popular inner canyon South Kaibab and Bright Angel Trails.	10 trails including the popular inner canyon North Kaibab Trail; an extensive network of rim hikes.
Overlooks	18 developed viewpoints	7 developed viewpoints, one accessible by foot from the Grand Canyon Lodge. Folks with 4WD can take the 17-mi. dirt route to Point Sublime.
Other activities	Train travel; tours; mule and horse rides; camping; fine dining; guided hikes; ranger programs; shopping.	Biking, horseback riding, picnicking, camping, and ranger programs.

9

☎ *702/638–3300, 800/634–6801* ⊕ *www.scenic.com.* **Sundance Helicopters** ☎ *702/736–0606, 800/653–1881* ⊕ *www.sundancehelicopters.com.*

Hiking Tours. The Grand Canyon Field Institute leads a full program of educational guided hikes around the canyon year-round. Topics include everything from archaeology and backcountry medicine to photography and natural history. Reservations are essential and cost from $115 to $895. For a personalized tour of the Grand Canyon and surrounding sacred sites, contact Marvelous Marv, whose knowledge of the area is as extensive as his repertoire of local legends.

Contacts Grand Canyon Field Institute ☎ *928/638–2485, 866/471–4435* ⊕ *www.grandcanyon.org/fieldinstitute.* **Marvelous Marv** ☎ *928/707–0291* ⊕ *www.marvelousmarv.com.*

Jeep Tours. If you'd like to see parts of the park that are accessible only by dirt road, a jeep tour can be just the ticket. Rides can be rough; if you've had back injuries, check with your doctor before taking a jeep tour. Offerings include trips into the Kaibab Forest, sunset tours, Old West tours, inner canyon trips, and helicopter/jeep combos. Grand Canyon Old West Jeep Tours also offers an all-day adventure to the inner canyon on the Hualapai Reservation. This trip departs year-round from Williams and the South Rim's Grand Canyon Village.

Contacts Grand Canyon Jeep Tours and Safaris ☎ *928/638–5337, 800/320– 5337* ⊕ *www.grandcanyonjeeptours.com.* **Grand Canyon Old West Jeep Tours** ☎ *928/638–2000, 866/638–4386* ⊕ *www.grandcanyonjeeps.com.*

Special-Interest Tours. The National Park Service sponsors all sorts of free Ranger Programs at both the South and the North rims. These orientation activities include daily guided hikes and talks. The focus may be on any aspect of the canyon—from geology, flora, and fauna to history and early inhabitants. Programs change seasonally. For schedules, go to Grand Canyon Visitors Center on the South Rim or the Contact Station on the North Rim.

Several of the free programs are designed especially for children. Seasonally, there are also Junior Ranger Discovery Packs for children that include field guides, binoculars, magnifying glasses, and other exploration tools that can be checked out, but they go fast.

Contacts Ranger Programs ☎ *928/638–7888* ⊕ *www.nps.gov/grca.*

VISITOR INFORMATION

Every person arriving at the South or North Rim is given a detailed map of the area. Centers at both rims also publish a free newspaper, the *Guide,* which contains a detailed area map; it's available at the visitor center, entrance stations, and many of the lodging facilities and stores. The park also distributes *Accessibility Guide,* a free newsletter that details the facilities accessible to travelers with disabilities. Grand Canyon National Park is the contact for general information.

Several websites are useful for trip-planning information, including the National Park Service's website, which has information on fees and permits. You can use the Xanterra Parks & Resorts Grand Canyon website to make reservations for park lodging, mule rides, bus tours, and some smooth-water rafting trips.

In summer, transportation-services desks are maintained at El Tovar, Bright Angel, Maswik Lodge, and Yavapai Lodge in Grand Canyon Village; in winter the one at Yavapai is closed. The desks provide information and handle bookings, sightseeing tours, taxi and bus services, mule rides, and accommodations at Phantom Ranch (at the bottom of the Grand Canyon). The concierge at El Tovar can also arrange most tours, with the exception of mule rides and lodging at Phantom Ranch.

Grand Canyon Lodge has general information about local services available in summer when the North Rim is open.

Visitor Info Grand Canyon Chamber of Commerce ☎ 928/638–2901 ⊕ www. grandcanyonchamber.com. **Grand Canyon National Park** ☎ 928/638–7888 recorded message ⊕ www.nps.gov/grca. **Grand Canyon National Park Lodges** ☎ 303/297–2757 ⊕ www.grandcanyonlodges.com.

SOUTH RIM

278 miles east of Las Vegas.

Visitors to the canyon converge mostly on the South Rim, and mostly during the summer. Grand Canyon Village is here, with most of the park's lodging and camping, trailheads, restaurants, stores, and museums, along with a nearby airport and railroad depot. Believe it or not, the average stay in the park is a mere four hours; this is not advised! You need to spend several days to truly appreciate this marvelous place, but at the very least, give it a full day. Hike down into the canyon, or along the rim, to get away from the crowds and experience nature at its finest.

GETTING HERE AND AROUND

By car, travel south on U.S. 93 to Kingman, Arizona; Interstate 40 east from Kingman to Williams; then Route 64 and U.S. 180 to the edge of the abyss. The South Rim is open to car traffic year-round, though access to Hermits Rest is limited to shuttle buses from March through November. Roads leading to the South Rim near Grand Canyon Village and the parking areas along the rim are congested in summer as well. If you visit from October through April, you can experience only light to moderate traffic and have no problem with parking.

When driving off major highways in low-lying areas, watch for rain clouds. Flash floods from sudden summer rains can be deadly.

There are also three free shuttle routes. Hermits Rest Route operates from March through November between Grand Canyon Village and Hermits Rest; it runs every 15 to 30 minutes from one hour before sunrise until one hour after sunset, depending on the season. The Village Route operates year-round in the village area from one hour before sunrise until after dark; it is the easiest access to the Grand Canyon Visitor Center. The Kaibab Trail Route travels from Grand Canyon Visitor Center to Yaki Point, including a stop at the South Kaibab Trailhead.

9

TOURS

Narrated motorcoach tours on the South Rim cover Hermits Rest Road and Desert View Drive. Other options include sunrise and sunset tours. Prices range from $21 to $59 per person.

ESSENTIALS

Park Info South Rim ☎ 928/638–7888, 877/444–6777 campground reservations ⊕ www.nps.gov/grca ◲ $25 per car, $12 per individual; $18 per night/campsite at Mather Campground, $12 per night/campsite at Desert View Campground ◷ 24/7.

Shuttle Service Arizona Shuttle ☎ 928/226–8060, 877/226–8060 ⊕ www.arizonashuttle.com.

Tours Xanterra Motorcoach Tours ☎ 928/638–2631, 928/638–3283 ⊕ www.grandcanyonlodges.com.

SCENIC DRIVES

Desert View Drive. This heavily traveled 23-mile stretch of road follows the rim from the East entrance to Grand Canyon Village. Starting from the less congested entry near Desert View, road warriors can get their first glimpse of the canyon from the 70-foot-tall Watchtower, the top of which provides the highest viewpoint on the South Rim. Eight overlooks, the remains of an ancestral Puebloan dwelling at the Tusayan Ruin and Museum, and the secluded and lovely Buggeln picnic area make for great stops along the South Rim. The Kaibab Trail Route shuttle bus allows you to ride round-trip without getting off at any of the three stops: South Kaibab Trailhead, Yaki Point, and Pipe Creek Vista.

Hermit Road. The Santa Fe Company built Hermit Road, formerly known as West Rim Drive, in 1912 as a scenic tour route. Nine overlooks dot this 7-mile stretch, each worth a visit. The road is filled with hairpin turns, so make sure you adhere to posted speed limits. The historic roadway reopened after an extensive rehabilitation in 2008. As part of the project, a 3-mile Greenway trail now offers easy access to cyclists looking to enjoy the original 1913 Hermit Rim Road. From March through November the improved Hermit Road is closed to private auto traffic because of congestion; during this period, a free shuttle bus will carry you to all the overlooks and to some places regular cars aren't allowed. Riding the bus round-trip without getting off at any of the viewpoints takes 75 minutes; the return trip stops only at Mohave, Hopi, and Maricopa points.

HISTORIC SITES

Kolb Studio. Built over several years beginning in 1904 by the Kolb brothers as a photographic workshop and residence, this building provides a view of Indian Garden, where, in the days before a pipeline was installed, Emery Kolb descended 3,000 feet each day to get the water he needed to develop his prints. Kolb was doing something right; he operated the studio until he died in 1976 at age 95. The gallery here has changing exhibitions of paintings, photography, and crafts. There's also a bookstore. During the winter months, a ranger-led tour of the studio illustrates the role the Kolb brothers had on the development of the Grand Canyon. Call ahead to sign up for the tour. ⊠ *Grand*

Canyon Village near Bright Angel Lodge ☎ *928/638–2771* ⊕ *www. grandcanyon.org/kolb* 🖃 *Free* ☉ *Apr.–mid-Oct., daily 8–7; mid-Oct.– Apr., daily 8–5.*

Tusayan Ruin and Museum. Completed in 1932, the museum offers a quick orientation to the lifestyles of the prehistoric and modern Indian populations associated with the Grand Canyon and the Colorado Plateau. Adjacent, an excavation of an 800-year-old dwelling gives a glimpse at the lives of some of the area's earliest residents. ⊠ *About 20 miles east of Grand Canyon Village on Desert View Dr.* ☎ *928/638–7888* 🖃 *Free* ☉ *Daily 9–5.*

SCENIC STOPS

The Abyss. At an elevation of 6,720 feet, the Abyss is one of the most awesome stops on Hermit Road, revealing a sheer drop of 3,000 feet to the Tonto Platform, a wide terrace of Tapeats sandstone about two-thirds of the way down the canyon. From the Abyss you'll also see several isolated sandstone columns, the largest of which is called the Monument. ⊠ *About 5 miles west of Hermit Rd. Junction on Hermit Rd.*

★ **Desert View and Watchtower.** From the top of the 70-foot stone-and-mortar watchtower, even the muted hues of the distant Painted Desert to the east and the Vermilion Cliffs rising from a high plateau near the Utah border are visible. In the chasm below, angling to the north toward Marble Canyon, an imposing stretch of the Colorado River reveals itself. Up several flights of stairs, the watchtower houses a glass-enclosed observatory with powerful telescopes. ⊠ *About 23 miles east of Grand Canyon Village on Desert View Dr.* ☎ *928/638–2736* ☉ *Daily 8–8; hrs vary in winter.*

★ **Hermits Rest.** This westernmost viewpoint and Hermit Trail, which descends from it, were named for "hermit" Louis Boucher, a 19th-century French-Canadian prospector who had a number of mining claims and a roughly built home down in the canyon. Views from here include Hermit Rapids and the towering cliffs of the Supai and Redwall formations. In the stone building at Hermits Rest you can buy curios and snacks. ⊠ *About 8 miles west of Hermit Rd. Junction on Hermit Rd.*

★ **Hopi Point.** From this elevation of 6,800 feet, you can see a large section of the Colorado River; although it appears as a thin line, the river is nearly 350 feet wide below this overlook. The overlook extends farther into the canyon than any other point on Hermit Road. The unobstructed views make this a popular place to watch the sunset.

Across the canyon to the north is Shiva Temple, which remained an unexplored section of the Kaibab Plateau until 1937. That year, Harold Anthony of the American Museum of Natural History led an expedition to the rock formation in the belief that it supported life that had been cut off from the rest of the canyon. Imagine the expedition members' surprise when they found an empty Kodak film box on top of the temple—it had been left behind by Emery Kolb, who felt slighted for not having been invited to partake of Anthony's tour.

Continued on page 332

THE STORY OF THE
COLORADO RIVER
THE GRAND CANYON, HOOVER DAM

By Carrie Frasure

High in Colorado's Rocky Mountains, the Colorado River begins as a catch-all for the snowmelt off the mountains west of the Continental Divide. By the time it reaches the Grand Canyon it has become a raging river, red with silt as it sculpts spectacular landscapes. Even though it's partially tamed by a network of dams, the Colorado is still a mighty river.

D LAKE MEAD

As the primary artery of the Colorado River Basin, the Colorado River provides a vital lifeline to the arid southwest. Its natural course runs 1,450 miles from its origin in Colorado's La Poudre Pass Lake to its final destination in the Gulf of Colorado. Along the way it gathers strength and speed from a multitude of tributaries. In northern Arizona, it's known as the primary sculptor of the Grand Canyon, where it now flows 4,000 to 6,000 feet below the rim. The river takes a lazy turn at the Arizona–Nevada border, where Hoover Dam creates the reservoir at Lake Mead. The river continues at a relaxed pace along the Arizona–California border, bringing energy and irrigation to people in Arizona, California, and Nevada before flowing into northwestern Mexico.

CREATION OF THE GRAND CANYON

Considered one of the seven natural wonders of the world, the Grand Canyon stretches along 277 miles of the Colorado River, ranging in width from 4 to 18 miles. Nearly 2 billion years of geologic history is revealed in exposed layers cut up to a mile deep in the Colorado Plateau. As uplift raised the plateau, the river and its tributaries slowly cut into the canyon's layers. Under the sculpting power of wind and water, the shale layers eroded into slopes and the harder sandstone and limestone layers created terraced cliffs, resulting in the canyon profiles seen today.

ENVIRONMENTAL CONCERNS

When the Grand Canyon achieved national park status in 1919, only 44,173 people made the grueling overland trip to see it. Today, the park receives nearly 5 million visitors a year. The construction of Lake Powell's Glen Canyon Dam and the tremendous increase in visitation has greatly impacted the fragile ecosystems. Air pollution has affected visibility, non-native plants and animals threaten the extinction of several native species, wildfire suppression has led to the dangerous overgrowth of forest landscapes, and the constant buzz of aerial tours has disturbed the natural solitude. ■TIP➔ Help ease the South Rim's congestion by taking the free shuttles, which have comprehensive routes along both Hermit Road and Desert View Drive as well as throughout Grand Canyon Village.

WHO LIVES HERE

Paleo-Indian artifacts show that humans have inhabited the Grand Canyon for more than 12,000 years. The plateau-dwelling Hualapai ("people of the tall pines") live on a million acres along 108 miles of the Colorado River in the West Rim. The Havasupai ("people of the blue green water") live deep within the walls of the 12-mile-long Havasu Canyon—a major side canyon connected to the Grand Canyon at the Colorado River—as they have for nearly 1,000 years.

Above, & Right views of Colorado River in Grand Canyon from Toroweap.

BEST CANYON VIEWS

- Hopi Point, South Rim
- Yavapai Point, South Rim
- Lipan Point, South Rim
- Grandview Point, South Rim
- Bright Angel Point, North Rim
- Cape Royal, North Rim
- Point Sublime, North Rim

HOOVER DAM

HISTORY

Hoover Dam was built in 1935 and was the world's largest hydroelectric power plant and tallest dam. It has since lost these titles; however, it's still the tallest solid concrete arch-gravity dam in the western hemisphere. The dam was completed two full years ahead of the six year construction schedule during the Great Depression.

ENVIRONMENT VERSUS ECONOMY

Prior to the dam's construction, the river, swollen by snowmelt, flooded the lowlands along the California-Arizona border each spring before drying up so drastically that water levels were too low to divert for crops each summer. The dam tamed the mighty river and today provides a stable, year-round water supply for 18 million people and more than one million acres of farmland. However, the lack of flooding and the controlled waters have negatively affected the backwater riparian habitats bringing several native fish species to the brink of extinction.

WHAT'S IN A NAME?

Even though it was located in the Black Canyon, the Hoover Dam was originally referred to as the Boulder Dam Project. The dam was officially named

ARTISTIC LEANINGS

Hoover Dam is an engineering marvel *and* a work of art. The design features the flowing lines of Modernism and Art Deco used by architect Gordon B. Kaufmann, designer of the Los Angeles Times Building. Artist Allen True, whose murals are prominent in the Colorado State Capitol, used Native American geometric designs in the terrazzo floors. But it's the pair of 30-foot bronze statues—*Winged Figures of the Republic*—that dominate the dam. The striking figures were sculpted by Oskar J.W. Hansen, who also created the five bas-reliefs on the elevator towers and the bronze plaque memorial for the 96 workers who died during the construction.

after Herbert Hoover in 1931. When Hoover lost his bid for re-election to Franklin D. Roosevelt in 1932, Harold Ickes took the office of the Secretary of the Interior and immediately issued notice to the Bureau of Reclamation to refer to the structure as Boulder Dam. In 1947, Hoover was vindicated when the naming controversy was settled with a resolution signed by President Harry S. Truman, restoring the name to Hoover Dam—much to the retired Ickes' indignation.

Above, Hoover Dam and *Winged Figures of the Republic*. Opposite, Hoover Dam.

DID YOU KNOW?

Hoover Dam was the biggest man-made masonry marvel to surpass the Great Pyramid of Giza. The dam is made of more than 5 million barrels of cement and 4.5 million cubic yards of aggregate—enough to pave a standard 16-foot-wide highway stretching from San Francisco to New York City.

LAKE MEAD

HISTORY

Prior to the construction of Hoover Dam, the canyon lands and river valleys along this western section of the Colorado River were home to settlements including the towns of St. Thomas and Kaolin as well as hundreds of Native American archaeological sites. After the dam was built, these towns and sites became submerged by Lake Mead.

ENVIRONMENT

The lakes's cool waters are surrounded by the stark drama of the Mojave Desert—North America's hottest and driest. Nearly 96% of its water comes from snowmelt in Colorado, New Mexico, Utah, and Wyoming. This means the water level is at its highest in early spring and late fall. Levels drop in summer when agricultural demands are at their highest and the surrounding desert heats up.

TODAY

Construction of Hoover Dam created Lake Mead's 100-mile long reservoir, which was named after Bureau of Rec-lamation Commissioner Elwood Mead. This enormous reservoir became the United States' first National Recreation Area in 1964. Today, more than 9 million people visit this wonderland each year.

TOMORROW

Over the last few years, Lake Mead's water levels have dropped drastically. As one of the largest reservoirs in the world, it provides water to residents and farmers in Arizona, California, Nevada and northern Mexico. An extended drought and the increased demand for this critical resource have exceeded the amount of water deposited into the lake by the Colorado River. Already the dramatic drop in the lake's water level has led to the exposure of parts of St. Thomas, as well as a series of islands in Boulder Basin. A recent study by the Scripps Institution of Oceanography shows that if the current conditions continue, there's a 50% chance that Lake Mead may be dry by 2021.

Above, Lake Mead. Opposite, sailing on the lake.

SPORTS IN THE AREA

Water recreation dominates the placid waters of Lake Mead. The dramatic scenery of the surrounding Mojave Desert just adds to the year-round draw. Some of the favorite sporting activities at this far-reaching reservoir include:

■ fishing for striped bass and rainbow trout
■ relaxing on a houseboat
■ exploring hidden coves by canoe or kayak
■ swimming at Boulder Beach
■ hitting the wakes on water skis
■ scuba diving at North Boulder Beach's Dive Park

CLOSE UP

Ride the Rails

Grand Canyon Railway. There is no need to deal with all of the other drivers racing to the South Rim. Sit back and relax in the comfy train cars of the Grand Canyon Railway. Live music and storytelling enliven the trip as you journey past the landscape through prairie, ranch, and national park land to the log-cabin train station in Grand Canyon Village. You won't see the Grand Canyon from the train, but you can walk or catch the shuttle at the restored, historic Grand Canyon Railway Station. The vintage train departs from the Williams Depot every morning, and makes the 65-mile journey in 2¼ hours. You can do the round-trip in a single day; however, it's a more relaxing and enjoyable strategy to stay for a night or two at the South Rim before returning to Williams. ☎ 800/843–8724 ⊕ www. thetrain.com ⊠ $75–$190 round-trip.

Directly below Hopi Point lies Dana Butte, named for a prominent 19th-century geologist. In 1919, an entrepreneur proposed connecting Hopi Point, Dana Butte, and the Tower of Set across the river with an aerial tramway, a technically feasible plan that fortunately has not been realized. ⊠ *About 4 miles west of Hermit Rd. Junction on Hermit Rd.*

★ **Mather Point.** You'll likely get your first glimpse of the canyon from this viewpoint, one of the most impressive and accessible (and most crowded) on the South Rim. Named for the National Park Service's first director, Stephen Mather, this spot yields extraordinary views of the Grand Canyon, including deep into the Inner Gorge and numerous buttes: Wotan's Throne, Brahma Temple, and Zoroaster Temple, among others. The Grand Canyon Lodge, on the North Rim, is almost directly north from Mather Point and only 10 miles away—yet you have to drive 215 miles to get from one spot to the other. ⊠ *Near Grand Canyon Visitor Center.*

Fodor'sChoice **Yavapai Point.** This is also one of the best locations on the South Rim
★ to watch the sunset. Dominated by the Yavapai Observation Station, this point displays panoramic views of the mighty gorge through a wall of windows. Exhibits here include videos of the canyon floor and the Colorado River, a scaled diorama of the canyon with national park boundaries, fossils and rock fragments used to re-create the complex layers of the canyon walls, and a display on the natural forces used to carve the chasm. Rangers dig even deeper into Grand Canyon geology with free ranger programs daily. Check ahead for special events, guided walks, and program schedules. There's also a bookstore. ⊠ *Adjacent to Grand Canyon Village* ⊠ *Free* ۞ *Daily 8–8; hrs vary in winter.*

VISITOR CENTERS

Desert View Information Center. Near the Watchtower, at Desert View Point, the Grand Canyon Association offers a nice selection of books, park pamphlets, and educational materials. ⊠ *East entrance* ☎ *928/638–7893* ۞ *Daily 9–5.*

Grand Canyon Visitor Center. The park's main orientation center, known formerly as Canyon View Information Plaza, near Mather Point, provides pamphlets and resources to help plan your sightseeing as well as engaging interpretive exhibits on the park. Rangers are on hand to answer questions and aid in planning canyon excursions. A bookstore is stocked with books covering all topics on the Grand Canyon, and a daily schedule of ranger-led hikes and evening lectures is posted on a bulletin board inside. A 25-minute film about the history, geology, and wildlife of the canyon plays every 30 minutes in the new theater. There's ample parking by the information center, though it is also accessible via a short walk from Mather Point, a short ride on the shuttle bus Village Route, or a leisurely 1-mile walk on the Greenway Trail—a paved pathway that meanders through the forest. ⊠ *East side of Grand Canyon Village, 450 State Rte. 64, Grand Canyon* ☎ *928/638–7888* ⊕ *www.explorethecanyon.com* ☉ *Daily 8–5, outdoor exhibits may be viewed anytime.*

Verkamp's Visitor Center. After 102 years of selling memorabilia and knickknacks on the South Rim, Verkamp's Curios moved to the park's newest visitor center in 2008. The building now serves as a bookstore, ranger station, and museum with exhibits on the pioneer history of the region. ⊠ *Across from El Tovar Hotel, Grand Canyon Village* ☎ *928/638–7146* ☉ *Winter 8–6, summer 8–7.*

Yavapai Geology Museum. Shop in the bookstore, catch the park shuttle bus, or pick up information for the Rim Trail here. ⊠ *1 mile east of Market Plaza, Grand Canyon* ☎ *928/638–7890* ☉ *Daily 8–8; hrs vary in winter.*

HIKING

Although permits are not required for day hikes, you must have a backcountry permit for longer trips (⇨ *See Permits at start of this section*). Some of the more popular trails are here; more detailed information and maps can be obtained from the Backcountry Information Center. Also, rangers can help design a trip to suit your abilities.

Remember that the canyon has significant elevation changes and, in summer, extreme temperature ranges, which can pose problems for people who aren't in good shape or who have heart or respiratory problems. ■TIP➔ Carry plenty of water and energy foods. The majority of each year's 400 search-and-rescue incidents result from hikers underestimating the size of the canyon, hiking beyond their abilities, or not packing sufficient food and water.

⚠ Under no circumstances should you attempt a day hike from the rim to the river and back. Remember that when it's 80°F on the South Rim, it's 110°F on the canyon floor. Allow two to four days if you want to hike rim to rim (it's easier to descend from the North Rim, as it is more than 1,000 feet higher than the South Rim). Hiking steep trails from rim to rim is a strenuous trek of at least 21 miles and should only be attempted by experienced canyon hikers.

9

EASY

Fodor's Choice ★ **Rim Trail.** The South Rim's most popular walking path is the 12-mile (one-way) Rim Trail, which runs along the edge of the canyon from Pipe Creek Vista (the first overlook on Desert View Drive) to Hermits Rest. This walk, which is paved to Maricopa Point and for the last 1.5 miles to Hermits Rest, visits several of the South Rim's historic landmarks. Allow anywhere from 15 minutes to a full day, depending on how much of the trail you want to cover; the Rim Trail is an ideal day hike, as it varies only a few hundred feet in elevation from Mather Point (7,120 feet) to the trailhead at Hermits Rest (6,650 feet). The trail also can be accessed from several spots in Grand Canyon Village and from the major viewpoints along Hermit Road, which are serviced by shuttle buses during the busy summer months. *Easy.* ■TIP➜ On the Rim Trail, water is only available in the Grand Canyon Village area and at Hermits Rest.

NEED A BREAK? If you've been driving too long and want some exercise, along with great views of the canyon, it's an easy 1.25-mile-long hike from the Information Plaza to El Tovar Hotel. The Greenway path runs through a quiet wooded area for about 0.5 mile, and then along the rim for another 0.75 mile.

MODERATE

★ **Bright Angel Trail.** This well maintained trail this is one of the most scenic hiking paths from the South Rim to the bottom of the canyon (9.6 miles each way). Rest houses are equipped with water at the 1.5- and 3-mile points from May through September and at Indian Garden (4 mi) year-round. Water is also available at Bright Angel Campground, 9.25 miles below the trailhead. Plateau Point, on a spur trail about 1.5 miles below Indian Garden, is as far as you should attempt to go on a day hike; plan on spending six to nine hours.

Bright Angel Trail is the easiest of all the footpaths into the canyon, but because the climb out from the bottom is an ascent of 5,510 feet, the trip should be attempted only by those in good physical condition and should be avoided in midsummer due to extreme heat. The top of the trail can be icy in winter. Originally a bighorn sheep path and later used by the Havasupai, the trail was widened late in the 19th century for prospectors and is now used for both mule and foot traffic. Also note that mule trains have the right-of-way—and sometimes leave unpleasant surprises in your path. *Moderate.* ⊠ *Trailhead: Kolb Studio, Hermits Rd.*

DIFFICULT

★ **South Kaibab Trail.** This trail starts near Yaki Point, 4 miles east of Grand Canyon Village and is accessible via the free shuttle bus. Because the route is so steep (and sometimes icy in winter)—descending from the trailhead at 7,260 feet down to 2,480 feet at the Colorado River—and has no water, many hikers return via the less-demanding Bright Angel Trail; allow four to six hours. During this 6.4-mile trek to the Colorado River, you're likely to encounter mule trains and riders. At the river, the trail crosses a suspension bridge and runs on to Phantom Ranch. Along the trail there is no water and very little shade. There are no campgrounds, though there are portable toilets at Cedar Ridge (6,320 feet), 1.5 miles from the trailhead. Toilets and an emergency phone are also available at the Tipoff, 4.6 miles down the trail (3 miles past Cedar Ridge). The trail corkscrews down through some spectacular geology. Look for (but don't remove) fossils in the limestone when taking water breaks. *Difficult.* ■ **TIP→ Even though an immense network of trails winds through the Grand Canyon, the popular corridor trails (Bright Angel and South Kaibab) are recommended for hikers new to the region.** ✉ *Trailhead: Yaki Point, Desert View Dr.*

MULE RIDES

★ Mule rides provide an intimate glimpse into the canyon for those who have the time, but not the stamina to see the canyon on foot. ■ **TIP→ Reservations are essential and are accepted up to 13 months in advance.**

These trips have been conducted since the early 1900s. A comforting fact as you ride the narrow trail: no one's ever been killed while riding a mule that fell off a cliff. (Nevertheless, the treks are not for the faint of heart or people in questionable health.)

OUTFITTERS

Xanterra Parks & Resorts Mule Rides. These trips delve into the canyon from the South Rim to Phantom Ranch, or west along the canyon's edge to a famed viewpoint called the Abyss (the Plateau Point rides were discontinued in 2009). Riders must be at least 55 inches tall, weigh less than 200 pounds (225 pounds for the Abyss tour), and understand English. Children under 15 must be accompanied by an adult. Riders must be in fairly good physical condition, and pregnant women are advised not to take these trips.

The three-hour ride to the Abyss costs $120.65 (water and snack included). An overnight with a stay at Phantom Ranch at the bottom of the canyon is $497.89 ($879.43 for two riders). Two nights at Phantom Ranch, an option available from November through March, will set you back $701.38 ($1,170.05 for two). Meals are included. Reservations (by phone), especially during the busy summer months, are a must, but you can check at the Bright Angel Transportation Desk to see if there's last-minute availability. ☎ *888/297–2757* 🌐 *www.grandcanyonlodges.com* ✍ *Reservations essential* 🕒 *Phantom Ranch rides daily; Abyss rides mid-Mar.–Oct., twice daily; Nov.–mid-Mar., once daily.*

9

WHERE TO EAT

$$$ STEAKHOUSE 🍴 **Arizona Room.** The canyon views from this casual Southwestern-style steak house are the best of any restaurant at the South Rim. The menu includes such delicacies as chili-crusted pan-seared wild salmon, chipotle barbecue baby back ribs, and half-pound buffalo burgers with Gorgonzola aioli. For dessert, try the cheesecake with prickly-pear syrup paired with one of the house's specialty coffee drinks. Seating is first-come, first served, so arrive early to avoid the crowds. [$] *Average main: $24* ✉ *Bright Angel Lodge, Desert View Dr., Grand Canyon Village* ☎ *928/638–2631* 🌐 *www.grandcanyonlodges.com* ✍ *Reservations not accepted* 🕒 *Closed Jan. and Feb. No lunch Nov. and Dec.*

$ SOUTHWESTERN 🍴 **Bright Angel Restaurant.** The draw here is casual and affordable. No-surprises dishes will fill your belly at breakfast, lunch, or dinner. Entrées include such basics as salads, steaks, lasagna, fajitas, and fish tacos. Or you can step it up a notch and order some of the same selections straight from the Arizona Room menu including prime rib, baby back ribs, and wild salmon. For dessert try the warm apple grunt cake topped with vanilla ice cream. Be prepared to wait for a table: the dining room bustles all day long. The plain decor is broken up with large-pane windows and original artwork. $ *Average main: $12* ⊠ *Bright Angel Lodge, Desert View Dr., Grand Canyon Village* ☎ *928/638–2631* ⊕ *www. grandcanyonlodges.com* ⚑ *Reservations not accepted.*

$

AMERICAN

✕ **Canyon Café at Yavapai Lodge.** Open for breakfast, lunch, and dinner, this cafeteria in the Market Plaza also serves specials such as chicken potpie, fried catfish, and fried chicken. Fast-food favorites here include pastries, burgers, and pizza. There isn't a fancy bar here, but you can order beer and wine with your meal. Resembling an old-fashioned diner, this cafeteria seats 345 guests and has easy-to-read signs that point the way to your favorite foods. Hours are limited in winter—it's best to call ahead then. $ *Average main: $6* ⊠ *Yavapai Lodge, Desert View Dr., Grand Canyon Village* ☎ *928/638–2631* ⊕ *www.grandcanyonlodges. com/canyon-cafe-423.html* ⚑ *Reservations not accepted.*

$$$

SOUTHWESTERN

Fodor's Choice

★

✕ **El Tovar Dining Room.** No doubt about it—this is the best restaurant for miles. Modeled after a European hunting lodge, this rustic 19th-century dining room built of hand-hewn logs is worth a visit. The cuisine is modern Southwestern with an exotic flair. Start with the smoked salmon–and–goat cheese crostini or the acclaimed black bean soup. The dinner menu includes such hearty yet creative dishes as cherry-merlot-glazed duck with roasted poblano black bean rice, grilled New York strip steak with cornmeal-battered onion rings, and a wild salmon tostada topped with organic greens and tequila vinaigrette. The dining room also has an extensive wine list. ■ **TIP→** Dinner reservations can be made up to six months in advance with room reservations and 30 days in advance for all other visitors. If you can't get a dinner table, consider lunch or breakfast—the best in the region with dishes like polenta corncakes with prickly pear–pistachio butter, and blackened breakfast trout and eggs. $ *Average main: $29* ⊠ *El Tovar Hotel, Desert View Dr., Grand Canyon Village* ☎ *303/297–2757, 888/297–2757 reservations only, 928/638–2631* ⊕ *www.grandcanyonlodges.com/el-tovar-421.html* ⚑ *Reservations essential.*

$

AMERICAN

✕ **Maswik Cafeteria.** You can get a burger, hot sandwich, pasta, or Mexican fare at this food court, as well as pizza by the slice and wine and beer in the adjacent Maswik Pizza Pub. This casual eatery is 0.25 mile from the rim. Lines can be long during high-season lunch and dinner, but everything moves fairly quickly. $ *Average main: $7* ⊠ *Maswik Lodge, Desert View Dr., Grand Canyon Village* ☎ *928/638–2631* ⊕ *www.grandcanyonlodges.com* ⚑ *Reservations not accepted.*

WHERE TO STAY

For expanded reviews, facilities, and current deals, visit Fodors.com.

$

HOTEL

☾

★

🛏 **Bright Angel Lodge.** Famed architect Mary Jane Colter designed this 1935 log-and-stone structure, which sits within a few yards of the canyon rim and blends superbly with the canyon walls. **Pros:** some rooms have canyon vistas; all are steps away from the rim; Internet kiosks and transportation desk for the mule ride check-in are in the lobby;

good value for the amazing location. **Cons:** the popular lobby is always packed; parking is a bit of a hike; lack of elevators make accessibility an issue for lodge rooms. **TripAdvisor:** "best views," "comfortable historic cabin," "fantastic location." ⓢ *Rooms from: $82* ✉ *Desert View Dr., Grand Canyon Village* ☎ *888/297–2757 reservations only, 928/638–2631* ⊕ *www.grandcanyonlodges.com* ⧉ *37 rooms, 18 with bath; 50 cabins* ⓘ *No meals.*

$$$
HOTEL
Fodor's Choice
★
🏨 **El Tovar Hotel.** The hotel's proximity to all of the canyon's facilities, European hunting-lodge atmosphere, attractively updated rooms and tile baths, and renowned dining room make it the best place to stay on the South Rim. **Pros:** historic lodging just steps from the South Rim; fabulous lounge with outdoor seating and canyon views; best in-park dining on-site. **Cons:** books up quickly. **TripAdvisor:** "excellent location," "historical and beautiful," "old time luxury and fine dining." ⓢ *Rooms from: $178* ✉ *Desert View Dr., Grand Canyon Village* ☎ *888/297–2757 reservations only, 928/638–2631* ⊕ *www.grandcanyonlodges.com* ⧉ *66 rooms, 12 suites* ⓘ *No meals.*

$$
HOTEL
🏨 **Kachina Lodge.** On the rim halfway between El Tovar and Bright Angel Lodge, this motel-style lodge has many rooms with partial canyon views ($10 extra). **Pros:** partial canyon views in half the rooms; family-friendly; steps from the best restaurants in the park. **Cons:** check-in takes place at El Tovar Hotel; limited parking; pleasant but bland furnishings. **TripAdvisor:** "amazing views," "perfect location," "great accommodation." ⓢ *Rooms from: $173* ✉ *Desert View Dr., Grand Canyon Village* ☎ *888/297–2757 reservations only, 928/638–2631* ⊕ *www.grandcanyonlodges.com* ⧉ *49 rooms* ⓘ *No meals.*

$
HOTEL
☾
🏨 **Maswik Lodge.** Accommodations are far from crowds and noise and nestled in a shady ponderosa pine forest, with options ranging from rustic cabins to more modern motel-style rooms. **Pros:** larger rooms here than in older lodgings; good for families; affordable dining options. **Cons:** rooms lack historic charm and cabins as well as rooms in the South Section are quite plain; tucked away from the rim in the forest. **TripAdvisor:** "good location," "good night's sleep," "quite adequate lodgings for inside the park." ⓢ *Rooms from: $92* ✉ *Grand Canyon Village* ☎ *888/297–2757 reservations only, 928/638–2631* ⊕ *www.grandcanyonlodges.com* ⧉ *278 rooms* ⓘ *No meals.*

$
B&B/INN
🏨 **Phantom Ranch.** In a grove of cottonwood trees on the canyon floor, Phantom Ranch is accessible only to hikers and mule trekkers. **Pros:** only inner-canyon lodging option; fabulous canyon views; remote access

ARRANGING TOURS

Transportation-services desks are maintained at El Tovar, Bright Angel, Maswik Lodge, and Yavapai Lodge (closed in winter) in Grand Canyon Village. The desks provide information and handle bookings for sightseeing tours, taxi and bus services, mule and horseback rides, and accommodations at Phantom Ranch (at the bottom of the Grand Canyon). The concierge at El Tovar can also arrange most tours, with the exception of mule rides and lodging at Phantom Ranch. On the North Rim, Grand Canyon Lodge has general information about local services.

9

White-water rafting is just one of the many activities you can experience in the Grand Canyon.

limits crowds. **Cons:** accessible only by foot or mule; few amenities or means of outside communication. **TripAdvisor:** "great staff and place to rest," "great cabin," "well worth the months of planning." [$] *Rooms from: $43* ✉ *On canyon floor, at intersection of Bright Angel and Kaibab trails* ☎ *303/297–2757, 888/297–2757* 🌐 *www.grandcanyonlodges.com* 🛏 *4 dormitories and 2 cabins for hikers, 7 cabins with outside showers for mule riders* 🍴 *Some meals.*

$$ HOTEL **Thunderbird Lodge.** This motel with comfortable, simple rooms with the modern amenities you'd expect at a typical mid-price chain hotel is next to Bright Angel Lodge in Grand Canyon Village. **Pros:** partial canyon views in some rooms; family-friendly. **Cons:** rooms lack personality; check-in takes place at Bright Angel Lodge; limited parking. **TripAdvisor:** "fantastic location," "nice canyon view," "better than expected." [$] *Rooms from: $180* ✉ *Desert View Dr., Grand Canyon Village* ☎ *888/297–2757 reservations only, 928/638–2631* 🌐 *www.grandcanyonlodges.com* 🛏 *55 rooms* 🍴 *No meals.*

$ HOTEL **Yavapai Lodge.** The largest motel-style lodge in the park is tucked in a piñon and juniper forest at the eastern end of Grand Canyon Village, near the RV park. **Pros:** transportation-activities desk on-site in the lobby; near Market Plaza in Grand Canyon Village; forested grounds. **Cons:** farthest in-park lodging from the rim. **TripAdvisor:** "simple but very nice," "great location," "cozy if somewhat dated." [$] *Rooms from: $120* ✉ *Grand Canyon Village* ☎ *888/297–2757 reservations only, 928/638–2961* 🌐 *www.grandcanyonlodges.com* 🛏 *358 rooms* 🕒 *Closed Jan. and Feb.* 🍴 *No meals.*

NORTH RIM

276 miles northeast of Las Vegas.

The North Rim stands 1,000 feet higher than the South Rim and has a more alpine climate, with twice as much annual precipitation. Here, in the deep forests of the Kaibab Plateau, the crowds are thinner, the facilities fewer, and the views even more spectacular. Due to snow, the North Rim is off-limits in the winter. The park buildings are closed mid-October through mid-May. The road closes when the snow makes it impassable—usually by the end of November.

Lodgings are available but limited; the North Rim only offers one historic lodge and restaurant and a single campground. Dining options have opened up a little with the addition of the Grand Cookout, offered nightly with live entertainment under the stars. Your best bet may be to pack your camping gear and hiking boots and take several days to explore the lush Kaibab Forest. The canyon's highest, most dramatic rim views also can be enjoyed on two wheels (via primitive dirt access roads) and on four legs (courtesy of a trusty mule).

GETTING HERE AND AROUND

To get to the North Rim by car, take Interstate 15 east to Hurricane, Utah; Routes 59 and 389 to Fredonia; and U.S. 89 and Route 67 to the North Rim. The North Rim is closed to automobiles after the first heavy snowfall of the season (usually in late October or early November) through mid-May. All North Rim facilities close between October 15 and May 15, though the park itself stays open for day use from October 15 through December 1, if heavy snows don't close the roads before then.

Reaching elevations of 8,000 feet, the more remote North Rim has no services available from late October through mid-May. AZ 67 south of Jacob Lake is closed by the first heavy snowfall in November or December and remains closed until early to mid-May.

When driving off major highways in low-lying areas, watch for rain clouds. Flash floods from sudden summer rains can be deadly.

From mid-May to mid-October, the Trans Canyon Shuttle leaves Bright Angel Lodge at 1:30 pm and arrives at the North Rim's Grand Canyon Lodge at about 6 pm. The return trip leaves the North Rim each morning at 7 am, arriving at the South Rim at about 11:30 am. One-way fare is $85, round-trip $160. A 50% deposit is required. Reservations are required. There is post-season shuttle service from October 16 to 31 but schedule varies from regular season.

PERMITS

The North Rim may be accessed in the winter by hiking, cross-country skiing, or snowshoeing. Winter visitors must obtain a backcountry permit for overnight use. Between the North Kaibab trailhead and Bright Angel Point, all overnight visitors are required to stay at the North Rim Campground. Winter campers can camp at large at all other areas between the northern boundary and the North Kaibab trailhead.

9

ESSENTIALS

Park Info North Rim. North Rim ☎ *928/638–7888, 877/444–6777 campground reservations* ⊕ *www.nps.gov/grca* ✉ *$25 per car, $12 per individual* ☾ *Daily mid-May–mid-Oct.*

Permits Backcountry Information Center ☎ *928/638–7875* ⊕ *www.nps.gov/ grca.*

Shuttle Info Trans Canyon Shuttle ☎ *928/638–2820.*

SCENIC DRIVE

★ **Highway 67.** Open mid-May to mid-October (and often until Thanksgiving), the two-lane paved road climbs 1,400 feet in elevation as it passes through the Kaibab National Forest. .

HISTORIC SITES

Grand Canyon Lodge. Built in 1937 by the Union Pacific Railroad (replacing the original 1928 building, which burned in a fire), the massive stone structure is listed on the National Register of Historic Places. Its huge sunroom has hardwood floors, high-beam ceilings, and a marvelous view of the canyon through plate-glass windows. On warm days, visitors sit in the sun and drink in the surrounding beauty on an outdoor viewing deck, where National Park Service employees deliver free lectures on geology and history. ⊠ *Off Hwy. 67 near Bright Angel Point, 10 Albright St.* ☎ *928/638–2631* ⊕ *www.grandcanyonlodges.com.*

SCENIC STOPS

★ **Bright Angel Point.** This trail, which leads to one of the most awe-inspiring overlooks on either rim, starts on the grounds of the Grand Canyon Lodge and runs along the crest of a point of rocks that juts into the canyon for several hundred yards. The walk is only 0.5 mile round-trip, but it's an exciting trek accented by sheer drops on each side of the trail. In a few spots where the route is extremely narrow, metal railings ensure visitors' safety. The temptation to clamber out to precarious perches to have your picture taken could get you killed—every year several people die from falls at the Grand Canyon. ⊠ *North Rim Dr.*

Cape Royal. A popular sunset destination, Cape Royal showcases the canyon's jagged landscape; you'll also get a glimpse of the Colorado River, framed by a natural stone arch called Angels Window. In autumn, the aspens turn a beautiful gold, adding even more color to an already magnificent scene of the forested surroundings. At Angels Window Overlook, **Cliff Springs Trail** starts its 1-mile route (round-trip) through a forested ravine. The trail terminates at Cliff Springs, where the forest opens to another impressive view of the canyon walls. ⊠ *Cape Royal Scenic Dr., 23 miles southeast of Grand Canyon Lodge* ☎ *801/356–7076.*

⚠ Practice basic safety precautions to reduce the risks of summer-storm-related dangers. The safest place to be during a thunderstorm is in a building or in a vehicle with the windows closed.

Point Imperial. At 8,803 feet, Point Imperial has the highest vista point at either rim; it offers magnificent views of both the canyon and the distant country: the Vermilion Cliffs to the north, the 10,000-foot Navajo

Mountain to the northeast in Utah, the Painted Desert to the east, and the Little Colorado River canyon to the southeast. Other prominent points of interest include views of Mt. Hayden, Saddle Mountain, and Marble Canyon. ✉ *2.7 miles left off Cape Royal Scenic Dr. on Point Imperial Rd., 11 miles northeast of Grand Canyon Lodge.*

Fodor's Choice ★ **Point Sublime.** You can camp within feet of the canyon's edge at this awe-inspiring site. Sunrises and sunsets are spectacular. The winding road, through gorgeous high country, is only 17 miles, but it will take you at least two hours, one way. The road is intended only for vehicles with high-road clearance (pickups and four-wheel-drive vehicles). It is also necessary to be properly equipped for wilderness road travel. Check with a park ranger or at the information desk at Grand Canyon Lodge before taking this journey. You may camp here only with a permit from the Backcountry Information Center. ✉ *North Rim Dr., Grand Canyon; about 20 miles west of North Rim Visitor Center.*

VISITOR CENTER

North Rim Visitor Center. View exhibits, browse in the bookstore, and pick up useful maps and brochures. Interpretive programs are often scheduled in the summer. If you're craving coffee, it's a short walk from here to the Roughrider Saloon at the Grand Canyon Lodge. ✉ *Near parking lot on Bright Angel Peninsula* ☎ *928/638–7864* ☀ *Mid-May–mid-Oct., daily 8–6.*

HIKING

EASY

✿ **Transept Trail.** This 3-mile (round-trip), 1½-hour trail begins at 8,255 feet near the Grand Canyon Lodge. Well maintained and well marked, it has little elevation change, sticking near the rim before reaching a dramatic view of a large stream through Bright Angel Canyon. The route leads to a side canyon called Transept Canyon, which geologist Clarence Dutton named in 1882, declaring it "far grander than Yosemite." Check the posted schedule to find a ranger talk along this trail; it's also a great place to view fall foliage. Flash floods can occur any time of the year, especially June through September when thunderstorms develop rapidly. *Easy.* ✉ *Trailhead: near the Grand Canyon Lodge's east patio.*

MODERATE

⚠ Flash floods can occur any time of the year, especially from June through September, when thunderstorms develop rapidly. Check forecasts before heading into the canyon and use caution when hiking in narrow canyons and drainage systems.

Uncle Jim Trail. This 5-mile, three-hour loop trail starts at 8,300 feet and winds south through the forest, past Roaring Springs and Bright Angel canyons. The highlight of this rim hike is Uncle Jim Point, which, at 8,244 feet, overlooks the upper sections of the North Kaibab Trail. *Moderate.* ✉ *Trailhead: North Kaibab Trail parking lot.*

★ **Widforss Trail.** Round-trip, Widforss Trail is 9.8 miles, with an elevation change of 200 feet. Allow five to seven hours for the hike, which starts at 8,080 feet and passes through shady forests of pine, spruce, fir, and aspen on its way to Widforss Point, at 7,900 feet. Here you'll have good views of five temples: Zoroaster, Brahma, and Deva to the

If you're driving to the Grand Canyon from Las Vegas, a detour in Kingman will lead you to Route 66—the longest remaining uninterrupted stretch of the "Main Street of America."

southeast and Buddha and Manu to the southwest. You are likely to see wildflowers in summer, and this is a good trail for viewing fall foliage. It's named in honor of artist Gunnar M. Widforss, renowned for his paintings of national park landscapes. *Moderate.* ⊠ *Trailhead: across from the North Kaibab Trail parking lot.*

DIFFICULT

Ken Patrick Trail. This primitive trail travels 10 miles one way (allow six hours each way) from the trailhead at 8,250 feet to Point Imperial at 8,803 feet. It crosses drainages and occasionally detours around fallen trees. The end of the road brings the highest views from either rim. Note that there is no water along this trail. *Difficult.* ⊠ *Trailhead: east side of North Kaibab trailhead parking lot.*

North Kaibab Trail. At 8,241 feet, this trail, like the roads leading to the North Rim, is open only from May through late October or early November (depending on the weather). It is recommended for experienced hikers only, who should allow four days for the full hike. The long, steep path drops 5,840 feet over a distance of 14.5 miles to Phantom Ranch and the Colorado River, so the National Park Service suggests that day hikers not go farther than Roaring Springs (5,020 feet) before turning to hike back up out of the canyon. After about 7 miles, Cottonwood Campground (4,080 feet) has drinking water in summer, restrooms, shade trees, and a ranger. *Difficult.* ■**TIP→** For a fee, a shuttle takes hikers to the North Kaibab trailhead twice daily from Grand Canyon Lodge. ⊠ *Trailhead: 2 miles north of the Grand Canyon Lodge.*

OFF THE BEATEN PATH

Unpaved forested side roads branch off Highway 67 before the North Rim park entrance station, leading to several remote viewpoints not

WINTER ACTIVITIES

Due to heavy snows and extreme winter weather, the North Rim closes all of its services from mid-October through mid-May. However, Highway 67 stays open to the North Rim until snows force the closure of the road at Jacob Lake. After the road closes, the rim can be accessed by hiking, snowshoeing, and cross-country skiing. Winter visitors must obtain a backcountry permit for overnight use during the winter season (later October through mid-May). Between the North Kaibab trailhead and Bright Angel Point, all overnight visitors are required to stay at the North Rim Campground. Winter campers can camp at large at all other areas between the northern boundary and the North Kaibab trailhead.

seen by the majority of Grand Canyon travelers. At Crazy Jug Point, you'll see the Colorado River as well as several canyon landmarks, including Powell Plateau, Great Thumb Mesa, and Tapeats Amphitheater. Timp Point features spectacular canyon views and a glimpse of Thunder River. Check with the Kaibab Forest Visitors Center in Jacob Lake for maps and road updates. The Forest Service maintains everything north of the rim, which is monitored by the National Park Service.

MULE RIDES

Canyon Trail Rides. This company leads mule rides on the easier trails of the North Rim. A one-hour ride (minimum age seven) runs $40. Half-day trips on the rim or into the canyon (minimum age 10) cost $75. Weight limits vary from 200 to 220 pounds. Available daily from May 15 to October 15, these excursions are popular, so make reservations far in advance. ☎ *435/679–8665* 🌐 *www.canyonrides.com/grand_canyon_rides.html.*

WHERE TO EAT AND STAY

$ AMERICAN 🍴 **Deli in the Pines.** Dining choices are very limited on the North Rim, but this is your best bet for a meal on a budget. Selections include pizza, salads, deli sandwiches, hot dogs, homemade breakfast pastries, and soft-serve ice cream. Best of all, there is an outdoor seating area for dining alfresco. It's open for breakfast, lunch, and dinner. [$] *Average main: $120* ✉ *Grand Canyon Lodge, Bright Angel Point, North Rim* ☎ *928/638–2611* ✍ *Reservations not accepted* 🕒 *Closed mid-Oct.–mid-May.*

$$$ AMERICAN ★ 🍴 **Grand Canyon Lodge Dining Room.** The historic lodge has a huge, high-ceilinged dining room with spectacular views and decent food, though the draw here is definitely the setting. You might find pecan-glazed pork chop, bison flank steak, and grilled ruby trout for dinner. The filling, simply prepared food here takes a flavorful turn with Southwestern spices and organic selections. It's also open for breakfast and lunch. A full-service bar and an impressive wine list add to the relaxed atmosphere of the only full-service, sit-down restaurant on the North Rim. Dinner reservations are essential in summer and on spring and fall weekends. [$] *Average main: $24* ✉ *Grand Canyon Lodge, Bright*

Angel Point, North Rim ☎ *928/638–2611* 🌐 *www.grandcanyonforever.com* ⏲ *Closed mid-Oct.–mid-May.*

$$$$ AMERICAN 👶 🍴 **Grand Cookout.** Dine under the stars and enjoy live entertainment at this chuck-wagon-style dining experience—the newest addition to the North Rim's limited dining options. Fill up on Western favorites including barbecue beef brisket, roasted chicken, baked beans, and cowboy biscuits. The food is basic and tasty, but the real draw is the nightly performance of Western music and tall tales. Transportation from the Grand Canyon Lodge to the cookout is included in the price. Be sure to call before 4 pm for dinner reservations. Advance reservations are taken up to seven days in advance at the Grand Canyon Lodge registration desk. [$] *Average main: $24* ✉ *Grand Canyon Lodge, North Rim* ☎ *928/638–2611* ✍ *Reservations essential* ⏲ *Closed mid-Oct.–mid-May.*

$ HOTEL Fodor's Choice ★ 🏨 **Grand Canyon Lodge.** This historic property, constructed mainly in the 1920s and 30s, is the premier lodging facility in the North Rim area. **Pros:** steps away from gorgeous North Rim views; close to several easy hiking trails. **Cons:** as the only in-park North Rim lodging option, this lodge fills up fast; few amenities and very limited Internet access. **TripAdvisor:** "wonderful relaxing place to stay," "lovely views," "great location and comfortable accommodations." [$] *Rooms from: $118* ✉ *Grand Canyon National Park, Hwy. 67, North Rim, Arizona* ☎ *877/386–4383, 928/638–2611 May–Oct., 928/645–6865 Nov.–Apr.* 🌐 *www.grandcanyonforever.com* 🛏 *40 rooms, 178 cabins* ⏲ *Closed mid-Oct.–mid-May* 🍴 *No meals.*

WEST RIM: THE HUALAPAI TRIBE AND GRAND CANYON WEST

70 miles north of Kingman.

The plateau-dwelling Hualapai ("people of the tall pines") acquired a larger chunk of traditional Pai lands with the creation of their reservation in 1883. Hualapai tribal lands include diverse habitats ranging from rolling grasslands to rugged canyons, and travel from elevations of 1,500 feet at the Colorado River to more than 7,300 feet at Aubrey Cliffs. In recent years the Hualapai have been attempting to foster tourism on the West Rim—most notably with the spectacular Skywalk, a glass walkway suspended 70 feet over the edge of the canyon rim. Not hampered by the regulations in place at Grand Canyon National Park, Grand Canyon West offers helicopter flights down into the bottom of the canyon, horseback rides to rim viewpoints, and boat trips on the Colorado River.

The Hualapai Reservation encompasses a million acres along 108 miles of the Colorado River in the Grand Canyon. Peach Springs, on historic Route 66, is the tribal capital and the location of the Hualapai Lodge. The increasingly popular West Rim is more than 120 miles away on freeway roads.

GETTING HERE AND AROUND

Grand Canyon West is a 5-hour drive from the South Rim of Grand Canyon National Park or a 2½-hour drive from Las Vegas. The 14-mile stretch of road leading to Grand Canyon West has improved, with a 5-mile portion now being paved, and the rest graded and maintained. Motorcycles and RVs, however, may find the roadway rough going. Visitors can schedule Park & Ride services on Pierce Ferry Road for a fee; reservations are required.

The Hualapai Tribe requires visitors to purchase tour packages to access the different viewpoints, which include shuttle rides, entrance to the Native American Village, and live performances. In addition, more than 30 tour and transportation companies service Grand Canyon West from Las Vegas, Phoenix, and Sedona by airplane, helicopter, coach, SUV, and Hummer.

EXPLORING INDIAN COUNTRY

When visiting Indian reservations, respect tribal laws and customs. Remember you're a guest in a sovereign nation. Don't wander into residential areas or take photographs of residents without first asking permission. Possessing or consuming alcohol is illegal on tribal lands. In general, the Hualapai and Havasupai are quiet, private people. Offer respect and don't pursue conversations or personal interactions unless invited to do so.

ESSENTIALS

Visitor Info Grand Canyon West ✉ *Hualapai Reservation* ☎ *928/769–2636, 888/868–9378* ⊕ *www.grandcanyonwest.com* ✉ *Packages range from $30 to $71 per person, plus taxes and fees, with the latter including access to Skywalk;* ☉ *Daily 8–5, Oct.–March; 7–7 Apr.–Sep..*

EXPLORING

Visitors aren't allowed to travel in their own vehicles to the viewpoints once they reach the West Rim, but can purchase one of four tour packages, ranging from the $44 per person Hualapai Legacy to the $360 private VIP tour that includes entrance to Skywalk. Tour prices include a Hualapai visitation permit and shuttle transportation to places such as Eagle Point, where the Indian Village walking tour visits authentic dwellings; Hualapai Ranch, site of Western performances, cookouts, and horseback and wagon rides; and Guano Point, where the "High Point Hike" offers panoramic views of the Colorado River. For an extra cost you can add a helicopter trip into the canyon, a boat trip on the Colorado, or a horseback ride to the canyon rim. Local Hualapai guides add a Native American perspective to a canyon trip that you won't find on North and South Rim tours.

The **Skywalk** is a cantilevered glass bridge suspended nearly 4,000 feet above the Colorado River and extending 70 feet from the edge of the Grand Canyon; it that opened in 2007. Approximately 10 feet wide, the bridge's deck, made of tempered glass several inches thick, has 5-foot glass railings on each side making an unobstructed open-air platform. Visitors must store all personal effects, including cameras, cell phones, and video cameras, in lockers before entering the Skywalk. A professional photographer takes personal photographs on the walkway, which can be purchased from the gift shop. At this writing, a three-level, 6,000-square-foot visitor center was under construction at the site; the date of completion is currently uncertain, but eventually this complex is expected to include a museum, movie theater, VIP lounge, gift shop, and multiple restaurants. A short walk takes visitors to the Indian Village, where educational displays uncover the culture of five different Native American tribes (Havasupai, Plains, Hopi, Hualapai, and Navajo). Intertribal, powwow-style dance performances entertain visitors at the nearby amphitheater.

WEST RIM: THE HAVASUPAI TRIBE AND HAVASU CANYON

141 miles from Williams.

GETTING HERE AND AROUND

From Williams drive towards the head of Hualapai Hilltop, which is west on Interstate 40 and AZ 66, north on Indian Highway 18. Note: last gas is at junction of AZ 66 and Indian Highway 18.

Another option is a helicopter ride into the canyon with Air West Helicopters. Flights leave from Hualapai Hilltop and cost $85 per person each way. Reservations are not accepted and visitors are transported on a first-come, first-served basis. Tribal members are boarded prior to tourists.

SAFETY AND PRECAUTIONS

Pack adequate food and supplies. Prices for food and sundries in Supai are more than double what they would be outside the reservation. The tribe does not allow alcohol, drugs, pets, or weapons.

ESSENTIALS

Tours Air West Helicopters ☎ *623/516–2790* ◷ *Mid-Mar.–mid-Oct., Thurs., Fri., Sun., and Mon. 10–1; mid-Oct.–mid-Mar., Fri. and Sun. 10–1.*

Visitor Info Havasupai Tourist Enterprise ☎ *928/448–2141, 928/448–2121 general information, 928/448–2111, 928/448–2201 lodging reservations* ⊕ *www.havasupaitribe.com* ✉ *$35 entrance fee; $5 impact fee.*

EXPLORING

With the establishment of Grand Canyon National Park in 1919, the Havasupai ("people of the blue-green water") were confined to their summer village of Supai and the surrounding 518 acres in the 5-mile-wide and 12-mile-long **Havasu Canyon.** In 1975 the reservation was substantially enlarged, but is still completely surrounded by national park lands on all but its southern border. Each year, about 25,000 tourists fly, hike, or ride into Havasu Canyon to visit the Havasupai. Despite their economic reliance on tourism, the Havasupai take their guardianship of the Grand Canyon seriously, and severely limit visitation in order to protect the fragile canyon habitats. Dubbed the "Shangri-la of the Grand Canyon," the remote, inaccessible Indian reservation includes some of the world's most beautiful and famous waterfalls, together with streams and pools tinted a mystical blue-green by dissolved travertine.

Havasu Canyon, south of the middle part of Grand Canyon National Park's South Rim and away from the crowds, is the home of the Havasupai, a tribe that has lived in this isolated area for centuries. You'll discover why they are known as the "people of the blue-green water," when you see the canyon's waterfalls, as high as 200 feet, cascading over red cliffs into travertine pools surrounded by thick foliage and sheltering cottonwood trees.

The striking falls, plunging into deep turquoise pools, seem like something from Hawai'i or Shangri La. The travertine in the water coats the walls and lines the pools with bizarre, drip-castle rock formations. Centuries of accumulated travertine formations in some of the most popular pools were washed out in massive flooding decades ago, destroying some of the otherworldly scenes pictured in older photos, but the place is still magical.

MAIL BY MULE

Arguably, the most remote mail route in the United States follows a steep 8-mile trail to the tiny town of Supai in Havasu Canyon. Havasupai tribal members living deep within the confines of the Grand Canyon rely on this route for the delivery of everything from food to furniture. During a typical week more than a ton of mail is sent into the canyon by mule, with each animal carrying a cargo of about 130 pounds.

The 600 tribal members now live in the village of Supai, accessible only down the 8-mile-long **Hualapai Trail,** which drops 2,000 feet from the canyon rim to the tiny town. The quiet and private Havasupai mostly remain apart from the modest flow of tourists, which nevertheless plays a vital role in the tribal economy.

To reach Havasu's waterfalls, you must hike downstream from the village of Supai. The striking **Havasu Falls** dashes over a ledge into another pool of refreshing 70°F water. The last of the enchanting waterfalls is **Mooney Falls,** 2 miles down from Navajo Falls. Named after a prospector who fell to his death here in 1880, the falls plummet 196 feet down a sheer travertine cliff. The hike to the pool below is a steep descent down slippery rocks with only the assistance of chains suspended along a series of iron stakes.

The Havasupai restrict the number of visitors to the canyon; you must have reservations. They ask that hikers call ahead before taking the trek into the canyon. Hualapai Trail leaves from Hualapai Hilltop, 63 miles north on Indian Route 18 from Route 66. From an elevation of 5,200 feet, the trail travels down a moderate grade to Supai village at 3,200 feet. Bring plenty of water and avoid hiking during the middle of the day, when canyon temperatures can reach into the 100s. If you'd rather ride, you can rent a horse for the trip down for $187 round-trip, or $94 one-way. Riders must be able to mount and dismount by themselves; be at least 4 feet, 7 inches; and weigh less than 250 pounds. Reservations must be made at least six weeks in advance with Havasupai Tourist Enterprise, which requires a 50% deposit. You'll need to spend the night if you're hiking or riding.

DEATH VALLEY

The desert is no Disneyland. With its scorching summer heat and vast, sparsely populated tracts of land, it's not often at the top of the list when most people plan their California vacations. But the natural riches of Death Valley—the largest national park outside Alaska—are overwhelming: rolling waves of sand dunes, black cinder cones thrusting up hundreds of feet from a blistered desert floor, riotous sheets of wildflowers, bizarrely shaped Joshua trees basking in the orange glow of a sunset, tiny pupfish that enthrall youngsters, and a silence that is both dramatic and startling.

WHEN TO GO

Most of the park's 1 million annual visitors still come between late fall and early spring, taking advantage of moderate temperatures and the lack of rainfall. During these cooler months you will need to book a room in advance, but don't worry: the park never feels crowded. If you visit during summer, believe everything you've ever heard about desert heat—it can be brutal, with temperatures often topping 120°F. The dry air wicks moisture from the body without causing a sweat, so drink plenty of water. Bring sunglasses, a hat, and sufficient clothing to block the sun's rays and the wind. Flash floods are fairly common; sections of roadway can be flooded or washed away. The

wettest month is February, when the park receives an average of 0.3 inch of rain.

GETTING HERE AND AROUND

It can take more than three hours to cross from one side of the park to another, so it's important to choose an entrance point that makes sense for what you want to see. From Las Vegas enter from the north at Beatty, Nevada, or via the central entrance at Death Valley Junction.

Distances can be deceiving within the park: what seems close can be very far away. Much of the park can be viewed on regularly scheduled bus tours, but these often don't allow time for hikes to sites not seen from the road, such as Salt Creek, Golden Canyon, and Natural Bridge. The best option is to drive to a number of the sites, get out of the car, and walk.

When driving in Death Valley, reliable maps are important, as signage is often limited or, in a few places, nonexistent. Other important accessories include a compass, a mobile phone (though these don't always work in remote areas), and extra food and water (3 gallons per person per day is recommended, plus additional radiator water). If you're able to take a four-wheel-drive vehicle, bring it: many of Death Valley's most spectacular canyons are otherwise inaccessible. Be aware of possible winter closures or driving restrictions due to snow.

Driving Information California State Department of Transportation Hotline. Call this hotline for updates on Death Valley road conditions. ☎ 916/445–7623, 800/427–7623 ⊕ www.dot.ca.gov.

California Highway Patrol. The California Highway Patrol offers the latest traffic incident information. ☏ *800/427–7623 recorded info, 760/872–5900 live dispatcher* ⊕ *cad.chp.ca.gov.*

VISITOR INFORMATION

PARK CONTACT INFORMATION

Death Valley National Park ☏ *760/786–3200* ⊕ *www.nps.gov/deva.*

PARK FEES AND PERMITS

The entrance fee is $20 per vehicle and $10 for those entering on foot, bus, bike, or motorcycle. The payment, valid for seven consecutive days, is collected at the park's entrance stations and at the visitor center at Furnace Creek. (If you enter the park on Highway 190, you won't find an entrance station; remember to stop by the visitor center to pay the fee.) Annual park passes, valid only at Death Valley, are $40.

PARK HOURS

Most facilities within the park remain open year-round, daily 8–6.

VISITOR CENTERS

Furnace Creek Visitor Center and Museum. The exhibits and artifacts here provide a broad overview of how Death Valley formed; you can pick up maps at the bookstore run by the Death Valley Natural History Association. This is also the place to sign up for ranger-led walks (available November through April) or check out a live presentation about the valley's cultural and natural history. The recently renovated center offers 12-minute slide shows about the park every 30 minutes. Your children are likely to receive plenty of individual attention from the enthusiastic rangers. Ongoing renovations to the center and museum are improving the displays and level of hands-on interactivity. ⊠ *Hwy. 190, 30 miles northwest of Death Valley Junction* ☏ *760/786–3200* ⊕ *www.nps.gov/deva* ⊙ *Daily 8–5.*

Scotty's Castle Visitor Center and Museum. If you visit Death Valley, make sure you make the hour's drive north from Furnace Creek to Scotty's Castle. In addition to living-history tours, you'll find a nice display of exhibits, books, self-guided tour pamphlets, and displays about the castle's creators, Death Valley Scotty and Albert M. Johnson. Fuel up with sandwiches or souvenirs (there's no gasoline sold here anymore) before heading back out to the park. ⊠ *Rte. 267, 53 miles northwest of Furnace Creek and 45 miles northwest of Stovepipe Wells Village* ☏ *760/786–2392* ⊕ *www.nps.gov/deva* ⊙ *Daily 8:30–5:30 (hrs vary seasonally).*

TOURS

Death Valley National Park and Red Rock Canyon Tours (*Death Valley Tours*). This one-day tour service will pick you up from your Las Vegas hotel and take you to some of the best Death Valley sites, including Devil's Golf Course and Zabriskie Point. Tours start at about $200 and include a Hummer option for those who want to do a little off-roading. ☏ *800/719–3768* ⊕ *www.deathvalleytours.net.*

Death Valley & Scotty's Castle Adventure Tour. These 11-hour luxury motorcoach tours of the park pass through its most famous landmarks. Tours include lunch and hotel pickup from designated Las Vegas–area hotels.

"On my drive into Death Valley I was rewarded at Zabriskie Point with this amazing view." —photo by Rodney Ee, Fodors.com member

Tours depart Tuesday and Thursday at 7 am and cost $199 per person. ☎ 800/719–3768 Death Valley Tours, 800/566–5868, 702/233–1627 Look Tours.

EXPLORING

HISTORIC SITES

Harmony Borax Works. Death Valley's mule teams hauled borax from here to the railroad town of Mojave, 165 miles away. The teams plied the route until 1889, when the railroad finally arrived in Zabriskie. Constructed in 1883, one of the oldest buildings in Death Valley houses the Borax Museum, 2 miles south of the borax works. Originally a miners' bunkhouse, the building once stood in Twenty Mule Team Canyon. Now it displays mining machinery and historical exhibits. The adjacent structure is the original mule-team barn. ⊠ Harmony Borax Works Rd., west of Hwy. 190, 2 miles north of Furnace Creek ☉ Daily 9–4:30.

Scotty's Castle. This Moorish-style mansion, begun in 1924 and never completed, takes its name from Walter Scott, better known as Death Valley Scotty. An ex-cowboy, prospector, and performer in Buffalo Bill's Wild West Show, Scotty always told people the castle was his, financed by gold from a secret mine. In reality, there was no mine, and the house belonged to a Chicago millionaire named Albert Johnson, whom Scott had finagled into investing in the fictitious mine. Despite the con, Johnson and Scott became great friends. The house functioned for a while as a hotel and still contains works of art, imported carpets, handmade European furniture, and a tremendous pipe organ. Costumed rangers, with varying degrees of enthusiasm, re-create life at the castle

DEATH VALLEY IN ONE DAY

DEATH VALLEY IN ONE DAY

If you begin the day in Furnace Creek, you can see several sights without doing much driving. Bring plenty of water with you, and some food, too. Get up early and drive the 20 miles on Badwater Road to **Badwater**, which looks out on the lowest point in the Western Hemisphere and is a dramatic place to watch the sunrise. Returning north, stop at **Natural Bridge**, a medium-size conglomerate rock formation that has been hollowed at its base to form a span across the canyon, and then at the **Devil's Golf Course**, so named because of the large pinnacles of salt present here. Detour to the right onto **Artist's Drive**, a 9-mile one-way, northbound route that passes **Artist's Palette**. The reds, yellows, oranges, and greens come from minerals in the rocks and the earth. Four miles north of Artist's Drive you will come to the **Golden Canyon Interpretive Trail**, a 2-mile round-trip that winds through a canyon with colorful rock walls. Just before Furnace Creek, take Highway 190 3 miles east to **Zabriskie Point**, overlooking dramatic, furrowed red-brown hills and the **Twenty Mule Team Canyon**. Return to Furnace Creek, where you can grab a meal and visit the museum at the Furnace Creek Visitor Center. Heading north from Furnace Creek, pull off the highway and take a look at the **Harmony Borax Works**.

circa 1939. Check out the Underground Tour, which takes you through a ¼-mile tunnel in the castle basement. ⊠ *Scotty's Castle Rd. (Hwy. 267), 53 miles north of Salt Creek Interpretive Trail* ☎ *760/786–2392* ⊕ *www.nps.gov/deva* ⊠ *$15* ☉ *Daily 8:30–5, tours daily 9–5 (hrs vary seasonally).*

SCENIC DRIVE

Artist's Drive. This 9-mile, one-way route skirts the foothills of the Black Mountains and provides intimate views of the changing landscape. Once inside the palette, the huge expanses of the valley are replaced by the small-scale natural beauty of pigments created by volcanic deposits. It's a quiet, lonely drive, and shouldn't be rushed. Reach Artist's Palette by heading north off Badwater Road.

SCENIC STOPS

Artist's Palette. So called for the contrasting colors of its volcanic deposits, this is one of signature sights of Death Valley. Artist's Drive, the approach to the area, is one way heading north off Badwater Road, so if you're visiting Badwater from Furnace Creek, come here on the way back. The drive winds through foothills of sedimentary and volcanic rocks. About 4 miles into the drive, a short side road veers right to a parking lot that's a few hundred feet before the "palette," whose natural colors include shades of green, gold, and pink. ⊠ *Off Badwater Rd., 11 miles south of Furnace Creek.*

Badwater. At 282 feet below sea level, Badwater is the lowest spot on land in the Western Hemisphere—and also one of the hottest. Stairs and wheelchair ramps descend from the parking lot to a wooden platform that overlooks a sodium chloride pool, a small but remarkably

9

persistent reminder that the valley floor used to contain a lake. You can continue past the platform on a broad, white path that peters out after a half mile or so. Badwater is one of the most popular and easily accessible sites within the park. From this lowest point, be sure to look across to Telescope Peak, which towers more than 2 miles above the valley floor. ⊠ *Badwater Rd., 19 miles south of Furnace Creek.*

Fodor's Choice   **Dante's View.** This lookout is more than 5,000 feet up in the Black
★   Mountains. In the dry desert air you can see across most of 110-mile-long Death Valley. The view is astounding. Take a 10-minute, mildly strenuous walk from the parking lot toward a series of rocky overlooks, where with binoculars you can spot some of Death Valley's signature sites. A few interpretive signs point out the highlights below in the valley and across, in the Sierra. Getting here from Furnace Creek takes an hour—time well invested. ⊠ *Dante's View Rd., off Hwy. 190, 35 miles from Badwater, 20 miles south of Twenty Mule Team Canyon.*

Devil's Golf Course. Thousands of miniature salt pinnacles carved into surreal shapes by the desert wind dot this wildly varied landscape. The salt was pushed up to the earth's surface by pressure created as underground salt- and water-bearing gravel crystallized. Get out of your vehicle and take a closer look; you'll see perfectly round holes descending into the ground. ⊠ *Badwater Rd., 13 miles south of Furnace Creek. Turn right onto dirt road and drive 1 mile.*

Golden Canyon. Just South of Furnace Creek, these glimmering mountains are perhaps best known for their role in the original *Star Wars.* The canyon is also a fine hiking spot, with gorgeous views of the Panamint Mountains, ancient dry lake beds, and alluvial fans. If you fork out a quarter for the small trail guide, be forewarned that several of the numbered signs it refers to are missing. ⊠ *Hwy. 178* ✛ *From the Furnace Creek Visitor Center, drive 2 miles south on Hwy. 190, then 2 miles south on Hwy. 178 to the parking area. The lot has a kiosk with trail guides.*

Racetrack. Getting here involves a 27-mile journey over a rough dirt road, but the reward is well worth the trip. Where else in the world do rocks move on their own? This phenomenon has baffled scientists for years and is perhaps one of the last great natural mysteries. No one has actually seen the rocks in motion, but theory has it that when it rains, the hard-packed lake bed becomes slippery enough that gusty winds push the rocks along—sometimes for several hundred yards. When the mud dries, a telltale trail remains. The trek to the Racetrack can be made in a sedan, but sharp rocks can slash tires; a truck or SUV with thick tires, high clearance, and a spare tire are suggested. ⊠ *27 miles west of Ubehebe Crater via dirt road.*

Sand Dunes at Mesquite Flat. These dunes, made up of minute pieces of quartz and other rock, are ever-changing products of the wind-rippled hills, with curving crests and a sun-bleached hue. The dunes are the most photographed destination in the park, and you can see them at their best at sunrise and sunset. Keep your eyes open for animal tracks—you may even spot a coyote or fox. Bring plenty of water, and note where you parked your car: it's easy to become disoriented in this ocean of sand. If you lose your bearings, climb to the top of a dune and scan the horizon for the parking lot. ✉ *19 miles north of Hwy. 190, northeast of Stovepipe Wells Village.*

Stovepipe Wells Village. This tiny 1926 town, the first resort in Death Valley, takes its name from the stovepipe that an early prospector left to indicate where he found water. The area contains a motel, restaurant, grocery store, campgrounds, and landing strip, though first-time park visitors are better off staying in Furnace Creek, which is more central. Off Highway 190, on a 3-mile gravel road immediately southwest, are the multicolor walls of **Mosaic Canyon.** ✉ *Hwy. 190, 2 miles from Sand Dunes, 77 miles east of Lone Pine.*

Titus Canyon. This is a popular 28-mile drive from Beatty south along Scotty's Castle Road. Along the way you'll pass Leadville Ghost Town, petroglyphs at Klare Spring, and spectacular limestone and dolomite narrows at the end of the canyon. Toward the end, a two-section of gravel road will lead you into the mouth of the canyon. ✉ *Access road off Scotty's Castle Rd., 33 miles northwest of Furnace Creek.*

Zabriskie Point. Although only about 710 feet in elevation, this is one of Death Valley National Park's most scenic spots, overlooking a striking panorama of wrinkled, multicolor hills. It's a great place to watch the sunrise, but it can be bustling any time of day. Pair it with a drive out to magnificent Dante's View. ✉ *Hwy. 190, 5 miles south of Furnace Creek.*

WHERE TO EAT

IN THE PARK

$ AMERICAN

🍴 **19th Hole.** Next to the clubhouse of the world's lowest golf course, this open-air spot serves hamburgers, hot dogs, chicken, and sandwiches. There is drive-through service for golfers in carts. [$] *Average main: $8* ✉ *Furnace Creek Golf Club, Hwy. 190, Furnace Creek* ☎ *760/786–2345* ⏲ *Closed June–Sept. No dinner.*

$ CAFÉ 👶

🍴 **Forty-Niner Cafe.** This casual coffee shop serves typical American fare for breakfast (except in the summer), lunch, and dinner. It's done up in a rustic mining style with whitewashed pine walls, vintage map-covered tables, and prospector-branded chairs. Past menus and old photographs decorate the walls. [$] *Average main: $15* ✉ *Furnace Creek Ranch, Hwy. 190, Furnace Creek* ☎ *760/786–2345* 🌐 *www.furnacecreekresort.com.*

$$$ AMERICAN Fodor's Choice ★

🍴 **Furnace Creek Inn Dining Room.** Fireplaces, beamed ceilings, and spectacular views provide a visual feast to match the inn's ambitious menu. Dishes may include such desert-theme items as crispy cactus fritters, and simpler fare such as salmon and free-range chicken and filet mignon all pair well with the signature prickly-pear margarita. There's a seasonal menu of vegetarian dishes, too. There's a minimal evening dress code (no T-shirts or shorts). Lunch is served, too, and you can always have afternoon tea in the lobby, an inn tradition since 1927. Breakfast and Sunday brunch are also served. Reservations are essential for dinner only. [$] *Average main: $28* ✉ *Furnace Creek Inn Resort, Hwy. 190, Furnace Creek* ☎ *760/786–2345* 🌐 *www.furnacecreekresort.com* ✍ *Reservations essential* ⏲ *Restaurant closed June–Sept.*

$$ AMERICAN 🍴 **Panamint Springs Resort Restaurant.** This is a great place for steak and a beer—choose among the 150 different beers and ales—or pasta and a salad. In summer, evening meals are served outdoors on the porch, which has spectacular views of Panamint Valley. Breakfast and lunch are also served. Reservations are suggested for dinner. [$] *Average main: $20* ✉ *Hwy. 190, 31 miles west of Stovepipe Wells* ☎ *775/482–7680.*

$$$$ STEAKHOUSE 👶 🍴 **Wrangler Buffet and Steakhouse.** This casual, family-style restaurant has a buffet for breakfast and lunch, and steak-house favorites (chicken, fish, barbecue platter) for dinner. It's slightly more formal than the other restaurant at the Furnace Creek Resort, the Forty-Niner Cafe. Still, there's no dress code and reservations aren't required. [$] *Average main: $31* ✉ *Furnace Creek Ranch, Hwy. 190, Furnace Creek* ☎ *760/786–2345* 🌐 *www.furnacecreekresort.com.*

OUTSIDE THE PARK

$$ AMERICAN 🍴 **Crowbar Café and Saloon.** In an old wooden building where antique photos adorn the walls and mining equipment stands in the corners, the Crowbar serves enormous helpings of regional dishes such as steak and taco salads. Home-baked fruit pies make fine desserts, and frosty beers are surefire thirst quenchers. [$] *Average main: $15* ✉ *Rte. 127, Shoshone* ☎ *760/852–4123.*

$ AMERICAN 👶 🍴 **Randsburg General Store.** Built as Randsburg's Drug Store in 1896, this popular biker and family spot is one of the area's few surviving ghost-town buildings with original furnishings intact, such as tin ceiling, light fixtures, and a 1904 marble-and-stained-glass soda fountain. You can still enjoy a phosphate soda from that same fountain, cool down with a draft beer, or lunch on the signature Yellow Aster ham-and-cheese sandwich and blueberry milk shake along with chili, barbecue, and breakfast. [$] *Average main: $10* ✉ *35 Butte Ave., Randsburg* ☎ *760/374–2143.*

$ AMERICAN 🍴 **Mt. Whitney Restaurant.** A boisterous family-friendly restaurant with a 50-inch television, this place serves the best burgers in town—but in addition to the usual beef variety, you can choose from ostrich, venison, and buffalo burgers. [$] *Average main: $10* ✉ *227 S. Main St., Lone Pine* ☎ *760/876–5751.*

WHERE TO STAY

For expanded reviews, facilities, and current deals, visit Fodors.com.

IN THE PARK

During the busy season (November through March) you should make reservations for lodgings within the park several months in advance.

$$$$ HOTEL Fodor's Choice ★ 🏨 **Furnace Creek Inn.** This is Death Valley's most luxurious accommodations, going so far as to have valet parking. **Pros:** refined; comfortable; great views. **Cons:** a far cry from roughing it; expensive. **TripAdvisor:** "cool comfort in the desert," "beautiful location and great facilities," "clean and rustic." [$] *Rooms from: $375* ✉ *Furnace Creek Village, near intersection of Hwy. 190 and Badwater Rd.* ☎ *760/786–2345* 🌐 *www.furnacecreekresort.com* 🛏 *66 rooms* ⏲ *Closed mid-May–mid-Oct.* 🍽 *Breakfast.*

$$ **Furnace Creek Ranch.** Originally crew headquarters for the Pacific
RESORT Coast Borax Company, the four buildings here have motel-style rooms
that are good for families. **Pros:** good family atmosphere; central loca-
tion. **Cons:** rooms can get hot despite air-conditioning; parking near
your room can be problematic. **TripAdvisor:** "nice," "good hotel and
amenities," "a great stay." $ *Rooms from: $135* ✉ *Hwy. 190, Furnace
Creek* ☎ *760/786–2345, 800/528–6367* ⊕ *www.furnacecreekresort.
com* ⤴ *224 rooms* ❙◯❙ *Breakfast.*

$ **Panamint Springs Resort.** Ten miles inside the west entrance of the
B&B/INN park, this low-key resort overlooks the sand dunes and peculiar geo-
logical formations of the Panamint Valley. **Pros:** slow-paced; friendly;
there's a glorious amount of peace and quiet after sundown. **Cons:**
far from the park's main attractions. **TripAdvisor:** "nice campsites,"
"quaint and a good bargain," "quiet, restful nights." $ *Rooms from:
$95* ✉ *Hwy. 190, 28 miles west of Stovepipe Wells* ☎ *775/482–7680
* ⊕ *www.deathvalley.com/psr* ⤴ *14 rooms, 1 cabin* ❙◯❙ *No meals.*

$$ **Stovepipe Wells Village.** If you prefer quiet nights and an unfettered
HOTEL view of the night sky and nearby sand dunes, this property is for you.
Pros: intimate, relaxed; no big-time partying; authentic desert-commu-
nity ambience. **Cons:** isolated; a bit dated. **TripAdvisor:** "tons of character," "basic accommodation in a stunning landscape," "over-priced."
$ *Rooms from: $140* ✉ *Hwy. 190, Stovepipe Wells* ☎ *760/786–2387
* ⊕ *www.escapetodeathvalley.com* ⤴ *83 rooms* ❙◯❙ *No meals.*

9

Travel Smart
Las Vegas

WORD OF MOUTH

"If you just want to stick to the Strip and not go out of town on your own, get the 24 hour pass on "The Deuce," which is a double deck bus that runs up and down the Strip. Last time I bought one it was $7. There is a free monorail between 3 of the hotels at the southern end of the Strip. If you decide you want to go out to see Red Rocks or Valley of Fire, you may have to get a car for the day."

—tomfuller

GETTING HERE AND AROUND

The modern, sprawling Western city of Las Vegas is fairly easy to get around by car, as it's laid out largely in a grid and crisscrossed by freeways. The only pitfall is traffic. Lots of it.

In fact, traffic along the Strip and intersecting roads, as well as parallel Interstate 15, can be horrendous. It's especially challenging on weekend evenings and when there are conventions in town, but traffic jams can spring up virtually any time of day or night. Give yourself plenty of time when you're traveling to or from the Strip. And be sure to keep your cool.

Parking is free at virtually every resort on the Strip (although some Downtown garages and lots charge a fee, the rate's often free if you get your ticket stamped by the casino cashier).

Outside the Strip, the city sprawls in all directions, and renting a car is the best way to get around, especially if you're staying in Lake Las Vegas, Summerlin, or another area more than a few miles from the Strip. Vegas is served by public buses, but it's impractical for visitors to rely on them.

▌ AIR TRAVEL

Flying times to Las Vegas: from New York, 5 hours; from Dallas, 2 hours; from Chicago, 4 hours; from Los Angeles, 1 hour; from San Francisco, 1½ hours.

If you're leaving Las Vegas on a Sunday, be sure to arrive at the airport at least three hours before your scheduled departure time. Though the TSA has improved its operation at McCarran International, security lines on busy days still seemingly stretch forever, and inevitably, travelers miss flights.

A couple of Vegas hotels, including MGM Grand, offer off-site baggage check-in on the baggage-claim level, which allows hotel guests to obtain boarding passes and check their luggage directly at the hotel.

Of course, even where off-site luggage check-in is not available, you can always save time by checking in online and printing out your boarding pass (or accessing it via app) before you depart for the airport.

Airline Security Issues Transportation Security Administration ⊕ *www.tsa.gov.*

AIRPORTS

The gateway to Las Vegas is McCarran International Airport (LAS), 5 miles south of the business district and immediately east of the southern end of the Strip. The airport, just a few minutes' drive from the Strip, is well served by nonstop and direct flights from all around the country and a handful of international destinations. The airport is consistently rated among the most passenger-friendly airports in the United States. In June 2012, a 2.4 billion expansion of Terminal 3 was completed, opening an additional 14 gates for domestic and international service.

Also, McCarran's close enough to the Strip that if you ever find yourself with a few hours to kill, you can easily catch a 5- to 15-minute cab ride to the Hard Rock or one of the South Strip casinos (Mandalay Bay and Luxor are closest), and while away some time. Additionally, as you might expect, McCarran has scads of slot machines to keep you busy.

Airport Information McCarran International Airport (LAS) ☎ *702/261–5211* ⊕ *www. mccarran.com.*

GROUND TRANSPORTATION

By shuttle van: This is the cheapest way from McCarran to your hotel. The service is shared with other riders, and costs $5 or $6 per person to the Strip, $7 to $15 to Downtown, and $10 to $30 to outlying casinos. The vans wait for passengers outside the terminal in a marked area. Because the vans make numerous stops at different hotels, it's not the best means of transportation if you're in a hurry.

By taxi: The metered cabs awaiting your arrival at McCarran are the quickest way of getting to your destination. *See ⇨ Taxi Travel below for more information.*

By town car: These rides are a bit more expensive than the average taxicab, but are much cleaner and nicer.

Contacts Bell Trans ☏ *702/739–7990, 800/274–7433* ⊕ *www.bell-trans.com.* **CLS shuttle** ☏ *702/740–4545* ⊕ *www.clsnevada. com.* **Gray Line** ☏ *702/384–1234, 800/634–6579* ⊕ *www.graylinelasvegas.com.*

FLIGHTS

All the major airlines operate frequent service from their hub cities and, as a whole, offer one-stop connecting flights from virtually every city in the country. In addition to nonstop service from the usual hub cities (e.g., Atlanta, Chicago, Cincinnati, Dallas, Denver, Houston, Minneapolis, Newark, Phoenix, Salt Lake City, San Francisco), nonstop service is offered to many other destinations, sometimes by smaller airlines. Southwest remains the dominant airline (carrying nearly double the number of passengers as its closest competitor, United), and it offers frequent flights to many cities in the South and West, including San Diego, Los Angeles, San Francisco, Oakland, Seattle, Salt Lake, Denver, Albuquerque, and Phoenix. Be sure to check the rates of the other discount airlines that serve Las Vegas, such as, jetBlue, Frontier Airlines, Alaska Airlines, and Horizon Air.

Airline Contacts Alaska Air ☏ *800/252–7522* ⊕ *www.alaskaair.com.* **American Airlines** ☏ *800/433–7300* ⊕ *www.aa.com.* **Delta Airlines** ☏ *800/221–1212* ⊕ *www.delta.com.* **Frontier Airlines** ☏ *800/432–1359* ⊕ *www. frontierairlines.com.* **Horizon Air** ☏ *800/252–7522* ⊕ *www.horizonair.com.* **jetBlue** ☏ *800/538–2583* ⊕ *www.jetblue.com.* **Southwest Airlines** ☏ *800/435–9792* ⊕ *www. southwest.com.* **United Airlines** ☏ *800/864–8331* ⊕ *www.united.com.* **Virgin America** ☏ *877/359–8474* ⊕ *www.virginamerica.com.*

▐ BUS TRAVEL

GREYHOUND

Greyhound provides regular Las Vegas service; the bus terminal is Downtown. Visit its website for fare and schedule information. Cash and credit cards are accepted, but reservations are not. Seating is on a first-come, first-served basis. The most frequent route out of Las Vegas is the one to Los Angeles, with departures a few times a day; the trip takes five to eight hours, depending on stops. Fares start around $35 one way. Arriving at the bus station 30 to 45 minutes before your bus departs nearly always ensures you a seat. On Sunday evening and Monday morning, arriving an hour or more before departure is recommended.

CAT

The county-operated Citizens Area Transit (CAT) runs local buses throughout the city and to most corners of sprawling Las Vegas Valley. The overall quality of bus service along the main thoroughfares is good. Nonlocals typically only ride CAT buses up and down the Strip, between Mandalay Bay and the Stratosphere. Some continue on to the Downtown Transportation Center. If you're heading to outlying areas, you may need to change buses Downtown. Mornings and afternoons the buses are frequently crowded, with standing room only. The fare for residential CAT buses is $2

THE DEUCE

The Deuce is a special double-decker CAT bus that rides the Strip for $5 (exact change required; $1 bills are accepted). All Deuce fares include transfers on residential CAT routes as well. The Deuce, which began service in 2005, certainly is a unique way to explore new and old Vegas alike. Buses stop on the street in front of all the major hotels every 12–17 minutes (in a perfect world) between 7 am and 2:30 am and every 21 minutes between 2:30 and 5:30 am. Because traffic is quite heavy along the Strip, delays are frequent. Also, because the bus route has become popular among tourists, 24-hour passes ($7) and three-day passes ($20) are available.

Bus Information Citizens Area Transit ☎ *702/228–7433* ⊕ *www.rtcsouthernnevada. com.Greyhound* ☎ *800/231–2222* ⊕ *www. greyhound.com.*

∎ CAR TRAVEL

Though you can get around central Las Vegas adequately without a car, the best way to experience the city can be to drive it. A car gives you easy access to all the casinos and attractions; lets you make excursions to Lake Mead, Hoover Dam, and elsewhere at your leisure; and gives you the chance to cruise the Strip and bask in its neon glow. If you plan to spend most of your time on the Strip, a car may not be worth the trouble, but otherwise, especially given the relatively high costs of taxis, renting or bringing a car is a good idea.

Parking on and around the Strip, although free, can require a bit of work. You'll have to brave some rather immense parking structures. Valet parking is available but can take a while at busy times and requires that you tip the valets ($1 to $2). Still, it's usually less expensive to rent a car and drive around Vegas, or to use the monorail (or even—gasp!—to walk), than to cab it everywhere.

NAVIGATING THE CITY

The principal north–south artery is Las Vegas Boulevard (Interstate 15 runs roughly parallel to it, less than a mile to the west). A 4-mile stretch of Las Vegas Boulevard South is known as the Strip, where a majority of the city's hotels and casinos are clustered. Many major streets running east–west (Tropicana Avenue, Flamingo Road, Desert Inn Road, Sahara Avenue) are named for the casinos built at their intersections with the Strip. Highway 215 and Interstate 15 circumnavigate the city, and the Interstate 515 freeway connects Henderson to Las Vegas and then to Summerlin. Because the capacity

of the streets of Las Vegas has not kept pace with the city's incredible growth, traffic can be slow at virtually any time, especially on the Strip, and particularly in the late afternoon, in the evening, and on weekends. At those times drive the streets parallel to Las Vegas Boulevard: Koval Lane and Paradise Road to the east; Frank Sinatra Drive and Industrial Road/Dean Martin Drive to the west. The Industrial Road shortcut (from Tropicana Avenue almost all the way to Downtown) can save you an enormous amount of time. You can enter the parking lots at Caesars Palace, the Mirage, Treasure Island, Fashion Show Mall, and Circus Circus from Industrial Road. Exit Frank Sinatra Drive off Interstate 15 North, and you can access the hotels from Mandalay Bay to Bellagio (including CityCenter).

∎TIP→ Visitors from Southern California should at all costs try to avoid traveling to Las Vegas on a Friday afternoon and returning home on a Sunday afternoon. During these traditional weekend-visit hours, driving times (along Interstate 15) can be more than twice as long as during other, nonpeak periods.

GASOLINE

It's easy to find gas stations, most of which are open 24 hours, all over town. There aren't any gas stations along the main stretch of the Strip, but you will find them within a mile of the Strip in either direction, along the main east–west cross streets. Gas is relatively expensive in Las Vegas, generally 30¢ to 40¢ per gallon above the national average. There's no one part of town with especially cheap or pricey gas, although the stations nearest the airport tend to charge a few cents more per gallon—it's prudent to fill up your car rental a few miles away from the airport before returning it.

PARKING

You can't park anywhere on the Strip itself, and Fremont Street in the casino district Downtown is a pedestrian mall closed to traffic. Street parking regulations are strictly enforced in Las Vegas, and meters are continuously monitored, so whenever possible it's a good idea to leave your car in a parking lot or garage. Free self-parking is available in the massive garages and lots adjacent to virtually every hotel, although you may have to hunt for a space, and you can wind up in the far reaches of immense facilities. You can avoid this challenge by paying for valet parking (charges vary greatly from property to property; at some casinos, such as Planet Hollywood, valet parking is free). Parking in the high-rise structures Downtown is generally free or inexpensive, as long as you validate your parking ticket with the casino cashier.

RENTAL CARS

The airport's rental-car companies are off-site at McCarran Rent-a-Car Center, about 2 miles from the main airport complex, and visitors must take shuttle buses from just outside the baggage claim to get there. The new facility reduces congestion in and around the airport, and offers visitors the opportunity to check bags for flights on some airlines without stepping foot in the main terminal. Still, the centralized location is so far from the airport that it can add anywhere from 15 to 20 minutes to your travel time. The bottom line: if you rent a car, be sure to leave yourself plenty of time to return the vehicle and catch your flight.

RENTAL CAR RATES

The Las Vegas average is anywhere from $20 to $70 a day for intermediate to full-size cars—usually you can find a car for under $30 a day (and at very slow times for less than $20), but during very busy times expect sky-high rates, especially at the last minute. Las Vegas has among the highest car-rental taxes and surcharges in the country, however, so be sure to factor in the 8.1% (in Clark County) sales tax, a 2% rental fee, 10% government services fee and a 2% county return fee. If you rent your car at the airport, an additional $3.75 "customer facility charge" applies. Owing to the high demand for rental cars

and significant competition, there are many deals to be had at the airport for car rentals. During special events and conventions, rates frequently go up as supply dwindles, but at other times you can find bargains. For the best deals, check with the various online services, or contact a representative of the hotel where you'll be staying, as many hotels have business relationships with car-rental companies.

Although there are several local car-rental companies along the Strip itself, they tend to be more expensive than those at the airport or elsewhere in the city.

RENTAL CAR REQUIREMENTS

In Nevada you must be 21 to rent a car, and some major car-rental agencies have a minimum age of 25. Those agencies that do rent to people under 25 often assess surcharges to those drivers. There's no upper age limit for renting a car. Non-U.S. residents will need a reservation voucher, a passport, a driver's license, and a travel policy that covers each driver when picking up a car.

Rental Center McCarran Airport Rent-a-Car Center ☎ 702/261–6001 ⊕ mccarran. com/03_carrentals.aspx.

ROAD CONDITIONS

It might seem as if every road in Las Vegas is in a continuous state of expansion or repair. Orange highway cones, road-building equipment, and detours are ubiquitous. But once the roads are widened and repaved, they're efficient and comfortable. The city's traffic-light system is state of the art, and you can often drive for miles on major thoroughfares, hitting green lights all the way. Signage is excellent, both on surface arteries and on freeways. The local driving style is fast and can be less than courteous. Watch out for un-signaled lane changes and turns.

There are rarely weather problems in Las Vegas, but flash flooding can wreak havoc. For information on weather conditions, highway construction, and road closures, visit the website of the Nevada Department of Transportation (⊕ *www.*

nevadadot.com/traveler_info/traveler_information.aspx) or call the department by dialing 511 in Nevada.

ROADSIDE EMERGENCIES

Call 911 to reach police, fire, or ambulance assistance. Dial *647 to reach the Nevada Highway Patrol.

RULES OF THE ROAD

Right turns are permitted on red lights after coming to a full stop. Nevada requires seat-belt use in the front and back seats of vehicles. Chains are required on Mt. Charleston and in other mountainous regions when snow is fresh and heavy; signs indicate conditions.

CHILDREN

Always strap children under age five or under 40 pounds into approved child-safety seats. In Nevada children must wear seat belts regardless of where they're seated.

DWI

The Las Vegas police are extremely aggressive about catching drunk drivers—you are considered legally impaired if your blood-alcohol level is .08% or higher (this is also the law in neighboring states).

SPEED LIMITS

The speed limit on residential streets is 25 mph. On major thoroughfares it's 45 mph. On the interstate and other divided highways within the city the speed limit is a fast 65 mph; outside the city the speed limit is 70 or 75 mph. Police officers are highly vigilant about speeding laws within Las Vegas, especially in school zones, but enforcement in rural areas is rare.

▌ MONORAIL TRAVEL

The monorail, which has fallen on hard economic times recently, gives Las Vegas an even more Disney-esque look. It stretches from MGM Grand, in the south, to the property formerly known as the Sahara, to the north, with several stops in between, including the Las Vegas Convention Center. All told, the trains make the 4-mile trip in about 14 minutes. To the

north, a Downtown monorail extension is in the planning stages but completion is several years away. The monorail runs Monday through Thursday 7 am–2 am, Friday through Sunday 7 am–3 am. Fares are $5 for one ride, $12 for a one-day pass, and $28 for a three-day pass. You can purchase tickets at station vending machines or in advance online, where special deals on passes are sometimes offered.

A number of west-side Strip properties also are connected by free trams that run roughly every 10 to 15 minutes, 9 am–1 am. There's one that runs between Excalibur and Mandalay Bay, one that runs between the Mirage and Treasure Island, and a new one that stretches from Monte Carlo through CityCenter to Bellagio.

Contact Las Vegas Monorail Company
☎ *702/699–8200* ⊕ *www.lvmonorail.com.*

▌ TAXI TRAVEL

Cabs aren't allowed to pick up passengers on the street, so you can't hail a cab New York–style. You have to wait in a hotel taxi line or call a cab company. If you dine at a restaurant off the Strip, the restaurant will call a cab to take you home.

FARES

The fare is $3.30 on the meter when you get in and 20¢ for every 1/13th mile (there's also a $30 per-hour charge for waiting). Taxis are limited by law to carrying a maximum of four passengers, and there's no additional charge per person. No fees are assessed for luggage, but taxis leaving the airport are allowed to add an airport surcharge of $1.80.

The trip from the airport to most hotels on the south end of the Strip should cost $11 to $14, to the north end of the Strip should cost $14 to $25, and to Downtown should cost $20 to $23.

TIPPING

Drivers should be tipped around 15% for good service (⇨ *Tipping in Essentials*). Some drivers cannot accept credit cards (and those that do usually add a surcharge); all drivers carry only nominal change with them.

SUGGESTED ROUTES

■TIP→ Be sure to specify to your driver that you do not want to take Interstate 15 or the airport tunnel on your way to or from the airport. This is always the longer route distance-wise, which means it's the most expensive, but it can sometimes save you 5 to 10 minutes on the trip if traffic is heavy on the Strip. Drivers who take passengers through the airport tunnel without asking are committing an illegal practice known as "long-hauling." You have every right to ask your driver about the routes he or she is using; don't be afraid to speak up. If you have trouble with your cab driver, be sure to get his or her name and license number and call the Taxi Cab Authority to report the incident.

Taxi Cab Authority ☎ *702/668–4000* ⊕ *www. taxi.state.nv.us.*

Taxi Companies Desert Cab ☎ *702/386– 4828.* **Yellow/Star** ☎ *702/873–2000.* **Whittlesea** ☎ *702/384–6111.*

ESSENTIALS

▮ BUSINESS SERVICES AND FACILITIES

Las Vegas is one of the nation's leading convention destinations, and all the town's major hotels have comprehensive convention and meeting-planning space and services. The best business centers in town are run by the chain FedEx Office, which has about a dozen locations throughout the area; the Hughes Center Drive outpost (open 24 hours) is closest to the Strip.

Contact FedEx Office & Print Center ✉ *395 Hughes Center Dr.* ☎ *702/951–2400* ⊕ *www. fedex.com.*

▮ DAY TOURS AND GUIDES

BOAT TOURS

The *Desert Princess*, a 300-passenger Mississippi River–style stern-wheeler, cruises Lake Mead. Tours include 90-minute sightseeing cruises, two-hour pizza party cruises, two-hour dinner and champagne brunch cruises, and three-hour dinner-and-dancing excursions.

Tour Operator Lake Mead Cruises ✉ *Lake Mead marina* ☎ *702/293–6180* ⊕ *www. lakemeadcruises.com.*

BUS TOURS

Gray Line and several other companies offer Las Vegas city and neon-light tours; trips to Red Rock Canyon, Lake Mead, Colorado River rafting, Hoover Dam, and Valley of Fire; and longer trips to different sections of the Grand Canyon.

Tour Operator Gray Line Tours ☎ *800/634– 6579, 702/384–1234* ⊕ *www.graylinelasvegas. com.*

HELICOPTER TOURS

Helicopters do two basic tours in and around Las Vegas: a brief flyover of the Strip and a several-hour trip out to the Grand Canyon and back.

GREAT READS

Some of the most memorable literary works that have featured Sin City include Larry McMurtry's *Desert Rose*, which relates the tale of a showgirl struggling to prevail in Vegas as her age catches up with her; and Hunter S. Thompson's vaunted classic, *Fear and Loathing in Las Vegas,* a gripping work of gonzo journalism that takes us through a drug-induced road trip to Las Vegas. *Fools Die* is one of mob-chronicler Mario Puzo's most entertaining novels about Vegas, offering an up-close glimpse of the city's infamous casino culture. Poker fans will love James McManus's *Positively Fifth Street,* about the rise of the now-famous World Series of Poker.

Tour Operators Maverick Helicopter Tours ☎ *702/261–0007, 888/261–4414* ⊕ *www. maverickhelicopter.com.* **Papillon Grand Canyon Helicopters** ☎ *702/736–7243, 888/635– 7272* ⊕ *www.papillon.com.* **Sundance Helicopters** ☎ *702/736–0606, 800/653–1881* ⊕ *www.sundancehelicopters.com.*

▮ HEALTH

The dry desert air in Las Vegas means that your body will need extra fluids, especially during the punishing summer months. Always drink lots of water even if you're not outside very much. When you're outdoors, wear sunscreen and always carry water with you if you plan a long walk.

▮ HOURS OF OPERATION

Las Vegas is a 24-hour city 365 days a year. Casinos, bars, supermarkets, almost all gas stations, even some health clubs and video stores cater to customers at all hours of the day and night (many people work odd hours here).

Most museums and attractions are open seven days a week.

Most pharmacies are open seven days a week from 9 to 7. Many, though, including local outposts of Walgreens, Rite Aid, and CVS pharmacy, several of them on the Las Vegas Strip, offer 24-hour and drive-through services.

Shopping hours vary greatly around town, but many stores are open weekdays and Saturday from 9 or 10 until 9 or 10 and Sunday 10 or 11 until 5 or 6. The souvenir shops on the Strip and Downtown often remain open until midnight, and some are open 24 hours. Quite a few grocery stores are open around the clock.

▌MONEY

Prices in Las Vegas can be gratis or outrageous. For example, you can get a sandwich wrap at one of the rock-bottom casino snack bars (Riviera, Four Queens) for $3–$4, or you can spend upward of $20 for a pastrami sandwich at the Carnegie Deli in the Mirage. A cup of coffee in a casino coffee shop or Starbucks will set you back $2 to $5, while that same cup is free if you happen to be sitting at a nickel slot machine when the cocktail waitress comes by. A taxi from the airport to the MGM Grand goes as low as $11 if you tell the driver to take Tropicana Avenue and there's no traffic, or runs as high as $25 if you take the Airport Connector and there's a wreck on the freeway. The more you know about Las Vegas, the less it'll cost you.

▌**TIP→** Prices throughout this guide are given for adults. Substantially reduced fees are almost always available for children, students, and senior citizens.

ATMs are widely available in Las Vegas; they're at every bank and at virtually all casinos, hotels, convenience stores, and gas stations. Casino ATMs generally tack on a fee of up to $4 per transaction (this, of course, is on top of any fees your bank might charge). In addition, all casinos have cash-advance machines, which take credit cards. You just indicate how large a cash advance you want, and when the transaction is approved, you pick up the cash at the casino cashier. But beware: you pay up to a 18% fee in addition to the usual cash-advance charges and interest rate for this "convenience"; in most cases, the credit-card company begins charging interest the moment the advance is taken, so you will not have the usual grace period to pay your balance in full before interest begins to accrue. To put it another way, don't obtain cash this way.

▌PACKING

Ever since the original Frontier Casino opened on the Los Angeles Highway (now the Strip), visitors to Las Vegas have been invited to "come as you are." The warm weather and informal character of Las Vegas render casual clothing appropriate day and night. However, there are some exceptions. A small number of restaurants require jackets for men, and some of the city's increasingly exclusive and overhyped "ultralounges" and high-profile dance clubs have specific requirements, such as no sneakers or jeans, or that you must wear dark shoes or collared shirts. At a minimum, even if there's no set dress code, you're going to fit in with the scene if you make some effort to dress stylishly when heading out either to the hipper nightclubs or even trendier restaurants (i.e., those helmed by celeb chefs or with trendy followings and cool decor). Just as an example, where jeans and T-shirts might be technically allowed at some establishments, try to wear plain, fitted T-shirts versus those with logos and designs, and choose jeans that are appropriate for a venue (crisp and clean for a nice restaurant, designer labels for a top club). It's always good to pack a few stylish outfits for the evening, and when you're making dinner reservations at an upscale spot or considering a visit to a nightclub, ask for the dress-code specifics. Also, flip-flops are best kept to pool areas

FOR INTERNATIONAL TRAVELERS

CURRENCY

The dollar is the basic unit of U.S. currency. It has 100 cents. Coins are the penny (1¢); the nickel (5¢), dime (10¢), quarter (25¢), half-dollar (50¢), and the very rare golden $1 coin and even rarer silver $1. Bills are denominated $1, $5, $10, $20, $50, and $100, all mostly green and identical in size; designs and background tints vary. You may come across a $2 bill, but it's rare.

CUSTOMS

Information **U.S. Customs and Border Protection** ⊠ *5757 Wayne Newton Blvd., Airport* ☏ *702/736-2253* ⊕ *www.cbp.gov.*

DRIVING

Driving in the United States is on the right. Speed limits are posted in miles per hour (usually between 55 mph and 70 mph). Watch for lower limits in small towns and on back roads (usually 30 mph to 40 mph). Most states require front-seat passengers to wear seat belts; many states require children to sit in the backseat and to wear seat belts. In major cities rush hour is between 7 and 10 am and 4 and 7 pm.

Highways are well paved. Interstates—limited-access, multilane highways designated with an "I–" before the number—are fastest. Interstates with three-digit numbers circle urban areas, which may also have other limited-access expressways, freeways, and parkways. Tolls may be levied on limited-access highways. U.S. and state highways aren't necessarily limited-access, but may have several lanes. If your car breaks down on an interstate, pull onto the shoulder and wait for help, or have your passengers wait while you walk to an emergency phone (available in most states). If you carry a cell phone, dial *55, noting your location on the small green roadside mileage marker.

ELECTRICITY

The U.S. standard is AC, 110 volts/60 cycles. Plugs have two flat pins set parallel to each other.

EMERGENCIES

For police, fire, or ambulance, dial 911 (0 in rural areas).

EMBASSIES

Contacts **Australia** ☏ *800/345-6541* ⊕ *www.austemb.org.* **Canada** ☏ *202/682-1740* ⊕ *www.canadianembassy.org.* **United Kingdom** ☏ *212/745-0200 New York, 310/481-0031 L.A.* ⊕ *ukinusa.fco.gov.uk/en.*

HOLIDAYS

New Year's Day (Jan. 1); Martin Luther King Day (3rd Mon. in Jan.); Presidents' Day (3rd Mon. in Feb.); Memorial Day (last Mon. in May); Independence Day (July 4); Labor Day (1st Mon. in Sept.); Columbus Day (2nd Mon. in Oct.); Thanksgiving Day (4th Thurs. in Nov.); Christmas Eve and Christmas Day (Dec. 24 and 25); and New Year's Eve (Dec. 31).

MAIL

You can buy stamps and send letters and parcels in post offices. Most hotels sell stamps as well. You may find stamp-dispensing machines in airports, bus and train stations, office buildings, drugstores, and convenience stores.

U.S. mailboxes are stout, dark blue steel bins; pick-up schedules are posted inside the bin (pull down the handle to see them). Parcels weighing more than a pound must be mailed at a post office or at a private mailing center.

Within the United States a first-class letter weighing 1 ounce or less costs 45¢; each additional ounce costs 20¢. Postcards cost 32¢. An airmail letter to most foreign countries starts as low as 85¢.

Most hotels will collect and send mail, but there are post offices throughout Las Vegas. The closest Strip one: 4632 South Maryland Parkway. The closest Downtown one: 201 Las Vegas Boulevard South. Most branches are open 8:30 until 5 on weekdays, and some are open Saturday (but with shorter hours). There are drop boxes for overnight delivery services all over town as well as at UPS Stores in most strip malls.

Contacts DHL ☎ *800/225-5345* ⊕ *www.dhl. com.* **UPS** ☎ *800/742-5877* ⊕ *www.ups.com.* **United States Postal Service** ☎ *800/275- 8777* ⊕ *www.usps.com.*

PASSPORTS AND VISAS

Visitor visas aren't necessary for citizens of Australia, Canada, the United Kingdom, or most citizens of European Union countries coming for tourism and staying for fewer than 90 days. If you require a visa, the cost is $140, and waiting time can be substantial, depending on where you live. Apply for a visa at the U.S. consulate in your place of residence; check the U.S. State Department's special Visa website for further information.

Visa Information U.S. Department of State ☎ *202/663-1225* ⊕ *travel.state.gov/ visa/visa_1750.html.*

PHONES

Numbers consist of a three-digit area code (702 in the Las Vegas region) and a seven-digit local number. Within many local calling areas you dial only the seven digits; in others you dial "1" first and all 10 digits—just as you would for calls between area-code regions. The same is true for calls to numbers prefixed by "800," "888," "866," and "877"—all toll-free. For calls to numbers prefixed by "900" you must pay—usually dearly.

For international calls, dial "011" followed by the country code and the local number. For help, dial "0" and ask for an overseas operator. Most phone books list country codes and U.S. area codes. The country code

for Australia is 61, for New Zealand 64, for the United Kingdom 44. Calling Canada is the same as calling within the United States, whose country code, by the way, is 1.

For operator assistance, dial "0." For directory assistance, call 555-1212 or occasionally 411 (free at many public phones). You can reverse long-distance charges by calling "collect"; dial "0" instead of "1" before the 10-digit number.

Instructions are generally posted on pay phones (though with the rise of cell phones, there are fewer of these). Usually you insert coins in a slot (usually 25¢-50¢ for local calls) and wait for a steady tone before dialing. On long-distance calls the operator tells you how much to insert; prepaid phone cards, widely available in various denominations, can be used from any phone.

CELL PHONES

The United States has several GSM (Global System for Mobile Communications) networks, so multiband mobiles from most countries work here. It's also becoming more commonplace to find pay-as-you-go mobile SIM cards in the United States; these allow you to avoid roaming charges without having to buy a phone. That said, cell phones with pay-as-you-go plans are available for well under $100. The cheapest with decent national coverage are the GoPhone from AT&T and Virgin Mobile, which only offers pay-as-you-go service.

Contacts AT&T ⊕ *www.att.com.* **Virgin Mobile** ☎ *888/322-1122* ⊕ *www. virginmobileusa.com.*

and men should avoid wearing sandals (of any kind) pretty much anywhere.

Although the desert sun keeps temperatures scorching outside in warmer months, the casinos are ice-cold. Your best insurance is to dress in layers. The blasting air-conditioning may feel good at first, but if you plan on spending some time inside, bring a light sweater or jacket in case you feel chilly.

Always wear comfortable shoes; no matter what your intentions, you cover a lot of ground on foot.

▌ RESTROOMS

Free restrooms can be found in every casino; you don't have to be gambling in the casino to use them. Many restrooms have attendants who expect tips for fetching you everything from breath mints to hand towels. You're not obligated to tip.

▌ SAFETY

The well-known areas of Las Vegas are among the safest places in the world for visitors. With so many people carrying so much cash, security is tight inside and out. The casinos have visitors under constant surveillance, and hotel security guards are never more than a few seconds away. Outside, police are highly visible, on foot and bicycles and in cruisers. But this doesn't mean you can throw all safety consciousness to the wind. You should take the same precautions you would in any city—be aware of what's going on around you, stick to well-lighted areas, and quickly move away from any situation or people that might be threatening—especially if you're carrying some gambling cash. When Downtown, it's wise not to stray too far off the three main streets: Fremont, Ogden, and Carson between Main and Las Vegas Boulevard.

Be especially careful with your purse and change buckets around slot machines. Grab-and-run thieves are always looking for easy pickings, especially Downtown.

Apart from their everyday vulnerability to aggressive men, women should have few problems with unwanted attention in Las Vegas. If something does happen inside a casino, simply go to any pit and ask a boss to call security. The problem will disappear in seconds. Outside, crowds are almost always thick on the Strip and Downtown, and there's safety in numbers. Still, be aware of pickpockets.

Men in Las Vegas also need to be on guard against predatory women. "Trick roller" is the name of a particularly nasty breed of female con artist. These women are expert at meeting single men by "chance." After getting friendly in the casino, the woman joins the man in his hotel room, where she slips powerful knockout drugs into his drink and robs him blind. Some men don't wake up. Prostitution is illegal in Clark County.

■TIP➡ Distribute your cash, credit cards, IDs, and other valuables between a deep front pocket, an inside jacket or vest pocket, and a hidden money pouch. Don't reach for the money pouch once you're in public.

▌ TAXES

The Las Vegas and Reno-Tahoe international airports assess a $6 departure tax, or passenger facility charge. The hotel room tax is 12% in Las Vegas.

The sales tax rates for the areas covered in this guide are: Las Vegas, 8.10%; Arizona, 6.6%; and California, 7.25% (though in the latter two cases, individual counties can and do add their own).

▌ TIME

Nevada and California are in the Pacific time zone. Arizona is in the Mountain time zone and doesn't observe daylight saving time.

▌ TIPPING

Just as in other U.S. destinations, workers in Las Vegas are paid a minimal wage and rely on tips to make up the primary part of their income. A $1 tip per drink is appropriate for cocktail waitresses, even when they bring you a free drink at a slot machine or casino table. On package tours, conductors and drivers usually get $10 per day from the group as a whole; check whether this has already been figured into your cost. For local sightseeing tours, you may individually tip the driver-guide $5 if he or she has been helpful or informative. Tip dealers with the equivalent of your average bet once or twice an hour if you're winning; slot-machine change personnel and keno runners are accustomed to a buck or two. Ushers in showrooms may be able to get you better seats for performances for a gratuity of $5 or more. Tip the concierge 10%–20% of the cost of a ticket to a hot show. Tip $5–$10 for making dinner reservations or arrangements for other attractions.

TIPPING GUIDELINES FOR LAS VEGAS	
Bartender	$1 to $5 per round of drinks, depending on the number of drinks
Bellhop	$1 to $5 per bag, depending on the level of the hotel
Coat Check Personnel	$1 to $2 per item checked; if there's a fee, nothing
Hotel Concierge	$5 or more, if he or she performs a service for you
Hotel Doorman	$1 to $2, if he helps you get a cab
Hotel Maid	$1 to $3 a day (either daily or at the end of your stay, in cash)
Hotel Room-Service Waiter	$1 to $2 per delivery, even if a service charge has been added
Porter at Airport or Train Station	$1 per bag
Restroom Attendants	$1 or small change
Skycap at Airport	$1 to $3 per bag checked
Taxi Driver	15% to 20%, but round up the fare to the next dollar
Valet Parking Attendant	$1 to $2, but only when you get your car
Waiter	15% to 20%, with 20% being the norm at high-end restaurants; nothing additional if a service charge is added to the bill

▮ VISITOR INFORMATION

Before you go, contact the city and state tourism offices for general information. When you get there, you might want to visit the Las Vegas Convention and Visitors Authority, next door to The LVH, for brochures and general information. Hotels and gift shops on the Strip have maps, brochures, pamphlets, and free-events magazines—*What's On in Las Vegas, Showbiz*, and *Las Vegas Today*—that list shows and buffets and offer discounts to area attractions.

Anthony Curtis's *Las Vegas Advisor*, a monthly print newsletter and website, keeps track of the constantly changing Las Vegas landscapes of gambling, accommodations, dining, entertainment, Top Ten Values (a monthly list of the city's best deals), complimentary offerings, coupons, and more, and is an indispensable resource for any Las Vegas visitor. Send $5 for a sample issue, or buy a five-day membership to the *Advisor's* online version by logging on to ⊕ *www.lasvegasadvisor. com*. Annual online memberships start at $37 per year.

Another great resource: the Internet site, VegasChatter.

Contacts Las Vegas Advisor ☎ *702/252–0655* ⊕ *www.lasvegasadvisor.com*. **Las Vegas Convention and Visitors Authority** ✉ *3150 Paradise Rd., Paradise Road* ☎ *702/892–0711, 877/847–4858* ⊕ *www.visitlasvegas. com*. **Nevada Commission on Tourism** ☎ *775/687–4322, 800/638–2328* ⊕ *www. travelnevada.com.***VegasChatter** ⊕ *www. vegaschatter.com*.

ONLINE TRAVEL TOOLS
ALL ABOUT LAS VEGAS

VEGAS.com advertises that in Las Vegas "it's who you know." Part of the Greenspun Media Group, which also publishes the *Las Vegas Sun*, VEGAS.com offers information about and instant booking capabilities for everything from hotels to shows. The *New York Times*–owned About.com has an excellent online "Las

Vegas for Visitors" guide, which includes dozens of original articles and reviews as well as links to many other Vegas resources.

One of the oldest sites is the Las Vegas Leisure Guide, which is full of hotel, restaurant, and nightlife info. Las Vegas Online Entertainment Guide has listings for hotels and an online reservations system, plus local history, restaurants, a business directory, and even some gambling instruction. Only Vegas, the official Las Vegas tourism website, has a little bit of everything going on in Sin City. Find out about events, book hotels, get special deals, and find out other vital travel info; the Las Vegas Convention and Visitors Authority, which runs the site, also broadcasts great deals and updates on Twitter (⊕ *www.twitter.com/vegas*). The City of Las Vegas has its own website, which is a great resource for service-related information, including how to pay a ticket or citation. Remember, what happens in Vegas, stays in Vegas.

MARRIAGE LICENSES

If you plan on getting hitched during your Vegas stay, you might want to check out the Clark County website for necessary marriage license information.

Contacts About.com ⊕ *govegas.about. com*. **City of Las Vegas** ☎ *702/229-6011* ⊕ *www.lasvegasnevada.gov*. **Clark County** ☎ *702/455-0000* ⊕ *www.clarkcountynv.gov*. **LasVegas.com** ⊕ *www.lasvegas.com*. **Las Vegas Leisure Guide** ⊕ *www.lasvegas-nv. com*. **Las Vegas Online Entertainment Guide** ⊕ *www.lvol.com*. **Las Vegas Review-Journal** ⊕ *www.lvrj.com*. **Only Vegas** ⊕ *www. visitlasvegas.com*. **VEGAS.com** ⊕ *www.vegas. com*.

INDEX

PHOTO CREDITS

1, MGM Mirage. 3, Michelle Chaplow/Alamy. Chapter 1: Experience Las Vegas: 6-7 Travel Pix Collection/age fotostock. 9, Tomasz Rossa. 10 (top right), Liane Cary/age fotostock. 10 (top left), Hank Delespinasse/age fotostock. 10 (bottom right), LVCVB. 10 (bottom left), Ian Dagnall/Alamy. 12, Buzz Pictures/Alamy. 13 (left), Las Vegas News Bureau/LVCVA. 13 (right), Corbis. 14 (left), Tomasz Rossa. 14 (top center), MGM Mirage. 14 (top right), Las Vegas Ski & Snowboard Resort. 14 (bottom right), Hervè Donnezan/age fotostock. 15 (left), CityCenter Las Vegas. 15 (top center), Brent Bergherm/age fotostock. 15 (bottom center), JTB Photo/Alamy. 15 (right), MGM Mirage. 16, Darius Koehli/age fotostock. 17, Pictorial Press Ltd/Alamy. 18 (left and right), Library of Congress Prints & Photographs Division. 18 (center), wikipedia.org. 19 (top left), Harrah's Entertainment. 19 (bottom left), CSU Archive / age fotostock. 19 (right), Pictorial Press Ltd/Alamy. 20 (left), wikipedia.org. 20 (bottom center), Content Mine International/Alamy. 20 (right), Pictorial Press Ltd/Alamy. 21 (top left), Allstar Picture Library / Alamy. 21 (bottom left), By Carol M. Highsmith [Public domain], via Wikimedia Commons. 21 (right), LOOK Die Bildagentur der Fotografen GmbH/Alamy. 22, david sanger photography/Alamy. 23, Ron Niebrugge/Alamy. 24, Konstantin Sutyagin/Shutterstock. Chapter 2: Exploring Las Vegas: 25, Nevada Commission on Tourism. 26, Hard Rock Hotel & Casino. 28, MGM Mirage. 32, Scott Frances. 36, Las Vegas Sands Corp. 40, LVCVB. 43, by Marcin Wichary www.flickr.com/photos/mwichary/4972813369/ Attribution-NonCommercial License. 46, lake las vegas by Ed Schipul www.flickr.com/photos/eschipul/5761020172/ Attribution-NonCommercial-ShareAlike License. 48, Green Valley Ranch. 50, Judy Crawford/Shutterstock. 52, (c) trekandshoot | Dreamstime.com. 53, Chee-Onn Leong/Shutterstock.Chapter 3: Where to Stay: 55, Wynn Resorts Holdings- LLC. 56, LVCVB. 59-61, Thomas Hart Shelby. 63, Brad Mitchell / Alamy. 64-65, Mike Briner/Alamy. 67, SuperStock / age fotostock. 69, Greg Anderson Photography/MGM Mirage. 71, (c) Rabbit75 | Dreamstime.com. 73, (c) Icefields | Dreamstime.com. 74, Marla Lampert / Alamy. 75, MGM Mirage. 77, CityCenter Las Vegas. 79, MGM Mirage. 81, Stuart Pearce/World Pictures/age fotostock. 83, Thomas Hart Shelby. 85, Jerry Sharp/Shutterstock. 87, Emmanuel Coupe / Alamy. 89, Scott Frances. 90, LVCVB. 91, Rubens Abboud / Alamy. 93, Wynn Resorts. 95, Courtesy of The Palazzo. 97, (c) Minyun9260 | Dreamstime.com. 99, Wynn Resorts Holdings- LLC. 103, CityCenter Las Vegas. 105 (left), MGM Mirage. 105 (top right), Michelle Chaplow/Alamy. 105 (bottom right), Green Valley Ranch Resort, Spa and Casino. 106 (top), Palms Casino Resort. 106 (bottom), Russell MacMasters. 107 (top left), Digital Vision. 107 (bottom left), Digital Vision. 107 (top right), Hard Rock Hotel & Casino. 107 (bottom right), MGM Mirage. 108, (top left), Harrah's Entertainment, Inc..108 (top right and bottom), MGM Mirage. 109 (top left), Harrah's Entertainment, Inc. 109 (top right), Denise Truscello. 109 (bottom), Green Valley Ranch Resort, Spa and Casino. Chapter 4: Gamble: 113, The Venetian. 114, Lise Gagne/iStockphoto. 121, Greg Vaughn/Alamy. 126, Lee Foster/Alamy. 129, Photo Network / Alamy. 136, Javier Larrea/age fotostock. 138, Danita Delimont / Alamy. 139, Mark Harmel / Alamy. 142, cloki/Shutterstock. 146, www.imagesource.com. 150, Lee Foster/Alamy. 153, Harrah's Entertainment, Inc.. 157, Jeff Thrower (WebThrower)/Shutterstock. 158, M. Timothy O'Keefe / Alamy. Chapter 5: Where to Eat: 167-78, MGM Mirage. 184, Werner Dieterich / Alamy. 187, O'Gara/Bissell Photography/MGM Mirage. 188 (top left), MGM Mirage. 188 (bottom left), Francis George/MGM Mirage. 188 (right), O'Gara/Bissell Photography/MGM Mirage. 189 (all), Brian Leatart. 190 (left), Melanie Dunea. 190 (top right), Enoteca San Marco. 190 (bottom right), B&B Ristorante. 191 (all) and 192 (both), MGM Mirage. 215 (top), Station Casinos. 215 (bottom left), Marie-Louise Avery/Alamy. 215 (bottom right), Harrah's Entertainment Inc. 216 (top), Wynn Las Vegas. 216 (bottom), Profimedia.CZ s.r.o./Alamy. 217 (top), LVCVB. 217 (bottom), Rough Guides/Alamy. 218 (top left), Bill Sitzmann/Alamy. 218 (top right), Barbara Kraft/Wynn Resorts. Chapter 6: Shopping: 221, Harrah's Entertainment. 224-25, Grand Canal Shoppes. 227, Studio J Inc. 234, Starwood Hotels & Resorts. 235, MGM Mirage. 236 (top), Wynn Las Vegas. 236 (bottom), Las Vegas Sands Corp. 237 (top and bottom), MGM Mirage. 238 (top and bottom), Harrah's Entertainment. 239 (top and bottom), MGM Mirage. 240, Trump Las Vegas. 244, Harrah's Entertainment. 255 (top and bottom left), Matt Villano. 245 (top right), Wynn Las Vegas. 245 (bottom right), Harrah's Entertainment. 249, Town Square Las Vegas. Chapter 7: Shows: 251, Ricardo Funari/age fotostock. 255, Tomasz Rossa. 257, David Hawe/©BMP. 258, Gerard Schachmes. 262 (top and bottom), Harrah's Entertainment. 270, MGM Mirage. Chapter 8: After Dark: 273, Douglas Peebles Photography/Alamy. 278, O'Gara/Bissell Photography/Mirage. 283, Marquee Nightclub & Dayclub. 287 (left), Trinette Reed/Brand X Pictures/Jupiter Images. 287 (top right), Adam Taplin. 287 (bottom right), Pedro Coll/age fotostock. 288 (top left), Nick Leary. 288 (top right), foodfolio/Alamy. 288 (bottom left), Chloe Johnson/Alamy. 288 (bottom right), Stuart Pearce/age fotostock. 289 (top left), Trinette Reed/Brand X Pictures/Jupiter Images. 289 (top right), foodfolio/Alamy. 289 (bottom left), Mode Images Limited/Alamy. 289 (bottom right), Pierre D'Alancaisez/Alamy. 290 (top), MGM

ABOUT OUR WRITERS

Dante Drago currently lives in New Jersey, and has more than 10 years of experience dealing table games in Atlantic City. His specialty is baccarat and blackjack, but he also deals many other games. When he is not working, he puts his collective experience and knowledge to use as a recreational gambler in Atlantic City and Las Vegas, which he has frequented many times. He can also be found doling out gambling advice and rarely known "tips" to his inquisitive friends on Facebook, who are curious about the inner workings of the casino and desire the perspective of an insider who has stood on both sides of the gaming table. He updated the Gambling chapter of this book.

Xazmin Garza is an award-winning fashion and beauty writer for the *Las Vegas Review-Journal*. She's lived in Sin City, and enjoyed its fabulous shopping and beautiful spas, for five years. When she's not blogging she's busy researching material for this book's Shopping chapter. Prior to her current position, Garza worked as editor of *Where* magazine in Las Vegas.

Matt Villano is a writer and editor based in Healdsburg, California. He contributes to *Time* magazine, the *Wall Street Journal*, the *New York Times, Sunset,* and *Entrepreneur*. He also blogs about outdoor adventure for DiscoverAmerica. com. When he's not researching stories or working on the guide's Exploring and Where to Stay chapters (among others), he's playing with his daughters.

Mike Weatherford came to us well prepared for the task of revising the Shows and Side Trips chapters of this book. He's lived in Las Vegas since 1987, is the author of *Cult Vegas—The Weirdest! The Wildest! The Swingin'est Town on Earth,* and, as the entertainment reporter for the *Las Vegas Review-Journal,* sees all the shows.